OF PLACE AND GENDER: WOMEN IN MAINE HISTORY

OF PLACE AND GENDER

WOMEN IN MAINE HISTORY

edited and with introductions by Marli F. Weiner

THE UNIVERSITY OF MAINE PRESS
ORONO, MAINE 2005

09 08 07 06 05   1 2 3 4 5

ISBN: 0-89101-105-6

The paper used in this publication meets the minimum requirements of the American National Standard for Information Sciences—Permanence of Paper for Printed Library Materials, ansi z39.48–1984. Printed and bound in the United States of America. Book design by Michael Alpert.

For my students,
who have taught me so much

CONTENTS

Tip O'Neill's famous quip that all politics is local might just as well apply to history. While sweeping national and international events are compelling, many people who are interested in history want to know the local story. Many towns have local historical societies that are devoted to preserving the history of that particular town, distinct from its neighbors. Countless volumes of community history are published every year and find a ready audience in people in that community and those who trace their roots to it. Even national events are often viewed through the local lens. Wars, for example, remain a key focus of attention, but what many people want to know about them is how people from their communities participated and what particular military units were doing at any given time. Such interest typically stems from the service of a loved one in that unit or its origins within a local area. Similarly, many people turn to history to help them answer questions about their ancestors, if not as individuals, then at least as members of racial, ethnic, or religious groups. Interest in immigration often stems from the fact that one's grandparents came from a particular place at a particular time. Members of minority groups push to have information about themselves included in school curricula and textbooks.

Interest in history as local history also extends to gender. Although textbooks have not always recognized it, women have had a different history from men, a subject increasingly explored in recent years. Many people want to know about women's lives: about their families, their work, their education, their opportunities, their efforts to improve their circumstances. Curiosity about famous women's achievements and ordinary women's accomplishments is widespread. The history of daily life—chores like cooking and cleaning, activities like giving birth and caring for the sick, events like weddings and funerals—fascinates many people, some of whom flock to living history museums to watch costumed actors performing those chores that seem both familiar and yet very foreign to how we accomplish the same tasks today. In addition, biographies and autobiographies of women are being published in great quantities, some intended to fill the desire for female role models for young women.

A volume of essays on Maine women's history fills a real need, helping to answer questions about what women were doing in local communities and highlighting their similarities and differences from women elsewhere. Maine women were sometimes in the forefront of change and sometimes lagged behind; most of the time they were preoccupied with the tasks of daily life, as were women elsewhere. However, the details of women's activities at home and in the community, like the context in which they were done, helps to set Maine women apart from women elsewhere. The essays in this volume offer insight into a rich variety of Maine women, some famous and some ordinary, some intent on changing their lives and their society and others struggling to survive, some confined by family and work to farm or village and others able to travel the world. Taken together, their stories enrich our understanding of Maine, of women, and of history.

* * *

Most of the essays in this collection were first written for a conference on the History of Women in Maine sponsored by the Margaret Chase Smith Library and the Maine Historical Society in 1997 and organized by Polly Welts Kaufman and Eileen Eagan. Even at the time, Polly envisioned a volume of essays drawn from the conference. The Margaret Chase Smith Library was instrumental in the organization of this volume, and an editorial board was created to help define the project.

Once many of the essays were chosen and preliminary editing work done, Polly was awarded a Fulbright to spend a year in

Norway, and so I assumed responsibility for writing the introduction and completing the book. Although not a scholar of Maine women, I was eager to participate in a project that raised questions about gender and place; my own work on women in South Carolina raised similar questions in a very different part of the country.

The volume would not have been possible without the help and support of numerous individuals. These include Greg Gallant of the Margaret Chase Smith Library, Michael Alpert and Betsy Rose of the University of Maine Press, Dick Judd of the University of Maine Department of History, and Mazie Hough of the Women in the Curriculum/Women's Studies Program at the University of Maine. The editorial board included Michael Alpert; Joyce Butler of the Maine Historical Society; Diana Long of the Department of History, University of Southern Maine; Dave Richards of the Margaret Chase Smith Library; and me. Several people were kind enough to read the introduction and save me from errors, including Andrea Constantine Hawkes, Mazie Hough, Pamela Dean, Dick Judd, and Polly Welts Kaufman.

Like many books trying to open new fields of inquiry by bringing together the work of many people, this book has seen several different visions of what it should be. The process has been similar to the book's subject of Maine women: complex, diverse, and open to interpretation. It is my hope that the result will offer Maine's people a new way of understanding themselves and their history.

–M. F. W.

OF PLACE AND GENDER: WOMEN IN MAINE HISTORY

The historian's job is to generalize: to move from myriad available facts to telling a coherent story, to move from the particular to the general without losing sight of the particular. Trying to make sense of the many kinds of individual stories that compose history means paying attention to what sets individuals apart from one another as well as what they have in common. It means respecting singular voices even while trying to conduct them into a not always harmonious chorus. It requires careful listening and even more careful arranging. If done with the proper care, the historian's work can reveal people, both individuals and communities, to themselves, helping them to understand who they are and how and why they came to be that way.

In recent years, historians struggling to advance such understandings of the human experience have looked to various aspects of individual identity as a means of explaining people's behavior. Such aspects of identity as race, gender, class, ethnicity, and religion have been used to gather individuals into coherent groups with similar experiences and to explain why members of those groups act as they do. Recognizing that individual identity is composed of all of these factors and more, historians have sought to explore not only the ways in which aspects of identity influence individual experience, but also their impact on one another, in the process turning them into categories of analysis. For example, black women are understood to be shaped by both race and gender, with gender separating them from black men and race from white women. Yet black women themselves are divided by class, education, age, and other factors that render their experiences distinct from one another even as they share membership in the category of black women. Similarly, while white women share race and gender identities, they are also divided by a range of factors. All of these aspects of identity reveal both the commonalities and divergences in women's experiences.

Perhaps the newest addition to the list of factors shaping identity is place. Where a person is from, where she lives, where she calls home, all shape her experience as clearly as other aspects of her identity, although we do not always recognize this as explicitly as the seemingly more apparent factors like race and gender. The invisibility of place has been particularly true in the Northeast, which has too often been considered as the unmarked norm by historians quick to write about the South or the West as regions diverging from that norm, but slow to consider the Northeast as a region.

Yet place as a category of identity has a particular resonance in Maine. Mainers have taken pride in their distinctiveness, believing themselves to have a unique history and experience, shaped in part by their difficult climate and poor soil, proximity to Canada, and Yankee heritage. Maine remained a frontier long after the rest of New England, becoming a state in the same year as Missouri. Its boundary with Canada was only settled when the rest of the nation was turning its attention to fighting with Mexico. It did not share many of the experiences historians associate with modernization in the rest of the nation. To be from Maine, tucked as it is into a corner of the nation, has a particular meaning to people in the state. It implies sharing a set of assumptions and traditions rooted in its history and culture. While many Mainers did not share these assumptions and experiences, they have come to characterize the state's sense of itself.

Maine's history and culture have shaped the characteristics associated with its people. Typed as self-sufficient and independent, hardworking and hard-driving, taciturn and dry-humored, competent and thrifty, Mainers have sometimes self-consciously adopted these qualities as their own. Mainers have also drawn distinct boundaries around their experiences, to this day noting a clear demarcation between natives and those "from away." To be from away means not to share the state's history and culture or its characteristics; in the eyes of natives, even long residence cannot convey these qualities. Thus, the characteristics associated with identification with place have mutated into stereotypes that cannot accurately define anyone's experience, although as stereotypes they have seemed to have great explanatory power.

Many of the stereotypes associated with Maine in both local eyes and those of the nation have been explicitly masculine: when we think of Maine, we think almost automatically of rugged fishermen and loggers, hunters and outdoorsmen. These male stereotypes were self-consciously cultivated as Maine transformed itself into a tourist paradise over the course of the later nineteenth and into the twentieth century. Maine became known—and knew itself—as a place to escape the effete comforts of the city for the rigors of the outdoors, providing a place for middle class urban businessmen to cultivate the challenges of the hunt and the ruggedness of outdoor life during their annual vacations. These masculine images left little room for women, however, and women's identity in Maine was never part of the state's sense of place, despite the efforts of Sarah Orne Jewett and several other notable Maine women writers.

Masculinist stereotypes belied the reality of many women's lives. On the one hand, the images seemingly excluded women, while on the other, women have shared many of the masculine activities associated with Maine life, although often from a vantage point that did not perceive them as challenging those images. Maine, for example, has since the mid-twentieth century a strong tradition of political participation by women, including large numbers of women in elective office, an experience that seemingly did not until recently threaten the prevailing view that politics was the province of men. Similarly, women whose view of their own work responsibilities included filling in for husbands away in the woods or at sea did not necessarily garner much private or public recognition for their efforts. Maine women's identity with place can be located in this gap between the stories Mainers believed about themselves and the realities of their experiences.

The sense of place Mainers have developed for themselves as well as the masculinist stereotypes it has engendered have been complicated by regional differences within the state. In the nineteenth century, these differences were most noticeable between the coast and the interior, while more recently they have taken the form of the concept of "two Maines." The divisions between the coast and the interior were noted by the relative isolation of the interior as compared with the coast's access to the outside world via the sea; these divisions led to economic differences that made many coastal communities far more prosperous and cosmopolitan than their inland counterparts. As a result, throughout the nineteenth century, many interior communities were plagued by limited economic opportunities that led to persistent out-migration by young people; along the coast, people were better able to provide for the next generation.

In the mid-twentieth century, these divisions were transformed into those between north and south, as the southwestern corner of the state became increasingly part of the orbit of development around Boston and more generally part of the industrialized corridor stretching from Washington northwards. The rest of the state, meanwhile, became increasingly isolated from economic development and the cultural and social complexity that went with it. By the turn of the twenty-first century, Maine's sense of place varied considerably depending on whether focus turned to the widespread poverty and depopulation in the northern and downeast sections of the state or to the thriving cities and suburbs of York and Cumberland counties in the southwest.

Maine's sense of place also varied according to the identity of the individual. In particular, ethnicity divided people in the state, separating those of English descent from those from French Canada, Ireland, or elsewhere, as well as from Native Americans. Ethnic differences were religious as well, since those of English descent, the original Yankees, were Protestant while many of the newcomers were Catholic and a few were Jewish. Even in the nineteenth century, mill towns in particular could include a rich variety of peoples. French-speaking Catholics migrating southward from Canada, the majority of the newcomers to the state, sought to replicate familiar institutions and cultural patterns, creating churches and parochial schools that served as cultural centers for their neighborhoods and educated generations of children. Like most of the other newcomers, they experienced widespread discrimination; ethnicity divided Mainers and complicated the sense of place they felt. While in recent decades some of those differences began to fade along with the French language, ethnicity remains a strong force shaping individual identity and experience within the state. Since the mid-nineteenth century, ethnic differences have been closely tied to those based on class, which also divided Mainers from one another. While economic and social distances between rich and poor might not be dramatic in rural areas, they could easily feel that way, and in more urban areas they were readily apparent.

These divisions within the state complicate understandings of Mainers' identification with place throughout the nineteenth and twentieth centuries. Contending versions of

Maine based on region within the state, class, religion, and ethnicity meant that identification with place could not be simple. At the same time, Maine's comparative homogeneity and commitment to its own distinctiveness have served to unify the state despite these differences. Mainers adopted identities for themselves that sometimes seemed astonishingly local, but set against a larger canvas, they understood Maine itself to be at the heart of the matter.

The question of identification with place becomes particularly important when we consider the state's difficult relationship to social change throughout these centuries. On the one hand, Maine has a strong tradition of championing unpopular political causes from abolition to temperance, among many others. It provided important early leadership for the Republican party that was committed to free soil and free labor and opposition to the extension of slavery. On the other hand, Maine has an equally strong political tradition of opposing innovation and reform, rejecting Shepard-Towner Act funds providing food and health care for mothers and children in 1921 and voting against Franklin Roosevelt in all four elections. Maine's commitment to traditions of self-sufficiency and Yankee independence made its leaders reluctant to accept outside aid; for much of the twentieth century, the state's economy was so depressed that its people became accustomed to taking care of their own and doing without. Its contradictory political sympathies allowed it to host both the International Workers of the World and the Ku Klux Klan. In its recent history Maine seems simultaneously to occupy a position ranging from the cutting edge of social change, especially in environmental issues, to digging in its heels to prevent any erosion of what it has perceived as its traditional values.

Historians tend to view cities as the centers of change of all sorts: economic, social, political. Cities, after all, became the center of industrial enterprise and thus home to business leaders as well as the waves of immigrants who transformed American culture. Those eager to escape the stultifying effects of the countryside were attracted to the promise of economic opportunity inherent in cities as well as the chance to promote new causes, new styles, new ways of doing things. Historians have sometimes painted those who stayed behind as uninterested in progress, as backward in social ideas, as resistant to change. Rural areas were considered to be in conflict with the vibrant possibilities inherent in urban life, which suffered disproportionately from the problems that plagued America but also offered a disproportionate share of the solutions. Such stereotypes hold rich explanatory power, yet they do not do justice to either city or countryside. Still, the realities that gave rise to these stereotypes have had significant impact in such an overwhelmingly rural state as Maine. Like other rural peoples, Mainers have sometimes seen their state as a place to be from, to leave, but not to transform from within. Those committed to economic opportunity and social change have had to decide whether to flee for the cities or accept limited chances at home.

Maine's overwhelmingly rural character also shaped the state's identity. With the exception of Portland, Lewiston, Bangor, Augusta, and a handful of smaller cities, the state's demographic portrait was one of tiny towns and scattered communities whose residents could be counted on to be familiar with one another's business and personalities, prospects and foibles. While some valued the intimacy of such familiarity, others found it stultifying in a larger society that increasingly valued individualism. Along with the close scrutiny of neighbors, rural society bred an isolation that remained unappealing to generations of young people as well as many of their parents; some of them used it as an excuse to flee the state.

Rural isolation took many forms in Maine. Men isolated for the winter in logging camps while their wives tended farm and family at home, or women isolated in coastal communities while their husbands were on fishing or merchant ships experienced particularly gendered forms of isolation. While the increase in railroad mileage in the nineteenth century and the spread of the interstate highway system in the twentieth brought improved access to the outside world, many in Maine remained bound to small communities with only limited ties beyond them. Winter could impose its own form of isolation. Still, for many, Maine's isolation was relative. Those left behind in coastal communities were in regular, if infrequent, communication with ships visiting ports around the globe. In the nineteenth century Chataqua performers, traveling theaters, and lyceum lectures brought cultural events even to remote corners of the state, at least in the summer. Later, new technologies like radio and television brought the rest of the nation into every Maine living room, reducing isolation dramatically, although this did not stop the flow of population away from the state.

★ ★ ★

These various threads—masculinist images; geographical, ethnic, and economic differences within the state; contradictory ideas about opportunity and social change; rural isolation—help to form the fabric of life and history in the state. The pattern they create becomes significantly more complex when we focus attention on the state's women, for women's experiences have differed in significant ways from men's. There are multiple possibilities for understanding Maine's women. Throughout the nineteenth century and for much of the twentieth, the prevailing set of assumptions in the nation defined women as inferior to men in most respects: weaker, less capable of engaging in the rough and tumble of the competitive economic world, unfit to make important decisions. This rhetoric offered women something of an ideological consolation prize, however: while their inferiority prevented them from participating in the public world, they were deemed more moral and virtuous than men, and so granted full control over the domestic realm, at least in theory. While this schematized version of society was often violated in practice, its realities shaped the parameters of possibility for many white, native-born, Protestant women, who were systematically denied access to education, jobs, politics, and other arenas of life deemed unsuitable for them. These exclusions effected such women in Maine no less than the rest of the nation; they touched the lives of other categories of Maine women as well, albeit in more complex ways.

Men throughout the state shared these views of women's potential and used them to justify limiting their options. Like women in most of the rest of the nation, Maine women were excluded from voting until 1920. Women had some opportunity for higher education, since the University of Maine and some of the private colleges admitted them in the nineteenth century, but women were generally expected to attend the state's normal schools for teacher training. Maine's laws and practices on most social questions assumed a patriarchal family structure; although the state was one of the first to allow married women to control the property they brought into the marriage and, later, their wages, this policy was the exception to a more restrictive norm and was not designed to enhance their economic status. While the details varied from state to state, Maine women shared the exclusions implicit in the rhetoric of domesticity with their peers in the rest of the nation.

At the same time, Maine's rural women were expected to cope with the state's difficult environment and the demanding work required to extract a living from it. Whether the men in their families earned a living by hunting, fishing, logging, farming, or something else, Maine women were expected to do the work necessary to sustain daily life. They did so without the conveniences available in more urban areas, no matter what those conveniences might have been at any given time: purchased cloth or shoes in the nineteenth century, purchased bread or preserved food in the twentieth. Rural women did without the benefits of indoor running water, electricity, and central heating long after their more urban counterparts could take them for granted. All of this meant that throughout the nineteenth and twentieth centuries, most women's days were filled with the tasks of domestic life, which were difficult and time-consuming. Here, too, Maine women were little different from their rural counterparts elsewhere.

For many women, those domestic tasks were accompanied by the similarly challenging work of helping their husbands in the chores of wresting a living from the generally inhospitable land or sea. The rigors of these occupations made having as many hands as possible available to do the work a necessity. Women typically rose to the occasion, routinely performing those tasks necessary to help their husbands along with their own domestic labor as part of a united, family effort to eke out a livelihood under harsh conditions. Later, as jobs outside the home became more available, women combined waged with domestic work to supplement the family economy. They routinely did all of these kinds of work while pregnant or nursing, for reliable birth control was largely unavailable until the mid-twentieth century, and for many, unthinkable.

Maine women's experiences were distinguished from those of many other rural women by the occupational pluralism that characterized the state's economy. Few families could earn their entire living from farming, fishing, or lumbering; most engaged in a multitude of income-generating activities that varied with the season. In addition to their primary employments, Maine's men and women were forced to undertake many kinds of activities in order to make ends meet, from harvesting ice in the winter to serving the tourists in the summer to selling surplus garden produce to canning fish in factories to making Christmas wreaths. Much of the time, these seasonal, temporary activities were not registered as work when done by women, particularly because for the most part they were done under the rubric of caring for their families and within the confines of domestic life rather than in a factory. Nevertheless, the multitude of productive as well as reproductive tasks that occupied women's time and the significant contributions their non-domestic labor made to the family economy set Maine women apart from rural women whose families could depend on earning a living from one kind of activity.

Maine's urban women had a rather different experience, one more like those of urban women in the rest of the nation. For the most part, they enjoyed more access to education and to regular waged work than women in the rest of the state. They formed neighborhood networks of friends and relatives who worked and played together, helping one another with housework and childcare, finding jobs and gaining education. They joined a wide variety of organizations to enhance their lives and those of their communities, engaging in reform, social, cultural, and other activities both with men and alone. Whether formal or informal, the groups they created were usually based on ethnic or class as well as gender identities, as women typically stayed within their communities to socialize and to create change; occasionally they joined with one another across differences to organize on a state or even national level. Urban women shared with those in rural areas an identity as Mainers, but their experiences were rather removed from those that defined the majority of the state's women. Yet many urban women had migrated from rural areas and retained close ties to them, bridging the distance between city and country. Many of them also retained a rural outlook, focusing on the differences that separated their experiences from those of women in larger, more diverse cities farther south.

As place, then, Maine shaped women's experiences by emphasizing their differences from women elsewhere, even from those of many other rural women. Maine's environment was too harsh, the demands of its occupations too rigorous and too uncertain, to allow all but a small percentage of women to enjoy the full control over the domestic realm that ideologues promised women in exchange for their absence from the public world. Full control over the domestic world they may well have had, but for most of them, it meant little other than work and more work and not the protections from the harsher aspects of life supposedly necessary for women's delicate constitutions.

Many women, of course, enjoyed the challenge of Maine's difficult life, yet even the hardiest of them were likely to find the winters long and the work arduous. Some found solace in religious faith or the closeness of family ties or the promise of better lives for their children. They committed themselves to working with their husbands as they believed women ought, to enhance family survival. Neither able to enjoy the limited protections offered by domesticity nor granted recognition for the full extent of their labors, most women simply made the best of a bad bargain. Such women rarely rejected conformity to familiar, traditional roles or challenged the assumptions informing them; instead, they worked hard to fulfill what was expected of them. They drew their identities from traditional notions of women's behavior as articulated in virtually every public forum in and out of the state as well as from the examples of their mothers and grandmothers.

Other women were less willing to accept identities shaped by familiar expectations of appropriate behavior. Rather than making the best of a bad bargain, they were determined to seek opportunity wherever they could find it, rejecting conformity and traditional roles in the process. Many such rebellious women were young and unmarried and thus unencumbered in their search for new meanings in their lives; many would later abandon their search in favor of marriage and children in the pattern of their mothers. Still, particularly in the decades around the turn of the twentieth century, many women in Maine and the rest of the nation chose to seek new opportunities and lives. Some of these women found that they had to leave the state to do so, joining a steady migration of young people of both sexes to the cities of the Northeast. Others were unwilling to relinquish their connections to Maine even as they sought opportunity; their actions would help to transform what it meant to be a Maine woman. These women may well have drawn from ideas about Yankee independence and self-sufficiency, interpreting these traits not as justifications to remain on isolated farms and impoverished villages but as inspirations for rebellion against the limits of such places. In essence, they reinterpreted some of the key tenets of Maine identity in ways never anticipated by those who used these ideas to reinforce tradition.

Still other women never had such choices to make. Native American women, immigrant women, the very poor, the unlucky rarely were able to make self-conscious choices about their identities as women; the terms in which the debate was framed were too foreign and too inaccessible to make reinterpretation possible. Still, such women did make choices about their lives, and their sense of themselves must be considered part of the complexity of the discussion of identity. Forced to contend with definitions of womanhood that excluded them from full participation, such women forged their own identities within the limits of what was possible.

* * *

Being a Maine woman could have many meanings. Some women who claimed that identity had long roots in the state, in the case of Native Americans stretching back even beyond the arrival of the first Europeans. Others with long roots were early English settlers and their descendants, who moved northward beginning before the Revolution hoping to exploit the economic promise in the relatively cheap land and abundant resources, and Acadians, who moved into the St. John Valley in the northern part of the state for similar reasons. Other Maine women came to the state much later, in the waves of immigrants from French- or English-speaking areas of Canada or from across the Atlantic, to take advantage of newer economic opportunities in the factories of the southern part of the state. Still others, whose roots were so shallow as to be virtually non-existent, were temporary visitors, part of the tourist culture that became so much a part of the state's economy in the late nineteenth century; some purchased land and joined the ranks of "summer people" whose ties to the state were more sentimental than anything else. Yet another category of Maine women were those who left the state, simultaneously fleeing its isolation and lack of opportunity and drawn to the seemingly richer life of urban areas. Women in each of these categories understood their identities as "Maine women" somewhat differently from the others; each had different relationships to the complex of factors that defined the history and experience of the state.

The essays in this volume are arranged chronologically into three approximate time periods: the mid-nineteenth century, the fifty or so years around the turn of the twentieth century, and the mid-twentieth century. Within each time period, the essays are grouped according to the approximate length of time the subjects had been in the state, in order to illuminate the changing meanings of identity for Maine women.

The essays, however, by no means explore every aspect of those identities and many important issues are not included in this volume. A comprehensive history of Maine women remains to be written. Even the most careful reader will learn little from this collection about Maine women before the mid-nineteenth century or in recent decades. The book includes little on women's experiences during the Civil War, or any other war for that matter. It includes nothing of the history of woman suffrage in the state, or of women's participation in the temperance cause, or of women's clubs, or other kinds of reform activity. We do not hear of Maine's black women, Italian women, Jewish women, or members of other groups within the state's population. We hear little of women's education, women's health, women's writings. While the historians cited in the bibliography have explored some of these subjects, they and others too numerous to mention suggest how much more there is to learn in order to develop a full understanding of the chorus of Maine women's voices.

The essays in this volume are but a beginning. They offer an opportunity to explore some of the ways in which identities of place and gender resonate with one another. In a nation in which localism has remained a vibrant force and in which gender is central to individual identity, these essays can help us to understand not just Maine history, but the history of the nation as well.

PART ONE

THE MID-NINETEENTH CENTURY

Like much of the rest of the nation, Maine in the middle decades of the nineteenth century was infused with optimism. The economy was booming, and in spite of periodic downturns, most people hoped that it would continue to boom for the foreseeable future. Social problems existed, but most Americans outside of the South believed that these could be easily solved; reformers were devoting plenty of time and attention to them and would presumably have them taken care of in short order. The nation and the state were young and expanding; nothing was likely to stop them from achieving their God-given promise of glory and achievement. After all, the new nation had successfully warded off the British not once but twice, defeated Mexico, expanded across the continent. Everything was possible.

The reality, of course, was far from the optimistic stories that Americans told themselves, as the presence of reformers and fears of economic downturns suggested. Slavery was only the most visible of the many inequities prevalent in the nation. Native Americans were in the process of being removed from their land, enclosed in smaller and smaller territories, although most Americans understood this as a sign of progress since it freed new land for white settlement. Immigrants were flooding in from Europe and finding themselves limited by poverty and discrimination to dismal factories and squalid tenements. The unbridled competition of industrial capitalism was polluting the environment, exploiting and injuring workers, and creating growing inequality.

Like people in the rest of the nation, Mainers at mid-century vacillated between optimism and anxiety for their futures. The state's economy was increasingly open to regional markets, which promised higher incomes but also increased vulnerability.

Social problems were less severe than elsewhere, as relatively few immigrants were drawn to the state, but improved transportation and communication made them seem closer—and some immigrants did arrive to work in granite quarries and textile factories, many of them French-speaking Canadians who began to arrive in large numbers in the 1870s. The disruptions of the Civil War were felt most deeply by those families with men off fighting, but people throughout the state were unsettled by the transformations in politics, the economy, and ideology it created.

Maine's native-born, white women shared these feelings of optimism and anxiety. Expanding opportunities enabled them to contribute in new ways to the economic well-being of their families as increasing numbers of them engaged in production of domestic goods for market, mostly from their homes. Selling surplus butter, eggs, cheese, garden produce, thread, cloth, candles, soap, and the like allowed them to purchase some items they had previously produced for themselves, but it simultaneously increased the amount of time they spent working at repetitive tasks and decreased the control they exercised over that work. Nearly all white women in the state were literate, and opportunities for higher education increased for the daughters of affluent families, but not nearly to the same extent as did men's. Married women were granted some control over their own property, but in nearly every other respect, they remained legally subordinate to their husbands, unable to enter contracts, to gain custody of their children in cases of divorce, or to vote. Such restrictions may occasionally have galled happily married women; those who were unhappy had little recourse, for there were few means of gaining independence. Nearly all women were subordinate to their husbands, denied access to opportunity, and tied to their homes by the need to care for their families. Women were valued for their hard work and respectable behavior; those who transgressed were liable to censure by their communities.

Mid-nineteenth-century Maine women for the most part accepted these limitations on their opportunities, although a few began to object privately and an even smaller number publicly. Maine hosted abolitionist, temperance, and woman's rights speakers, and its people took advantage of the opportunity to hear and debate their ideas. Some also took advantage of wartime needs to organize societies to sew for soldiers and raise funds for hospitals. Isabella Fogg became a nurse after her son was injured; Dorothea Dix, originally from Hampden and nationally recognized for her work reforming prisons and institutions for the mentally ill, became superintendent of Army nurses in 1861. Other women gathered books, clothing, and other supplies to send to the South to help the former slaves adjust to freedom; at least one, Sarah Jane Foster, actually went there to teach them. These activities offered the mostly middle-class women who engaged in them the chance to learn important political skills such as organizing, fundraising, publicizing, and debating, all of which would serve them—and their daughters—well in the future. The vast majority, however, remained quietly at home, immersed in the demands of caring for their families and earning a living, and unable either to imagine or to realize a wider scope for their actions.

If optimism and anxiety characterized the nation's response to changing economic and social conditions in the mid-nineteenth century, so too did they characterize relationships between women and men. The debate over proper relationships was loud and long. For most antebellum commentators, women's proper place was in the home, where they could both be protected from the competitive masculine world and devote full attention to inculcating Christian morality into their husbands and children. Both men and women espoused these views, with increasing vehemence as the century advanced.

Their vehemence was occasioned by the growing claims being made by reformers and woman's rights advocates, who sought to open an ever-larger place for women in the public world. (It would take until well into the twentieth century for anyone to advocate men's participation in the private world as anything but the rulers of families.) Woman's rights advocates sought to open educational and occupational opportunities for women. They advocated improvements in women's legal position, including rights to property; access to divorce and child custody, especially in cases of wife-beating; and citizenship rights, including the vote. They also sought less tangible goals, including dress reform, equality within marriage, and access to positions of leadership in religion.

The debates stirred by these demands demonstrate how deeply anxiety about gender penetrated into American society. Older beliefs about masculinity and femininity were giving way in the face of the disruptions caused by social and economic change, leaving few people unscathed. Some clung to older beliefs with renewed commitment and self-consciousness, while others sought ways to integrate new notions into their everyday lives. While these issues were perhaps most deeply felt in areas of the country where modernization had developed most fully, their influence was pervasive throughout the nation. No region or state remained untouched by the crisis in gender provoked by economic change and the demands of reformers. In Kathryn Tomasek's essay, we see this debate as manifested in mid-nineteenth-century Bangor.

"NOT A NERVOUS MAN":
GENDER ANXIETY AND WOMEN'S RIGHTS
IN ANTEBELLUM BANGOR, MAINE

Kathryn Tomasek

When women's rights advocate Jane Sophia Appleton asked former Maine governor and fellow Bangor resident Edward Kent to write a brief literary piece for a charitable project, her request brought to the surface a host of gender anxieties centered on Kent's belief that "unwomanly" reformers like Appleton were encroaching on men's domain. He expressed these anxieties in a utopian short story entitled "A Vision of Bangor in the Twentieth Century." Since Kent's story attacked not only her editorial practices but also her interests in such reforms as women's rights and Fourierism, Appleton defended herself in her own utopian short story entitled "Sequel to the Vision of Bangor in the Twentieth Century." Both stories were published in *Voices from the Kenduskeag*, edited by Appleton and Cornelia Crosby Barrett, in 1848.[1]

Kent and Appleton debated gender and women's rights through their arguments about appropriate behavior for women and men, arguments that were grounded in opposing economic ideologies. Kent imagined a future in which capitalism and masculine competitiveness had triumphed over Fourierism, a socialist economic alternative that he saw as a threat to the family and to traditional gender roles. In contrast, Appleton proposed a future in which cooperation had replaced competition and Fourierism had led to the development of more egalitarian gender roles than those idealized by Kent. The exchange between Appleton and Kent demonstrates the connections among ideas about gender, economic systems, and women's rights in antebellum Bangor.[2]

Fourierism was a popular and influential movement for economic and social reform that challenged both the capitalist economic system that relied on competition and the accompanying family ideal that hid women's labor and kept them economically dependent on male wage earners. Based on the theories of French utopian Charles Fourier (1772–1837), the reform was introduced to the United States by New Yorker Albert Brisbane in 1840. In the context of the depression that followed the Panic of 1837, the reform sought to create communities that offered men of the working and middle classes the promise of economic security and the opportunity to share their labor with others. Fourierism promised women economic autonomy because communities would pay them for housework and would treat them as economic individuals, keeping separate accounts for each community member. The movement attracted tens of thousands of adherents. Between 1842 and 1846, Fourierist enthusiasts established twenty-four communities in nine states and territories from New Jersey to Iowa, and the Transcendentalist community at Brook Farm converted to Fourierism. Outside the communities, Fourierists established local Fourier clubs in New England, western New York, and the Ohio Valley.[3] In Maine, Brisbane's propaganda and the organizational efforts of lecturer John Allen yielded Fourierist adherents in Hallowell, Winthrop, Vassalboro, Bowdoinham, Portland, Ellsworth, and Bangor.[4] Notice of Brisbane's propaganda began to appear in the *Bangor Daily Whig and Courier* in 1842, when editor John S. Sayward noted that Brisbane "makes the subject highly attractive and calculated to make a deep impression on the public mind."[5] Sayward reprinted some of Brisbane's columns, and he suggested that Fourierist communities might represent a viable alternative for men who found themselves out of work.[6] Sayward noted the existence of "friends to the Fourier plan" in Bangor by 1843; the next year, the Fourierist newspaper the *Phalanx* reported the existence of a Fourier club in the city.[7]

The popularity of the Fourierist movement aroused concern among its opponents in Bangor and elsewhere, and Edward Kent's "Vision of Bangor" marked him as such an opponent. The story's ardent defense of both capitalism and masculinity revealed how thoroughly Kent's own gender identity was rooted in the successes of the capitalist economic system that prevailed in the city. By the 1840s, Bangor had become a prosperous medium-sized city whose most ambitious citizens hoped that it would rival both Portland and Boston in importance.[8] Founded as Kenduskeag Plantation in 1769 and located at the point where the Kenduskeag Stream joins the Penobscot River, Bangor had gone through a frontier phase in the late eighteenth and early nineteenth centuries.[9] It had become a boom town by the 1820s. The city's prosperity was founded on the thriving lumber trade, in which pine logs were cut upstream and driven down the Penobscot to be milled at such nearby places as Veazie, Orono, and Old Town.[10] From Bangor, which had a harbor deep enough to accommodate ocean-going vessels, the city's lumber barons shipped their boards to destinations along the eastern and Gulf coasts of the United States as well as to markets in the West Indies and Europe.[11] Incorporated as a city in 1834, Bangor suffered economic downturns beginning in 1836, when the bottom fell out of a land market based on rampant speculation. National economic troubles brought by the Panic of 1837 and the depression that followed hindered the city's recovery.[12] But like the rest of the nation, Bangor had been restored to economic equilibrium by the mid-1840s.[13] As historian Stewart Holbrook described the city in his influential book *Holy Old Mackinaw* (1938), by mid-century it was a masculine paradise of "booze, bawds, and battle" in which rough-hewn loggers and rivermen shared with elite lumber barons a taste for rum and raw capitalism.[14] Edward Kent presented a city somewhat removed from such boom-town rowdiness, but he celebrated the ties among capitalism, competition, and masculinity nonetheless. Bangor's economic resiliency attested to the strength of capitalism, and for Kent, that strength also signalled masculine power. In his "Vision of Bangor," he ellided threats to capitalism with threats to masculinity.

Kent defended both capitalism and masculinity against such threats in response to an invitation to contribute to *Voices from the Kenduskeag,* and this encounter with women reformers provoked the gender anxiety he expressed in "Vision of Bangor." *Voices from the Kenduskeag* was a charitable project, a gift book whose sales would benefit the Bangor Female Orphan Asylum (BFOA). Typical of antebellum voluntary associations, the organization was a classic example of women's benevolent work. Like similar organizations in other cities throughout the United States, the BFOA brought elite women together to aid their less fortunate sisters.[15] The organization had originally been established as the Union Female Education Society in 1835, with the goal of aiding indigent women.[16] When it incorporated as the BFOA, first in 1836 and again in 1839, the organization aimed to provide education, work and support for orphaned girls.[17] Such goals required funding, and the gift book had become a familiar fundraiser by 1848, the best known example being the *Liberty Bell,* the abolitionist gift book edited by Boston's Maria Weston Chapman. Benevolent women solicited poetry, fiction, and essays from well-known figures in hopes that their friends and acquaintances would support their charitable project through purchase of the book. As editors, Appleton and Barrett enlisted the aid of Bangor's leading citizens to benefit the BFOA. Contributors included not only the editors and other ladies such as Barrett's sister, Henrietta Crosby Ingersoll, but also local authors Eliza Leland Crosby and John E. Godfrey, Unitarian pastor Frederic Henry Hedge, and political and business leaders such as Edward Kent. In the "Advertisement" that followed the title page of *Voices from the Kenduskeag,* Barrett emphasized the cooperation of these leading citizens and the charitable purpose of the book (3). Such a project might seem unlikely to arouse the ire of its contributors, but Edward Kent objected less to either the gift book or the goals of the BFOA than he did to its editors, particularly Jane Sophia Appleton.[18]

Like Kent and her co-editor Cornelia Crosby Barrett, Jane Appleton belonged to Bangor's elite, but unlike either she was dedicated to the causes of women's rights and Fourierism.[19] Her father, Thomas A. Hill, had been one of the earliest practitioners of law in the city.[20] Also active in local political and business affairs, Hill was wealthy enough by the mid-1830s to have new homes built for himself and for his two daughters and their husbands near the city's commercial district. His sons-in-law, John Alfred Poor and Moses L. Appleton, were also Bangor attorneys.[21] Jane Appleton was the younger of Hill's daughters. A well-educated woman who read German and wrote poetry, she published an essay on women's education in Sarah Josepha Hale's *American Ladies' Magazine* in 1835.[22] She may have learned of Fourierism from Mary Poor, to whom she was related by marriage; Mary Poor was treasurer of the local Fourier club in 1848.[23] Although Appleton's name did not appear in newspaper references to the Fourier club, her "Sequel to the Vision of Bangor" attests to her strong interest in Fourierism as a way to achieve education, economic autonomy, and equality of opportunity for women.

Appleton's interest in Fourierism and women's rights distinguished her from her co-editor, Cornelia Crosby Barrett, whose concerns were more conventional. In addition to the advertisement that opened *Voices from the Kenduskeag* and the "Poetical Introduction" that she co-wrote with Appleton, Barrett contributed three prose pieces to the book. In a temperance fable entitled "Asa Glover, Esq.", Barrett suggested the punishment that awaited men who profited from the immiseration of others through the sale of alcohol. Her other two stories made similar moral points. In "First Impressions" she lamented the dangers of gossip, and in "The Resolve" she praised the value of Christian self-improvement and extolled behavior that "exhibited in a life of active usefulness, the renovating power of divine truth" (219).

In contrast, four of the six poems that Appleton contributed in addition to her utopian short story suggested an interest in more radical forms of social change. She seemed, for example, to be an advocate of the peace movement. In "Lenora" she translated German poet Gottfried August Bürger's influential Romantic ballad about a woman whose dead lover bore her away to his resting place during the night. One source of the poem's appeal to Appleton may have been its anti-war implications: the lover had died in a war the poem characterized as "dissension" born of "ruthless spirits" (129). Appleton also voiced her opposition to war in "The Macedonian," which celebrated the use of a captured British warship to transport grain for the relief of hunger in Ireland. She specifically linked humanitarian goals to women in "Woman, Is It By Thee?", in which she lamented a gift presented to a military commander by a group of women. Citing "the lesson . . . / of Love, and Peace, and Mercy taught / By Blood and Cross" (31), she called for Christian women to oppose the U.S.–Mexican War. Her concern for women's proper role contributed to her sense of frustration with the way her society treated women. This frustration came through in her humorous poem "On Hearing Ladies Toasted as the 'Poetry of Life,'" which showed her low opinion of the way flowery descriptions of women ignored their hard work and kept them from "our lawful claim" (114). In these poems, as in her "Sequel to the Vision of Bangor," Appleton revealed herself as more interested in fundamental social change than Barrett.[24] It was this interest and the unfeminine vigor with which she pursued it that Kent found objectionable.

Edward Kent's tale in fact speaks volumes about the anxieties created by women's reform activism in one man who thoroughly identified with the perquisites of masculinity. Kent had made a successful career in the two most masculine professions of the nineteenth century—law and politics. Law put to good use masculine characteristics that society generally viewed as negative. While the profession of law fostered such masculine weaknesses as aggressiveness and worldliness, it also represented the best possible use of such masculine traits as dominance and reason since it employed them in the pursuit of justice.[25] Similarly, traits Americans associated with men were perceived to serve the public good in the political arena. Although such negative masculine attributes as conflict and competitive self-interest characterized the partisan politics of the second quarter of the nineteenth century, men who engaged in politics as candidates and voters participated in a masculine culture that emphasized the strength and power of government.[26] In his own successful political career, Edward Kent embodied Alexis de Tocqueville's observation that lawyers in the United States formed "the highest political class."[27] As such, Kent benefited greatly from the prerogatives of masculinity, and it was clearly these prerogatives that he defended from encroachments by women like Appleton in his "Vision of Bangor in the Twentieth Century."

Kent's short story followed a fairly typical form for utopian fiction, a dream or vision of the future brought on by extraordinary circumstances in the author's daily life. Such stories often contain a frame narrative in which the author appears as himself (or infrequently herself—the time traveler is usually male), and the utopia proper as an internal narrative that the author relates as an account of a dream or trance.[28] Kent had used this device in a short story entitled "The Field of the Incurables," which he published in 1826 and which Appleton and Barrett reprinted in *Voices from the Kenduskeag*. A humorous story about hypochondria, this earlier piece had also shown Kent's admiration for Lord Byron, inspired perhaps by Kent's interest in the Greek struggle for independence.[29] As an epigraph, Kent quoted Byron's 1816 poem "Darkness": "I had a dream, which was not all a dream" (100).[30] Kent used this dream conceit again in his "Vision of Bangor in the Twentieth Century." Self-deprecating humor marked this later work as well, but the humor thinly concealed an undercurrent of criticism for Appleton's unfeminine behavior.[31] In his frame narrative Kent gave his account of Appleton's efforts to persuade him to write the story; his utopia recounted a dream of a visit to Bangor in the year 1978. In that dream he envisioned a world in which women like Appleton did not exist.

Why would his story express such hostility toward Appleton that she would feel compelled to respond? Edward Kent represented himself as an unwilling contributor to *Voices from the Kenduskeag* (to which he belittlingly referred as the "Bangor book"), but his dispute with Jane Appleton went far deeper than this unwillingness, extending to some of the ambivalences that surrounded masculinity in the mid-nineteenth century. If law and politics made use of negative masculine traits for higher purposes, writing had more feminine connotations as a profession. The great male authors of the American Renaissance, for example—Emerson, Hawthorne, Melville, Whitman—perceived themselves as alienated from the aggressive and self-interested standards of nineteenth-century masculinity, and Kent's story suggests that others also saw writers as less than manly.[32] In fact, lawyers as a group self-consciously rejected the writing of literature when they defined law as a masculine, public profession in the late eighteenth and early nineteenth centuries.[33] Kent himself had mixed literature and law early in his career. "The Field of the Incurables" was published the year after he moved to Bangor and began to practice law in the city. The story had seemed to hold few implications for his gender identity; it was merely an amusing tale about human folly. But when Jane Appleton asked Kent to take up his pen again over twenty years later, the writing of literature seemed to hold a much deeper and more portentous meaning for him. As a successful lawyer and politician, he had much more to lose, and now the act of writing called up serious gender anxieties for Kent. The frame narrative of Kent's utopia suggests a deep fear of the writer he harbored secretly within himself. As the person who called that writer to the fore, Appleton became the embodiment of danger and gender confusion.

This confusion manifested itself in Kent's presentation of his encounters with Appleton as a perverse seduction. Edward Kent was, he assured his readers, "not a nervous man," but he also described himself as "one of the unfortunate victims, selected, I know not on what principle," to contribute to Appleton's project—that is, an endangered innocent of the sort found in gothic fiction (61).[34] In Kent's story, Jane Appleton was the demonic seducer, "calm, confident and secure," who made him feel "like the entwined fly in the web of the spider" (62). Though she frequently left him alone to contemplate his fate, this "inexorable woman" returned again and again to remind him that he must bow to her will (61). This seduction narrative implied that Kent faced a dire fate if he acceded to Appleton's demands. He described a greater and greater loss of his gender identity as Appleton drew him more and more into her plan. At first, he was able to fend off her assaults by losing himself in masculine pursuits like business, but as time wore on, he found himself more and more in her power. He began to feel a desire to write, and this sign of his weakness was followed by a feminization Kent described as an illness sure to have a "fatal result":

> I found myself parting my hair, and smoothing it down and opening my vest and turning down my collar *à la Byron*. I saw myself in the mirror, and there was a new and most ludicrously grotesque, sentimental, half-poetic and half-transcendental, and altogether lackadaisical stare of the eyes, and dropping of the eyebrows. The case began to look alarming. (62)

After another visit from Appleton, "feeling like one spellbound," Kent went home, where he fell asleep to dream of orphans, writing implements, and Bangor's future (63). In the end Kent suffered a dire fate indeed. Feminized, he became a writer.

Edward Kent took his revenge for this feminization by imagining a future for Bangor and for the nation that was aggressively masculine. In his persona as time-traveler, Kent entered the Bangor of 1978 a stranger, but soon found himself at home in a city in which the values of the marketplace prevailed and both Fourierism and feminism had failed.[35] Kent's future Bangor belonged to a nation that, following the pattern set by the U.S.–Mexican War, had extended its borders south all the way to Cape Horn. Capitalist competition and technological innovation had made it possible to travel from

Bangor to Boston in four minutes. Kent's narrator visited the Mount Hope Cemetery and the banks of the Kenduskeag, and back in the city he learned that Bangor no longer made its fortune in lumber but now engaged in trade and in the manufacture of "'cotton, woollen [sic] and mixed goods'" (69). Indeed, he surmised with satisfaction: "The dollar still remained the representative of value, and the idol of men" (69). Kent's future Bangor differed only in details from the city he knew in 1848.

If affirmation of national expansion and capitalist values characterized the observations of Kent's time-traveler, the crux of his utopia remained the proper relationship between women and men, just as that relationship was the central if unstated theme of his frame narrative. After asking his guide about the business life of the city, Kent's narrator inquired about "'social arrangements,'" by which he meant Fourierism. The guide replied: "'O, . . . that nonsense died a natural death, and with it the kindred absurdities of women's rights to participate in government and to direct affairs out doors as well as in.'" According to the guide, only an occasional "'old, cross-grained or disappointed maid'" raised "'a sort of snarl'" about women's rights, but on the whole, the women of 1978 had returned to the ways of the past. "'Our women,'" the guide assured Kent's narrator, "'bake and darn stockings and tend the babies, and mend their husbands' clothes, teach their children the way they should go, and walk with them in it, and read their bibles and as many books as they can find time to.'" Having experimented with women's suffrage, these women had found that "'nature was too strong for abstract theories'" and had agreed "'to compromise, and let the *women* rule indoors, and the *men* out'" (70, emphasis in the original). In Kent's utopia, women knew their place.

When Kent's narrator pressed his guide on the question of women's rights, the guide recounted a story that ridiculed the entire movement. According to this story, women had been granted suffrage, but the experiment had failed because of the impossibility of meshing feminine frailties with the masculine seriousness of the political process. Women had insisted on voting for candidates based on looks rather than qualifications, and when they had themselves been elected to public office, the work of the legislature had been delayed for such frivolities as shopping, fashion, and childcare.[36] In the case of a particularly serious matter that had required great secrecy, women's loose tongues had created a political disaster. Reforms that altered the nineteenth-century gender system were doomed, in Kent's eyes, because that system represented the only correct relationship between women and men. Its benefits were evident in an idyllic view of twentieth-century Bangor, in which children played marbles, rolled hoops, and batted balls beneath the branches of elm trees. When women knew their place, all was right with the world.

Kent's final visions expressed his utter hostility to women like Appleton, who refused to remain in their place. As he passed along the street, he noticed that some of the children were reading such classics as *Mother Goose*, *Robinson Crusoe* and *Pilgrim's Progress*. "It seemed there were some books," he noted, "that would *never* be consigned to oblivion" (72, emphasis in the original). Of course, oblivion was precisely the fate he reserved for Appleton's book. Entering a bookstore, he saw other classics on the shelf: the King James Bible, *Don Quixote*, and works by Shakespeare, Milton, and Robert Burns. When he asked for a copy of the "Bangor Book," the proprietor had never heard of it. Only one person in the store remembered it, "a little dried-up specimen of a man" who had seen the book in a corner of the Antiquarian Society, an alcove labelled "'the day of small things'" (72). Edward Kent took his final revenge by imagining Bangor's orphanage as "a substantial, elegant, and commodious building," inhabited by "healthy, happy, and well conditioned children" (73).[37] The BFOA's larger goal had survived the test of time much better than had Appleton's "Bangor Book." In the end, Appleton and her project were superfluous.

In response to Kent's efforts to put her in her place through his masculinist and capitalist vision of Bangor's future, Jane Appleton proposed an alternative future for the city. Taking its cue from the first line of Kent's story, her epigraph discounted his utopia as an old man's illusion—the biblical quotation read, "'Your young men shall see visions, and your old men shall dream dreams'" (243).[38] In "Sequel to the Vision of Bangor in the Twentieth Century," Appleton presented a much more detailed description of the relationship between women and men in Bangor's future and of the material conditions that fostered this relationship. She appropriated not only the form of Kent's story but also—in a move that might well have confirmed his gender anxiety—his persona as male time-traveler. Appleton, too, dreamed that she visited Bangor as Kent's time-traveler in 1978, but she replaced Kent's guide, whom she described as "'a cross-grained, conservative old creature'" known for "'venting his indignant ire against the progress of the sex'" (254). Her own guide resembled Clement C. Moore's description of Santa Claus in his 1823 poem "A Visit from St. Nicholas": "a hale, hearty old gentleman, with a right honest countenance, and an eye wherein a spice of roguery was bewitchingly blended with a deep, manly earnestness" (243–44).[39] Appleton's guide showed her a future Bangor in which women and men were intellectual and economic equals. Based on Fourierist plans for cooperative housekeeping, Appleton's utopia disputed Kent's assessment of the impracticability of Fourierism and predicted a more feminist future.

Jane Appleton began her description of Bangor's future with a series of observations that attacked masculine competitiveness and exclusivity and promoted cooperation and benevolence. In keeping with her poetical repudiations of war in general and the U.S.–Mexican War in particular, her guide showed her narrator a museum that displayed "'weapons of war'" as "'curiosities'" and memorials to the "'atrocities'" wrought by false notions of national honor (244). Expressing approval of "the great moral advance of society" represented by the end of war, Appleton's narrator also saw evidence that even disputes among churches had ended (244). And just as religious harmony and the peace museum indicated an end to competition, the guide's tale of the end of the Independent Order of Odd Fellows signalled the end of masculine exclusivity in the form of secret societies.[40] In a story that ridiculed the rites practiced by members of such organizations, the guide described the infiltration of an Odd Fellows' lodge by "'a parcel of wags'" (246). According to the guide, once the Odd Fellows had been dissolved, some of the former members had formed a benevolent society that performed good works "'without the drawbacks of secrecy and ceremony'" (250). For Appleton, war, religious differences, and secret societies highlighted the follies of men, while peace, cooperation, and benevolence—features associated with Fourierism, women's reform activism, and other movements for social change—pointed to a better way.

Like Kent's story, Appleton's turned from a set of general observations about her future Bangor to the question of relationships between women and men. She began this part of her story with a scene that contrasted nineteenth-century attitudes toward women with her vision of equality between the sexes. In this scene, Appleton's version of Kent's narrator encountered a woman in an art gallery and responded to her according to the custom of the nineteenth century. Noticing her "grace and dignity," he attempted to break the ice by flattering her (250). When the woman only laughed at his efforts, the time-traveler's guide explained that gender relations had changed in Bangor since the nineteenth century. "'Woman is no longer considered as a mere object for caresses and pretty words,'" the guide declared. "'She is not now petted and pacified with adulation . . . when she only asks for *justice. Your* age *fondled* woman. *Ours* honors her. You gave her *compliments. We* give her *rights*'" (251, emphasis in the original). Whereas "woman" had formerly been seen as "'a mere *adjunct* to man,'" she was now "'regard[ed] . . . as *complete in herself.*'" (252, emphasis in the original). In Appleton's utopia, women were not "poetry" but men's equals.

Women in Appleton's utopia enjoyed this egalitarianism because Fourierism had given them an autonomy unknown in the nineteenth century. Like some other women in the 1840s, Appleton saw in Fourierism the promise of independence through cooperative housekeeping.[41] In her utopia, eating houses and cooperative housework had given women the free time they needed to cultivate their minds. They were economically self-sufficient because Appleton's Fourierist Bangor "'gave due compensation to all industry, whether in man, woman or child'" (255). In fact, changes in women's work and compensation marked the most significant innovations Appleton's guide described. Resistance to such changes had been overcome as a result of "'the impossibility of getting female domestics for an occupation which brought so much social degradation and wear and tear of body and clothes'" (255). The burdens of housekeeping had been lightened through the use of "'steam, machinery, division of labor, [and] economy of material'" (256–57). Appleton described a community laundry as well as changes in cooking, "'window cleansing, carpet shaking, moving, sweeping, and dusting, too'" (257). And far from finding this work demeaning, women in her utopia "'[took] part in all these very processes,'" choosing the labor that suited them best and receiving fair wages for it (258). The economic independence they enjoyed as a result freed them from the necessity of marrying for money. Consequently, Appleton's guide reported, "'The family and the home are indeed sacred, and the bond broken only by death'" (258). Changes in women's work had far-reaching social consequences.

These changes did not mean, however, that women participated in electoral politics. In his "Vision," Edward Kent had imagined assertive women as masculinized and power-hungry creatures who threatened his own gender identity, but Jane Appleton self-consciously rejected masculine power. As she described them, the women of her future Bangor had no interest in participating in the political and economic activities of the public sphere. According to Appleton's guide, the story about women and politics that Kent had recounted had been the result of a prank. Some "'female wags'" had resorted to the joke as a way to silence men who misinterpreted every assertion of women's rights as an appeal for suffrage (260). In Appleton's view, electoral politics held no interest for women.

In fact, Appleton used the issue of women and suffrage to instruct men on their proper role, much as Kent had used the issue to do the same for women. Recalling perhaps Kent's celebration of the fact that money had remained "the idol of men," Appleton's guide described to her time-traveler an incident in which women had been forced to take part in public affairs because men had neglected their responsibilities. According to the guide, men had at one time become "'completely eaten up with the love of money,'" a disease that had discolored their skin and eyes and deranged their minds (260). As a result of this "'money-leprosy,'" men had become unable to meet their public responsibilities, and whenever questions had arisen about anything other than money, they had all deferred to their wives (260). Forced to take over the affairs of state, women had used unspecified "domestic" measures to restore "order and beauty . . . to society" and to assure that "men became men again" (261). For Appleton as for Kent, gender-appropriate behavior—which included men in control of political affairs—ensured the smooth running of society.

Appleton's story closed with a description of a party that highlighted the similarities and differences in Appleton's and Kent's gender ideals as well as the strength of the disagreement between them. At the party, Appleton's narrator observed the effects of her new gender system in practice. Although the party looked on the surface much like "festive gatherings" of the nineteenth century, her time-traveler perceived a subtle difference: "The courtly manners, the graceful exteriors, veiled a *spirit*. Man was there in his manly sincerity, as well as pride, and woman in her majesty, as well as beauty" (262, emphasis in the original). And both were there "to meet each other as friends and companions, as spirits bound to the same haven, and created for the same objects" (262–63). The women and men of her utopia preserved their gender differences in the service of a higher equality. Each not only knew his or her place but also felt its higher purpose. Different but equal, they respected each other for their separate contributions to their common goals. Appleton showed her antagonism to anyone who disagreed with her utopian ideal in a final vision that echoed the end of Kent's earlier story "The Field of the Incurables" and may have been a play on his description of himself as a writer. Her narrator saw an interloper at the party whom her guide described as an "exquisite" (265). Effeminate in dress and manner, this intruder was—like those afflicted with "money-leprosy"—a man who did not know his own place. Appleton's narrator found him "grotesque," from his elaborately groomed hair to his lavish clothing and jewelry. The exquisite disrupted the party with a hideous laugh that was "part squeal, part cackle, and part a suppression of both" (265). When Appleton's narrator and guide found themselves unable to keep from joining in this "infectious" laughter, their "unearthly noises" caused an earthquake that brought Appleton's vision to a violent end (265). A figure of ridicule who inappropriately crossed gender boundaries, Appleton's exquisite paralleled Edward Kent in his inimical relationship to her utopia.

As chilling as her description of the exquisite may have been, Appleton's criticism of the marketplace and her lack of interest in politics might have been even more threatening to Kent and the prerogatives of masculinity he sought to defend. Jane Appleton directly criticized the love of money that Edward Kent celebrated, and she dismissed as foolish masculine paranoia the notion that women would want to vote. Her position on suffrage might have been a relief to Kent in one way. If his worst nightmare was women's involvement in politics, his fears should have been relieved by Appleton's disavowal of the franchise as a goal. But in another way, her outright dismissal of politics—the profession to which Kent had devoted much of his adult life—might have been quite a blow. If politics was ultimately of little interest or importance to women like Appleton, would not Kent himself become the "dried-up specimen" of his own story, who concerned himself with "small things"? The threat of such inconsequence might have been enough to make him a nervous man indeed.

He might have grown even more nervous had he paid close attention to Appleton's statement of her own goals. She represented those goals as simple and reasonable—intellectual equality, freedom from the tedium of housework, economic independence, mutual respect between women and men. These goals did not speak directly to Kent's fears about women's rights and the possible effects for men, but they did suggest that Kent's fears were to a certain degree well-founded. Men, after all, had more to lose than control over electoral politics. Jane Appleton did indeed seek to challenge the power of men in such arenas as education and domestic decision-making, and she sought to end women's economic dependence on men. She was an assertive woman who advocated a form of social and economic change that rejected the capitalist foundations of masculinity and promoted gender equality. She thus represented a multifaceted threat to a masculinity founded on notions that women should "rule indoors, and . . . *men* out." Edward Kent's reaction to Jane Appleton's practices as an editor and to her interests in Fourierism and women's rights exposes the fragility of masculinity in the volatile capitalist economy that he celebrated.

An earlier version of this paper was presented at the 1996 conference of the Northeast Modern Language Association in Montréal and before a faculty group at Wheaton College. The author would like to thank Bonnie Anderson, Susan Lynch Foster, Andrea Constantine Hawkes, Mazie Hough, Polly Welts Kaufman, Darby Lewes, Jeem Trowbridge, Michael Tomasek Manson, and the anonymous readers for this volume.

1. [Cornelia Crosby Barrett and Jane Sophia Appleton, eds.], *Voices from the Kenduskeag* (Bangor, Maine: David Bugbee, 1848). Contributors and editors were anonymous; attribution of authorship is based on later lists of contributors in copies in the Bangor Public Library, Bangor, Maine. Parenthetical citations refer to this volume. Both Kent's "Vision of Bangor in the Twentieth Century" and Appleton's "Sequel" were reprinted in *American Utopias: Selected Short Fiction*, ed. Arthur O. Lewis, Jr. (New York: Arno, 1971). An abridged version of Appleton's "Sequel" may also be found in *Daring to Dream: Utopian Stories by United States Women, 1836–1919*, ed. Carol Farley Kessler (Boston: Pandora, 1984), 49–64.

2. The literature on nineteenth-century gender systems is vast and constantly growing. The classic works on women and nineteenth-century gender ideology are Barbara Welter, "The Cult of True Womanhood: 1820–1860," *American Quarterly* 18 (Summer 1966): 151–74; Kathryn Kish

Sklar, *Catharine Beecher: A Study in American Domesticity* (New Haven, Conn.: Yale University Press, 1973); and Nancy F. Cott, *The Bonds of Womanhood: "Woman's Sphere" in New England, 1780–1835* (New Haven, Conn.: Yale University Press, 1977). On men and masculinity, see Michael Gordon, "The Ideal Husband as Depicted in the Nineteenth-Century Marriage Manual," in *The American Man*, ed. Elizabeth H. Pleck and Joseph H. Pleck (Englewood Cliffs, N.J.: Prentice-Hall, 1980), 145–57; E. Anthony Rotundo, *American Manhood: Transformations in Masculinity from the Revolution to the Modern Era* (New York: Basic Books, 1993).

3. On Fourierism in the United States, see Carl J. Guarneri, *The Utopian Alternative: Fourierism in Nineteenth-Century America* (Ithaca, N.Y.: Cornell University Press, 1991); Arthur E. Bestor, Jr., "American Phalanxes: A Study of Fourierist Socialism in the United States (With Special Reference to the Movement in Western New York)," 2 vols. (Ph.D. diss., Yale University, 1938). For Fourier's theories, see *Oeuvres complètes de Charles Fourier* (Paris: Anthropos, 1966–1968); Frank E. Manuel, *The Prophets of Paris* (Cambridge, Mass.: Harvard University Press, 1962); Nicholas V. Riasanovsky, *The Teaching of Charles Fourier* (Berkeley: University of California Press, 1969); Jonathan Beecher and Richard Bienvenu, trans. and eds., *The Utopian Vision of Charles Fourier: Selected Texts on Work, Love, and Passionate Attraction* (Boston: Beacon Press, 1971; reprint, Columbia: University of Missouri Press, 1983); Jonathan Beecher, *Charles Fourier: The Visionary and his World* (Berkeley: University of California Press, 1986).

4. *Phalanx* 1, 10 (18 May 1844): 148; *Phalanx* 1, 17 (24 August 1844): 255; *Harbinger* 4, 4 (2 January 1847): 64; *Harbinger* 6, 14 (5 February 1848): 110.

5. *Bangor Daily Whig and Courier*, 30 July 1842.

6. For reprints of Brisbane's column, see for example, *Bangor Daily Whig and Courier*: 19 April 1843, 28 April 1843, 5 May 1843, 12 May 1843; for Fourierist communities as a solution to unemployment, see *Bangor Daily Whig and Courier*: 26 October 1842, 24 April 1843.

7. *Bangor Daily Whig and Courier*, 8 April 1843; *Phalanx* 1, 10 (18 May 1844): 148.

8. Carol N. Toner, *Persisting Traditions: Artisan Work and Culture in Bangor, Maine, 1820–1860* (New York: Garland, 1995), 30.

9. "City of Bangor," in *The Bangor Directory; Containing the Names of the Inhabitants, Their Occupations, Places of Business, and Dwelling Houses, and the City Registers, with Lists of the Wharves, the City Officers, Public Officers, Banks and Societies, and Other Information* (Bangor: James

Burton, Jr., 1834), 9; James B. Vickery, "The Settlement of Old Kenduskeag," in *An Illustrated History of the City of Bangor, Maine*, ed. James B. Vickery (Bangor, Maine: Bangor Chamber of Commerce Bi-Centennial Committee, 1969), 15–21.

10. Richard W. Judd, "Maine's Lumber Industry," in *Maine: The Pine Tree State from Prehistory to the Present*, ed. Richard W. Judd, Edwin A. Churchill, and Joel W. Eastman (Orono: University of Maine Press, 1995), 270–71.

11. David C. Smith, "Lumbering and Shipping in Bangor Port: The Halcyon Days of the Nineteenth Century," in *Illustrated History*, ed. Vickery, 29–38; Richard G. Wood, *A History of Lumbering in Maine, 1820–1861*, University of Maine Studies, Second Series, No. 33 (Orono: University of Maine Press, 1935), 200–25.

12. John Christopher Arndt, "'The Solid Men of Bangor': Economic, Business and Political Growth on Maine's Urban Frontier, 1769–1845" (Ph.D. diss., Florida State University, 1987), 142–254.

13. Toner, *Traditions*, 19–38.

14. Stewart Holbrook, *Holy Old Mackinaw* (New York: Macmillan, 1938). The quotation is from an excerpt, "The Flowering of a Lumber Town," in *A History of Maine: A Collection of Readings on the History of Maine, 1600–1976*, ed. Ronald F. Banks (Dubuque, Iowa: Kendal/Hunt, 1976), 246–51, quotation on 247.

15. Barbara J. Berg, *The Remembered Gate: Origins of American Feminism, The Woman and the City, 1800–1860* (New York: Oxford University Press, 1978); Mary P. Ryan, "A Women's Awakening: Evangelical Religion and the Families of Utica, New York, 1800–1840," in *Women in American Religion*, ed. Janet Wilson James (Philadelphia: University of Pennsylvania Press, 1980), 89–110; Nancy A. Hewitt, *Women's Activism and Social Change: Rochester, New York, 1822–1872* (Ithaca, N.Y.: Cornell University Press, 1984); Anne M. Boylan, "Women in Groups: An Analysis of Women's Benevolent Organizations in New York and Boston, 1797–1840," *Journal of American History* 71 (1984): 497–523; Anne M. Boylan, "Timid Girls, Venerable Widows and Dignified Matrons: Life Cycle Patterns Among Organized Women in New York and Boston, 1797–1840," *American Quarterly* 38 (1986): 779–97; Lori D. Ginzberg, *Women and the Work of Benevolence: Morality, Politics, and Class in the Nineteenth-Century United States* (New Haven, Conn.: Yale University Press, 1990); Anne Firor Scott, *Natural Allies: Women's Associations in American History* (Urbana: University of Illinois Press, 1991).

16. Abigail Ewing Zelz and Marilyn Zoidis, *Woodsmen and Whigs: Historic Images of Bangor, Maine* (Virginia Beach, Va.: Donning, 1991), 110.

17. *Private and Special Acts of the State of Maine, Passed by the Sixteenth Legislature, At its Session, held in January, 1836. Published Agreeably to the Resolve of June 28, 1820.* (Augusta, Maine: Smith and Robinson, 1836), 303; *Private and Special Acts of the State of Maine, Passed by the Nineteenth Legislature, January Session, 1839. Published Agreeably to the Resolve of June 28, 1820.* (Augusta, Maine: Smith and Robinson, 1839), 647–48. The 1839 incorporation made the organization tax exempt. The number of incorporators had declined from 1836, as had the amount of real estate and income allowed the organization, perhaps a reflection of the economic depression affecting Bangor and the nation. On the significance of incorporation for women's benevolent associations, see Ginzberg, *Benevolence*, 48–53.

18. Similar complaints about the editors of the volume marked William Paine's "Correspondence" (138–45).

19. Neither Appleton nor Barrett were listed among the incorporators of the BFOA named in 1836 or 1839, but the women whose names were included came from the same business and professional elite to which Appleton and Barrett belonged.

20. John E. Godfrey, "Memoir of Hon. Edward Kent, LL.D.," *Collections of the Maine Historical Society* 8 (Portland, Maine: Hoyt, Fogg & Donham, 1881), 452.

21. Deborah Thompson, *Bangor, Maine, 1769–1914: An Architectural History* (Orono: University of Maine Press, 1988), 83–86 and 67–68; James H. Mundy and Earle G. Shettleworth, Jr., *The Flight of the Grand Eagle: Charles G. Bryant, Maine Architect and Adventurer* (Augusta, Maine: Maine Historic Preservation Commission, 1977), 41–42. John Alfred Poor practiced law in Bangor until he moved to Portland in 1846 to pursue his interests in railroad promotion; see Charles W. Tuttle, "Hon. John Alfred Poor, of Portland, Me.," *New-England Historical and Genealogical Register and Antiquarian Journal* 26, 4 (October 1872): 357–75; Joel W. Eastman, "Transportation Systems in Maine, 1820–80," in *Pine Tree State*, ed. Judd et al., 311–19. Born in Waterville, Maine, in 1811, Moses L. Appleton graduated from Waterville College in 1830, studied law in Cambridge, and moved to Bangor in 1834. In addition to his legal practice he served as Bangor's representative to the state legislature in 1848 and 1849; see Henry A. Ford, *The History of Penobscot County, Maine* (Cleveland: Williams, Chase & Co., 1882).

22. *Bangor Daily Whig and Courier*, 1 April 1884.

23. I have been unable to find a complete membership list for the Bangor Fourier Club. Partial lists appear in: *Harbinger* 6, 20 (18 March 1848): 157; *Harbinger* 7, 2 (13 May 1848): 12–14; *Harbinger* 7, 22 (30 September 1848): 176. On the Poor family, see Alfred D. Chandler, Jr., *Henry Varnum Poor: Business Editor, Analyst, and Reformer* (Cambridge, Mass.: Harvard University Press, 1956); James R. McGovern, *Yankee Family* (New Orleans: Polyanthos, 1975). On Mary Poor, see Janet Farrell Brodie, *Contraception and Abortion in Nineteenth-Century America* (Ithaca, N.Y.: Cornell University Press, 1994), 9–37; Ronald J. Zboray and Mary Saracino Zboray, "Political News and Female Readership in Antebellum Boston and Its Region," *Journalism History* 22, 1 (1996): 2–14.

24. Appleton's other two contributions were more conventional. "The Veiled Donor" paid homage to an anonymous woman who had donated two hundred dollars to the BFOA (273), and in "The Child's Spring Song" Appleton celebrated the free spirit of a child who could imagine himself or herself outdoors even when a mother bid the child to "mind" (266–67).

25. Rotundo, *American Manhood*, 171–72.

26. Rotundo, *American Manhood*, 217–19.

27. Alexis de Tocqueville, *Democracy in America*, trans. Henry Reeve (New York, 1945), 1:288, quoted in Rotundo, *American Manhood*, 172.

28. Darko Suvin, *Metamorphoses of Science Fiction: On the Poetics and History of a Literary Genre* (New Haven, Conn.: Yale University Press, 1979), 170–93. For mention of the difficulty of analyzing Kent's utopia, see Lyman Tower Sargent, "Utopia—The Problem of Definition," *Extrapolation* 16, 2 (1975): 137–47.

29. Godfrey, "Memoir," 452–53.

30. George Gordon, Lord Byron, *The Complete Poetical Works of Lord Byron*, Cambridge Ed., ed. Paul Elmer More (Boston: Houghton Mifflin, 1905), 189–90.

31. On Kent's sense of humor, see Godfrey, "Memoir," 461–68.

32. David Leverenz, *Manhood and the American Renaissance* (Ithaca, N.Y.: Cornell University Press, 1989).

33. Michael Grossberg, "Institutionalizing Masculinity: The Law as a Masculine Profession," in *Meanings for Manhood: Constructions of Masculinity in Victorian America*, ed. Mark C. Carnes and Clyde Griffen (Chicago: University of Chicago Press, 1990), 133–51.

34. D.A. Miller, "*Cage aux folles*: Sensation and Gender in Wilkie Collins's *The Woman in White*," in *Speaking of Gender*, ed. Elaine Showalter (New

York: Routledge, 1989), 187–215; see also Eve Kosofsky Sedgwick, *Between Men: English Literature and Male Homosocial Desire* (New York: Columbia University Press, 1985).

35. I use the anachronistic term "feminism" advisedly. Women who sought to change women's status as women used the term "woman's rights" rather than "feminism" in the nineteenth century, and the latter term did not come into general use in the United States until the early twentieth century; see Nancy F. Cott, *The Grounding of Modern Feminism* (New Haven, Conn.: Yale University Press, 1987). In this instance, the term provides a convenient shorthand for a focus on broadening women's educational opportunities and reducing women's economic dependence on men.

36. Duties such as shopping and childcare made up a significant proportion of middle-class women's work by the mid-nineteenth century; see Jeanne Boydston, *Home and Work: Housework, Wages, and the Ideology of Labor in the Early Republic* (New York: Oxford University Press, 1990).

37. Bangor's Children's Home was not built until 1869; Zelz and Zoidis, *Woodsmen*, 110.

38. The quotation is from Acts 2:17.

39. These two descriptions are somewhat ambiguous and may represent a rebuke directed at Kent since both may in fact describe him. While the former certainly expresses Appleton's opinion of Kent the author of "A Vision of Bangor," the latter may well represent a tribute to Kent the city father who was well known for his sense of humor. On the significance of Moore's description of Santa Claus, see Stephen Nissenbaum, *The Battle for Christmas* (New York: Knopf, 1996), 49–89.

40. The Independent Order of Odd Fellows came to Bangor in 1844; see *The Bangor Directory; Containing the Names of the Inhabitants, Their Occupations, Places of Business, Residence, City Officers, Banks, Churches, and Other Useful Information* (Bangor, Maine: Samuel S. Smith, 1846), 87. On the relationship between masculinity and secret societies in the nineteenth century, see Mark C. Carnes, *Secret Ritual and Manhood in Victorian America* (New Haven, Conn.: Yale University Press, 1989).

41. Dolores Hayden, *The Grand Domestic Revolution: A History of Feminist Designs for American Homes, Neighborhoods, and Cities* (Cambridge, Mass.: MIT Press, 1981); Barbara C. Quissell, "The New World That Eve Made: Feminist Utopias Written by Nineteenth-Century Women," in *America as Utopia*, ed. Kenneth M. Roemer (New York: Burt Franklin, 1981), 148–74.

Mid-nineteenth-century men and women who debated the proper place for women in society simultaneously struggled to define the nature of ideal relationships between themselves. Economic changes were reducing older patterns of mutual interdependence between husbands and wives, patterns based on reciprocal labor within a family economy. These were being replaced with a contradictory ideal of marriage that valued both the separation of spheres and love and companionship between spouses. These changes occurred gradually and not without conflict. Men who rejected ideas about women's rights in favor of domesticity and subordination could simultaneously want their wives to understand and sympathize with their concerns. Women who sought equality in the public world did not demand it in private. Yet for many couples the nature of marriage was changing.

Individuals might first notice the changing nature of marriage in the ways young people courted. While arranged marriages had never been common on this side of the Atlantic, in colonial times the young at least paid lip service to their parents' wishes, and often valued their advice. Prospective husbands were evaluated on their economic potential, wives on their housekeeping skills, and young people recognized their parents' superior skill at assessing these matters. During the nineteenth century, however, romantic love increasingly became paramount when choosing a marriage partner. Women recognized that they would be expected to defer to husbandly authority, and so sought to make sure that authority would not sting.

One of the most dramatic changes in marriage nationwide over the course of the nineteenth century was the declining birth rate. While the details varied, overall women averaged seven children at the beginning of the century and only three or four by the end. Fewer children did not necessarily mean less work for women, however, for the declining birth rate was accompanied by rhetoric that demanded more individual attention to each child. Similarly, while industrialization meant that there was less domestic labor to be done, a declining birth rate meant fewer hands to help do it.

Both changes in courtship expectations and the declining birth rate helped to redefine the reality of marriage and family for white couples across the nation. While for the most part men and women continued to inhabit separate spheres with separate concerns, they simultaneously sought to develop closer personal relationships with their spouses than had previously been the norm. Constance Fournier describes some of the ways these tensions were felt by mid-century maritime couples.

"HOME FOLKS": MARITIME COUPLES OF PENOBSCOT BAY SUSTAIN FAMILY AND COMMUNITY ASHORE AND AT SEA

Constance Anne Fournier

In 1939, Maine writer Mary Ellen Chase described the lives of her grandmother's circle of sea-widowed friends as not being restricted by the "tidy, enclosed life" of a Maine village. Instead, she wrote, they were "alive and free, patient and wise, unflurried and fearless."[1] Marriage to sea captains offered nineteenth-century Maine women an opportunity to extend and enhance their traditional female roles; they became important agents in linking sea and shore activities. Managing a household alone ashore or taking the family aboard their husbands' vessels enhanced maritime women's independence of spirit, strength of character, and knowledge of certain male skills and responsibilities. An examination of the correspondence of seafaring families also demonstrates the complexity of long-distance marriages and the strategies husbands and wives employed to preserve the family bond.

Letters between nineteenth-century Maine sailing captains and their wives reveal how both partners struggled to maintain marital intimacy and a sense of family and community. To cope with the ever present uncertainties and fears inherent in seafaring and to reduce the stress of long separations and frequent comings and goings, partners developed strategies to help them redefine their roles and establish flexible

Figure 1. Captain Joseph Griffin of the ship *Lillias*, Stockton Springs, Maine. Private collection.

relationships. In their absence, mariners depended upon wives to manage family and business affairs and maintain social networks at home.[2] When wives chose to sail with their husbands, they played an integral role in establishing community aboard ship and in port where they visited and celebrated with their seafaring neighbors.

Maritime couples strengthened their marriage bonds through frequent letter writing, anticipating reunions, and sailing together aboard ship. Their correspondence challenges the popular belief that Victorians were emotionally isolated and illustrates how husbands and wives made confidants and companions of one another.[3] Their letters reveal the high degree of stress repeated separations placed upon relationships and how much husbands and wives struggled to keep communication and intimacy alive. Wives at home worried about their husbands' health and safety at sea, while captain husbands feared losing contact with their family and community affairs ashore. Left behind ashore, wives complained of feeling trapped by the responsibilities of housekeeping and mothering; at sea, husbands complained of the loneliness of authority aboard ship and the isolation from family and community ashore. Both partners were forced to confront their own loneliness and dependency, the stress of homecomings, the possibility of marital infidelity, and the fear of death of a spouse.

Extended families were often essential in sustaining the maritime couple by offering support and companionship to a wife while her husband was away at sea. The mariner often counted on relatives to look after his immediate family in his absence. When Joseph and Abbie Griffin were married in 1867, they moved into a portion of Joseph's parents' home in Stockton Springs on Penobscot Bay.[4] The Griffin relatives were influential in town and helped Joseph obtain positions aboard ship and acquire capital for trading ventures. Joseph became captain of the *Lillias*, a Maine-built coaster[5] which chartered Maine cargo (mostly lumber and stone) to be delivered along the East Coast and the West Indies in exchange for other goods.[6] From 1868 to 1872, Joseph's parents and other relatives served as a support system for his wife and children while he was away at sea.

Figure 2. Abbie and Guy Griffin, wife and son of Joseph Griffin, Stockton Springs, Maine, 1870. Private collection.

Abbie and Joseph Griffin socialized mostly with Joseph's large extended family with whom they corresponded regularly and shared their lives emotionally, socially, and economically. They were related to nearly everyone in Stockton Springs, and Abbie lived in the same house with Joseph's parents and younger siblings. When Joseph and Abbie sailed together, they received letters from Joseph's many relatives in Stockton Springs who kept them informed of news at home.

When Abbie was at home, caring for her small children, she wrote Joseph about how thoughtful her in-laws were. Joseph's mother often brought Abbie her dinner and his cousins brought up her wood. Not having yet received her husband's wages, Abbie told him that Uncle Henry Staples, proprietor of a general store, supplied her with necessities on credit. She explained: "I have had to get some things at Uncle Henry's on tic, as you tell about. I hated to awfully, but I have needed money for so many things this winter. It has taken a good deal to run me, but those who dance must pay the fiddler. I will try and do the very best I can."[7]

On December 6, 1871, Joseph's father, Isaac Griffin, wrote Joseph that Abbie had given birth to a baby girl that day, and that Aunt Miranda had felt proud to help the doctor with the delivery. Joseph's father noted: "Your little tiny daughter weighs 8 pounds and 5 ounces, all rigged and ready for sea!"[8]

Joseph's extended family, who owned shares in several coasters sailing out of their harbor, helped each other in times of financial need, shared holidays and special events, and visited each other daily. Their honesty and loyalty to one another helped them to endure the hardships of seafaring life and maintain a tight-knit sense of community upon which they could depend for moral and financial support.

As the nineteenth century progressed, the increased demands of seafaring required that captain husbands spend less and less time with their families. In a letter to Abbie written shortly after their marriage, Joseph Griffin worried about earning enough to support his family through the long, hard Maine winter: "I do not admire the job quite as well as I should if I were getting the same wages toting lumber from Bangor so I could drop in home once in a while and get a clean shirt. But in this job it isn't what I like, it is the dollars I am after. We shall need some to lie back on this winter if I stay at home and I suppose I shall."[9] Preparing for long, cold winters without work, mariners often were forced to work particularly hard during the warmer seasons to make up for winters when fewer shipping charters were available.

Women shared their husbands' perceptions of the necessity of going to sea, when opportunities for making a living were better there than ashore. By the end of the nineteenth century, however, mariners were less able to defend their maritime occupation because American shipping and its profits were declining. Wives became more ambivalent about their husbands' careers as seafaring became more competitive and less profitable.[10] As early as 1828, Lucy Grey of Yarmouth, Maine foresaw a dismal future for deep water sailing. Sick with fever, she wrote her husband: "I wish you would give up the sea and turn farmer as navigation appears to be more and more discouraging."[11] Abbie Griffin expressed her willingness to move to the South Carolina port town of Little River (a timber trade destination) if it would improve their financial situation and allow them to be together. She admitted that "most anything is better than going to sea and not making anything. I would go anywhere for the sake of having you at home with me, for I don't think it is very pleasant to have a husband and have him gone all of the time."[12]

For the husband who placed a high priority upon his relationship with his wife and family, the job aboard ship became more and more difficult over time. Captain Josiah Mitchell of Yarmouth returned to sea in 1850 after a pleasant visit at home. He felt torn between his desire to be with his family and his duty as a provider, stating: "Sometimes I think I ought not to have come away at all, but on the whole I believe I did right in coming—if not I hope to be forgiven." Seventeen years later Captain Mitchell explained to his daughters in Yarmouth that he felt forced to continue going to sea after his wife's death because expenses had increased so drastically that he now felt quite poor. He said that it was necessary "in order to preserve for my darling children what little I have got that while my health is spared I must continue to work. I would prefer a situation on shore that would enable me to have all my children with me, but if I cannot get that, why I must take what I can get."[13]

A Stockton Springs couple, Captain Henry Edward Clifford and Henrietta (Etta) Park Blanchard Clifford maintained a lengthy correspondence between 1852 and 1860 while Edward was away at sea. Etta resided with Edward's family in Searsport where she gave birth to their son Benjamin in 1855. Torn between trying to earn a decent living and being with his family, Edward confessed his feelings of isolation and his ambivalence about being a mariner: "I am homesick, but I suppose I ought not to stop home for I cannot hardly get a living if I go to sea all the time but what is the good of living if we can't enjoy part of the time with friends, a person that follows the sea . . . is deprived of all of his friends all good society."[14]

Without the family and community support which sustained wives ashore, shipmasters found themselves isolated in their seat of command aboard ship. Relating their troubles and fears to their wives gave husbands some emotional relief from the burdens of being at sea. Perhaps they also hoped that by revealing the trials of seafaring, their wives would more easily tolerate and understand their erratic behavior during their visits home. Maritime husbands and wives constantly had to readjust their expectations and behavior to accommodate the difficult conditions of their marriages.

Maritime couples assuaged their loneliness by acknowledging romantic and nostalgic feelings in frequent correspondence. By openly expressing their feelings in the privacy of their letters, they strengthened their marital bonds and defined their love and commitment to one another. In 1871 Abbie Griffin wrote her husband about how their feelings for one another were intensified by the distance between them:

"We can't know how much we enjoy each other's company until we are separated from each other do we?"[15]

This mutual dependency upon letter writing, however, had its obstacles, particularly when one partner corresponded more frequently than the other could or would. Joseph Griffin's major complaint was that Abbie "doled out" too few letters, which made him feel neglected and anxious about what was happening at home. Shortly after their marriage he began an on-going complaint about the scarcity of her letters. Joseph admonished his wife: "As you do not think it worthwhile to write me whether there has been any rains at home, do not know which way to turn, so a fair wind may blow fifty dollars into my pocket and may blow a hundred out."[16]

Joseph discovered early in his marriage that his wife was no match for him as a correspondent, nor was she disposed to apologize for her infrequent and often brief letters. Abbie let him know she had more pressing things to occupy her time, such as keeping house and rearing a family alone. She wrote in no uncertain terms that loneliness was no easier for her to endure: "Don't think you spend any more time thinking of me than I do of you. One can think and work too you know, but as to lieing awake nights, I do not. . . . I have got nicely settled keeping house, but I don't have such a bully time as you think." Abbie's sharp retorts did not prevent Joseph from fussing about what he called her "sour little scribbles," which he felt came too infrequently.[17]

Occupied with taking care of her two children, Abbie had difficulty in finding time to write. The couple's differing expectations about the frequency of correspondence became a source of contention which they often camouflaged with humor or sentimentality. Allowing self-pity to take over when Abbie's letter writing did not meet his expectations, Joseph complained: "When I get no letters, I feel as if you cared as little about me as you do a holey stocking that has no mate. . . . Sometimes I feel so cross because you do not write more often that I could say things that would make you bawl for a month, but at the same time would walk a dozen miles to see you and give as many dollars for just one hour's chat, and think I could then go back about my business as contented as a bear in a cornfield."[18] His insistence upon a continuous flow of letters from home showed his lack of understanding of the heavy demands housekeeping and child-rearing placed upon women.

Captains often wrote about idle times in port, waiting for cargo to be unloaded and loaded, and assumed that their wives, too, had ample free time to take up pen and write. Responding to one of Joseph's scoldings, Abbie described the all-consuming care their sick son Guy demanded: "He has got so he lies in the cradle most of the time, but he has to be rocked all of the time. I am rocking him now, I had to hire my washing done last week, for I couldn't get time to do it." Three years later, Abbie struggled to make it through a snowy, cold January with a new baby daughter to care for in addition to their young son. Although her in-laws were close by to give her emotional support and run errands, Abbie was in charge of her small family and had to care for her children alone. She felt that Joseph could not possibly understand what it was like to be home with a newborn baby and a boy at a difficult age. She unabashedly told Joseph her limits: "I tell you [you] don't know anything about what it is to have a little baby and be all alone. I did my washing myself this week. Got it out at half past eleven in the morning, before the baby was up. I got along with it nicely, and that is all I have done this week."[19]

In spite of his frequent complaints, Joseph may have realized that he had to forego being showered with correspondence for the more practical benefits of having a wife with enough ambition and practical knowledge to maintain affairs at home. A seafaring husband might imagine an idealized Victorian woman by the hearth, but a practical "downeaster" like Joseph Griffin acknowledged that a "sick doll may be an agreeable companion when one is home, but not a profitable one to a poor man, or a comfort to think of when one is away all of the time."[20] He expected his wife to be his economic "helpmate," like wives of an earlier era, as well as his companion. Abbie knew she would have been a better helpmate if she could have worked outside the home for a wage, as single women in the village were earning money during the winter doing piece work at a garment shop. However, she described making her son a suit out of Joseph's old navy coat and reminded him how lucky he was to have a wife who saved money by doing all her own work. Abbie was proud of her thriftiness and often related her money-saving devices to her husband, letting him know that she contributed to their economic security.

Mariners like Joseph Griffin and Edward Clifford expressed a fear of losing contact with activities in their families and communities. They assumed their wives would nurture them as well as their children; men often expected this attention to continue in their absence. Edward Clifford worried about not receiving more letters from his wife Etta: "I shall almost think you have left me for you said if I would write often that you would do the same and I know that no man writes more letters than I do, but many write better ones, and I think no man thinks of his wife oftener than I do." Edward's letters repeated over and over again how much he missed his wife and child. Feeling increasingly sorry for himself, Edward confessed: "I am lonesome without you, I have nothing to love me when I come aboard and get my clothes and hug me when I am sick or tired."[21] Edward revealed his feelings of powerlessness, similar to those expressed in the diaries and letters of nineteenth-century women relegated solely to home and family life.

Continuously missing his wife, Edward Clifford wrote: "I want to see you dear Etta, last night when I went to bed I thought of home, I did laugh and almost cry when I thought how you would lay and kiss me, you would turn back to the baby if you do love him so well—you love me better."[22] Such "feminine" sentiments coming from a man's pen were not uncommon among nineteenth-century mariners writing to their wives at home. Captain Josiah Mitchell valued the expression of feelings and emotions: "but let fools laugh at such feelings if they will, for my part I would give but little for a man that was devoid of them."[23]

Private correspondence reveals that "tender feelings and sympathetic emotions" had become an important aspect of the Victorian male role. Masculine role expectations required, however, that men hide the emotional part of their natures and only express their emotions in private to the women they loved.[24] Nineteenth-century mariners may have been "unique in their willingness to express their softer sides, perhaps because of their distance away from home and their women," according to historian Margaret Creighton. American men expressed "more feminine attributes when female and male occupational worlds were more distant."[25] Most mariners voiced longings to be united once again with their wives and children, giving little validity to the popular assumption that mariners were cold-hearted men who went to sea to get away from them.[26] Mariners' ambivalent feelings about leaving their families ashore present us with a different picture of seafaring life.

Camouflaging his feelings with humor, Joseph Griffin expressed a loneliness as severe as any experienced by a stereotypical waiting wife.[27] Wanting his wife and son Guy to accompany him aboard ship, he wrote:

> I have finally come to the conclusion I had rather sleep three in a bed than sleep alone so long. . . . Do not think I will allow such a thing as your staying at home so long as there is the slightest prospect of

coaxing you at sea, for I am just sick enough to be cross and to need a cheerful wife to calm the troubled waters, and yet well enough to be thankful for such agreeable company . . . for I am so everlasting lonesome I would rather tend out a sick child than sit and wink alone like a sick goose on a mud puddle.

In contrast, Abbie noted simply and practically that she was unable to accompany him at sea: "I suppose you are as lonesome as I am, but misery likes company you know. I thought when you went away I would not wait until December, but I find I have had to. I think, though, that it is better for you to go alone, as you seem to fat on it." Although Joseph wrote Abbie that he wanted "a young wife as I am so nervous," he had settled for the company of a "great shaggy Newfoundland dog," that he struggled to bathe aboard a tossing ship.[28]

Discords in the maritime marriage were usually caused by the partners' different expectations, the difficulty of communication over long distances, and the loneliness inherent in physically isolated spheres of activity. Letter writing allowed maritime men and women to express their feelings and keep their affections and intimacy alive.[29] Sometimes the severest test was not sustaining romantic feelings for one another while apart, but maintaining a working relationship that could adjust to their comings and goings.[30]

Reunions were particularly stressful. The returning seafarer never found home the same as the one he imagined during his absence, nor was he the same for those awaiting him. Although wives equated home with a husband's presence, the mariner seemed to equate home with wife, friends, and relatives left behind, and not with housekeeping, childrearing, and other essential duties.

Wives regretted their husbands' limited happiness during their brief visits home. When her husband "dropped by for a clean shirt," Margaret Hannah Gray of Yarmouth, Maine, remembered the work she had to do: "When Nicholas left for foreign voyages, he would take with him fifty-two white shirts, with fine pleats and ruffles. Thus supplied, he had one clean shirt for every Sunday service that he conducted on shipboard."[31] Nicholas' arrival home inevitably meant she had fifty-two shirts to wash, starch, and iron before he left on the next long voyage. Needing to continue domestic duties while the husband was at home could precipitate his "crabbedness" at being neglected. Husbands used to being in command aboard ship wanted to take command of their households upon returning from sea. Wives, in turn, were not always willing or able to relinquish domestic authority; discords between couples on this account were common. Couples counted upon a companionate marriage characterized by emotional, social, and economic interdependence to carry them through long separations, but the reality was far more complex.

Separations often forced these men and women to re-evaluate and even change their accustomed roles and behavior. Once again alone at sea or at home, both husbands and wives had the opportunity to reflect upon the values of family life and their behavior toward one another during reunions. Upon returning to sea, husbands sometimes expressed regret for their contrary moods while at home. In his first letter to his bride, Joseph Griffin apologized for leaving Abbie a "widow" and for his own shortcomings as a husband: "I have come to the conclusion to remember you in your widowhood, partly to apologize for my crabbedness while at home."[32]

Edward Clifford also berated himself for not being a better husband: "You are kind to me dear Etta, you are a good wife and I wish you had a good husband but you have not, but I love you Etta and I think there is not one quite so good as you are and still I will often vex you, you will overlook it in me and only think of my better actions if I have any." Feeling similarly guilty about her unpleasant behavior, Etta confessed: "I have not forgotten how kind you always were to me when I was sick and how cross I used to be to you." She added: "Oh, Eddy, can you ever forgive me for such unkindness to you who was always so kind to me? But I hope you will not lay it up against me I know you cannot forget it, I was so ugly I shall try to do better at another time."[33]

Joseph Griffin reminded Abbie of a cool greeting he once gave her on his return home in answer to her hearty one, which he now regretted: "I have had it in my mind's eye to apologize to you for my coolness a good many times when we have been together. I could never pucker myself enough into being sentimental enough to do it, and look you square in the eye while apologizing." He was sorry for all his "matrimonial delinquencies" and the times he had "wounded her feelings, though I did not really mean to do so, for the fault was in my head not my heart."[34]

Couples who experienced difficulites adjusting to repeated separation and reunion could consider going to sea together. Men who were anxious about their families at home and women who were ambivalent about unaccustomed responsibilities often resorted to this alternative. Abbie Griffin admitted that she preferred sailing with her husband to remaining at home alone. Recognizing that her husband's ship felt more like home than anywhere else, she confessed: "Think I am about as poor a hand alone as you are to go to sea alone." A year later Abbie became even more insistent: "I do want you to get into a larger vessel for my sake, so I can go with you, for as to staying at home here alone I am not going to."[35]

Most captains longed to have their families aboard and were happy to have their wives make their ships more homelike. Returning to sea alone after having had his wife aboard, Edward Clifford missed his wife: "Is it of any use for me to

Figure 3. Searsport ship captains and families aboard the ship Electric
Spark. Courtesy Penobscot Marine Museum, Searsport, Maine.

say that I miss the one that has been my constant companion
for the last 16 months? . . . It does not seem like the same
pleasant home that it has been, I miss the dresses, the roses
and the baskets and most of all I miss my kind wife. I won't
think of it without crying."[36] Having a family aboard not only
eased a husband's loneliness, but it also made it easier to
socialize with other seafaring families, sharing visits, parties,
and outings while in port. The captain husband was once
again part of the family unit, a social ideal for couples forced
to spend so much time alone.

Wives joined their husbands aboard ship to keep marital
intimacy alive and satisfy the social expectation that husband and wife should be together. Often both captain and
wife recognized from experience that the implacable enemy
of their marriage was separation. Captains desirous of enjoying the comforts of home aboard ship rarely resisted taking
their wives and families to sea with them. Younger families

Figure 4. Cabin view of the ship Joesphus, built at Damariscotta, Maine, in 1876. The man in the photo is Capt. Joseph Henry Park. Courtesy Penobscot Marine Museum, Searsport, Maine.

believed it was crucial to stay together, not only to strengthen the bonds of a new marriage, but also for the children to grow up in the presence of their fathers. Many women accompanied their husbands continuously, even when they were expecting a child, but it was nearly always the wife's decision whether or not she chose to go to sea.[37]

Although wives reconstructed their traditional family roles aboard ship to meet the exigencies of seafaring, some wives' insistence on accompanying their husbands could also be viewed as a challenge to the pervasive ideology that a woman's place was in the home. Abbie Griffin explained why she wanted to sail with Joseph: "I think I shall have fully as easy a time going to sea as I shall staying at home—probably easier. I shan't have any fires to build in the morning."[38] Transferring the home to their husband's ship also gave women an opportunity and an excuse to go beyond their kitchens and see the world. Mary Ellen Chase, observing these seafaring women growing old in her native Blue Hill, claimed: "To men who earned their livelihood from the sea, its life became a matter of course; to women it meant a breaking of bonds, a sudden entrance into freedom."[39]

The decision to go to sea required a difficult choice for women between living without their husbands' company or without family, friends, and community. Leaving the security of their New England villages and the support of their families and friends was a real sacrifice. Their sea journals are filled with expressions of grief on parting from their "dear ones" ashore. Leaving older children behind to attend school was particularly difficult for mothers. Often sailing wives mentioned how much they missed their churches and families, especially on Sundays and holidays. In 1890, Jenny Prescott, homesick on the Fourth of July, which was her birthday as well, wrote to her folks in Woolwich, Maine: "I suppose the India crackers are snapping all round you; and the house is cool and fragrant with roses and new hay. Someone will remember my birthday, I think."[40] Letter writing was an important way to to keep up-to-date with loved ones and what was going on ashore.

Downeasters, the square-rigged merchant vessels built cooperatively by families living in the sheltered harbors of Maine, were well-suited for family life. They were comfortable, stable, and dry, with plenty of space on the after deck for a family to stroll, read, write letters, embroider, and have school lessons. Although family quarters were cramped, they could be luxuriously decorated and required less housekeeping than a home ashore. Most sailing wives busied themselves with traditional women's work, continuing such chores as sewing, ironing, and caring for their children. In addition, they had leisure to pursue fashionable Victorian hobbies. Clara Baker of Gardiner, Maine installed an organ and played Gilbert and Sullivan tunes, painted china and pictures, kept scrapbooks, and made pictures and wreaths of colorful, gelatin-laden seaweed from the Chincha Islands.[41]

Sailing wives were committed to family life and performed duties similar to those to which they were accustomed ashore. They had to accomplish their domestic tasks within tight quarters, amidst the pitch and roll of the ship, with fewer amenities, and sometimes with less help than they had ashore. Jenny Prescott of Woolwich described her chores on a typical stormy day at sea: "I have done a big day's work today. Four button-holes. . . . It is blowing a gale and has been for twenty-four hours. . . . The ship is hove to under a lower-main-topsail. It is very rainy and the water comes in through the skylights. Attending to the children, the cat and dog, watching and reading the barometer and bearing patiently the rolling and pitching has made my day's work."[42]

Scott Dow, writing about his Maine seafaring family, explained that his mother sailed with three small children, while two older children were left ashore to finish school: "Four times she went to sea with a six weeks' old baby, taking a goat aboard to supply milk for the children. She had to do all the sewing for the family, wash and iron, and administer old family remedies whenever someone was sick. Yet she still found time to read the Bible through."[43]

Another Maine woman, Maria Higgins, sailing with her family in 1883, accomplished many domestic tasks and taught her children reading, spelling, and arithmetic each morning. She and the children also tended the chickens, hens, two sheep, two pigs, and a dog and cat. Watching her children "race around brown, wild and barefooted like Indians," she commented on how easily they adapted to sea life. Her boy required less attention than on land.[44]

Women aboard ship kept house, nursed sick seamen, provided religious instruction and learned navigation. A few even assumed command of the ship in an emergency, just as they had supervised their own households in their husbands' absences.[45] Many considered life upon the high seas preferable, in spite of its discomforts, to waiting years at home for their husbands' return. Saddened to leave loved ones behind, terrified by storms at sea, and bewildered by strange faiths in foreign lands, these women learned to adapt. Sailing wives accepted the challenge of taking on new roles as circumstances required, thus enabling them to expand beyond the confines of the domestic sphere.

Sustaining a sense of community outside of the narrow limits of the ship was important for nineteenth-century sailing families. Maine families enjoyed meeting each other ashore in ports in South America, the Caribbean, and the Pacific. Here ships gathered and sailing couples, often with their children, spent a few days or even months ashore where they met other sailing families. Maine families exchanged gifts, necessities, and mail from home while they visited and enjoyed outings and holidays together. Wives welcomed a rest from the hardships aboard ship and indulged in shopping, visiting, and churchgoing.

Families far from home looked forward with great anticipation to meeting their Penobscot Bay neighbors in foreign ports. Mattie Nichols aboard the ship *Frank Pendleton* described in her husband's shipboard newspaper, the *Ocean Chronicle*, her anticipation of arrival in some faraway port. The excitement of meeting old friends highlighted the joy of a safe arrival. She noted, however, that arrivals also caused anxiety: "The principal thought is to get in safely without accident to ship, or crew, then we can anticipate receiving letters from our dear ones at home; but often there is sadness in connection with the thought, for fear of what may have happened while we were so many days at sea."[46] For Annie Dow, arriving in the port of Genoa in 1870 meant receiving long-awaited letters from her daughters, ages six and ten, left behind in Searsport to attend school. She was also cheered to find a number of American ships anchored there with captains' families aboard, "so we ladies have very pleasant times together."[47]

In 1878, after a long Pacific voyage, Annie Dow wrote how happy she was to arrive safely in the port of Yokohama: "Jimmie and I have got along very well in the cabin, but I have gotten most tired of it." She looked forward to a Fourth of July celebration with families from other American ships anchored there. All the American captains were going to gather aboard a ship chosen by committee. She was honored that their ship, the *Clarissa B. Carver*, was chosen for the celebration by two committees of American captains. She wrote her son in Searsport: "It was a rainy day but nevertheless the ship and the men of war were gaily decked with bunting. I never saw so many flags flying in one day before." Wishing that her son Freddie could have been with them, she described the "gala day": "We had the cabin all trimmed up with green. They commenced bringing roast pig and roast turkey. . . . Music was furnished by the bands from the different men of war that came on board at different times of the day." Her daughter Sarah danced with two Russian officers who had brought presents for the children. The celebration was even written up in the Yokohama paper.[48]

During Annie Dow's stay in Yokohama, she spent many days ashore with Mrs. Blanchard. The Blanchards' vessel, the *Henrietta*, was anchored nearby, enabling the Dow children, Clytie and Scott, and the Blanchard children to visit each other. "They were together all the time," Annie Dow said, "day and night, and Clytie and Nora had such nice times together, playing with paper dolls, etc." Annie wrote how sad she felt to see the Blanchards' ship depart, leaving her without female company: "Capt. Blanchard is so jolly, we shall be left quite alone. There is not another lady in the fleet." Describing how much they would miss the Blanchards, Annie Dow's letter demonstrated the strength of local community abroad: "Have had a real family gathering, a real Searsport crowd, all together with the children we numbered 13. Quite a lot of Searsport people to meet in a foreign port."[49]

Annie Dow later remembered that this was the last time they were to see Captain Blanchard, who lost his life along with one of his sons in an Atlantic storm. Captain Blanchard's six brothers all lost their lives at sea—a poignant reminder of the heavy toll the sea could take on a family. This constant fear unfortunately became a reality for both Etta Clifford and Abbie Griffin, whose marriages ended prematurely when their husbands were lost at sea. Less than two months before his thirty-second birthday, Captain Clifford and his five-year-old son drowned in a gale off Cape Cod, leaving Etta with newly-born twin girls. On April 19, 1874, Joseph Griffin was lost at sea just before his thirty-first birthday during a storm off Cape Hatteras. Abbie was expecting her third child, Josephine, who was born six months later.

Whether at home, far out at sea, or in foreign ports, Maine sailing couples struggled to keep their families and communities together in spite of the demands of seafaring. Sea captain husbands wrote letters to their wives expressing intense loneliness, exacerbated by isolation from family and society aboard ship. While wives ashore also expressed loneliness, it was mitigated by the constant care and company of children as well as visiting relatives and neighbors. The correspondence between maritime couples challenges the popular view that seafaring males preferred the exclusively masculine world of seafaring to family and community. Historians have debated whether marriage in the second half of the century was predominantly companionate or paternalistic in nature. In their correspondence, maritime couples demonstrated the companionate nature of their relationships through their desire to hold each other close. After difficult reunions when misunderstandings seemed especially painful, couples, again separated by vast oceans, would long for one another's company. They would again write sentimental love letters to draw one another close, confess their misunderstandings and beg forgiveness for unpleasant reunions, and always anxiously wait to be united once again. When they sailed together they never lost sight of their home community. They wrote letters, kept journals, published shipboard newspapers, entertained themselves and one another, "spoke" to their neighbors at sea, carried neighbors' letters home, and socialized with "home folks" in their Victorian ships' parlors in foreign ports. Against tremendous odds, the seafaring families of Penobscot Bay struggled to maintain and rejuvenate their marriages, family, and home community whenever and wherever they happened to be.

This paper is based upon the correspondence (1850–1872) of two Penobscot Bay couples, supplemented by excerpts from the letters of several other Maine captains writing about similar circumstances during the same time period. Some of these sources were used in a doctoral dissertation on the experiences of New England sea wives; other sources are from an ongoing research project with the Penobscot Marine Museum in Searsport for a prospective exhibit, "Penobscot Bay as an Ocean-Going Community at Sea and Ashore in the Nineteenth Century."

1. Mary Ellen Chase, *A Goodly Fellowship* (New York: Macmillan, 1939), 22.
2. During the colonial period, women took on male duties while their husbands were away as soldiers, seafarers, or foreign ambassadors. They were termed "deputy husbands." See Laurel Thatcher Ulrich, *Good Wives: Image and Reality in the Lives of Women in Northern New England, 1650–1750* (New York: Oxford University Press, 1980); Mary Beth Norton, *Liberty's Daughters: The Revolutionary Experience of American Women,*

1750–1800 (Boston: Little, Brown, 1980); Elisabeth Anthony Dexter, *Colonial Women of Affairs: Women in Business and the Professions in America Before 1776* (Boston: Houghton Mifflin, 1931) and *Career Women of America, 1776–1840* (Francestown, N.H.: M. Jones Co., [1950]; reprint, Clifton, N.J.: Augustus M. Kelley Publishers, 1972); Carolyn Bird, *Enterprising Women* (New York: W. W. Norton, 1976); Lyle Koehler, *A Search for Power: The "Weaker Sex" in Seventeenth-Century New England* (Urbana: University of Illinois Press, 1980).

3. Karen Lystra discusses the role of romantic love in nineteenth-century America and how couples strengthened their emotional ties by expressing their most intimate feeling in their private correspondence. Karen Lystra, *Searching the Heart: Women, Men, and Romantic Love in Nineteenth-Century America* (New York: Oxford University Press, 1989).

4. Ralph H. Griffin, Jr., ed., *Letters of a New England Coaster, 1868–1872* (Westwood, Mass.: n.p., 1968). Boarding with relatives was common in mid-nineteenth-century Maine. Few captains just starting out in the sea trade owned their own homes. See Scott J. Dow, "Captain Jonathan Dow, The Seafaring Days of Our New England Family," 1948 manuscript at the Penobscot Marine Museum, Searsport, Maine.

5. Coasters were any vessel involved with the coastal trade. In the nineteenth century Atlantic, coasters usually were sloops or schooners.

6. Downeast vessels were built for particular captains who, with their friends or relatives, took shares in the enterprise, often gaining a controlling interest. The main burden of the ship's business was carried on by the captain, who could choose to take his family to sea with him. Joanna Colcord, "Domestic Life on American Sailing Ships," *American Neptune* 2 (July 1942): 193.

7. Griffin, *Letters*, 209, 217, 243. Although tradition and the hard climate had taught Maine housewives to be frugal and resourceful, maritime women often became dependent upon relatives, neighbors, and shipping agents for favors or for money. In the Maine Maritime Museum in Bath there is a collection of notes from nineteenth-century mariners' wives to shipping agents requesting cash advances and news of their husbands' whereabouts.

8. Griffin, *Letters*, 211–13.

9. Griffin, *Letters*, 9. Bangor, Maine was the world's largest exporter of timber in the late nineteenth century. Since Bangor was just thirty-five miles up the Penobscot River, Joseph would have had more opportunities to visit his family than he had sailing the southern trade route.

10. Lisa Norling, in an article on New Bedford whaling wives, writes that wives often urged husbands to give up going to sea because long separations frustrated their ideal of the companionate marriage. See Lisa Norling, "'How Frought with Sorrow and Heart-pangs': Mariners' Wives and the Ideology of Domesticity in New England, 1790–1880," *The New England Quarterly* 65 (1992): 441–42.

11. Lucy Grey to Joshua Grey, Yarmouth, Maine, Hooker Collection of family letters, Schlesinger Library for Women's History, Radcliffe Institute, Cambridge, Massachusetts.

12. Griffin, *Letters*, 206. Economic security seemed to be a more immediate need during an era when women were discouraged from working for wages. If their husbands died at sea, as many did, with no property ashore, wives were left "high and dry" so to speak, unless they had the opportunity to remarry. Susan Griggs, in her study of re-marriage in nineteenth-century Newburyport, Massachusetts, attributes the large number of young widows "to the frequent exposure of mariners to premature death by drowning or disease," and sees mariners moving to less hazardous occupations in middle age. Susan Griggs, "Toward a Theory of Re-Marriage: A Case Study of Newburyport at the Beginning of the Nineteenth Century," *Journal of Interdisciplinary History* 8 (1977): 198–200. My own analysis of letters and diaries of New England coastal wives points to a pattern which emerged in the mid-nineteenth century. As middle-class women became more confined to the private sphere of domestic life as the century progressed, diminishing their opportunities to earn money through business and trade as many earlier maritime women had done, they became more dependent upon their husbands' financial support. Consequently, wives began urging husbands to take up farming or some other less hazardous and more secure occupation which would give them financial security, especially after a husband's death, when they might inherit property.

13. Josiah Mitchell to his wife, about 1850; Josiah Mitchell to his children, April 1867. Letters of Captain Josiah Angier Mitchell to his wife and children, Yarmouth, Maine, 1850–1873, from the private collection of Judith Ann Read Elfring, Yarmouth, Maine.

14. Edward Clifford to Henrietta Clifford, November 1852, Stockton Springs Historical Society, Stockton Springs, Maine. Wives sometimes traveled to various North Atlantic ports to meet their husbands while they were ashore.

15. Griffin, *Letters*, 188. For a discussion of the nineteenth-century assumption that the pain of separation gives meaning to love and sorrow defines

happiness, see Lystra, *Searching the Heart*, 50. Joanna Colcord, in writing about her life at sea, disagreed with the idea that the seafaring family was weakened by separation. Instead she claimed that "the alternation of close association and prolonged separation during which unaccustomed pens learned the art of holding each other close by long journal-letters, seemed to work quite the other way—seafaring families have remained among the most close-knit of any in the world." Colcord, "Domestic Life," 200.

16. Griffin, *Letters*, 43.

17. Ibid., 197.

18. Ibid., 71.

19. Ibid., 35, 228.

20. Ibid., 72.

21. Edward Clifford to Henrietta Clifford, 27 February 1856; 14 April 1860.

22. Edward Clifford to Henrietta Clifford, 12 February 1856. Etta had sailed with her husband more frequently before their son was born. Before his birth she had lost two daughters soon after birth, perhaps making her reluctant to bring their only surviving child to sea.

23. Josiah Mitchell to his wife, about 1850.

24. Lystra, *Searching the Heart*, 123–25.

25. Margaret S. Creighton, "Davy Jones' Locker Room," *Iron Men, Wooden Women: Gender and Seafaring in the Atlantic World, 1700–1920*, ed. Margaret S. Creighton and Lisa Norling (Baltimore: Johns Hopkins University Press, 1996), 125.

26. Historian Linda Grant DePauw challenges the popular misconception that seafaring men were such misogynists that they went to sea to get away from women: "The extraordinary strains placed on family life by long separations actually made families in seafaring communities stronger because their members appreciated each other more and held their affections together with prayers and letters, while families not so tested took their relationships for granted." Linda Grant DePauw, *Seafaring Women* (Boston: Houghton Mifflin, 1982), 11–12.

27. Popular culture and literature imagines the mariner's wife as a lonely woman pacing the shoreline or a rooftop "widow's walk" searching for sight of her husband's ship—a suitable role for a Victorian woman. The correspondence of maritime couples, instead, illuminates the loneliness of seafaring husbands, "pacing their decks" longing for wives and family at home—a view that contradicts the popular image of ultra-masculine seafaring men in such classic sea tales as Herman Melville's *Moby Dick* and Jack London's *Sea Wolf* who appear content to be away from their womenfolk.

28. Griffin, *Letters*, 47–48, 80, 61.

29. The pain of absence was aggravated by slow and difficult communication. Letters between ship and shore moved slowly down and across the Atlantic, around the Horn and across the Pacific. One whaling husband received only six of the more than one hundred letters his wife in New England had sent him. Letters would be sent by every ship sailing to where the intended recipient was believed to be. Men at sea also sent letters by every ship they met, in port or in passing on the ocean, that seemed likely to reach home before they would. "A large percentage of letters were hopelessly delayed or went astray entirely." Elmo Hohman, *The American Whaleman: A Study of Life and Labor in the Whaling Industry* (New York: Longsmans, Green, and Cole, 1928), 86–88. See also: A. B. C. Whipple, "The Whalers," in *The Seafarers* (Alexandria, Va.: Time-Life Books, 1979), 109–10.

30. Maritime marriages encompassed a wide spectrum of different kinds of unions, ranging from what Carl Degler describes as a companionate marriage to what Brian Strong describes as an emotionally distant marriage. Strong suggests that sentimentality may have been used to obscure deeper problems within the nineteenth-century family. Middle-class families emphasized "fitting together" and avoided deeper problems of identity, especially women's, and that "at best, marriages were often adjustments in which couples managed to live *not* unhappily." Brian Strong, "Toward a History of the Experimental Family: Sex and Incest in the Nineteenth-Century Family," *Journal of Marriage and the Family* 35 (1973): 458–60; Carl Degler, *At Odds: Women and the Family in America from the Revolution to the Present* (New York: Oxford University Press, 1980), 38.

31. Julianna FreeHand, *A Seafaring Legacy: The Photographs, Diaries, Letters, and Memorabilia of a Maine Sea Captain and His Wife, 1859–1908* (New York: Random House, 1981), 21–22.

32. Griffin, *Letters*, 7.

33. Edward Clifford to Henrietta Clifford, 17 November 1855; Henrietta Clifford to Edward Clifford, 15 April 1855.

34. Griffin, *Letters*, 72.

35. Ibid., 197, 249.

36. Edward Clifford to Henrietta Clifford, 4 April 1855.

37. John Battick, in his research on thirty-six Searsport wives who accompanied their husbands to sea in 1880, discovered that half were sea captains' daughters. The thirty-six represented 40% of the 89 ship masters' wives in Searsport that year. See John F. Battick, "The Searsport 'Thirty-

six': Seafaring Wives of a Maine Community in 1880," *The American Neptune* 44 (1984): 151–52. Joanna Colcord writes that the town of Searsport incompletely lists the names of seventy children born at sea, and only one fatality is remembered to have occurred among them. William Blanchard assisted his wife's delivery of their six children who were all born aboard ship. When a doctor could not be reached during a typhoon, the Blanchards together delivered a baby successfully for another sailing couple in the harbor of Kobe, Japan. Another Searsport woman grew up to tell the tale of how she was born in an open boat at sea, after her father's ship had been destroyed by fire. Colcord, "Domestic Life," 194. Women who expected to give birth while at sea could make special arrangements. A Searsport midwife known as Grandma Searles made a career of going to sea with expectant women to deliver their babies. Most women relied on their husbands who were trained as ships' doctors to deliver their babies. DePauw, *Seafaring Women*, 173.

38. Griffin, *Letters*, 53.

39. Chase, *Goodly Fellowship*, 22.

40. Jenny Prescott's Journal, 4 July 1890, in *Woolwich Times*, Woolwich Historical Society, Woolwich, Maine.

41. Charles G. Bolte, ed. *Portrait of a Woman Down East: Selected Writings of Mary Bolte* (Camden, Maine: Down East Books, 1983), 168, 174–75; DePauw, *Seafaring Women*, 165–66.

42. Jenny Prescott's Journal, 2 September 1890.

43. Scott J. Dow, "The Story of Captain Jonathan Dow," transcript, May 1948, Penobscot Marine Museum, Searsport, Maine.

44. Maria Higgins to her family, 21 January 1884, 5 February 1884, 19 October 1884, Maine Maritime Museum, Bath, Maine.

45. Constance Anne Fournier, "Navigating Women: Exploring the Roles of Nineteenth-Century New England Sailing Wives," *Maine History* 35 (1995): 46–61. Although maritime women, like others of their day, were relegated to the private domestic sphere and did not take an active part in the male seafaring enterprise aboard ship, they were prepared to take over male tasks if necessary. Captain husbands often taught their wives navigation skills, and celestial navigation was included in the curriculum of a number of New England female academies. Wives who were not particularly fond of, or adept at, feminine domestic pursuits found that life aboard ship offered them the opportunity to try their hand at traditional "masculine" activities, such as navigation, seamanship, or keeping the ship's log and accounts.

46. Mattie Nichols, "Sailing and Arriving," *The Ocean Chronicle, Published by Captain E. P. Nichols on board the Bark* Clara *and Ship* Frank Pendleton, *1878–1891* (Searsport, ME: Penobscot Marine Museum, 1941). Both Mattie and Captain Nichols wrote in this self-published newspaper aboard ship; it served as a chronicle of their voyages for their family and friends back in Searsport.

47. Dow, "Captain Jonathan Dow, The Seafaring Days of Our New England Family."

48. Dow, "The Story of Captain Jonathan Dow."

49. Ibid.

PART TWO

THE TURN OF THE TWENTIETH CENTURY

By the last decades of the nineteenth century and the first of the twentieth, Americans were struggling to cope with changes far greater than those that had perplexed them earlier. In the aftermath of Civil War, industrial development had reached unprecedented, unimaginable levels that disrupted earlier understandings of work, credit, banking, labor relations, even time. Periodic economic downturns, culminating in the Great Depression of the 1930s, brought bankruptcy and unemployment to many, along with eviction, hunger, and misery. Even in good times, farmers throughout the nation struggled to survive; so did the increasing numbers of workers, both immigrant and native born. A small number of men amassed enormous fortunes while ever-growing multitudes of immigrants, African Americans, and the poor eked out miserable livings in the squalor of burgeoning cities. Corruption, both civic and moral, was ubiquitous. Railroad magnates, industrial leaders, and politicians enjoyed the seemingly unquestionable right to arrange law and society to enhance their ability to make money without regard for the environment, the health and safety of their workers, quality of life, or any other concerns.

Americans were not reluctant to protest against these conditions, although their protests were often ineffectual. Farmers organized themselves into granges and created an economic and political movement known as populism in order to protect themselves from rapacious railroads, discriminatory banks, and other groups they considered harmful to their interests. Workers formed unions and went on strike for recognition of their right to organize, better wages, job security, and improved working conditions; often their efforts were met with violence. Some turned to socialism or other radical forms of political organization as a means of encouraging a thorough reworking of society; these groups, too, met with violence. Middle-class reformers, alarmed by the disorder they saw around them, turned to experts to help find solutions. Known as Progressives, these reformers sought ways to purge government of corruption and make it more efficient and responsible, which included extending protection to the weakest and most vulnerable in society. Others responded to the growing uncertainty of life by attempting to confine what they considered troublesome elements in society, and racism and nativism flourished in the form of the Ku Klux Klan, immigration restriction, and scapegoating.

Across the nation, women participated in many kinds of organizations designed to promote their interests. Working women, rejected by most male-dominated unions, instead formed their own, striking in large numbers in New York City, Lawrence (Massachusetts), and Chicago, and in smaller numbers elsewhere. Middle-class women by the millions joined women's clubs, the Women's Christian Temperance Union, and suffrage organizations in hopes of improving themselves and their society. Women in vast numbers also began agitating for more personal kinds of change, transforming relations with their husbands by refusing subordination, practicing birth control, changing their clothing and hair styles, riding bicycles and driving cars, and generally engaging in freer, more independent forms of expression.

Maine was not immune from these national trends. While it perhaps did not experience them on the same scale or with as much intensity as other places, Maine had its share of labor unrest, nativist violence, and radical organizations, as well as Progressive reformers. Linked as elsewhere to economic change, this turmoil stemmed in Maine more from the contradictions inherent in a resource-based economy in an industrializing society than from vertical integration or the scale of enterprise, which remained for the most part small. Industrial activity boomed, although in ways that meant uncertainty for individual owners and workers. Maine experienced a significant influx of immigrants in these decades, principally from French Canada, but also from many countries in Europe. The Ku Klux Klan was quite large and influential, turning its attention primarily against Catholic Franco Americans. Politically, the state was dominated by Republicans, who were usually successful at preventing incursions from opponents of any sort, not just Democrats but most reformers as well.

While Maine remained conservative in terms of party politics, women across the state championed Progressive causes and worked hard to improve society as well as their own status. Women's efforts to gain the franchise were routinely defeated by the legislature and, in 1917, the voters, although the legislature did ratify what became the Nineteenth Amendment. This marked the culmination of a decades-long campaign that recruited many women to assume new political roles and led them to develop innovative means of organizing in rural areas. Maine had active women's clubs, WCTU chapters, and other single-sex organizations. In addition, women were active in many mixed groups such as the state's granger movement, which allowed them complementary participation with men and reserved some offices specifically for them.

While organizing for change appealed to many of the state's women, most continued to spend their time engaged in the more traditional tasks of caring for their families. They continued to work at the mixture of domestic tasks and household production for market familiar to earlier generations; the details shifted from time to time as markets and resources changed, but the context remained the same. Opportunities for wage earning increased, particularly in the textile industry in the southern part of the state, attracting large numbers of immigrant women to work in the mills. Women with some education and a good command of English might find jobs as clerical workers, telephone operators, or in sales, but relatively few kept these jobs after they married and had children. Family continued to be the center of women's lives; work outside the home either a means of earning money before marriage or a way to enhance the family economy after it.

White women were not the only Mainers who had to find ways to respond to cultural change around the turn of the century. Native American women also negotiated the tensions between traditional roles and new realities, an undertaking framed by the ongoing struggle to sustain cultural identity in the face of white encroachments. Native American women seeking a place for themselves did so in a context marked by erosion of traditional ways of earning a living, loss of land, and denial of opportunity. They did so in the face of persistent discrimination coupled with a growing fascination with them as "exotic" that left them vulnerable to personal and commercial exploitation.

Native American women like Lucy Nicolar who sought recognition by whites as well as in their own communities did so in the context of a national debate about how best to understand and deal with Indians. In 1887, the Dawes Severalty Act had dissolved Indian tribes as legal entities and ordered the division of tribal lands. In 1924 Indians born in the United States were granted full citizenship, in a move designed to eliminate their separate status and deny their histories and cultures. Clearly, assimilation was on the national agenda. In various parts of the country Native Americans were forced to abandon their languages as well as tra-

ditional dress and hair styles; children were forcibly taken from their parents to be educated at boarding schools where they were isolated from any knowledge of their own cultures.

At the same time, white fascination with their cultures inspired many Native Americans to new ways of thinking about stereotypes and exploitation, assimilation and identity. Adding gender to these considerations only complicated the process by which women sought to claim and reclaim autonomy and integrity. Maine women who made and sold baskets for tourists, marketing their wares in traditional costumes while singing traditional songs, or who performed Native culture before Indian and white audiences did so in an effort to explore and explain their identities as Native American women. Bunny McBride here introduces us to one such woman, whose experiences in both cultures force us to consider the complex workings of overlapping identities.

PRINCESS WATAHWASO:
BRIGHT STAR OF THE PENOBSCOT

Bunny McBride

Lucy Nicolar[1] always had more than her share of self-confidence. In January 1900, at age 17, this bold and comely Penobscot Indian from Maine visited the Women's Debating Society in New York City. At the end of a lively discussion about immigration, the debaters resolved that it was "dangerous and threatening to all true Americans." According to a journalist who wrote about the event, Nicolar—also known as Princess Watahwaso—took their conclusion as her cue:

> She arose to speak, her stately form commanding instant recognition. In a sweet but audible voice, she said, "I believe I am the only true American here. I think you have decided rightly. Of all my forefathers' country, from the St. John [River] to the Connecticut, we have now but a little island one-half-mile square. There are only about 500 of us now. We are very happy on our island, but we are poor. The railroad corporations, which did their share of robbing us of our land, are now begrudging us half-rate fare.
>
> "But we forgive you all."
>
> There was a long silence, and the subject was laid on the table. The president said that the musical feature would have to be omitted as the pianist was sick, and "would someone please volunteer?" No one had the courage to try an impromptu before that large audience.
>
> When at last who should beg to be allowed to try but Wah-Ta-Waso, who played some selections from Chopin with the greatest ease and sang a plaintive air which touched the hearts of all those present and made them feel like doing anything in the world for her.[2]

In the years that followed, such juxtapositions of art and politics became the hallmark of Lucy Nicolar's life as an Indian entertainer and activist. Time and time again, she used artistry as a means to a political end—to help win public school access for Penobscot children, to convince the state to build a bridge linking her island reservation to the mainland, to gain voting rights for her tribe. Perhaps most significant of all, she used it to squelch public assumptions that Indian cultures should and would melt into mainstream society. In 1942, her artful activism prompted one local journalist to write, "It is a recognized fact that, wherever any move is afoot on the reservation for public betterment, Princess Watawaso, well known Penobscot singer and actress, is involved somewhere."[3]

Nicolar's life story is fascinating in and of itself. More than this, it is a bold-faced example of how Native women responded to turn-of-the-century socioeconomic challenges and opportunities. Looking at her life helps us understand why American Indians and "Indianness" have survived despite relentless pressure to assimilate.

CHILDHOOD

Lucy Nicolar's life began June 22, 1882 on Indian Island, 315 acres of reservation land sitting in the Penobscot River just opposite Old Town, Maine. In the century leading up to her birth, Penobscot territory had been whittled down from hundreds of thousands of acres to just 140 small islands lying in the 30-mile stretch of river between Old Town and Mattawamkeag. Hunting, the mainstay of Nicolar's forefathers, had diminished greatly, mainly due to new game laws, the destruction of forests, competition from white hunters (settlers and lumber crews), and declining fur markets. Pressed by these changes, Penobscots sought other livelihoods. Most, anxious to retain a measure of their traditional liberty, avoided the miserable confines of factory jobs where one worked long hours for paltry wages. Some acquiesced to the farming of small plots, spurred by crop bounties paid by a government hoping to settle and assimilate the Native population. Many younger men labored seasonally as river drivers. Both men and women made moosehide moccasins used in logging camps and the sturdy woodsplint baskets that settlers needed for harvesting and household storage.

But, more than anything else, nineteenth-century Penobscots began to capitalize on mainstream society's romantic ideal of primitive naturalism. Born of ambivalent racism coupled with a reaction to industrialization, the primitivist ideal provided a ready audience for Indians willing to act out generic versions of tribal traditions and prompted a handful of Penobscot men and women to become entertainers in vaudeville and medicine shows. Moreover, it lured summer tourists and sport hunters to Maine. A fair number of Penobscot men became hunting guides, and many women began making fancy splint and sweetgrass baskets, designed to suit the Victorian tastes of well-to-do visitors. Usually, men cut the ash trees and transformed them into weavable splints, and women gathered the sweetgrass and wove the baskets. Men and women alike ventured to coastal resorts to market their wares.

By the time Nicolar was born, Penobscot women had come to the fore as major cash-earners by producing and selling crafts and in a few cases performing in road shows. This was a striking shift. Traditionally, women in Maine's several tribal groups had significant roles in the economic well-being of their families, but little power beyond the domestic sphere. Their expanding sphere of influence is evident in the fact that by 1900 two-thirds of the households on Indian Island depended on baskets as their primary source of income—and women were the major makers and marketers.[4]

Nicolar entered the world twelve years after her older sister Emma and two years before her younger sister Florence. These girls landed in the arms of remarkable parents. Their father, Joseph Nicolar, was a keen-witted and much-respected man whose reputation reached well beyond the shores of Indian Island. Born to Tomer (Thomas) Nicola and Mary Malt (Martha) Neptune in 1827, he hailed from a notable line of Penobscots. His maternal grandfather, Lt. Governor John Neptune, was one of the most impressive Penobscot chiefs of all time. On his father's side, his great-grandfather was the famous "Half-Arm" Nicola, who survived the 1724 English attack of the Kennebec Indian village of Norridgewock—and lost part of an arm in the massacre.[5]

Intellectually ambitious from childhood, Joseph attended school in several Maine towns, and may well have had "the best education of all the Indians of his time."[6] At age thirty-one he served his first term as tribal representative to the state legislature, an elected position he held with distinction and won more often than any other Penobscot.[7] People on and off the reservation referred to him as the lawyer of the tribe. They also called him the tribe's scribe, for he often wrote short news items about Penobscots, as well as feature stories about their crafts, traditions and history, for various newspapers.[8] He also wrote a book, *The Life and Traditions of the Red Man*, published in 1893. A handsome man and an able orator, Joseph frequently received invitations to lecture about Penobscot life.[9] On top of this, he did a bit of land surveying and proved highly successful at tilling the soil. For a while, he served as superintendent of farming for the tribe and offered written reports to the Indian Agent.[10] Moreover, like most Penobscot men of his day, Joseph hunted and fished "for the pot" and helped market baskets made by his wife and daughters.[11] In Nicolar's estimation, "he was the grandest man who ever lived."[12]

Nicolar's mother, Elizabeth Josephs Nicolar, was twenty-one years younger than her husband, and people called her Lizzie. Described by a local newspaper as "respected," "intelligent," and "superior in many ways," she was considered "a power for good" in "all the doings" of her people. She was also beautiful.[13] As skilled at public relations as she was at basketry, Lizzie traveled throughout New England to market her craft. She participated in major sportsmen's exhibits and other shows where she sold her wares while espousing the virtues of Penobscot traditions.[14] A born leader, she often organized social and charitable events on the reservation.[15] In 1895 she helped found the Wabanaki Club of Indian Island, which gained membership in the State Federation of Women's Clubs in 1897. As the club's first vice president, she played a key role in defining and carrying out its purpose "to collect and preserve the history and legends of the aboriginal inhabitants of Maine and to establish an industrial union to which each member shall contribute her own work, the sale of which shall form a fund to be used as the society directs."[16] Lizzie, as much as Joseph, was a role model for Nicolar.

Nicolar and her family lived on the southeast side of the island in a comfortable, two-story home with clapboard siding and a mansard roof. Between the well-furnished house and the river lay her father's potato field and smaller plots where he grew beans, vegetables, and wheat.[17] Although the Nicolars were relatively prosperous among Penobscots, theirs was hardly the only house on the reservation that defied the public notion that Indians still lived in wigwams— or in squalid shacks.[18]

Home life centered on the big wood stove in the kitchen. There, the heady odor of pipe tobacco smoke mingled with the tempting smells of fresh bread or roasting venison and the sweet scent of grass and ash strips used for basketmaking. Basketry played an important role in her family's livelihood—

as it did in most Penobscot households at the time. Lizzie knew how to weave an array of baskets and passed the skill on to her three daughters. Together they participated in sweetgrass braiding parties with other women and girls on the island. And every summer they joined the great exodus from the island, heading to the coast to sell their handiwork to tourists. Each household targeted a particular resort community year after year. For Nicolar's family it was Kennebunkport.[19] Usually, but not always, Joseph went with them.

In early July the family packed up great batches of finished baskets—plus a good supply of raw basket-making materials—and traveled by train to the seaside. Once there, they set up camp and began weaving on the spot. Demonstrations helped promote sales, as did dressing in Indian garb and having the children dance for tourists. Even as a little girl, Nicolar was a willing performer, always ready to offer a dance or a song. People especially enjoyed her singing, and when she realized this, she began charging a penny for a song. When no one balked at the fee, she upped her price to a nickel.[20] And who could resist buying a basket after hearing her sing? Scenes like this occurred at countless summer resorts and lingered in the minds of passersby, making baskets and Maine Indians all but synonymous. The Nicolars remained at the coast until they sold out their inventory, usually by August 1. They had another run on baskets during the Christmas season, when they shipped the goods to various shops and individuals around New England.[21]

As an economic mainstay, baskets figured in many aspects of Penobscot life. When a family hit upon hard times, women got together and made up a batch of saleable baskets to help the family get by.[22] The sale of donated baskets also financed numerous church renovations.[23] And every year Penobscots celebrated the first of May by decorating each other's doors with beautiful May baskets.[24] At home and in the public eye, baskets had become a symbol for Penobscot culture, and as they gained prominence, so did the women who made them.

In Nicolar's day, many Penobscots played musical instruments and sang. They enjoyed traditional Penobscot music as well as varieties of Western music picked up in lumber camps and taught at the Catholic mission school on the island. Throughout Nicolar's growing-up years, impromptu house concerts were common at parties and sweetgrass braiding get-togethers, and local musicians played often for events at the reservation's community hall. These included minstrel shows, dramatic presentations, and lectures—some of which were organized to raise funds for the church.[25] Also, at least once a year, Penobscots invited folks from the mainland to a grand ball or a big wedding dance, where island musicians played a musical potpourri of classical waltzes, Irish jigs, and traditional Penobscot dances.[26]

Across the river, a parade of entertainers passed through Old Town during the summer months. Vaudeville shows were on the rise, circuses and menageries were many, and at least one Indian medicine show came to town each year. If you could not afford a ticket to the actual event, you could always watch the free ballyhoo used by most performers to drum up an audience. A variety of other entertainments appeared year-round at the Old Town City Hall.

In 1892 Nicolar's father hired City Hall with fellow tribesman Frank Loring for a performance that presented the customs of their people.[27] The event, which Nicolar surely saw, is of special note. Loring, a celebrated showman known as "Big Thunder," had left Indian Island as a boy in the 1830s, looking for work. After a stint with the great P.T. Barnum, he spent half a century producing, directing, and acting in "Indian entertainments" throughout New England. His life echoed that of many other Indians who, in the course of the nineteenth century, resorted to commodifying their cultures to make a living. Despite a life on the road, Loring was never a stranger to Indian Island, and in 1890 he settled there as a sort of entertainer-in-residence. He maintained a small museum, heralded by a birchbark sign that read: "Big Thunder, Indian Relics and Traditions Told." And he lived out an old friendship—and slight rivalry—with his age-mate, Joseph.[28] In their twilight years, both men still commanded attention—Joseph as a dignified presence accustomed to writing seriously about Penobscot traditions and speaking on behalf of his people in the halls of state government; and Loring as a seasoned entertainer who could package any tradition and bring it to life for public consumption. Their joint City Hall performance, as described in the local paper, showcased their contrasting skills and personalities. "Mr. Nicolar" gave an "articulate" lecture and "Big Thunder" quickened everyone's pulse with his "very amusing" enactment of Indian customs.[29] We can assume Nicolar's father appeared in a suit and tie, while Loring donned an Indian costume, including his signature ostrich plume headdress. In the years that followed, echoes of that evening resounded in Nicolar's performances as she gave audiences something in between the decorum of her father and the flamboyance of Big Thunder.

NICOLAR TAKES THE STAGE

In 1878, four years before Nicolar's birth, the Sisters of Mercy had come to Indian Island to establish a Catholic primary school. Until their arrival, formal education for Penobscot children had been a haphazard endeavor. But the sisters brought missionary zeal to the task and awakened scholastic curiosity in the community. The school they started continued for generations to come, but seems to have reached its heyday in terms of effectiveness and community support during Nicolar's childhood. In 1890 the average daily attendance

was forty pupils—70 percent of all eligible boys and girls.[30]
The nuns taught music—piano playing and singing in particular—along with the requisite three R's and catechism. And
the children performed in school concerts tied to religious
holidays. Nicolar was among the most zealous students in
the group. At age fourteen, three years after her father's death
in 1894, she determined to become the first girl from Indian
Island to attend high school in Old Town. Making the leap
there from the reservation school required special preparation, so she began working with a tutor to catch up to her
peers on the mainland.[31]

The nuns and Nicolar's father may have been the force
behind her early formal education, but it was her mother who
taught her how to make baskets and market them in sophis-
ticated ways. Especially after her husband's death, Lizzie
guided her daughters to seize upon the few economic opportunities available to Native women. Under her tutelage,
Nicolar and her sister Florence graduated from singing and
dancing for tourists at their summer basket stand in
Kennebunkport to participating in major sportsmen's shows
from Boston to New York to Baltimore. These grand exhibits
touted the pleasures of "rusticating"—the special sort of
tourism for which Maine had become famous. They featured
displays that promoted wilderness equipment, from canoes
and fishing rods to pack baskets, snowshoes, and hiking
boots. No show was complete without an Indian encampment to conjure up romantic images of life in the wilderness,
and no encampment was complete without a cast of real
Indians, such as Lizzie and her daughters. They spent their
days at the site, making and selling baskets and snowshoes.
The encampment sometimes featured a miniature lake where
visitors could have the pleasure of being paddled about in a
canoe by lovely "Indian maidens."[32] To these events Nicolar
brought a rare flair, born of natural beauty and charisma

Figure 1. "Belle of the Penobscots." Nicolar at age 14, as depicted in a
Lewiston, Maine newspaper. (Collections of Maine
Historical Society, Portland, Maine.)

enhanced by a mix of traditional and formal education. She
had "black snapping eyes—so bright and dark that you could-
n't see the pupils."[33] Those eyes, her flow of sable hair, and
everything else about Nicolar began to captivate journalists.
At age fourteen she appeared in an article titled "Belle of the
Penobscots." It included two full-length portraits of her—one
depicting her wearing an "Indian costume" and holding a
rifle, the other showing her dressed in modern clothing and
commandeering a bicycle. The text said, in part:

> Lucy is a young miss of marked beauty, and wherever she goes with
> baskets or Indian exhibits, many a young American who looks upon
> the Indian maiden feels that the land of the Penobscots must be "the

land of handsome women." Just now Lucy is receiving private instructions that she may enter Oldtown High School. Her instructor tells me that she is bright in her studies and that mathematics is her forte. Lucy is perhaps the most proficient piano player on the island, being the owner of an instrument. She also sings pleasantly. But the skill of the tribe is not forgotten by this young member, for she can make baskets, etc. etc., as well as some of the older ones. [34]

Among those charmed by Nicolar was Montague Chamberlain, who wore several administrative hats at Harvard College in the 1890s, including Assistant Dean of Men. By avocation a naturalist, Chamberlain had a keen interest in the traditions of American Indians—especially Nicolar's people, because a Penobscot had saved his grandfather's life.[35] He first visited Indian Island in 1897, and early the next year he wrote a lengthy sympathetic article about contemporary Penobscot life for the *Cambridge Tribune*.[36] Becoming an advocate for the education of young Penobscots, he gathered books and funds to set up a library on the reservation, hosted picnics and sports competitions for youngsters, and sought scholarships and other educational opportunities for them.[37]

Nicolar met Chamberlain when she was preparing for high school on the mainland. Although she later claimed to have been the first girl from Indian Island to attend school in Old Town, there is no proof of this.[38] She may be missing from school records because she attended informally or too briefly to be noted. It is also possible that Chamberlain plucked her up and took her to Boston before she even started at Old Town—for it is certain that she spent several years in his household, beginning in 1898 or 1899. With Chamberlain's help Nicolar received the best in educational and musical advantages.[39] He also offered on-the-job-training by taking her on as an assistant.[40] His elite Harvard connections opened doors for Nicolar in Boston and New York; and when she

Figure 2. Nicolar as the "pet of New York Society," 1900.
(Courtesy of Robert Anderson)

walked through those doors, people took notice. While showing herself to be comfortable with the manners of white society's cultural elite, she played into their romantic notions of
what it meant to be Indian and began introducing herself as
"Princess Watahwaso" ("Bright Star"). By 1900, as one journalist noted, "Wah-Ta-Waso, an educated and refined girl, is
often the pet of New York society."[41]

Around 1901 Chamberlain left Harvard and became an
independent accountant. Nicolar continued to work for him,
playfully bragging that she was better at numbers than he
was.[42] At age twenty-three, she married a wealthy Boston
doctor and later moved to Washington, DC, with him. Little
else is known of this marriage.[43]

In 1913 Nicolar turned thirty-one, divorced her first husband and moved to Chicago, where she studied piano at the
Music School of Chautauqua.[44] By now she had developed a
concert program of Indian songs, legends, and dances, and she
had performed in various venues—schools, women's clubs,
benefits. But a man named Tom Gorman had a bigger vision
for her talents. Although he was a lawyer for the state of
Illinois, Gorman's passion lay in another field: theater. When
he came to know Nicolar, he offered to become her manager—and her husband. She said yes to both.[45] Before long, successful bookings in various midwestern cities led to a contract with the Redpath Lyceum Bureau as a performer on the
prestigious Redpath Chautauqua Circuit.

The Redpath Circuit had its roots in two popular forms of
nineteenth-century adult education: lyceums and Chautauquas. Lyceums, which in the U.S. date back to the 1820s,
were institutions that organized weekly lectures, debates, and
other secular educational events. Chautauquas sprang from a
summer camp for religious teachers, founded in 1874 on the
shores of Lake Chautauqua in New York. In order to keep
participants awake and refreshed, camp founders punctuated

their religious classes with recreational activities. Soon, musical offerings and lectures by authors, explorers, and political leaders found their way into the curriculum, and it was not long before hundreds of self-styled Chautauquas cropped up in communities all across the nation. Typically, their programs of "constructive entertainments" combined local talent with features acquired through lyceum bureaus.[46]

The standard bearer among lyceums was the Redpath Bureau, with branches in several cities.[47] In 1904 Redpath's Chicago manager came up with the idea of "circuit Chautauquas"—packaged programs put together by his office and marketed across the nation. By 1913 he had proved that he could deliver a "better program at a more competitive price" than most Chautauqua groups could independently. Circuit Chautauquas all but eclipsed community-produced programs. Other lyceums stepped forward to grab some of the business, but the Redpath Bureau won the lion's share and assembled programs that outshone all others.[48]

When Nicolar stepped into Chicago's Redpath office, its director recognized the Penobscot "princess" as "a find." Her first contract with the Bureau marked out a thirty-week tour at a fine salary: $75 per week in 1917, with a possible renewal at $112.50 the following year and $150 the year thereafter.[49] She stayed with the circuit two years and gained a reputation as a noted and memorable performer. Forty years after seeing her on stage as part of Redpath's "Deluxe Seven Day Circuit," the Bureau's former treasurer wrote:

> As the days went on the programs became even better. The fourth night opened with the Spanish cellist, followed by beautiful and aristocratic Princess Watahwaso. She was a full-blooded Penobscot Indian from Maine, "flower of one of the last pure Indian families," the program said. She sang tribal songs, told tribal legends, and danced in tribal costumes, including a feathered war bonnet.[50]

Figure 3. Nicolar on the Redpath Chautauqua Circuit, 1917.
(Redpath Chautauqua Collection,
University of Iowa Library)

Circuit itineraries were grueling, with shows in some twen-ty-seven towns a month. Nicolar selected her own accompa-nists, and Redpath, in turn, drew up contracts with them. Often she appeared with Thurlow Lieurance, a well-known composer-pianist especially noted for making written, as well as phonographic, recordings of Indian melodies, chants, songs, and prayers. It is a measure of Nicolar's stature that she earned $15 more per week than he did.[51]

Like other Indian performers, Nicolar succeeded, in part, because she played into popular notions of romantic exoti-cism. She did not really have a choice, but she knew exactly what she was doing, and therein lay her strength. Seeing her-self as an ambassador for all American Indians, she pointed out distinguishing aspects of the songs, legends, and dances of the various tribes represented in her program. But she also adjusted her presentations to suit popular taste, aware that Chautauqua's white audiences were curious about other cul-tures, but would not tolerate anyone who challenged their "civilized" biases. Bicultural and broadly educated, the Indian princess from Maine was both alluring and safe to circuit crowds. She fulfilled the noble savage ideal dictated by popu-lar stereotypes of the time, while making it clear that she was well versed in the cultural etiquette of her hosts. How well she merged the strengths of her father and Big Thunder![52]

Nicolar came to Redpath as a self-assured and accom-plished woman, and her work with the Bureau made her all the more so. She shared the bill with a rotating cast of cele-brated opera singers and illustrious speakers. Women sup-plied at least half of the talent in the circuit, and they must have been emboldened as they watched one another criss-cross the country, hauling luggage, dealing with strangers, and working out all the details and difficulties of life on the road.[53] Since its inception in 1868, the Bureau had gained a reputation for booking lecturers whose views matched the liberal opinions of its founder, James Redpath. They included women's rights advocates such as Susan B. Anthony and Elizabeth Cady Stanton. The tradition continued with the Redpath Chautauqua Circuit, which featured such leading suffragists as Carrie Chapman Catt and Anna Howard Shaw. Indeed, the fight for women's rights waxed eloquent and passionate in Chautauqua tents. This was especially true during Nicolar's 1917–1919 stint with the circuit, which marked the final run toward the passage of the Nineteenth Amendment. Typically, local women raised a "suffrage tent" within a stone's throw of the Chautauqua tent and thrust literature into the hands of every passerby.[54] None of this was lost on Princess Watahwaso, for American Indian women as well as men had neither citizenship nor the right to vote. In the years ahead she would become one of the strongest advocates for correcting these injustices.

Nicolar left the Redpath Circuit in the spring of 1919 just before her thirty-seventh birthday. Although she made special appearances on Chautauqua stages over the next few years, she never signed another thirty-week contract with Redpath. After traveling home to Indian Island for a visit, she and Gorman moved to New York City. He set up an office in the New York Hippodrome and worked as liaison between entertainers and top vaudeville houses, from Marcus Loew to Keith-Albee to the Orpheum. In preparation for a recording contract, Nicolar took classes at a voice studio. There she came to know such opera celebrities as Rosa Ponselle and Anna FitzHugh, who came to her New York debut at Aeolian Hall, April 7, 1920. Billed as a "song recital in costume" by the "Indian Mezzo-soprano Princess Watahwaso," Nicolar's concert featured an Italian aria and Indian songs adapted by Thurlow Lieurance and other noted composers.[55] It coincided with the release of the Victor Record Company's recordings of Nicolar singing Lieurance's compositions, including "By the Waters of Minnetonka" (which would become her most popular recording) and "By the Weeping Waters" (her favorite). The company sent Nicolar on promotional tours from Colorado to California to Mexico.[56]

In June 1921 Nicolar went home to participate in a big celebration on Indian Island—an event that foreshadowed the great pageants she would help organize in years to come. Penobscot spokesman Newell Francis told the *Lewiston Evening Journal* that his tribe staged the event "to renew old times and customs, so the ways of our fathers will not be forgotten by our children." For the occasion Penobscots hoisted canvas "wigwams" on the point near the ferry landing, arranging them in half-moon formation and draping them with skins and branches. Some 2,000 visitors flocked to the gathering, which featured traditional dance performances, canoe races and foot races, as well as displays of tribal "treasures" that had been passed down through the generations. The Penobscot band, dressed in beads and feathers, played much of the day, and in the afternoon Nicolar gave one of her grand solo "entertainments" for the crowd. That evening a small group of Penobscot musicians known as the "famous Francis Orchestra" provided music for a dance.[57]

During the 1920s, Nicolar performed on numerous vaudeville circuits, no doubt booked by Gorman. Now in her forties, she gathered up younger American Indian performers and took them on the road. In January 1927 she teamed up with three entertainers half her age for a weeklong engagement at a Keith-Albee theater in Passaic, New Jersey. A glowing review paid tribute to Princess Watahwaso as "a lady of brilliant attainments, an authority on Indian lore and a Victor Record artiste." In contrast, her co-stars were painted in a youthful light: Princess Wantura as "a combination of all the feminine graces," possessing "youth, talent and beauty . . . and a soprano voice of rare tonal purity"; Molly Spotted Elk as a dancer "with an innate understanding of poetry in motion"; and accompanist Tommie Little Chief as "a modern young fellow whose greatest enjoyment is a visit to the rendezvous of the jazz set, where the girls are pretty and good dancers, the music intoxicating—and the lights low."[58]

After the New Jersey booking, Nicolar organized a new troupe. It included herself, Penobscot dancer Molly Spotted Elk (embarking on her own road to fame), and five other budding performers—a Comanche, an Onondaga, a Pawnee, and two Kiowas. Setting out on a two-month tour on the renowned Keith-Albee-Orpheum Circuit, they played major theaters in Ohio, Michigan, and New York. Nicolar's various numbers included one with Bruce Poolaw, a twenty-four-year-old Kiowa rodeo star from Oklahoma. Promoted as "Chief Poolaw" ("Prairie Wolf"), Poolaw sang "Indian Love Call" with Nicolar in front of a painted backdrop of a tepee in a forest clearing. This unlikely duet between a dignified middle-aged woman and a cocky young Kiowa proved to be providential.[59]

Nicolar and Poolaw had met earlier in 1927 at one of the Wednesday night dinners she hosted for Indians in New York. According to Poolaw's niece Linda Poolaw, "Everyone had to bring food, and those who didn't had to sing for their meal." Poolaw, fresh out of Oklahoma and struggling to get by, sang for his supper along with fellow Kiowa Tommie Little Chief. "They sang some Kiowa song," said Linda, "and it made them so lonesome that tears started rolling down their cheeks. But after that Lucy signed them up and led them around" on the vaudeville circuit.[60]

By the end of the decade, vaudeville had fizzled under the weight of the Great Depression and competition from the new "talkies" that superseded silent films. In response, Nicolar teamed up with Poolaw and developed a new act for schools, summer camps, and clubs. Crisscrossing the nation

Figure 4. Nicolar with her troupe on the Keith-Albee Vaudeville Circuit,
1927 (l–r: Bruce Poolaw, Princess Watahwaso, Princess Wantura,
Tommie Little Chief). (Courtesy of Charles Shay)

by car, they stopped at Indian reservations in their path, picking up Native costumes, props, and ideas.[61] Meanwhile, soon after the Wall Street crash of 1929, Tom Gorman grabbed most of his and Nicolar's assets and took off to Mexico.[62]

MRS. BRUCE POOLAW
PLAYS TO THE HOME CROWD

For Nicolar, all roads led home to Indian Island. Since leaving the reservation as a teenager, she had visited at least once a year, even after her mother's death in 1924. Sometimes she came to Maine to perform, and sometimes when she came to see family, she ended up performing. For instance, in the summer of 1926, she gave a recital for the Maine Federation of Women's Clubs in Kennebunkport,[63] and in the summer of 1930, she made a guest appearance with the Downie Brothers Circus in Lewiston.[64] Reports of her return usually made it into Maine newspapers. On June 26, 1930, a page-one headline in the *Old Town Enterprise* announced: "Princess Watawaso, Famous Penobscot Tribe Daughter in Old Town on Visit." The article noted that "the princess" had come home to rest "after an extensive tour of the south and southwest" and announced that she would give a concert in the reservation's community hall "in response to the urgent request of her friends on the island reservation, as well as many others in Old Town and the surrounding vicinity. . . . The princess has done much for the uplift of her people during her public career, both locally and nationally." This time, Nicolar's visit turned into a permanent move back to the island. By the end of the year she had settled into her new abode next to the ferry landing. Indicative of her worldliness, she had bought a modular house in Chicago and had it shipped by train to Old Town and hauled to the island on a raft.

Soon after Nicolar moved into her new house, so did Poolaw. Some say their relationship was strictly business, others call it a unique love affair. According to Nicolar's grand-nephew Robert Anderson, who lived with the couple as a boy from 1935 to 1944, Nicolar "went for" Poolaw because "she liked young men and she got caught up in that show biz thing." More significantly, they needed each other. Poolaw lacked Nicolar's formal education, social finesse, and cross-cultural scope, but he could sing and dance and captivate an audience. In short, she educated him and he assisted in her shows—driving her from venue to venue and adding new spice to her act.[65]

When Nicolar resettled on Indian Island, she brought with her decades of experience dealing with people from every station in life. She could hold her own with society's movers and shakers, whether they were politicians, businessmen, or scholars. She knew how to draw a crowd, please them, and win their favor. And now she had come to a point in her life and a place in the world where she had an opportunity to make a more lasting mark. As she saw it, there was much to do on the home front: Penobscots were in an economic slump, compounded by the Great Depression. The only primary school education option for Penobscot children was the reservation school, which was falling short. Indian Island residents could not register to vote in Old Town. And, without a bridge to the mainland, the community was too isolated for its own good. Nicolar determined to do something about these problems. She had help from her sister Florence, who, with her husband and children, also returned to the island in 1930.

Florence had walked a very different path from her sister. Several years after graduating from Old Town High School at age twenty-two,[66] she had married Leo Shay, a bright, hard-working Penobscot fellow six years her junior. For a time they had lived on the reservation. Then, as their son Bill recalls, they moved to Connecticut in 1923 "for economic opportunity and to put us kids in school some place other than with the nuns." By 1930 the Depression had chased them home, and now, for the first time in thirty years, Florence and Nicolar both lived on the island.[67]

The sisters brought contrasting strengths to their endeavors. Nicolar's fun-loving spirit and flamboyance caught one's eye, and her gift for gab grabbed one's ear. A powerful presence, she could be intimidating to anyone who crossed her. Florence was a quiet but firm presence, a careful thinker more likely to voice her views with pen than tongue.[68] Nicolar referred to her as the "tribal scholar."[69] They joined forces with Florence's sister-in-law Pauline Shay to revive the Indian Woman's Club (which their mother had helped found thirty-five years earlier) with the purpose of promoting "Indian welfare, education and social progress."

Immediately the women took up a task Pauline Shay had already begun—pressing for legislation that would give Penobscot parents the option of sending their children to the public schools of Old Town instead of to the reservation's Catholic school. As they saw it, the nuns of the day offered too much catechism and too little standard education. In 1931 they won their cause—about the same time their club reaffiliated with the Maine Federation of Women's Clubs. But victory came at a price: "expulsion" from their church.[70] Consequently, with twice-married Nicolar leading the way, a group of Penobscots set out to establish a Protestant church on the island. After a mighty struggle, they succeeded— becoming Baptists by fire.[71]

Meanwhile, Nicolar's entertainment work with Poolaw continued. On February 2, 1931, they staged an Indian pageant in the island's community hall. Two weeks later they rented Old Town City Hall for a powwow and dance, open to anyone who had the 50-cent entry fee. Both events had an inter-tribal flavor, with Penobscot boys and girls trained and costumed by the Kiowa "chief" and the Penobscot princess.[72]

That spring, Poolaw drove back to Oklahoma to see his Kiowa family and friends, but returned east in time to join Nicolar for engagements she had arranged at several Maine camps. While they were on tour, a journalist caught up with them in Lewiston. As usual, Nicolar used the interview to expound on some of her causes. She mentioned the Indian Woman's Club and its efforts in the areas of education and cultural preservation. She said she planned to assemble a "representation of Maine Indian craftsmanship" for the National Indian Exposition in New York at the end of the year. And she promoted the "Inter-tribal Ceremonial" about to take place in Bangor on July 23. *Of course* she and Chief Poolaw would participate in that. The gala's co-sponsors, the Penobscot Valley Country Club and the Maine Development Commission, had modeled it after the Pendleton Round-up in Oregon. They touted it as "an event of entertainment, education and historical value to preserve the customs and crafts of our Maine Indians and to bring real financial benefits to the State." On the day of the pageant, some forty Penobscots and Passamaquoddies showed up to perform, along with their Kiowa "guest." They presented an elaborate melodrama—a sort of hybrid Pocahontas/Hiawatha story—featuring numerous traditional dances and songs, including cameo performances by Nicolar and Poolaw. Basketmakers and local business people promoted their wares and everyone involved garnered accolades.[73]

The following year Old Town's Chamber of Commerce determined to profit from its proximity to Indian Island and host a spectacular three-day Indian pageant that would outdo the Bangor event.[74] In early May the Chamber's secretary came up with a basic script for the August pageant, as well as what he saw as a catchy title: "Shadowy Sachem." Two weeks later, spurred by Nicolar and Poolaw, the Penobscot tribe pledged its cooperation. Poolaw even convinced his brother Justin to drive up from Oklahoma and help with preparations.[75] In late June the *Old Town Enterprise* announced that Princess Watahwaso, Chief Poolaw, his brother, and their helpers had been "industriously at work" constructing the "Princess Wattawasso Indian Village," midway between Old Town and Stillwater. Designed to be the pageant's centerpoint, the village featured bark tepees, a sweat lodge, and an archery range, plus a "large workshop tent" where tribespeople would make Indian crafts in public view, and a "commodious" gift shop tent for the selling of "baskets, bows & arrows, bead work, Navajo blankets, etc."[76]

Largely due to Nicolar's theatrical experience and the rigorous rehearsal schedule she imposed, the pageant surpassed everyone's wildest expectations. As reported in the local paper, thousands flocked to Old Town to witness a spectacle based on a story line that went like this: Penobscot Indians seek and find a camping site, set up a "real Indian Village," and then go about daily traditional life. Passamaquoddies come to the village carrying wampum and seeking approval for a marriage between one of their braves and a Penobscot maiden. A grand wedding ceremony begins, only to be interrupted by the sound of guns in the distance. Soon, a group of white men arrive. Seeing the richness of the land, the newcomers "cheat the trusting Indians, give them fire-water, etc., and finally come in such numbers that the Indians are robbed and killed and driven from their lands" to the reservation.[77]

The town chronicle went on to describe the pageant in detail. Events on day one, it said, began with "gorgeously arrayed" Indians arriving at the town's ferry landing by canoes and by road. From there, the mounted and unidentified "Shadowy Sachem" led Princess Watahwaso and "scores of Indian braves, squaws and children" up Stillwater Avenue to their village. Chief Poolaw consecrated the site with a prayer song and pipe ceremony. Then came an array of demonstrations and performances: men built a canoe and fabricated paddles. They made bows and arrows and showed young boys how to use them. And they pounded an ash log to make wood strips for baskets. Women wove baskets, rocked "papooses" in cradleboards hanging from low tree boughs and prepared a mid-day feast. Boys and girls played traditional games and sports. That evening a great crowd of people filled the bleachers and hundreds more stood for a program of dances, songs, and legends. Princess Watahwaso "covered herself with glory as the conductor of the program," standing before the microphone in the glow of electric floodlights. On day two the Penobscot-Passamaquoddy wedding ceremony and the arrival of white settlers took place, followed by another evening program. The final morning belonged to Old Town citizens and their parade of some two dozen floats decorated by local merchants and organizations. Then came swimming and canoe races and other water sports, held in the stretch of river between Old Town and Indian Island. Festivities concluded that night with a curious cultural combination: a Grand Colonial Ball with music by the Indian Orchestra.[78]

After the pageant, the *Old Town Enterprise* ran a front-page photo of Nicolar under this headline: "Special Commendation Is Given to Princess Watawasso for her Excellent Work as General-Director of the Penobscot Indians who without Her Aid the Indian Pageant Would Have Been in Vain." A brief accompanying article described her "tireless" effort in commandeering 112 Indians, which had resulted in "one of the best Indian performances known in New England."[79]

If Nicolar had mixed feelings about commodifying Penobscot culture, she did not show it. Rather, she took hold of white society's fascination with Indians and used it to her

Figure 5. Indian Pageant, Old Town, Maine, 1933. Nicolar sits in lead canoe, waving. (Courtesy of Jean Archambaud Moore)

favor. In 1933, she topped the 1932 pageant, adding three dramatizations to the program: a legend about the origins of the Red Man, a story about star-crossed Indian lovers, and an historic reenactment of "The Norridgewock Massacre." The last was a graphic portrayal of the devastating English attack that gave Nicolar's forefather his name, "Half-Arm" Nicola. Putting this gruesome piece of Maine history on stage brought damning specificity to the previous year's generic presentation of Indians being driven away by white settlers. In blatant understatement, the Old Town paper described this daring piece of political theater as simply "a fine performance."[80]

Some time in the early 1930s, Nicolar divorced Gorman, and in 1937 she married Poolaw. But before she and Poolaw made their vows, he had an affair with Margaret Ranco, another woman on the island, who gave birth to his daughter, Irene. In the years that followed, Nicolar reached out to the child and treated her "like a daughter."[81]

Because the two- and three-day pageants of 1932 and 1933 were such huge undertakings, the event diminished and ultimately disappeared in the course of the decade. But in 1940 Nicolar and Poolaw produced a one-day pageant on the reservation.[82] And the following year, hired by Old Town, they acted as co-stars and co-directors of a full-scale revival of the 1933 pageant—offering a welcome diversion from the gloom of World War II.[83] In the years that followed, the pageant came and went. After 1947, neither Nicolar nor Poolaw directed the event, but they always participated in one way or another. Although large portions of the pageants played into Indian stereotypes, these grand events also offered Penobscots a ritual for identifying and holding on to their ethnic distinctiveness year after year. In fact, they provided a cultural platform on which the tribal community could regroup, redefine, and reclaim themselves as a people. Certainly they gave Nicolar the high profile she needed to boost her causes.

Of course, Lucy and Bruce Poolaw needed to make a living. This they did by continuing to organize Indian programs at summer camps and various events around the state and beyond. Sometime in the early 1940s, they opened an Indian novelty shop alongside their house, near the ferry landing. In 1947, when Nicolar was sixty-five and Poolaw forty-four, they decided to transform their store into a high profile enterprise. After tearing down an old house next to the landing, they hired the island's Baptist minister along with Nicolar's nephew, Bill Shay, to build a wooden two-story tepee on the site. As Shay recalls, "We used the materials from the house. It took us six to eight weeks. Aunt Lu and Bruce opened the shop right away." Painted white with deep red trim, the structure was highly visible from the mainland and it quickly became a destination point for tourists. Inside one could buy everything from baskets, rattles, war clubs, and beaded moccasins to miniature tepees, toy birchbark canoes, and balsam pillows. And one could meet and chat with the shop's famous owners. To keep up inventory and attract customers—and to provide jobs for members of the tribe—Nicolar and Poolaw hired basketmakers to weave at their shop for about $3 a day. They also encouraged Penobscot children to come over to the teepee and dance for visitors. Usually, they outfitted the youngsters and guided them in their dancing. According to Poolaw's daughter, Irene, Nicolar had a gift for teaching. "If kids were slow to learn, she would help them along by demonstrating rather than saying do this or do that. She gave you the feeling for the dance and then left room for you to do it your way."[84] By the end of the day, the kids had won a few coins and Poolaw's Tepee had won a few more customers.[85]

Nicolar and Poolaw seized every promotional opportunity for their shop. Nicolar's grand-nephew, Robert Anderson, said: "I've never met a promoter like Bruce. He and Lucy liked publicity. It meant that eventually someone would come to the shop and buy a basket from them at their store. Any time a politician or a star was around, they stepped forward. They even did a thing with Jack Benny." They also "did a thing" with U.S. First Lady Eleanor Roosevelt, who came to Maine in 1943 to christen a mine detection boat built at Camden Ship Yard. The coordinator of the ceremony liked the idea of an Indian interlude in which Penobscots made Mrs. Roosevelt an honorary member of the tribe. At the event "Chief" Poolaw instructed "Muskrat" (young Robert Anderson) to start a council fire. Then, lighting the "pipe of peace," Poolaw announced, "I will sing to the Great Spirit of the North, the East, the South and the West, to ask the Great Spirit's protection for the big war canoe." Next, Nicolar sang the "woman's song," and Anderson and two other Penobscot children danced. Finally, Ted Bear Mitchell proclaimed, "As governor of the Penobscot Indians, I, the Bear, deem it a great privilege to make you, Eleanor Roosevelt, an honorary member of our tribe. I will ask Princess Watawahso to place the band of wampum upon your head. Your name in the tribe is *Owduleesul*—'Many Trails.'" Press photos of the event show Nicolar and Poolaw with a grinning Roosevelt who is clutching a Penobscot basket and wearing a band of wampum around her hat.[86]

The Poolaws often included Penobscot youngsters in their programs around the state. They received modest (some say stingy) payment, but, in the words of Nicolar's grand-niece,

Figure 6. Nicolar and Poolaw making U.S. First Lady Eleanor Roosevelt an honorary member of the Penobscot Tribe on the occasion of a boat christening at Camden Ship Yard, Maine, 1943. Note Penobscot basket in Roosevelt's hand and the wampum Nicolar has just placed around her hat. (Courtesy of Jean Chevari)

Emma Nicolar, "When Aunt Lu and Bruce got a group of us to go out and do parades, that said to us, 'There's an opportunity here. You have to learn to grab hold of it!'" Those who performed with Nicolar and Poolaw all remember riding with them in their "BIG Cadillac." The couple's ostentatious cars and personalities, along with their relative prosperity, rankled many people on the island, as did Nicolar's relentless drive to found the Protestant church. But many others were drawn to the showy duo, especially to Nicolar. As Poolaw's daughter Irene Pardilla put it, "To kids, Lucy was like a pied piper. She would organize plays and use them to teach us things. She gave you a feeling that there wasn't anything you couldn't do."[87] No matter what people said or felt about them, there is no doubt that Nicolar and Poolaw's presence—especially their tepee store—helped put food on the table of Penobscots who made baskets and other crafts.[88]

Factionalism and gossip were nothing new on the reservation and did not greatly bother Nicolar. She was far more troubled by the social and economic gap between tribal members and mainstream society. In her eyes, living on an island exacerbated the problem, and she set her mind on getting the state to build a bridge to the mainland. Emma Nicolar recalls that Nicolar pressed for the bridge because "she wanted people to get to work and young people to get out and see the world, especially to go to school. She influenced me. She told me, 'Get out, get an education, get off Indian Island.' I thought she was pushing me away from here, but now I see that that's where her advantages came from and that's what she wanted for me."[89] Beyond this, a bridge would solve the problem of dangerous river crossings and drownings caused by sudden freezing or thawing, running ice and shifting currents and water levels.[90] Also, although Nicolar did not mention this, it certainly would not hurt business at Poolaw's

Figure 7. "Chief Poolaw's Tepee," Nicolar and Poolaw's shop on Indian Island. This photo was taken circa 1949, shortly after the teepee was built. In the foreground is the "sawdust trail" over the ice, which served as a winter track from the mainland to the island until a bridge was built in 1950. (Maine Folklife Center, University of Maine, Orono, Maine)

Figure 8. Poolaw and Nicolar selling baskets and other Indian novelties inside Poolaw's Tepee. From a postcard printed circa 1951. (Author's collection)

Tepee. Nicolar spoke about the bridge so often in her public appearances that some people thought she was raising money to build it. To this day rumors abound on the island that she collected bridge donations and pocketed them for herself.[91] Robert Anderson says that is nonsense. "I traveled with them more than anybody and *never* did I hear them mention money for the bridge—only that we *needed* a bridge. They spread the idea and pushed politicians to act on it."[92] Ultimately, politicians did act. On November 29, 1950, Nicolar stood on the newly erected bridge, along with various dignitaries and island residents, for the dedication. As program committee chair for the event, she acted as master of ceremonies, introducing speakers, including Maine's Governor Frederick Payne, who became an honorary tribal member that day and received a Plains Indian war bonnet to mark the occasion.[93]

★　★　★

In 1924 American Indians had gained U.S. citizenship and with it the right to vote in federal elections. However, in Maine, Indians living on state reservations still could not register to vote and therefore had no voice in state and federal elections. This stemmed from their legal position as "wards of the state"—a status that also exempted them from paying taxes of any kind. Many Penobscots were wary of a change in the status quo, quite willing to surrender voting to avoid taxation. As Nicolar saw it, her people should have the right to vote *and* to be tax free. After 1924 both she and Florence had voted without a problem when living outside Maine. But, as Florence later wrote, when they moved back home and tried to register as citizens in Old Town, they "met with a distinct refusal [because] an obsolete law of the State of Maine forbids the registration and voting by Indians, and in that law we are classed with criminals, paupers and morons." The sisters made several other attempts to vote in Maine and for three decades pressed state legislators for an Indian suffrage bill. Florence wrote letters, while Nicolar did her lobbying face-to-face. No doubt Nicolar drew inspiration from her Chautauqua days, when she heard the eloquent pleas of leading suffragists. During the war years she told anyone who would listen that Penobscots were "as patriotic as any Americans," pointing out that thirty-three men from Indian Island were in the service, including five draftees. Florence, a mother, made the same point in a more personal manner: "I have four sons and I feel that the government has not the right to draft my boys for service without giving us the right to vote." Eventually, the sisters prevailed, and in 1953 Maine law changed, giving reservation Indians the right to vote without altering their tax status.[94] The following year, at least one Maine newspaper ran a photograph of Nicolar, then seventy-two years old, dropping her vote into the ballot box. The caption read: "INDIANS VOTE FOR THE FIRST TIME— Princess Watawaso of the Penobscot Indian Tribe at Old Town casts the first vote of an Indian on a reservation in Maine."[95]

THE QUIET YEARS

Nicolar stayed active throughout her life, although she traveled less in her final years. Beyond maintaining Poolaw's Tepee with Poolaw, she remained devoted to the island's Baptist church. She served as church pianist and organist for twenty-five years, always singing as she played. "You could hear her above everyone," recalls her nephew, Charles Shay. "Her voice wasn't what it used to be, but it still had *volume.* I remember one time when my father was half-asleep in his rocking chair, Aunt Lu decided to sing a little something for my new wife, Lilli. When she opened her mouth, Pa almost fell out of his chair!"[96]

Three months before her eighty-seventh birthday, Nicolar sang her last note. News of her death on March 27, 1969 appeared in newspapers from Maine to New York City. The *New York Times* reported that "Princess Watawaso had lectured and sung the songs of her people in most of the United States," and went on to recount the many venues of her artistry. The local paper chronicled more than her stage career, such as her role in the church and her service as a Tribal Council member and as an officer in various non-Native organizations.[97] To accommodate a large and varied crowd, her family held funeral services at the United Baptist Church in Old Town. But they laid Nicolar to rest in the tribal cemetery on Indian Island—beneath a headstone that had Poolaw's named etched next to hers. Despite this engraved invitation, he never joined her there. Several years after her death, he packed up most of their belongings and returned to Oklahoma. In 1984, he passed away among his own people, and they buried him there.

When Poolaw left Indian Island, a struggle ensued over property inheritance between his daughter and Nicolar's relatives. Irene and her family moved into the house, and she and her husband ran Poolaw's Tepee until Nicolar's kin gained legal possession of the buildings. In 1988 Irene relocated the business to Old Town's main street, where it quickly became a landmark in its own right. Ten years later, a terrible fire consumed the shop. Ironically, that same year the original tepee received a facelift, as did Nicolar's home—thanks to her nephew, Charles Shay. True to his aunt's worldliness, Shay lives most of the year in Vienna with his Austrian wife, Lilli. But much of his heart, history, and family are on Indian Island, and he spends his summers in

Nicolar's old home next to the landmark tepee, a stone's throw from the bridge.[98]

In Nicolar's vaudeville days, folks who really knew her may have chuckled when they saw her play the role of a delicate forest maiden singing "Indian Love Call," since, in fact, she was a strong, independent self-provider. In this sense she was like so many other turn-of-the-century women in the Penobscot community. But there was more to her than that.

At the time of Nicolar's birth, most people, including Penobscots, assumed her small tribe would vanish through assimilation. She never accepted that idea. Deeply rooted in Penobscot traditions, she could probably recount them more accurately than anyone else of her generation, and she spent a lifetime making sure they stayed in the public eye. The young Watahwaso who addressed the Women's Debating Society in 1900 might have forgiven her white audience for trespasses against her people, but she had no intention of letting them forget that Penobscots still existed. As an artful pragmatist, she altered traditions to win over audiences and politicians, but she also kept an essential core alive within the armor of theatrical packaging. Without her efforts, it is doubtful that Penobscots could have brought so much cultural vitality to their bold political moves to reclaim lost lands and rights in the 1970s and 1980s. In this sense, "Bright Star" has continued to shine.

I wish to thank several Penobscots who helped me piece together this story: Lucy's nephews, Charles Shay and the late Bill Shay, her grandnieces, Caron Shay and Emma Nicolar (all of Indian Island), her grand nephew Robert Anderson of Lincolnville, Maine, as well as Bruce's daughter, Irene Ranco Pardilla of Indian Island and his niece Linda Poolaw of Anadarko, Oklahoma. Others who helped include Carole Binette and the late Glenn Starbird (keepers of Penobscot genealogical information), James

Neptune at the Penobscot Museum and Jean Archambaud Moore, my reservation hostess and friend and a storehouse of information. Appreciation to Steve Green, former archivist at the Maine Folklife Center (University of Maine, Orono), for making me a copy of the Victor recording that features Watahwaso's most popular song, "By the Waters of Minnetonka." Finally, heartfelt thanks to my husband, Harald Prins, whose depth of knowledge on Maine Indian history has strengthened everything I have written in this area.

1. Although as an adult Lucy usually went by her stage name Watahwaso and/or by the names of her three husbands, here, for the sake of simplicity, she is referred to by her family name, Nicolar. There is some confusion concerning this family name, variously spelled as *Nicolar, Nicolas, Nichola* or *Nicola*. Introduced by the French in the early baptism ceremonies of Lucy's ancestors, the original spelling was *Nicolas*, the name of a Catholic saint. The English, not hearing the all-but-silent "s," spelled it *Nichola* or *Nicola*. Lucy's father, a literate man with a keen ear for language, added an "r" to certain words that ended with a vowel in order to indicate a particular pronunciation. This he did also with his own name, spelling it *Nicolar*. It appeared this way on the cover of his book, *The Life and Traditions of the Red Man*, and references to him in the annual Indian Agent Reports almost always followed this spelling, as did most newspaper articles mentioning him or his wife Elizabeth. Articles that mentioned Lucy or her sister Florence prior to their marriages also followed this spelling. The "r" in Nicolar—like the "s" in the French spelling—is imperceptible to the unknowing ear.

2. "Penobscotbelles," *Bangor Daily Commercial*, 12 January 1900.

3. "Little New Church Starts with Courage and Faith," *Bangor Daily News*, 9 February [1942?]. (Note: The year of publication is approximate, as that part of the date was clipped off this article before it was placed in the church's scrapbook.)

4. Montague Chamberlain, "The Penobscot Indians: A Brief Account of Their Present Condition," *Cambridge Tribune*, 8 February 1898. Reprinted in *Old Town Enterprise*, 4 March 1899. In a 1987 unpublished paper, "A Case Study in Political Ecology—Penobscots in Maine," Harald Prins analyzes the 1900 census for Penobscot and Piscataquis counties in Maine. He says this about Penobscots: "Nearly 100 of the 157 Indian Island adults who responded to the 1900 census listed basketmaking as their primary occupation. Another thirty said they were day laborers, and ten worked as guides.

Only one individual noted hunting as his employment, while one other said he made his living through a combination of hunting and guiding."

5. Fannie Hardy Eckstorm, *Old John Neptune and Other Maine Indian Shamans* (Portland, Maine: Southworth-Anthoensen Press, 1945), 31–32.

6. Fannie Hardy Eckstorm, *Indian Place Names of the Penobscot Valley and the Maine Coast* (Orono: University of Maine Press, 1978), 237.

7. Glenn Starbird, "A Brief History of Indian Legislative Representatives in the Maine Legislature" (unpub. paper, 1983).

8. Eckstorm, *Indian Place Names*, 237; *Report of the Agent of the Penobscot Tribe of Indians for the Year 1894* (Augusta: State of Maine), 10. In addition to newspaper correspondences mentioned by Eckstorm, Joseph Nicolar is surely "Fox"—the writer of "Old Town Island," a column that appeared weekly in the *Old Town Enterprise* during 1888 and 1889. I say this based on the rarity of Nicolar's literary skills, the pleasure he took in sending correspondences to newspapers, and the fact that many of these news snippets contained information to which someone outside of his immediate household would not be privy. Moreover, as Harald Prins pointed out to me, the column follows Nicolar's peculiar spelling of certain words.

9. Eckstorm, *Indian Place Names*, 237; "City Item," *Old Town Enterprise*, 27 February 1892, 5 March 1892; John R. Wiggins, "Indian Princess," *Down East* 13, 4 (November 1966): 28–30.

10. "Old Town Island," *Old Town Enterprise*, 1 December 1888; *Report of the Agent of the Penobscot Tribe of Indians for the Year 1879*, 8–9. Nicolar's farming success is also noted in the agent reports for 1882, 1883 and 1889.

11. "Old Town Island," *Old Town Enterprise*, 14 July 1888, 22 September 1888, 3 November 1888, 15 December 1888.

12. Wiggins, "Indian Princess."

13. "Belle of the Penobscots," unidentified Lewiston, Maine, newspaper, 11 December 1897, in M. A. Little, "History and Biography of Maine" (unpub. scrapbook in Maine Historical Society collection, Portland, Maine); "Old Town Island," *Old Town Enterprise*, 9 February 1889; "Old Town Island: Home of the Progressive Penobscots," *Old Town Enterprise*, 1 January 1910; "Died: Mrs. Elizabeth Nicolar," *Old Town Enterprise*, 11 December 1924.

14. "Items of Local Interest," *Old Town Enterprise*, 18 December 1897; "Local Doings," *Old Town Enterprise*, 15 April 1899, 23 September 1899, 4 November 1899, 2 December 1899; "Maine's Exhibit," *Old Town Enterprise*, 10 October 1900; "Local Doings," *Old Town Enterprise*, 24 November 1900; "Champion Canoeists: What the New York Sun Says About Indian Maidens," *Old Town Enterprise*, 20 March 1906.

15. "Local Happenings," *Old Town Enterprise*, February 1897.

16. Jennie June Croly, *The History of the Woman's Club Movement in America* (New York: Henry G. Allen & Co., 1898), 575–76.

17. *Report of the Agent of the Penobscot Tribe of Indians for the Year 1883*, 6; Lawrence "Bill" Shay, interview by author, Indian Island, Maine, 16 May 1998.

18. In "Home News," *Old Town Enterprise*, 29 April 1893, the writer muses about Penobscots participating in the Chicago World's Fair: "[They] will spend the summer living in a birchbark wigwam at the fair, which will be known as the Penobscot Camp. The Old Town Indians would represent the present generation of the Penobscot tribe better . . . by living in a commodious house fitted with modern furnishings, musical instruments, oil paintings, etc." See also, "New View of Indians," *Lewiston Journal*, 22 February 1896.

19. "Old Town Island," *Old Town Enterprise*, 13 July 1889. This is just one of many late-nineteenth-century references about this. For fuller accounts of the Penobscot summer exodus, see the Indian Agent Reports from the last quarter of the nineteenth century. See also the essay by Pauleena Macdougall in this volume.

20. Marion Gridley, *Indians of Today* (Crawfordsville, Ind.: The Lakeside Press, 1936), 121.

21. "Old Town Island," *Old Town Enterprise*, 15 December 1888.

22. "Old Town Island," *Old Town Enterprise*, 28 April 1888.

23. *Report of the Agent of the Penobscot Tribe of Indians for the Year 1880*, 10; see also the reports of 1888 (8) and 1890 (10–11).

24. "Old Town Island," *Old Town Enterprise*, 12 May 1888.

25. "Local Happenings," *Old Town Enterprise*, 21 November 1896; Bunny McBride, *Molly Spotted Elk: A Penobscot in Paris* (Norman: University of Oklahoma Press, 1995), 36–37.

26. "Penobscotbelles."

27. "City Items," *Old Town Enterprise*, 27 February 1892.

28. To date, the most complete account of Frank Loring's life appears in Harald Prins' article, "Chief Big Thunder (1827–1906): The Life History of a Penobscot Trickster," *Maine History* 37, 3 (Winter 1998): 140–58.

29. "City Items," *Old Town Enterprise*, 5 March 1892.

30. *Report of the Agent of the Penobscot Tribe of Indians for the Year 1889*, 6.

31. "Belle of the Penobscots"; Wiggins, "Indian Princess."

32. "Maine's Exhibit," *Old Town Enterprise*, 10 November 1900; "Local Doings," *Old Town Enterprise*, 24 November 1900; "Maine Sportsmen's Exhibit," *Old Town Enterprise*, 15 December 1900.

33. Emma Nicolar, interview by author, Indian Island, Maine, 21 May 1998. Emma, Lucy's grand-niece, lived with her "Aunt Lu" from age 11 to 13.

34. "Belle of the Penobscots."

35. Gridley, *Indians of Today*, 121; "Editor's Note," *Old Town Enterprise*, 4 March 1899; McBride, *Molly Spotted Elk*, 307; "Princess Watahwaso and Assisting Artists," promotional flyer, Redpath Lyceum Bureau, 1918, in Box 248F, Redpath Chautauqua Collection, Special Collections, Main Library, University of Iowa, Iowa City; Wiggins, "Indian Princess."

36. 8 February 1898. Reprinted in the *Old Town Enterprise*, 4 March 1899.

37. "Local Doings," *Old Town Enterprise*, 18 February 1899, 15 April 1899, 10 June 1899.

38. Wiggins, "Indian Princess"; Alumni Records, Old Town High School.

39. Gridley, *Indians of Today*, 121; see also Wiggins, "Indian Princess"; "Local Doings," *Old Town Enterprise*, 19 May 1900; and "Princess Watahwaso and Assisting Artists."

40. Wiggins, "Indian Princess."

41. "Penobscotbelles."

42. Employee Records, Harvard University Archives; Wiggins, "Indian Princess."

43. Wiggins, "Indian Princess." On New Year's Day in 1910, news about this marriage appeared in a page-one *Old Town Enterprise* article, "Old Town Indian Island: Home of the Progressive Penobscots and a Bit of their History": "When people heard [Nicolar] had married a Boston man who could claim no relationship to the tribe except that acquired by the marriage tie, they all wished her much happiness. She now lives in Washington, DC, and time does not seem to have changed her love of family or tribal feeling, as she spent last summer in company with her mother, Mrs. Lizzie Nicolar, at Kennebunkport."

44. Wiggins, "Indian Princess." This divorce is unusual, given Lucy's Catholic upbringing, and suggests that she was already beginning to break with the church.

45. Emma Nicolar, interview; "Local News," *Old Town Enterprise*, 14 April 1917. This news bit dubs Nicolar's husband as "Mr. Wattawaso" and notes "Mr. Goram [sic], a white lawyer on staff of state's attorney in Chicago. Married to Lucy Nicolar."

46. Joseph E. Gould, *Chautauqua Movement* (New York: State University of New York, 1961), 3–12; Harry P. Harrison, *Culture Under Canvas* (New York: Hastings House, 1958), 39–49; John E. Tapia, *Circuit Chautauqua* (Jefferson, N.C.: McFarland & Co., 1997), 19–24.

47. Gould, *Chautauqua Movement*, 74–75; Harrison, *Culture Under Canvas*, 31–38; Tapia, *Circuit Chautauqua*, 11–18.

48. Gould, *Chautauqua Movement*, 76–77; Harrison, *Culture Under Canvas*, 50–55; Tapia, *Circuit Chautauqua*, 25–47.

49. Box 248F of the Redpath Chautauqua Collection. It was Redpath's treasurer Harry P. Harrison, who referred to Lucy as "a find" (6 January 1917 letter to Mr. A. A. Fisk). Various other correspondences, along with Lucy's contract, show that Redpath covered transportation costs and Lucy was responsible for room and board. Since Chautauqua entertainers were often housed and fed by leading members of the communities where they performed, her expenses would be minimal. Even if she wanted or needed to stay in a hotel, a decent one ran no more than $15 a week.

50. Harrison, *Culture Under Canvas*, 7.

51. Box 248F of the Redpath Chautauqua Collection. Several letters and various promotional materials (programs, flyers) refer to joint appearances by Princess Watahwaso and Thurlow Lieurance. In his 17 October 1917 letter to four top Redpath administrators, "JPY" (Redpath's assistant treasurer J. P. Young) asks that Lucy's higher salary be kept secret.

52. McBride, *Molly Spotted Elk*, 145–46; Tapia, *Circuit Chautauqua*, 100.

53. Wiggins, "Indian Princess."

54. Harrison, *Culture Under Canvas*, 217–28.

55. In Wiggins, "Indian Princess," Nicolar says this recital took place April 19, but the actual program from the event says April 7. The program is among papers in Box 248F of the Redpath Chautauqua Collection, where there is also a letter of congratulations to Nicolar from Redpath Bureau treasurer, Harry P. Harrison.

56. Wiggins, "Indian Princess"; Emma Nicolar, interview. Thanks to Emma, the author had the pleasure of hearing a cassette tape copy of Nicolar's Victor recordings. Nicolar gave a brief, energetic introduction to each song and did not waste a second between speaking and breaking into song. Her high singing voice was strong, fluid, and embracing. Emma remembers that when she lived with Nicolar from age 11–13, she often asked, "Can I play your records, Aunt Lu?" and Nicolar always said, "Oh sure, go ahead."

57. "'Chief' Newell Francis . . . on Indian Island," *Lewiston Evening Journal*, 30 July 1921.

58. Unattributed 1927 newsclipping in Molly Nelson Archambaud's [Molly Spotted Elk] personal papers. These include letters, news clippings, manuscripts, photographs, and research notes, and are now in the Maine Folklife Center, University of Maine, Orono.

59. McBride, *Molly Spotted Elk*, 82–83.

60. Linda Poolaw, telephone interview by author, 13 December 1999.

61. "Princess Watawaso, Famous Penobscot Tribe Daughter In Old Town On Visit," *Old Town Enterprise*, 26 June 1930; Robert Anderson, interview by author, Lincolnville, Maine, 17 May 1998.

62. Poolaw, interview.

63. "Penobscot Indians Visit Lewiston: Princess Watawasa and Kiowa Chief en route to Western Maine Camps," *Lewiston Journal*, 15 July 1931. This article notes: "The princess has a well-trained voice and has been heard at the Maine Federation of Women's Clubs five years ago at Kennebunkport, and elsewhere at schools, clubs and camps."

64. A 1930 photograph of Downie Brothers Circus, by Miss Washburn of Lewiston, Maine, includes Nicolar and Poolaw in costume. This photo is in the possession of Nicolar's nephew, Charles Shay, a summer resident of Indian Island.

65. Anderson, interview.

66. Alumni Records, Old Town High School.

67. Lawrence "Bill" Shay, interview.

68. Anderson, interview; Emma Nicolar, interview; Lawrence "Bill" Shay, interview.

69. William H. Clark, "Penobscot Tribe Has Few Men Left at Oldtown, Me.," *Boston Sunday Globe*, 23 August 1942.

70. Florence Nicola Shay, *History of the Penobscot Tribe of Indians* (Old Town: Florence Shay, 1941), 6–9, 15. Her son Lawrence "Bill" Shay told the author that Florence wrote this 15-page booklet to sell at the 1941 Indian Pageant in Old Town. Also, he said that the woman's club was "formed for the purpose of political pull."

71. "Little New Church Starts With Courage and Faith," *Bangor Daily News*, 2 February [1942?]. This article credits Nicolar with initiating the church: "Three years or so ago, [Nicolar] spoke to a New York churchman of her acquaintance about establishing a church for the relatively few but interested Protestant residents of the island. The churchman took up the matter, and Jesse Starr, not then ordained, came to Old Town to investigate the situation." Starr and his family committed themselves to the cause, and moved to the island. At first, they "made their home in the novelty store operated during the summertime by Chief Poolaw and Princess Watowaso. There they conducted their services . . . and laid the foundation for the long, hard struggle to found a church in the community." Shay, *History of the Penobscot Tribe*, 6–7. In an interview with the author, Emma Nicolar refers to her aunt's efforts to found a Protestant church as the "long Catholic-Baptist war."

72. Charles Shay, interview by author, Indian Island, Maine, 16 May 1998. He has posters for both of these events.

73. "Penobscot Indians Visit Lewiston, Princess Watawasa and Kiowa Chief," unidentified newsclipping (perhaps *Lewiston Journal* or *Maine Sunday Telegram*), 15 July 1931; "The Pendleton Round-up is a World Famous Example," advertisement in *The Bar Harbor Times*, 22 July 1931; "Intertribal Indian Ceremonial" Program (Bangor, Maine: Penobscot Valley Country Club and the Maine Development Commission, 1931).

74. "The Indian Pageant, 'A Great Publicity Scheme' has just Recently been Published by the Boston Sunday Advertiser," *Old Town Enterprise*, 14 July 1932.

75. Several articles in *Old Town Enterprise* 1932: "The Shadowy Sachem," 12 May; "The Penobscots Co-operating," 19 May; "Detailed Program and Dates of the Great August Indian Festival," 2 June.

76. "Indian Village in Progress of Construction," *Old Town Enterprise*, 23 June 1932.

77. "Program, Great Old Town Indian Pageant," *Old Town Enterprise*, 4 August 1932.

78. Title missing, *Old Town Enterprise*, 11 August 1932.

79. "Special Commendation," *Old Town Enterprise*, 18 August 1932.

80. Several articles in *Old Town Enterprise*, 1933: "Governor of Penobscots Announces Present Plans: Indian Pageant in August," 20 July; "Putting Finishing Touches on Indian Pageant," 27 July; "Pageant Next Wed., Thurs., Fri.," 3 August; "Indians, Outnumbered 3000, Entertain Paleface Horde With Singing And Dancing," 10 August; "Shadowy Sachem Pageant . . . Scores Triumphant Success," 17 August.

81. Wiggins, "Indian Princess"; Irene Ranco Pardilla, telephone interview by author, 27 July 1998.

82. Several articles in *Old Town Enterprise*, 1940: "Indian Pageant May be Revived," 2 May; "Chamber of Commerce is Looking for Expert to Direct Indian Pageant," 9 May; "Chamber of Commerce Board of Directors Held Meeting," 30 May; "Indian Pageant Main Subject of Chamber of Commerce Meeting: Chief Poolaw, Princess Watawasso in Lengthy Discussion," 13 June; "Indian Pageant on Reservation to have Big Parade—Special Show," 29 August.

83. Several articles in *Old Town Enterprise*, 1941: "Airport, Pageant, Traffic Share Limelight," 8 May; "1941 Old Town Pageant is Certainty: Chief Poolaw, Princess Watowaso to Direct 3-Day Exposition," 29 May; "Gov. Sumner Sewall and Earle Doucett, Publicity Man, Wish Pageant

Well," 19 June; "Lovers' Leap, Origin of the Redman to be Shown at Indian Pageant," 3 July; "Indian Pageant Making Progress," 24 July; "Old Town's Indian Pageant to be Even Better than 1931 Show," 31 July; "Penobscots to Portray Story of Vanishing Red Man Today in Long Awaited Pageant," 7 August; "Indian Pageant Great Success," 14 August.

84. Pardilla, interview.

85. Emma Nicolar, interview; Lawrence "Bill" Shay, interview.

86. Barbara F. Dyer, *"Grog Ho!" The History of Wooden Vessel Building in Camden, Maine* (Rockland, Maine: Courier-Gazette, Inc., 1984), 104; Anderson, interview.

87. Emma Nicolar, interview; Pardilla, interview.

88. Lawrence "Bill" Shay, interview.

89. Emma Nicolar, interview.

90. Shay, *History of the Penobscot Tribe*, 13–15.

91. Jean Francis Chevari, interview by author, 16 May 1998; Jean Archambaud Moore, interview by author, 16 May 1998.

92. Anderson, interview.

93. "Governor Here Nov. 29 for Indian Bridge Ceremony," *Penobscot Times*, 9 November 1950; "Governor Dedicates New Bridge to Indian Island," *Penobscot Times*, 30 November 1950.

94. Shay, *History of the Penobscot Tribe*, 14; Clark, "Penobscot Tribe Has Few Men Left." For pro and con arguments on the voting issue, see H.P. 423, L.D. 470 ("Resolve Proposing an Amendment to the Constitution Permitting Indians to Vote") in the Legislative Record, House, 9 April 1953: 1118 and in the Legislative Record, Senate, 1 May 1953: 1962–63. See also "Maine Indians Demand Status as 'Free Nation,'" *Lewiston Sun*, 27 March 1957, and David L. Ghere, "Assimilation, Termination, or Tribal Rejuvenation: Maine Indian Affairs in the 1950s," *Maine Historical Quarterly* 24, 2 (Fall 1984): 250–52.

95. The photograph of Nicolar casting her vote appeared in an unidentified newspaper clipping saved by her grandniece Emma Nicolar. Nicolar makes note of this honor in Wiggins, "Indian Princess," 30.

96. Charles Shay, interview.

97. "Mrs. Bruce Poolaw, Singer Of Penobscot Indian Lore," obituary, *New York Times*, 21 March 1969; "Services Held For Penobscot Princess," *Penobscot Times*, 27 March 1969.

98. Charles Shay, interview.

The debate about women's proper place between Edward Kent and Jane Appleton of mid-nineteenth century Bangor described by Kathryn Tomasek was by no means the last word on the subject. Indeed, the decades surrounding the turn of the twentieth century were filled with impassioned rhetoric on all sides of the subject as women came closer to achieving at least some forms of public equality. Americans continued to vie with one another to find the most convincing arguments for preserving traditional roles or for challenging them.

Among the means adopted by many women for participating in these debates was writing. A less visible means of supporting social change than political organizing, writing nevertheless offered women an effective means of having their voices heard. Women throughout the country had long used writing as a way to push against the boundaries of acceptable behavior. Some developed careers as journalists or published magazines. Some were frankly commercial in their efforts to reach a mass audience with their novels. Still others, who perhaps preferred to view themselves as "serious" artists, mined the terrain of local color to provide inspiration for their writing. They wrote about small communities across the United States with sympathy and affection, but also with a significant degree of distance: they looked back to such communities with self-conscious awareness that they were becoming increasingly archaic—quaint, to use a word they used themselves—in an increasingly modern society. Many of these local color writers lived in that modern world and shared many of its sensibilities, in spite of their nostalgia. They were enormously popular with Americans alarmed by the rapidity of social change and eager to preserve familiar values, or what they believed those values to have been.

Women local color writers—and most of them were women—faced a perplexing contradiction. Unwilling to forego the modern world that had offered them the opportunity to write, at the same time they sought to celebrate a more traditional world that would have preferred women to keep silent. As a result, these women writers as a group offered mixed messages about gender, simultaneously celebrating women's independence and deploring the social changes that had called it forth.

The women Joan Radner describes are not among those usually considered local color writers, in part because they were not self-conscious in their stance, nor did they write for a national audience. Yet they shared the local colorists' concern for preserving community even as they sought to enhance their own place in it, while firmly rejecting the modernizing world. Their efforts to preserve and contest rural Maine culture speak eloquently to their similarities to and differences from women who chose to write for a larger public audience and for money, even if about the same sorts of communities.

Joan N. Radner

In a speech written to be delivered at a literary program of the Fryeburg Center Grange in the early spring of 1893, an anonymous author (probably a woman) chose to discuss progress in strikingly feminist terms:

> I heard some one say not long since, that they could not see any great improvement or progress in this generation. What a mistake! Are people blind or fools to utter such thoughts? Look back one hundred years and what did the people have to brag about?
>
> A woman had no rights, she could not hold property, she was even debarred the privilege of an education. The men would say no money shall go to educate a She. After a while they were allowed to go to school from eight until nine, for the boys must have the rest of the day. The women of those days were thought just about as much of as the oxen of the present time.
>
> Today a woman has as many privileges as a man: She has access to the colleges and universities, and can take any course that her brother does, and in many cases goes far ahead of him; she can hold as much property as she can get and the men cannot touch it.

Then the speaker brought forth her crowning argument:

> And think of the Literary Clubs now, how many have the privilege of belonging to one or more. The Maine State Federation can boast of fifteen hundred members and not yet six months old. . . .[1]

How can any one say, and know what they are saying, that there is no improvement in this generation?

The Grange speaker defined progress almost entirely in terms of women's rights, and especially of women's intellectual opportunities. At the very end of the speech, seemingly as an afterthought, she listed a few other "wonderful improvements since what we call the 'dark ages'": railroads, steam power, electricity.[2] But her delight was concentrated in her statement, "Today a woman has as many privileges as a man."

How could the Grange speaker make such a claim—especially with respect to small rural communities such as the one in which she was speaking? What intellectual "privileges" and opportunities were open to women in postbellum farming villages? Certainly—despite the speaker's exuberant optimism—not "as many" as were available to men, but nonetheless, farm women made themselves felt in the public intellectual life of even the most rural hamlets in northern New England. They did so by a means that, as Mary Neth and Nancy Grey Osterud have shown, was typical of rural women's strategic achievement of power: they used their organizing skills to integrate with men in social enterprises.[3] This integration was at once liberating and confining. New England farm women did indeed gain public voice and influence, as this essay will show—but to maintain that privilege in their patriarchal culture, they had to accept significant limitations.

★ ★ ★

It was of course true that the previous century had seen immense increases in women's literacy and education. William J. Gilmore's observation that the "increasing intellectual emancipation of ordinary American women" was "one of the central developments of the nineteenth century" certainly held true for western Maine.[4] Fryeburg Academy, founded in 1792, admitted female scholars as early as 1806. Despite its relatively small population, Fryeburg was home to two of the twenty-seven women's clubs included in the Maine Federation at its inception. But the Fryeburg Literary Club (founded in 1890), located in Fryeburg Village, and West Fryeburg's Stirling Club (1891) were both—as was the Academy—situated several miles away from more remote and rural Center Fryeburg, where the Grange woman was crowing her delight at such opportunities. Unlike the common schools, the Academy and the literary clubs benefited the middle and upper classes almost exclusively. Although such institutions were probably within the experience of this particular Grange speaker, her neighbors were likely to have experienced no more than the education provided by the local one-room schools. It requires some investigation and reflection, therefore, to understand how she could express such unqualified enthusiasm about the equality of women's privileges.

Patriarchy had many provinces, and women's voices were unwelcome in most of them. In rural neighborhoods not only were politics, law, and medicine male bastions, but women's access to informal public venues of discussion was certainly more restricted than men's. Typically, for instance, gatherings around the woodstove in stores were exclusively male. In the same decade as the enthusiastic Grange writer was claiming such striking advances in female privilege, her fellow member of the Fryeburg Center Grange, John F. Hobbs of nearby Lovell, wrote a comic essay describing the local village store group as "the Lovell Court of Law." He caricatures men as "Chief Justice," "judges," and "attorneys" of the back-store "court," including himself as one of the "Leading

Members of the Bar." Tongue always in cheek, he wrote of the importance of the "court" to the town:

> We need two physicians in this place and we have them: no matter which one you employ, before you die, you will wish you had had the other. We need a good minister and we have one; we need a good minister's good wife, and we have her. But, *over and above all*, we need that Court of Law, to settle law points, adjudicate quarrels, decide trades and to harmonize and regulate Community. That Court, although it *grinds slow*, yet it grinds *exceeding small*.

Despite John Hobbs' well-honed irony, his final point has a serious side: a long-standing, traditional social institution like the back-store gathering *was* important "to harmonize and regulate Community." But Hobbs was explicit that not everyone was included among the Court's harmonizers and regulators.

> No women are allowed to attend. If a woman has any matter to come before the Court, she must appear by Atty. I do not know the reason of this rule, except that the Chief Justice says *"He won't have um round."*

Hobbs was well aware of the irritant power of this exclusion:

> For some unaccountable reason the ladies of this Village, perhaps because they are not allowed to practice, look with disfavor upon this Court and stigmatize its Business, its *important Business*, as *loafing* and its *hard mental labor*, harder than sprouting potatoes, beating carpets, putting up stove funnels and making soap, as *Idleness*.[5]

What were the women missing? What they would have gained by "practicing" in the back-store court was not just relief from domestic chores. Like most such institutions, the Lovell back store provided a sociable public forum for discussion of the affairs of town, state, and country. As a visible and centrally-located gathering, the "court" was an authoritative vehicle of community opinion. It also constituted a stage for oratory and verbal wit, an arena for humorous repartee, and even a setting for literature. For the entertainment of the village store audience (and for other audiences as well), John Hobbs wrote and declaimed a series of essays[6] that included his composition about the "Lovell Court of Law" and often sported with the issue of women's place, as in the following example:

A few mornings ago we had a session of Court at Barnes' Back Store. It was a cold morning but Barnes had a good fire, and we all huddled round the stove, to have a good time and discuss Law Points. . . . Dora [Hobbs' wife] had sent me after some molasses, with orders to return immediately, but I felt it my duty to stay. . . . Eben had begun his speech, when all at once the store door opened and in darted a little Smith kid and said to Eben, "Your wife says your horse is down and if you don't come and take care of him I shall get someone that will."

If someone had taken each separate man of us by the seat of the pants and the knob of the neck and thrown us in the cold Kezar River, it wouldn't have been any more of a cooler. Eben behaved nobly, simply pausing to say that a horse on his feet wasn't worth over ten cents. He kept on with his speech. Barnes put in some more wood to counteract the cold that came in with Mary's message. But it was no use. *Female influence had reached us.* Henry G. thought of Kate and began to button up his coat to go. I thought how Dora had told me not to stop, and in a little while, Court adjourned, and we all went about our Business, full of hard thoughts of Mary.

Mary did wrong. What she ought to have done under the circumstances was to have sent a polite little note something like this— "Dear Eben—I know you are very busy with John Hobbs, Henry G. Walker, Clif Eastman and Jim Farrington, etc., but your horse is down. Do not read this aloud so as to disturb your Brother Lawyers, but when you can get away without making the others feel lonesome, please return. Yours lovingly, Mary."[7]

In a culture that enjoyed and applauded John Hobbs' misogynistic irony, how could that 1893 Grange writer claim that women had finally attained equal privilege with men? Despite the fact that most of her female neighbors would not have attended high school, the answer lies in her emphasis on access to education and literature as prime markers of women's progress. Hobbs' sallies were couched in literary writing; the privilege to which women laid claim included the power of literary rejoinder. Literature was an important arena for the battle—or maybe, more accurately, the tug-of-war—of the sexes in rural northern New England. Despite their exclusion from the wit and wisdom of the patriarchal back store, the women of Lovell and neighboring Fryeburg, like many other nineteenth-century farm women in the region, had developed a way to share in the influential culture that men like John Hobbs enjoyed. They did not storm the village store behind Mary Fox, waving a banner. Instead, they used the literary and intellectual attainments that the Grange author so heartily celebrated to create events that brought them into the midst of local intellectual life. Federated and thus obvious as part of a statewide and national movement, Women's Clubs were the most recent and visible of rural women's intellectual achievements, and perhaps for that reason the Grange speaker chose to cite them specifically. But they were by no means the first effective intellectual venture on the part of New England farm women. As the remainder of this essay will demonstrate, such women had been maintaining dynamic public literary events in their own villages since the mid-century.

At the center of their events was a female-edited "newspaper"—in Fryeburg named the *Toll Bridge Journal* (later the *Toll Bridge Graphic* and the *Grange Echo*) after the rural district along the Saco River that sponsored it. Between the 1850s and the end of the century, the village newspaper tradition was widely distributed in inland farming communities across Maine, New Hampshire, and Vermont. In addition to the Toll Bridge papers, surviving examples include, in Maine, the Kenduskeag *Meteor*, *The Veazie Light*, the *Embden Center Times*, *The Bean's Corner Sunbeam* (Jay), *The Mystic Tie* (Carthage/Weld), *The Ladie's Enterprise* (Sweden), and the South Levant Reading Club *Independent*; in New Hampshire, the Antrim *Literary News*, *The Gem of the Valley* (West Plymouth), *The Pleasant Pond/Lake Pleasant Transcript* (Deerfield), and *The Poplin Herald* (Fremont); and in Vermont, the West Danville Debating Club *Enterprise,* the East Cabot Debating Club *Monitor,* and the West Halifax *Evening Star.*[8] These papers, which generally aimed to appear weekly during the winter months, were not mechanically printed; they were handwritten, and usually there was only one copy of each issue. A woman—designated everywhere the "editress"—collected the "pieces" for the newspaper from her neighbors, arranged them in a deliberate order (and sometimes composed additional bits), and wrote out a fair copy of the whole.[9] Then at the area's weekly "Lyceum" or debating club, the paper would be read out loud—performed—before the general community audience.[10] (In some areas, as in Fryeburg Center, after Subordinate Granges were established later in the century the debates and newspapers were transferred to the literary programs of the Grange.)

Through her paper the editress exerted power in the community. She expressed herself as a persuasive intellectual force. If her neighbors did not see themselves as writers, she urged them to *become* writers. One Fryeburg editress—perhaps casting an oblique slur at the back-store "attorneys"—chided reluctant contributors:

> You say I can't write a piece for the paper, because I have no talent in that line. It is just what you ought to try to develop, a great writer said demand virtue and you will have it, demand taste for literature and you will obtain it. . . . There is no place of any size on earth but

> where there may be a literary circle, and how much better it would
> be to spend one's leisure hours in study than in idle gossip that drags
> downward all who become victims to its grasp. (*Toll Bridge Graphic*)

Once she had collected the pieces, the editress decided which
would be included in the paper; thus she had a direct effect
on the self-esteem of the contributors. Occasional representations of these dynamics exist: in Sophie May's 1871 novel
The Doctor's Daughter, for instance, young Judith and
Marian of fictitious Quinnebasset, Maine, submit a poem for
the first time to the editress of Salmagundi, then wait tremu-
lously to see if it will be read as part of the paper at the
Thursday evening Circle meeting.[11]

Not only did the editress solicit and select the pieces for
the paper, she also put her own spin on them by determining
their order, and even, if she wished, by composing not only
the expected editorial essay, but pieces of her own as well.
She chose a broad spectrum of her neighbors' offerings. They
contributed verse as well as prose; they wrote about politics,
about local farming events and mishaps, about courting and
marriage, about philosophical issues, about the importance of
writing for the paper. They submitted moral essays: "The
Influences of Bad Habits," "The True Wife," "Friendship,"
"The Charities That Sweeten Life." Occasionally they wrote
poetry appreciative of local life or landscape: "The Afterglow,
Suggested by a Sunset off Mt Kearsarge." There were
thoughtful pieces about economic issues, such as the 1885
discussion in the Antrim (N.H.) *Literary News* on the topic
"Does Farming Pay?"

But despite these serious pieces, the prevailing mood of the
community papers on most topics was comic, parodic, teasing. In his Historical Address for the centennial of Sweden,
Maine, on August 26, 1913, Wellington H. Eastman captured
what was, for him, the essence of the literary lyceums:

A part of the program usually consisted of a lyceum paper, filled with wisdom more or less wise, and bits of wit that were more or less witty. I particularly remember a humorous description of a strange foreign land, bearing the name of Black Mountain District [an actual neighborhood in Sweden]. It was made up of ingenious puns on the names of the residents, some of whom were exceedingly Smart, while others were extremely Poor. At one time in its past history, we are told, there was a Knight on one side of the road and a Day on the other, but at the time the article was written the Knight was perpetual. Yet notwithstanding the long Knights (I believe one was six feet two) had hard Frosts, they had Berrys the year round.[12]

A Toll Bridge writer's wry wit captured the local view of the excesses of temperance campaigning in the 1890s:

> The Gum Question.
> By the Apostles of Temperance
> and the Anti-Gum Question.

> It has been estimated that nine tenths of the crime and pauperism of this State are the direct results of gum-chewing. So alarming has been the growth of this terriable [sic] vice that it is hardly too much to say that we are a nation of gummards. Its ravages are visible everywhere. . . .
> The collection of the crude gum from the trees requires the labor of half the Mainiac population, men, women and dogs during the winter months: the rest of the year is spent in adulter[at]ing it for the market. (*Toll Bridge Journal/Grange Echo*, 1890s)

When the local County Commissioner's sleigh overturned and dumped him on his head in a snowbank, the paper carried sly allusions to the disaster in verse. When Toll Bridge farmers who should have known better purchased diseased pigs, again the inventive paper writers responded; one of their pieces on the subject, a mock announcement of a lecture on "hogology," combined a jest at the purchasers with a blunt nudge at the misogynistic John Hobbs, who was "respectfully requested not to be present as he might consider the lecture personal." The moods, the concerns, the events, and the amusements of the community were broadly represented in the lyceum newspapers. In fact, the papers seem intended to represent the community not only to itself, but even in playful competition with neighboring areas, as was implied by the smug tone of the mock obituary in the *Toll Bridge Journal* (c. 1870) when the *Jackson (N.H.) City News* ceased to appear: "it has gone and in the language of the poet, 'Let it went.'. . . 'Rest in peace' thou lovely sheet."

The lyceum papers spoke for the community in a woman's voice. In some villages where the position of editress rotated weekly or fortnightly, the editress herself would perform the public reading; in other areas the editress served a longer term, but different women took turns reading the paper aloud after the formal lyceum debate.[13] The paper reading gave gender balance to the lyceum evening. In most communities the participants in the debate were men (though this was not the rule in some areas, such as Kenduskeag), but the entire evening—unlike the village store gatherings—involved both men and women in key roles. The debate, a male-controlled oratorical enterprise, was followed and balanced by the reading aloud of the handwritten village newspaper, a woman-controlled literary enterprise.

In their verbal cleverness, their community focus, and their public rhetoric, the village lyceum papers had some similarity to the store "Court of Law." (The *Toll Bridge Journal* even drew upon the talents of some of the attorneys from the Lovell "court of law": John Hobbs, that acute practitioner at the bar, occasionally contributed humorous pieces to the *Journal*—and was also roundly teased in its pages, as in the "hogology" announcement.) Like the back-store "court," the lyceum papers were witty, but because more public, their jokes (and their comments on local events) were more risky, and were therefore buffered by containment in a formal structure: the public reading of anonymous written texts by a reader who was not necessarily the author of the pieces she was reading. Only the editress could identify the individual authors; she concealed their identity from the rest of the gathering by making a fair copy of the entire paper in her own handwriting before the lyceum met. Thus the editress was doubly powerful in the situation, controlling not only what messages went forth, but also the knowledge of whose messages they were.[14]

The lyceum evenings offered women a strong voice in the community, a share in the pleasures of public repartee, and an opportunity to mix with men as intellectual equals. However, this demonstration of what Hobbs termed "female influence" seems to be contradicted by the gender representations in the lyceum papers themselves. Despite their control of production and performance, in the contents of their papers women presented a very conservative Victorian gender paradigm.

This conservatism is all the more obvious because the topic of relations between the sexes bulks very large in the papers. Although men and women of all ages contributed pieces for the village papers, those most actively supporting the tradition were young and usually unmarried adults, who had fewer family responsibilities to keep them from writing literary pieces or from attending the evening gatherings. As a result the most productive and prevalent topic in the papers was romance: young people's hopes and affinities, their successes and failures at courting, the (mis)fortunes of marriage, and the tribulations of bachelorhood.[15]

The papers' writers were immensely inventive concerning romantic attachments. In papers sampled from some eighteen communities the topics of courting, marriage, and bachelorhood are represented in more than two dozen different literary genres—whose natures reveal the models on which the writers drew. Many of their pieces took their cue from the popular press. A mock advertisement, from the *Embden Center Times*, 29 November 1893:

Wanted

A wife one that can cook, wash, mop, dress deer and skin foxes.

—Elmer Berry

—and, a page later—

Wanted

A position as house wife, can cook, and dress all kinds of game should prefer a hunter as I am very fond of wild meat.   —Bell Bean

A business announcement (So. Levant *Independent*, 23 March 1881):

Dissolution

The copartnership hitherto existing under the name of Walker and Eldridge is hereby dissolved and after this date will be known as Griffin and Eldridge.

Signed Daniel Walker

Carrie Eldridge

A notice from East Bethel:

Lost and Found

Lost on the road between Beans Corner and Middle Intervale a young man's heart, any one returning the same to the Subscriber will be swiftly rewarded.

Fred Howe

Kimball Hill Dec 4th 1877

Found

Near the residence of JD Hastings an article resembling a human heart. The owner can have the same by proving property and paying charges.

Parody of advice columns:

Answers to Correspondents
Stevy Sawyer wishes to know what he shall do when the girls will not let him go home with them. We would advis[e] him to go home alone. (*The Ladie's Enterprise*, Sweden, 10 May 1877)

Given the inland location of virtually all the communities that produced these papers, the most ironic mock-journalistic genre was "Shipping News," depicting the courting adventures of local young men and women as if they were the movements of ships.

Ship News   Port of Veazie
The Steamer Hattie sailed from port commanded by Capt. Morris Buckly, Capt. Frost having resigned.

Outward Bound
Long voyage—The beautiful Steamship "May" commanded by Capt. P. T. Huckins. (*The Veazie Light*, 22 January 1877)

Traditional New England folklore and amusements provided other models for the local newspaper authors. For stories of wooing disasters, the ballad was the genre of choice, sometimes put into the mouth of the unfortunate suitor himself. Poor "Sam" in Fryeburg "went a courting," was told by the girl to leave, and suffered the rewards of clumsiness:

In my various avocations in my past persuits [*sic*] of life
My neighbors talked of nothing else but getting me a wife
But now they talk of my bad luck as I am well aware
How up to Mr Walker['s] I tumbled down the stairs.
(*Toll Bridge Journal*, Fryeburg, c. 1870)

In Kenduskeag in 1884 poor Willie Watson tried for twelve stanzas to find a girl willing to go skating with him,

> But Willie's rather bashful
> So many times he's been refused
> He don't think it's just fair
> The way that he's been used.
>
> *(The Meteor, 15 November 1884)*

Conundrums—a popular parlor pastime—drew on New England's love of punning on names:

> What kind of a dog does our Organist prefer?
> A Barker of course.
>
> . . .
>
> Which book in the New Testament is interesting to
> a certain young lady?
> The book of James.
>
> *(Toll Bridge Journal/Grange Echo, 1890s)*

Rhyming "comparisons" could suggest interesting relationships:

> As the corn is to the crow
> So is Abbie to Crockets Joe
>
> As the city is to the mayor
> So is Byron Webster to May Taylor.
>
> *(Bean's Corner Sunbeam, Jay, 20 March 1879)*

"Echo" couplets were widely popular:

> What makes Etta's face so long,
> Echo ans[wers]—Because Jim is gone. . . .
>
> What makes Tavie bite her lip,
> Echo ans—Because Proctor has given her the slip.
>
> (East Bethel lyceum paper)

The Bible readings that were part of every child's heritage furnished models for more elaborate parodies: Chronicles,

warning Epistles, "My Wife's Commandments" by a hen-
pecked husband, a Saco River flood depicted in the style of
Genesis. Common legal experience yielded the popular genre
of the versified mock will, whose couplets could pair up
everybody in the neighborhood:

> My will I've made, now free and clear
> I will all my things to my Children dear.
>
> . . .
>
> To Ossian Ripley and his Nellie
> I will give my Apple Jelly.
>
> . . .
>
> To Emma Niles and Grover Frank
> I give my dog that is so lank.
>
> . . .
>
> To Albertie Bean and Mamie T
> I give five cents to go on a spree.
>
> . . .
>
> This closes the list of all my wares
> to be given to my Children who live in pairs
> and any whom I've left behind
> may get all the dollars they can find.
>
> ("Aunt Jemima's Will," *Bean's Corner*
> *Sunbeam*, 16 January 1877)

Picking up on the legal theme, a contributor to the East
Bethel paper devised a set of "Blue Laws" for Kimball Hill,
the local neighborhood of most of the contributors, with such
prohibitions as:

> It shant be lawful for Etta Bartlett to be courted Sunday night unless
> her mother sits in the room and takes notes. . . .
> It shant be lawful for Jim Bartlett to kiss Etta more than three times
> a day unless by her request in writing.

Schoolwork—a recent and sometimes even a current experience for some of the younger contributors[16]—dictated the

form and tone of essays in the papers, and sometimes inspired unique literary inventions:

> Parsing Lesson
> Everitt Judkins is a preposition shows the relation between Jessie Brown and Lena Pratt. Alvin Judkins is a verb and agrees with [Le]ttie Bow. . . . Berdell Pratt is a regular transitive verb future tense and shall or will have Ella May Libby. Transitive verbs require an object to complete the sense. (*The Mystic Tie*, Carthage/Weld, January 1875)

Other common literary modes—letters, diaries, popular fiction—filled out the repertoire of the papers' contributors.

These homespun pieces presented courting as the means to settled marriage. Through the papers' light genres affinities were revealed and tested out, liaisons were proposed and rearranged. On occasion a girl was obliquely rebuked for coquetry; in 1875, for instance, *The Mystic Tie* carried "A sketch from Etta['s] diary," in which Etta revels in the memory of a week spent teasing her beaux. But far more frequently the boys were pilloried for clumsiness or bashfulness. And bachelors—always presented as men too inept to get wives, not as men who prefer not to marry—were teased mercilessly. Elias Gould of Bean's Corner was too nervous to propose to "one of the fairest of earth's creatures"; he begged sympathy for his "deep afflictions" and lamented "that I've 'no match made in Heaven,' and I must drag out my natural term of life in a dreary state of loneliness, and without a lovely better half. Sad but how true and yet how different it might have been" ("Elias' Soliloquy," *Bean's Corner Sunbeam*, 20 March 1879). "Aunt Jerusha's Will" sentenced another unsuccessful young man to a sour life:

> To Herman Grover he seems to be without a mate
> So I'll will him a few pickles in my blue plate.
> (*Bean's Corner Sunbeam*, 20 March 1879)

In their neighbor Hiram Kelsey Hobbs the *Toll Bridge Journal* writers created an archetypal scapegoat bachelor. In 1871 (when he was 33) the *Journal* carried supposed extracts from a week of "Kelsey's Diary." On Monday he lamented, "I cant endure the tortures of a single life much longer and what's more! I wont"—and set off, day by day, to propose to and be rejected by a different girl, promising on Friday that if he failed once more, "I will next week go to Boston to be Conductor on a Railway Car." Twenty years later he was still the butt of the *Journal*'s jokes: "Hiram K. says he would like to have the women vote, if one of them would only vote to marry him."

Marriage was presented as the primary goal of the young newspaper writers—and as every woman's fulfillment. In accord with the typical Victorian canon of domesticity,[17] every young village woman was to become "The True Wife": "a companion given by God to smooth the rough road to eternity," "she labors to make man happy, her household duties are accomplished with a cheerful mind and ready hand, neatness follows in her footsteps, and frugality in her actions" (*Toll Bridge Journal*, 12 March 1870); she is to make "The Anglo-Saxon Home" heavenly with "the sweet music of woman's voice . . . [and] the soft whisper of woman's love" (*Toll Bridge Journal/Grange Echo*, 1890s). But marriage should be entered into carefully and with realistic expectations:

> The Eastern Argus relates an instance of a beautiful young lady who having been blind regained her eyesight after marriage. I think that it is no uncommon thing for a persons eyes to be opened by matrimony.
>
> (*Toll Bridge Journal/Grange Echo*, 1890s)

In 1875 *The Mystic Tie* ascribed to Mansfield Brown of Carthage verses outlining the qualities of the wife he sought—beauty, youth, artistic accomplishments, patience, domestic skills, fidelity, abstinence from eating onions, and "far above all, the best dish of the feast, / Her Pa must be worth twenty thousand at least"; the answer, attributed to Flora Phiney, promised almost all the requisite qualities, except "one trifling thing I omit[t]ed to mention / I bring you a true heart but nary a pencion [sic]." Some papers carried comic "before" and "after" verses detailing the disillusionment of spouses.

Wives—in the abstract—were cautioned against shrewishness, willfulness, and improvidence. Occasionally the generic humor in the papers echoed the misogyny of the village store "court": "A wife should be like an almanac, for then a man could have a new one every year" (*Toll Bridge Journal/Grange Echo*, 1890s). Actual husbands in the community, on the other hand, were teased even about thoughts of infidelity.

> There is Seymour Hobbs, so pleasant and jolly
> He never lays awake for other mens folly
> He has a good wife, who his head often whirls
> Because he's a notion to be after the girls.
> (*Toll Bridge Journal*, c. 1870)

Generic jokes about men, or about husbands, were far less common in the papers than jokes about women.

Unlike bachelors, unmarried older women were not teased in the papers, though occasionally a young woman was forecast to be a "poor old maid," and in 1876 a letter in the *Veazie Light* predicted that in twenty years, Lue Spencer would be among the town's "confirmed old maids . . . disgusted at their futile attempts to get married," and would be running for the legislature as "the women's rights candidate." The papers' authors generally took a dim view of women's political ambitions. Although the topic of debate at the February 12, 1880, meeting of the West Plymouth (N.H.) Literary Association was "Resolved: that marriage does not increase the happiness of the sexes," two weeks later that Association's paper, *The Gem of the Valley*, carried a poem entitled "Women's Rights":

'Tis the right of a woman the babies to tend;
    To wash, bake and brew, to make and to mend;
Her right to be tidy, to sweep and to dust:
    In fact to do *all* that a housekeeper *must*;
Her right to be cheerful all the day through;
    Though her cares may be many, and her comforts but few.

For seven more stanzas the poem outlined her "right" to get dinner ready on time for her husband, keep the children quiet, visit and tend the sick, offer hospitality, weep and pray for the erring, care for the poor, and forgive wrongs. Only the final verse accorded her the slightest entitlement to speak for herself:

'Tis her right to be cared for; her right to be loved;
    And all her good deeds to be kindly approved.
All these are her rights: they'll number forty-four,
    So I will now mention only one more:
'Tis her right to be *firm* when she *knows* she is *right*
    Despite every opposition, Now I'll bid you "Good Night."[18]

Such items present a paradox that cannot be ignored. Even though a woman, the editress, had final control of each paper's messages, and the actual voice of a woman, the reader, delivered those messages to the assembled community, the implied voice as well as the message in many pieces is male. A *Veazie Light* essay signed with the audacious alias "Gay Spanker" advised Veazie girls to stop "simpering or playing the fool to some brainless mustached fox in the parlor"; "better set your cap for that young farmer or river driver at whom you have nearly died a laughing so many times. . . . Go to work, and be no longer the contempt of all the smart, active, go-ahead marriageable young men in Veazie" (22 January 1877).[19] Why, in an era when travelers, lecturers, and the popular press brought news of women's political and social activism to even the most remote rural areas, were the editresses so willing to have their papers push women toward exclusively domestic and local goals? There were very occasional traces of contention, as, for example, in an 1890s "Gossip about Town" submission to the Fryeburg editress: "Seymour says he wishes the women paid all the taxes; he should like so much better to collect of them," to which the author appended a brief comment: "The Brute." But the writer's objection is ambiguous at best: is s/he criticizing Seymour's flippant attitude towards women's rights, or only (if this is the Seymour Hobbs pilloried elsewhere for thoughts of infidelity) his womanizing tendencies?

How should we understand the seeming contradiction between the women's control of the lyceum papers and the patriarchal gender messages they broadcast? It was not uncommon for women in the nineteenth century to assert literary prerogatives while simultaneously—and even perhaps strategically—championing conventional female domesticity. But in northern New England women may have had an additional reason to advocate conservative traditions. The insistence of "Gay Spanker" that women marry local men gives us an important clue to the puzzle. The pervasive discussion of courtship and gender roles in the village papers needs to be heard in the context of the late nineteenth century, an era marked by economic change and progressive challenge to the traditional ideals of family farming valued by the older communities of northern New England. The underlying mission of the village editresses was nothing less than cultural preservation. More and more young people were leaving settled rural communities for the frontier or the industrial cities. The pull to move away was enormous; in Fryeburg and Lovell, for instance—the area that produced the *Toll Bridge Journal*—between 1860 and 1890 the population declined by 23%. (This statistic is even more dramatic when we consider that in the same period the population of the entire United States doubled.) For those who chose not to leave the farming villages of northern New England—"those who stayed behind," as historian Hal Barron has named them—handwritten newspapers, humorous as they often were, performed serious functions.[20] They expressed and taught and helped to maintain a consistent set of expectations and attitudes, among which the celebration of female domesticity, local matchmaking, and marriage were key elements.

The tradition of handwritten lyceum papers thus carried its own internal contradictions. Through the editing and performing of these papers women in rural northern neighborhoods counteracted gender separation and inequality by creating an influential community institution that integrated women and men and fostered mutuality between them. Women achieved public voice and expressed their power. No matter what the back-store "courts of law" might decree, through these little papers "female influence" reached the town, and a different and authoritative force was on hand to "harmonize and regulate the Community." But in the villages of postbellum northern New England, harmonizing and regulating the community seemed to call for the assertion of women's subordination. The lyceum papers filled the role Pauline Greenhill has described for "folk poetry" in general: they were "a significant medium for grassroots participation in and contestation of cultural change."[21] In fact, in themselves they embodied that contestation. The divergent gender messages projected by the papers' text and context offer us a

vivid illustration of the tensions educated rural women needed to negotiate a century ago. "Today a woman has as many
privileges as a man," wrote the Grange speaker in 1893. But
committed to the essentially conservative project of community survival, such women never tested the full implications
of that claim.[22]

1. The Maine Federation of Women's Clubs was founded in September,
1892, and by the time of its first Directors' Meeting, in February, 1893,
included some twenty-seven federated clubs. The movement grew rapidly
in Maine; by 1898, ninety-six clubs in forty-nine towns were federated,
with a total reported membership of 4,174 (eight clubs did not report membership totals). Although most of the clubs focused on the study of history
or literature, some specialized in music, art, travel, current events, law, or
language study. Georgia Pulsifer Porter, *Maine Federation of Women's
Clubs: Historical Sketches, 1892–1924* (Lewiston, Maine: Lewiston Journal
Printshop, 1925); *Manual of Maine Federation of Women's Clubs, 1898–99*
(Lewiston, Maine: n.p., 1899).
2. Hobbs papers, Lovell Historical Society, Lovell, Maine.
3. Mary Neth, "Building the Base: Farm Women, the Rural Community, and
Farm Organizations in the Midwest, 1900–1940," in *Women and Farming:
Changing Roles, Changing Structures*, ed. Wava G. Haney and Jane B.
Knowles (Boulder, Colo.: Westview Press, 1988), 339–55; Nancy Grey
Osterud, *Bonds of Community: The Lives of Farm Women in Nineteenth-
Century New York* (Ithaca, N.Y.: Cornell University Press, 1991).
4. William J. Gilmore, *Reading Becomes a Necessity of Life: Material and
Cultural Life in Rural New England, 1780–1835* (Knoxville: University of
Tennessee Press, 1989), 47.
5. Hobbs papers, Lovell Historical Society.
6. These compositions were known locally as the "Brown Paper Essays"
from his habit of writing them in pencil on brown butcher paper (see
Pauline W. Moore, *A Lady of Lovell: The Story of Charlotte Hobbs* [Lovell,
Maine: Lovell Historical Society, 1981], 2); several are now in the collection of the Lovell Historical Society.
7. Hobbs papers, Lovell Historical Society.
8. Papers such as those on which this essay draws are largely in private col-

lections and are only beginning to come to light, although since 1997, when this essay was written, I have discovered dozens more. Very few Maine and New Hampshire handwritten newspapers of this period have yet been identified and catalogued in libraries or historical society archives. In Maine, issues of *The Bean's Corner Sunbeam* (1877, 1879) and its successor, *The Academic Wreath*, have been donated to the Jay Historical Society, as has an issue of the South Levant Reading Club *Independent* (1881) to the Levant Historical Society. *The Embden Center Times* (November 29, 1893) is in the collection of the Embden Historical Society; *The Mystic Tie* (January 1875) is in the archives of the Weld Historical Society. Photocopies of the *Toll Bridge Journal, Toll Bridge Graphic,* and their 1890s successor the (Fryeburg Center) *Grange Echo* are in the archives of the Fryeburg Historical Society. The archives of the New Hampshire Historical Society include various issues of the (Antrim) *Literary News* (1885, 1886), *The Gem of the Valley* (West Plymouth, 1878, 1880, and 1870–80 records of the West Plymouth Literary Association), and the (Deerfield) *Pleasant Pond/Lake Pleasant Transcript* (1887?, 1897), as well as antebellum handwritten papers (many produced by secondary school students) from Hampton, Claremont, East Andover, Henniker, and Llandaff. Two issues of the *Poplin Herald* (1879, 1880) are in the hands of Matthew E. Thomas, Town Historian of Fremont, N.H. The John F. Hobbs papers are in the archives of the Lovell (Maine) Historical Society. Some Vermont lyceum papers—*The Enterprise* (W. Danville, 1884), *The Monitor* (E. Cabot, 1878), and *The Evening Star* (W. Halifax, n.d.)—are in the archives of the Vermont Historical Society.

9. In a few communities—particularly in the earliest, antebellum years of the village newspaper tradition, and particularly in New Hampshire and Vermont—there were male editors, or a male editor and one or more female editresses. The single issue of the *Hampton Budget* (20 October 1847) in the New Hampshire Historical Society archives seems to have been edited by a man, and alludes to a male editor of a contemporary village paper in nearby Epping (Collection No. 1990-166). The *Kearsarge Fountain* of East Andover, N.H., began in 1848 with a male editor, but by 1850 it was published by an editress (NHHS Collection No. 1989-092). When *The Gem of the Valley* was initiated in 1870 (under the title *The Weekly Advertizer*) as the paper of the West Plymouth Literary Association, it had both an editor and an editress who took turns producing the paper; by 1878 the position of editor had disappeared and only an editress is mentioned in the Association's proceedings (NHHS Collection No. 1961-4).

10. The local institutions by which the papers were sponsored went by various names: lyceum, literary association/society/circle/club/union, debating club. "Lyceum" was by far the most common term, and given the variety of activities these local gatherings encompassed, the tradition seems to validate the nineteenth-century definition of "lyceum" quoted by Joseph F. Kett: "a literary club of almost any description" (*The Pursuit of Knowledge Under Difficulties: From Self-Improvement to Adult Education in America, 1750–1990* [Stanford, Calif.: Stanford University Press, 1994], 45). Formal debates and the reading aloud of homegrown literary newspapers were central features of the village lyceums, setting them apart from the more urban and somewhat earlier nineteenth-century "lyceums" that sponsored for their subscribers series of lectures and presentations by traveling notables (cf. Carl Bode, *The American Lyceum: Town Meeting of the Mind* [New York: Oxford University Press, 1956]; Barbara Allen Hind, "The Lyceum Movement in Maine" [Master's Thesis, University of Maine, Orono, 1949]; Kett, *The Pursuit of Knowledge Under Difficulties*).

11. Sophie May [Rebecca Sophia Clarke], *The Doctor's Daughter* (Boston: Lee and Shepard; New York: Charles T. Dillingham, 1871), 62–67.

12. Philip W. Richards, *Sweden, Maine History, Volume Two: Adversity and Determination* (Sweden, Maine: Philip W. Richards, 1989), 4–5.

13. See, for example, the 1866 diary of Mary Frances Hodsdon of North Waterford, Maine, who reports and evaluates the performance of different readers of the paper of the North Waterford Debating Club (cf. Joan Newlon Radner, "'Performing the Paper: Handwritten Newspapers and Village Life in Postbellum Maine," *Northeast Folklore: Essays in Honor of Edward D. Ives*, ed. Pauleena MacDougall and David Taylor [Orono: University of Maine Press and Maine Folklife Center, 2000], 363–82). The Hodsdon diaries are in Box 279, f4 and f7, Special Collections, Fogler Library, University of Maine, Orono.

14. The pieces in the paper were almost always unsigned (or attributed falsely). Although in some cases the authors' identities would have been known or strongly suspected, conscious attempts were made to preserve anonymity. A pencilled note on the back of some teasing "Alphabetical Poetry" submitted to the editress of the *Bean's Corner Sunbeam* makes this explicit: "Miss Mary E. Webster, Pleas[e] not tell who wrote this."

15. For a wider view of courtship in this period, see, for instance, Karen Lystra, *Searching the Heart: Women, Men, and Romantic Love in Nineteenth-Century America* (New York: Oxford University Press, 1989); Ellen K. Rothman, *Hands and Hearts: A History of Courtship in America* (New York: Basic Books, 1984).

16. As I have pointed out elsewhere, the village newspaper tradition may have had its origin in similar publications created for lyceums by secondary school students (Radner, "Performing the Paper").

17. See Nancy F. Cott, *The Bonds of Womanhood:"Women's Sphere" in New England, 1780–1835* (New Haven, Conn.: Yale University Press, 1977); Barbara Welter, "The Cult of True Womanhood, 1820–1860," *American Quarterly* 18 (1966): 151–74.

18. Evidently these verses imitate and parody a popular type of poem, exemplified by "What Are the Rights of Women?" by Mrs. E. Little, published in *The Ladies Wreath* 2 (1848–49), 133. (Cited in Welter, "Cult of True Womanhood," 173.) A similar (anonymous) poem, "What Are Women's Rights," published originally in *New Dominion Monthly* (1867), is quoted by Fraser Sutherland, *The Monthly Epic: A History of Canadian Magazines, 1789–1989* (Markham, Ont.: Fitzhenry & Whiteside, 1989), 39. I am grateful to Elizabeth Hedler for these citations.

19. Contrast to this message the typical lyceum paper advice to young men about selecting wives, which again criticize women, as in the piece on "Young Ladies of Today" in *The Gem of the Valley* for 30 November 1878, which concludes: "My advice to every young man is to beware of a fashionable young lady. Never marry the girl who sits in the parlor while her mother stands in the kitchen."

20. See Hal S. Barron, *Those Who Stayed Behind: Rural Society in Nineteenth-Century New England* (New York: Cambridge University Press, 1984); Radner, "Performing the Paper."

21. Pauline Greenhill, *True Poetry: Traditional and Popular Verse in Ontario* (Montreal: McGill-Queen's University Press, 1989), 8.

22. For information and advice, and for locating, sharing, and copying some of the material cited in this essay, I would especially like to thank William D. Barry and Stephanie Philbrick, Maine Historical Society; Clyde G. Berry, Master of the Maine State Grange; Sue Black, Bridgton (Maine) Historical Society; Don and Jo Buzzell, Fryeburg, Maine; Paul Carnahan, Vermont Historical Society; Roberta Chandler and Irene Dunham, Lovell (Maine) Historical Society; Elizabeth Hamlin-Morin, New Hampshire Historical Society; Stanley R. Howe, Bethel (Maine) Historical Society; Diane Jones, Fryeburg (Maine) Historical Society; Emily Joseph, American University; Sean Minear, Weld (Maine) Historical Society; Winnie Moore, Denmark (Maine) Historical Society; Patricia P. Pickard, Bangor, Maine; Kimberly R. Sebold, University of Maine, Orono; Matthew E. Thomas, Fremont, N.H.; Margaret R. Yocom, George Mason University, Fairfax,

Virginia; and the staff of the Fogler Library, Special Collections Department, University of Maine, Orono.

I would greatly appreciate information about other handwritten papers of the period; please contact me at jradner@american.edu.

Early-twentieth-century debates about proper roles for women did not turn exclusively on the question of their participation in the public world. In addition, Americans debated questions of women's sexuality, struggling to pin down the shifting boundary between acceptable and unacceptable behavior. The assumption of women's fundamental passionlessness prevalent in the nineteenth century was giving way to recognition of them as sexual beings, both capable of and entitled to pleasure. Still, that sexuality was considered acceptable only within very narrow limits; premarital activity, lesbianism (a new term describing a newly self-conscious set of behaviors), and prostitution were all condemned as problematic deviations from the norm. As a result, sexuality became yet another arena in which conflicts between traditional and more modern ways of thinking were played out.

That conflict also focused on birth control, which allowed sexuality to be separated from reproduction, inspiring vigorous debate throughout the nation. Proponents considered it beneficial because it would free women to express their sexuality without the risk of pregnancy, creating happier marriages in the process; opponents abhorred the potential immorality and decline of traditional values they perceived it would bring. Most Americans, includ-

ing most in Maine, experienced the debate at something of a distance, as birth control information was not available in most communities, although the debate was widespread.

Debates about birth control pointed to a growing awareness of the sexual double standard, along with growing complaints about its hypocrisy. While premarital sexual activity by men was for the most part tolerated at the turn of the century, any expression of sexual intimacy by unmarried women was condemned; responsibility for remaining chaste was placed firmly in their hands. Birth control, where it was available, was reserved exclusively for the married; even its proponents for the most part did not advocate unrestricted sexual freedom. Yet in spite of the double standard, a few Americans, mostly following the lead of European sexologists, began to argue that women should be allowed to express their sexuality freely; not to do so was damaging to them physically and emotionally.

Of course, most Americans did not wait for sexologists' permission to engage in sexual activity of any sort. The gap between expectations and practice grew ever wider as the expectations themselves were subjected to debate. Americans, it seemed, were engaging in all sorts of illicit activity with increasing frequency. Mazie Hough offers a view of the consequences for one group of Maine women.

"TO TAKE THE PLACE OF HER OWN KIN": OLD PRACTICES AND NEW OPPORTUNITIES FOR UNWED MOTHERS IN BANGOR, MAINE

Mazie Hough

In 1928, Gertrude Atwood, superintendent of the Good Samaritan Home Agency in Bangor, Maine, wrote to the sister of a young unmarried woman who had travelled 185 miles from Fort Kent to deliver her child there. "We feel the girl is not at all a bad girl," Atwood wrote, "but is impulsive, and has made a mistake from the effects of which she is now passing through the bitterest experience a girl can go through, and it has come to us, although we are strangers to her, to take the place of her own kin."[1]

The Good Samaritan Home was one of only two homes for unwed mothers in the state between 1886 and 1940. Of the two, it attracted the larger number of pregnant women and wider community support. From 1902 to 1941, one hundred and three pregnant women sought its services. Both Catholic and Protestant, Franco-American and Anglo-Saxon, the women shared a common rural experience. While more than half went home with their babies, a substantial portion—a third—remained in Bangor. With the help of the Good Samaritans, they took jobs, left their children in the Home temporarily, and eventually most married. Often their husbands adopted their children.

The Home was one of over 200 similar institutions available for unwed mothers in the United States at the turn of the century. Historians have documented how these homes developed as the nation moved from a collection of island communities to an integrated industrialized nation.[2] They have described in detail a national discourse on unwed mothers that shifted from describing unwed mothers as victims of male seduction who needed support and encouragement to keep their children, to describing them as psychological deviants who needed casework and would be best served by giving up their children to adoption.[3]

An analysis of the case records from the Good Samaritan Agency, however, suggests that in rural Maine at least another paradigm of unwed motherhood prevailed.[4] This paradigm, operative throughout rural Maine, reflected a different attitude toward unwed mothers and suggested a different treatment for them. It was a conservative paradigm—one geared toward getting the most out of every member who belonged to a community and excluding all who did not—and it persisted almost without change well into the twentieth century. The Good Samaritan Home Agency mediated between this local paradigm and the changing national one. In the early part of the century, when wide community support enabled the Home to be autonomous, it built an institution that reflected rural values, but was located in the third largest city in the state. As a result, it enabled women and their families to feel comfortable with a move from their homes to Bangor and thus ultimately provided the women with an opportunity to escape from the confines of their rural communities. As social work became more professionalized and the state government began to enforce national standards, the Good Samaritan Agency was forced to adopt national practices that were increasingly at variance with local values. As a result the Home lost its ability to mediate successfully between local and national expectations, leaving Maine women without a viable option outside of their home communities.

At the turn of the century, Maine was an overwhelmingly rural state with close to 500 towns and only twenty cities.[5] Ever since the mid-nineteenth century, when railroads began to supplant coastal shipping as the primary system of transportation in the United States, most of these towns had experienced a gradual but steady economic decline. While most farmers owned their own land, competition from the west, as well as poor soil and climate conditions, limited the amount of wealth any one farmer could accrue. Limited opportunity drove many who were looking to improve their lives out of the state. Beginning in mid-century, newspapers, legislators, and educators spoke frequently of the constant outmigration of the state's youth and of the need to do something about it.[6] Conserving local resources became a state-wide concern.

Reflecting this concern, Maine state legislators and courts in the mid-nineteenth century maintained the original common law traditions regarding bastardy, seduction, and settlement.[7] These laws—the state's construction of legitimacy— served to protect communities from undue expense. They made careful distinctions between those who belonged and those who did not, emphasized the need for inter-generational rights and responsibilities, and encouraged residents to be self-sufficient, and to remain within and contribute to the community.[8]

Underlying this construction of legitimacy was Maine's settlement law, which required towns to provide basic support to all their residents. Although a person could not obtain a settlement in a town until he or she had lived there for five years without receiving any public support, the settlement laws could place a considerable burden on small communities. As a result, towns paid special attention to who did and who did not belong. Overseers of the poor could, and frequently did, send those seeking relief back to the town in which they had a settlement, or billed that town for the cost of the support. Overseers and the law also made sure that all families took care of their members before they turned to the town for help. Under Maine's settlement law, a single pregnant woman had the settlement of her father. First her family and then the town was obliged to provide for her delivery and the support of her and her child.

While Maine's settlement laws emphasized the responsibility of the family and community to take care of their own, Maine's bastardy law emphasized the responsibility of the father to take care of his child. Any woman who gave birth to or was pregnant with a "bastard" child could go before the justice of peace and bring suit against the putative father. The court would try the case before a jury and, finding the man responsible, could charge him with the costs of the suit, the expenses of the delivery, and regular payments for the support of the child for as long as the court deemed necessary. Recognizing the towns' vested interest in the outcome of a suit, the law allowed a town to join a suit once a woman had initiated it. Town selectmen could thus legitimately pursue a father attempting to flee his responsibility or provide a woman with legal counsel.[9]

Once initiated, the outcome of a bastardy trial relied almost exclusively on the requirement that a woman name the father of her child as she was giving birth. "It was deemed," the court concluded in 1852, "that in the hour of her agony and under the danger of immediate death, there would be little fear of the utterance of the falsehood or the concealment of truth on her part."[10] Once a woman had thus named a man during her labor, there was little the man could do to defend himself. It did not matter if the woman had asked someone else to marry her, had named someone else before the birth, or had intercourse with another a few days after conception. It was immaterial even that a woman had been a prostitute for the past three years. "In this court," the court stated emphatically, "the character of the complainant for chastity is not an issue."[11]

The requirement that a woman name the father of her child during labor not only gave importance to her testimony, but also required her to be with others when she gave birth, for she could not prove she had named the father unless someone else was there to hear her do so. This requirement, coupled with the law that punished single women who gave birth in secret, reinforced the community's ability to separate those who belonged—who accepted the community's interference—and those who did not.[12]

Letters from the Good Samaritan case records from the early twentieth century reveal that community practices and values continued to reflect the same values that were embodied in the bastardy and settlement laws. Like these laws, community members concerned about specific pregnant women emphasized communal self-sufficiency and individual responsibility. While they did not necessarily condone pregnancy outside of marriage, letter writers suggested that a woman's value was more dependent on her willingness to work hard and to accept community guidance than on her reputation for chastity. It was in the town's best interest, for example, that a single woman with a child marry, for then her husband would have to support her and her child. While the town relied on bastardy legislation to encourage a man to marry the mother of his child, it also encouraged other men to marry single mothers by emphasizing that their pregnancies were not a result of bad character but of youth, and that they were redeemable. The women were not bad, town members repeatedly insisted in their letters of reference to the Good Samaritan Home, only unfortunate and young. This was true even in the case of a fifteen-year-old who had been involved with more than one man. Though she had been "a little loose for a year or two," attorney Joseph W. Sawyer stated, "she is not what I would call a bad girl but one who is more unfortunate than anything else." The Rev. Alfred G. Davis concurred and added that with the right training she could "develop into a virtuous and respectable woman and I trust a useful member of the society." In another case, attorney William Waldron wrote that the girl had been in the habit of going out at nights more than a girl her age should. "From all I can learn," he added, "she is not a bad girl naturally, but she certainly was in danger of becoming a bad woman. She was young and thoughtless and liked a good time."[13] Since communities regarded the woman's pregnancy as the result of her youth, they held themselves as well as the pregnant woman responsible. The community had not provided adequate supervision. An eighteen-year-old girl whose parents were "anxious to have her come under the influence of the Home" was described by a Red Cross nurse as "a girl who left school when about fourteen and is more untaught than wayward."[14]

The community relied on older women to supervise younger ones. They did this by taking younger women into their homes to help with the work,[15] and they also did it through gossip. Gossip both informed older women how younger women were behaving and served to remind younger women (and men) of the behavior that was expected. While gossip made sure that no one escaped observation, it also allowed transgressions to be placed in their community context. A woman's sexual behavior, for example, could be balanced by her willingness to work. Eva Scates, field agent for the New England Home for Little Wanderers, wrote to Gertrude Atwood, Superintendent of the Home, about one girl whose mother had had three illegitimate children, all by different men. She admitted to Atwood that the "mother has had a very bad reputation." However, she added, she was "known to have been honest and very hard working and . . . took good care of her children." She pointed out that the mother "worked in the best families in town and although they knew of her reputation, they employed her because of her capability."[16]

The community used gossip to track down the man who might help support the child and to keep an eye on women who had already had one child out of wedlock. Scates advised Atwood to encourage a woman in the Home to name the father of her child. "I can keep track of his whereabouts through one of the sheriffs here who knows the engineer on the crew. As far as I can learn the man is not married. Also is earning good wages."[17] Another agent kept tabs on a woman who had left the Good Samaritans and boarded her baby in the country. The agent reported that the brother of the woman's employer "has a garage in Island Falls and he hears a great deal of gossip around the place. He has heard some of the 'hangers-on' of the town say that they had tried to make advances to Lena and that she had shown her French temper so I imagine they have not got along very well with her."[18]

If communities expected women to work hard and to be subjected to gossip, they expected families to help take care of female kin and their babies when it was necessary. In the same way that communities operated to determine who did and who did not belong, families made a distinction between kin and strangers. They made every effort to keep children born out of wedlock within the family and to avoid relying on strangers. "I don't believe God is pleased when we neglect our children," wrote one woman of a mother who had abandoned hers.[19]

The women who came to the Good Samaritan Home rarely placed their children for adoption and when they did, often placed them with extended family members. Ellen's brother-in-law was responsible for her pregnancy and her brother-in-law's sister adopted their child. When Atwood wrote that the child might be "backward," the sister replied: "We have no others to compare with so perhaps can not judge but we think she is darling. Of course we . . . took her on account of her parentage mostly and would probably have loved her anyway." The father of Irene's lover objected to their marriage and adopted the child himself. Hazel's priest objected to her marriage because her lover was "dissipated and shiftless." Nevertheless the lover wrote that though he could not get any money for a settlement, Hazel and her child should "come here to my people. We ain't got very much. But she will be welcome to what we got."[20]

This response to unwed mothers was not harshly punitive, but it was closed. Women had to depend upon families and communities that were fully aware—and did not forget—that they had been depended upon, and any new infant meant an additional economic burden on families that were often already strapped. The case records suggest that the women's lives within their communities were isolated, subject to intense gossip, and filled with hard work. The women who made great efforts to come to the Good Samaritan Home were often looking for a way out.

One woman expressed the thoughts of many when she wrote on her return home: "The harbor is all frozen over and this place is some dead. There's nothing here but snow." While the women repeatedly spoke of being lonely and isolated, they also acknowledged that whatever they did was noted by their neighbors. One woman, who "came to Caribou to work" as soon as she knew something was wrong, wrote that she would like her mother to know about her pregnancy. But, she commented, "she can't read her letters herself and she'll get a stranger to read this for her and then every one up home will know it." Another who returned to her family's poverty-stricken farm without her child suggested how actively the community kept tabs on young women. "I was very busy all day yesterday," she reported. "Many of the neighbors were in to see me and everybody on the line called me on the phone when they heard I was home."[21]

Gossip was not the only aspect of rural community life unwed mothers sought to escape. Invariably the women admitted to the Good Samaritan Home came from lives in which they were required to do hard physical labor. A number were orphans who had been placed out to earn their keep at age twelve. Atwood commented of one placed in this way: "She has done heavy manual labor in the fields, has milked six cows night and morning, and has had the privilege of attending school but little." Orphan girls were often adopted for their labor when they reached the age of twelve. Said a woman of her adopted daughter: "I took her because I had no girl and I needed help."[22]

Other women who left their families to work often sent money home on low wages. Atwood described one twenty-one-year-old who was crippled from infantile paralysis: "She has been supporting herself for some time, working as a domestic in a country town where she has done all kinds of heavy labor."[23] Those who were working on their own were often called back to help the family in times of crisis. Families called them home to maintain the household when their mothers became sick or died, but they also called on them to provide necessary field labor. Atwood wrote to the Immigration Service about Mattie: after she was called home to care for her invalid step-mother and insane step-sister, her life was "indescribably hard and lonely." "She tells me," Atwood wrote, "that she has taken the place of a man in the fields for years; that in the spring of '27 she herself planted thirty acres of potatoes, with a potato planter, . . . that she and her father did the haying, and that she was all the assistance he had in harvesting the crops."[24]

While some young women went off to work to help support their families, others were needed too much at home to leave. Jerrie was twenty-six when she applied for admission to the Home. Her father was a potato farmer and her mother wrote: "I didn't now why she didn't com home she nous my health is very poor and has been this last twelve year I have got a lame leg and hip and I have got a big family. . . . Jerrie . . . is all the help I have[.] I have had the hardest time since she went away."[25] Any young woman who did not labor was considered a burden, especially if she were pregnant. One young man, whose wife had become pregnant by another, admitted he might take her back, but only if she led a "good life supporting her self with honest labor without the help of outsiders."[26]

The women who appealed to the Home for support knew the value of their labor. It was common when writing the Home for them to comment: "I can work and I am very willing to do anything if you can only help me."[27] They made no attempt to deny their sexual conduct or blame others for their circumstances, but instead offered to work to make up for it.

A majority of the early Good Samaritan board members had themselves grown up in small Maine towns. In many ways they structured the Home to reflect the same practices and values as the communities from which they had come. Board members expected the unwed mothers to work hard and to assume responsibility. In contrast to the national social work discourse early in the century, the Good Samaritans emphasized the importance of age rather than gender and encouraged the mutual obligations that age imposed. In over 1,000 pages of minutes and reports spanning thirty-two years, Gertrude Atwood never blamed men for seducing women, except in cases where the men were considerably older.

Like community members writing to the Home on behalf of young women, Atwood faulted older women for not providing young girls with the supervision and training that they required. The residents, she insisted, were not degraded women who were habitual sinners, but "young girls who have missed even the most ordinary counsel against bad influence which even the plainest, most untaught mother might give," and were victims of "unguarded surroundings." With training they had the potential to become "fine Christian characters, a power for good in the community."[28]

Atwood's sympathy for the women she served was predicated on their youth; her annual fundraising appeals to the community described the "girls" who gave birth before they had scarcely entered the portals of womanhood. On the other hand, in admitting a twenty-six-year-old, she commented that her age was "not conducive to arouse our sympathy. The fact remains too that we do not derive the same sense of satisfaction in serving girls of such supposed maturity of judgement and horse sense."[29]

Atwood's commitment to age-appropriate behavior and responsibilities even outweighed her support for marriage. While she reported with a sense of satisfaction the number of residents who were married each year, she spoke with disapproval only of their marriages with men twice their age. "It is to be regretted," she commented, "that such marriages are not prohibited by statute, thus preventing the inclination of such ignorant parents to marry the girl off regardless of the consequences in their belief that such saves the family's reputation."[30]

If the women in the Home were misguided girls, as Atwood suggested, they could redeem themselves by accepting responsibility for themselves and their children. The Good Samaritans expected the women, no matter how young, to assume the support of their children. To this end it would help place them in jobs once their time in the Home was over and would board their babies for a minimal fee, as long as the women claimed responsibility for rather than abandoning their children. "I am sure it is not the policy of the Home to relieve the girls of their children," Atwood wrote to one, "and in your particular case I do not know what your reason for wishing to give her up is."[31]

Year after year Atwood commented that the Good Samaritans believed that accepting the responsibilities of motherhood served to redeem a young woman. "When these girls are desirous of being good mothers, with all that involves," she told the public, "they have retrieved the past, and should be shown the respect and dignity due them from a Christian People."[32]

If the residents redeemed themselves by assuming responsibility, they proved themselves worthy by hard work. The Home charged an entrance fee of fifty dollars "to guard against their becoming passive recipients of charity." It offered those who did not have the fee the opportunity to work out their indebtedness at five dollars a week. In addition, it required all residents to work in the Home for six months after delivery. As the Home boarded outside babies in addition to those born in the Home, it regularly housed twice as many children under three as adults. Paid staff were there only to supervise the work. The residents baked, cleaned, gardened, canned produce, washed diapers, mixed formulas, and assisted in deliveries. Every year they assisted in spring cleaning, which ordeal was "quite a strain on the tempers of both girls and workers."[33]

While the Good Samaritans subjected women to the same hard work, gossip, and expectation of responsibility as did the communities, it did so in another location. Thus it offered women another standpoint, a place from which to negotiate a new life, one perhaps less tied to isolation, scrutiny, and hard work. Providing a place outside of the community where women could receive supervision, child care, and a job offered them a choice. Women no longer had to marry the men who impregnated them, or rely on the charity of their home towns. They could settle in a city of over 20,000 where the opportunities were far greater than in the small towns from which the majority came.

Between 1930 and 1950, both Maine communities and the Good Samaritans went through profound changes. While the Depression pushed communities' self-sufficiency to the limit, it also opened the possibility of adoption for unwed mothers. Strangers from across the country applied in ever increasing numbers to the Good Samaritan Home and others like it for children to adopt. In 1941 there were 200 applications for six available children. Many applicants were professionals who owned their own homes and had high regular salaries. They offered children more immediate economic security than poor single rural women could dream of providing in a lifetime.

At the same time, state and national welfare organizations were defining a new vision of unwed mothers that was increasingly at odds with the Good Samaritans' policies and practices.[34] National professional standards called for treating out-of-wedlock pregnancy as a psychological or emotional rather than an economic problem, and for treating each individual "case" with counseling rather than hard work and responsibility. The new standards called for decreasing institutional care and for providing all unwed mothers with the opportunity to escape the stigma of their pregnancy by giving up their child to adoption.

Required to abide by state and national standards in order to acquire necessary licenses and to obtain funding, the Good Samaritan Home gradually decreased the length of stay in the Home and the amount of work it expected from the residents. In 1951 the Home hired its first professional social worker whose job, in part, was to explore the possibility of adoption with each resident. In 1954 the Good Samaritan Agency closed the home and replaced it with a system of individualized foster care. As the Home provided more services and relied less on residents' hard work, it was forced to charge higher fees and to end the offer to residents to "work out their indebtedness." Without an institutional stay supervised by a regular staff, the Good Samaritans no longer had an opportunity to get to know a resident's capabilities. It could therefore no longer provide job placement or recommendations. In short, the Good Samaritan Home could no longer offer or promote self-sufficiency and responsibility.

Even as the Good Samaritan Home dramatically changed its practices to conform more fully to national standards, small towns continued to operate on more traditional rural values. They continued to call on young women to provide hard physical labor in the service of their families and they still expected a woman and her family to be responsible for the care of her child. Even in 1951 the primary service offered by the Good Samaritan Agency's new social worker—adoption—was too foreign to the rural unwed mothers for them to accept comfortably. For the next three years, well over half of the women—far more than ever before—gave up their children for adoption, but only, their records make clear, because they could not afford to do otherwise. One woman, who was herself born out of wedlock, tried for a year to keep her child and then decided at last to give her up because, she commented, "I shall not be able to support her myself and I have no plans of getting married in the near future." She added, "It is not what I really want but I think that it is the only right thing to do."[35]

In 1951, however, when Aid to Dependent Children (ADC) became generally available in Maine, even reluctant acceptance of new policies ceased as unwed mothers shifted back to traditional practices. They either rejected outright the services offered by the Good Samaritan Agency or insisted on keeping their babies. Between 1951 and 1958, forty-four of the fifty-three women served by the Good Samaritans kept their children. The nine who did not were state wards, married, or in their second unwed pregnancy. As one mother of a pregnant woman who decided to keep her baby asserted: "People do not give their babies away."[36]

This was in direct contrast to standard national practice, where by 1955, separating the unwed mother and child had become the norm for social service agencies.[37] The first professional social worker hired full-time by the Good Samaritans struggled to understand this almost universal decision of the women to keep their children. She suggested in her reports that the decisions were made to get back at a mother, to find love, or to oblige a family eager for the additional money ADC would bring. At one point, on hearing that the Pentecostal Church encouraged women to keep their children, she commented: "I think that is why so many of the girls have been keeping their babies because of this influence from the Pentecostal Church."[38]

But the records suggest that the reason was not the church or an overbearing mother, but the community's continued insistence that a woman take care of her own. One resident told the social worker that she knew a girl who kept her baby and "had no difficulty in being accepted." Another considered giving hers up through adoption but was concerned that people "would hold it against her if she did not take the baby and bring it up." Another wrote with relief that her new husband had learned that she had given up her child for adoption but that he did not hold it against her as she thought he would.[39]

At times, the community even actively interfered to keep mother and child together. In 1958 three community members accompanied Kay when she came to pick up her child at the Good Samaritan Agency office. Kay had earlier claimed that she "wasn't remotely interested" in her son, and "didn't even want to know the color of his hair or eyes," her social worker asserted. Kay had signed a consent form to place her child for adoption and then changed her mind several times. Finally her minister, her cousin, and the woman for whom her mother worked came into the office. This last, the social worker wrote in her case notes, claimed "that pressure had been put on Kay to place the baby for adoption." The community members waited beside Kay as she told the Good Samaritan social worker that she wished to keep her child and then accompanied her out of the office.[40] Social workers accepted these choices with resignation. Commented one of an eighteen-year-old who had decided to keep her child at the family farm: "It is a good community and perhaps the child will be accepted and things work out better than we usually expect."[41]

While acceptance from families and communities and the financial support of ADC enabled women in the 1950s to keep their children by providing basic acceptance and support, the decision to return home with a child born out of wedlock was not necessarily an easy one. In many cases, it meant remaining within communities where women experienced isolation, hard work, and community scrutiny. As the social worker noted of one seventeen-year-old whose father was crippled with arthritis and unable to work: "I feel pretty sure that Anna will love her child, but that it will be just another case of a child being brought up in a very poor environment and with very little beyond the poorer necessities."[42]

There is little record of what happened to these later women. The Good Samaritan Agency stopped recording marriages of past residents, and stopped supervising them and reporting on their progress in different jobs. Many former residents did, however, write to the Good Samaritans of their desire to return to Bangor. One wrote in 1953: "It seems good to be home after four months but I have a lot of lonesome moments. My mother is starting to work all day instead of just afternoons . . . so it gives me a lot of time to be alone." Another seventeen-year-old wrote: "I wish I was back down there because I miss it. I work harder now than I did when I was down there." In another letter she noted: "I am just beginning to appreciate what Mrs. Merrill & you did for me. Remember when I was down there, well in the afternoon I didn't have to work but I am telling you I have to work afternoons now and I mean work too."[43] A number wrote requesting jobs at the Good Samaritans. Noted one: "I really miss the place a lot so that's why I like to work there."[44]

Women felt the conflict between their local communities and a larger world, between the work and isolation of their home towns and the promise of something else in the larger cities. One woman complained:

> I miss the girls awfully there isn't any girls up here that are of my age now. They are married or gone away. . . . Just been to town three times. Can't go when your picking you get so tired you like to go to bed as soon as possible. . . . There are a lot of potatoes yet to be dug.

Two months later she wrote: "I wanted to come here awfully bad when I was down there. Now I'm kinda lonesome for Bangor. There isn't much doing here. No movies or anything."[45] Her loneliness, like the circumstances and values that brought her to it, would have been familiar to many other women decades earlier.

The construction of legitimacy in Maine had long-lasting consequences. The emphasis on local community support and individual responsibility extended well into the twentieth century. While it promised women at least the minimal support necessary to survive, it reinforced their dependence on their families and their communities.

For the first four decades of the twentieth century, the Good Samaritan Home built on rural values and provided women with a unique opportunity to receive significant support in a relatively nonjudgemental way. By providing them with child care and job placements, the Home provided a transition between rural communities and urban Bangor. As a result it enabled the women to create new lives for themselves outside of their resource-limited communities. As national social work standards forced the Good Samaritans to meet national and not community imperatives, however, the opportunities offered by the Home no longer met the needs of women from rural Maine. As a result, the Home no longer offered a viable alternative, and the women had no option but to return home more dependent than ever on their families and their home communities. When the Home was able to acknowledge and work with the values and practices of local communities, it enabled the women it served to transcend the confines of those communities. When it became bound by national standards, it lost much of its ability to transform the lives of the women.

---

1. Good Samaritan Case Record #297-125, Gertrude Atwood to __, 2 April 1928. Located in the Good Samaritan Agency, 450 Essex Street, Bangor, Maine.

2. Richard Wiebe, *The Search for Order: 1877–1920* (New York: Hill and Wang, 1967).

3. See, for example, Regina G. Kunzel, *Fallen Women, Problem Girls: Unmarried Mothers and the Professionalization of Social Work, 1890–1945* (New Haven, Conn.: Yale University Press, 1993); Rickie Solinger, *Wake Up Little Susie: Single Pregnancy and Race Before Roe v. Wade* (New York: Harper & Row, 1992); and Marian J. Morton, *And Sin No More: Social Policy and Unwed Mothers in Cleveland, 1855–1990* (Columbus: Ohio State University Press, 1993).

4. The author had access to every fifth record in the Good Samaritan Case Files beginning in 1918. The names in each file were deleted for privacy. The names of the unwed mothers used in this report are pseudonyms. The Good Samaritan Home was renamed the Good Samaritan Agency in 1954 when the Agency replaced its home with a series of foster homes.

5. Works Progress Administration, *Maine: A Guide "Down East"* (Cambridge, Mass.: Riverside Press, 1937), 48.

6. James S. Leamon, Richard W. Wescott, and Edward O. Schriver, "Separation & Statehood, 1783–1820," in Richard W. Judd, Edwin A. Churchill, and Joel W. Eastman, eds., *Maine: The Pine Tree State from Prehistory to the Present* (Orono: University of Maine Press, 1995), 187–90; David C. Smith, "Toward a Theory of Maine History—Maine's Resources and the State" and Arthur M. Johnson, "The Maine Problem," in *Maine: A History Through Selected Readings,* ed. David C. Smith and Edward O. Schriver (Dubuque, Iowa: Kendall/Hunt, 1985), 207–16, 480–87.

7. This is in clear contrast to the legislators in other states who transformed bastardy and seduction laws to emphasize the importance of women's sexual behavior. See, for example, Mazie Hough, "'I'm a Poor Girl in Family and I Want to Know If You Be Kind': The Community's Response to Unwed Mothers in Maine and Tennessee, 1876–1954" (Ph.D. diss., University of Maine, 1997) and Michael Grossberg, *Governing the Hearth: Law and the Family in Nineteenth-Century America* (Chapel Hill: University of North Carolina Press, 1985).

8. One indication of the conservative nature of these laws was that they remained almost unchanged for over 100 years.

9. *Low v. Mitchell,* 18 Maine 372 (1841); *Harmon v. Merrill et al,* 18 Maine 150 (1841).

10. *Blake v. Junkins,* 34 Maine 237 (1852).

11. *Blake v. Junkins,* 34 Maine 238 (1852); *Beals v. Furbish,* 39 Maine 473 (1855); *Wilson v. Woodside,* 67 Maine 249 (1870).

12. *State of Maine v. Kirby,* 57 Maine 30 (1869) provides a history of this law.

13. #207-36, Joseph W. Sawyer to Gertrude Atwood, 25 October 1921, and Alfred G. Davis to Good Samaritans, 1 November 1921; #188-16, William Waldron to Gertrude Atwood, 16 July 1919.

14. #202-31, __ to Gertrude Atwood, 4 March 1921.

15. The files suggest that it was common practice for younger women in the community to move into another household to help with the work. See Laurel Thatcher Ulrich, *A Midwife's Tale: The Life of Martha Ballard,*

Based on her Diary, 1785–1812 (New York: Knopf, 1990) for a detailed description of this kind of mutual responsibility in a rural Maine community in an earlier period.

16. #392-220, Eva Scates to Gertrude Atwood, 6 March 1934. That men were also subjected to gossip is suggested by the fact that, as one young girl reported, the community shunned the man who got her pregnant, but accepted her. Fifteen-year-old Estelle wrote that she was entering her child's name in the cradle call in her church. "I have got the best carriage there is in Milford and I tell you I shine some," she said. At the same time she noted, "Everybody is death on Milliard now. Hardly anybody speaks to him." #201-30, __ to matron, 1 November 1921.

17. #215-44, Eva Scates to Gertrude Atwood, 7 October 1922.

18. #187-15, Laura Klippel to Miss Scoboria, 18 October 1921.

19. #256-84, __ to Gertrude Atwood, 25 January 1920.

20. #179-7, __ to Gertrude Atwood, 10 February 1921; #191-19, #196-24, __ to Gertrude Atwood, 31 May 1920; #317-145, __ to __, 26 June 1929.

21. #178-6, __ to Good Samaritans, 2 February 1920; #187-15, __ to Good Samaritans, 21 June 1919; #195-25, __ to Scoboria, 26 November 1920.

22. #196-24, __ to Good Samaritans, 31 May 1920; *Annual Report* 1923.

23. *Case Committee Report*, June 1931.

24. #297-125, Gertrude Atwood to Immigration, 20 September 1928 and 12 October 1928.

25. #195-23. Jerrie was one of the few who gave up her child for adoption before she returned home. One suspects she did not want to burden her family with one more child.

26. #257-85, Husband to Gertrude Atwood, 19 November 1925.

27. #173-1, __ to Good Samaritans, 17 January 1918.

28. *Annual Report* 1920, 5; *Annual Report* 1914, 13.

29. *Superintendent's Report*, March 1935.

30. *Superintendent's Report*, March 1935.

31. #240-69, Gertrude Atwood to __, 12 March 1927.

32. *Annual Report* 1924, 6, 7.

33. *Annual Report*, 1922; *Superintendent's Report*, April 1935.

34. For a history of the development of social work and its impact on the treatment of unwed mothers see Walter Trattner, *From Poor Law to Welfare State: A History of Social Welfare in America*, 2d ed. (New York: Free Press, 1979); Kunzel, *Fallen Women, Problem Girls*; and Solinger, *Wake Up Little Susie*.

35. #775-578, __ to Good Samaritans, 15 May 1949.

36. #988-793, casework notes, October 1954.

37. Rickie Solinger estimates that in 1955, ninety thousand single mothers gave up their children for adoption in the U.S. Solinger, "Race and 'Value': Black and White Illegitimate Babies, 1945–1965," in *Mothering: Ideology, Experience, and Agency* ed. Evelyn Nakano Glenn, Grace Chang, and Linda Rennie Forcey (New York: Routledge, 1994), 37. It is interesting to note that African American women—like rural Maine women—rarely gave up their children for adoption. See also Morton, *And Sin No More*.

38. #997-801, #986-791, #1094-935 and #971-776.

39. #885-690, 9 August 1951; #1004-811, 23 March 1955; and #604.

40. #1089-926, 27 February 1958.

41. #967-772, Eugenia Rugan to __, June 1954.

42. #1020-827, case notes, 15 January 1956.

43. #940-745, __ to Hayward, 2 December 1953; #705-512, __ to Mrs. Lovitt, 22 December 1946 and 11 January 1947.

44. #758-561, __ to Merrill, 20 June 1948.

45. __ to Hayward, 21 October 1943 and 7 December 1943. This sentiment was also reflected in the large number of women who returned home only to ask the Good Samaritans for a job.

*Women progressive reformers throughout the nation were commit-
ted to extending their traditional responsibility for domestic life
into the community. Determined to clean up their surroundings
the way they cleaned their homes, to protect the weak and vulnerable the way they protected their children, and to enhance
community life and health the way they enhanced their families'
quality of life, these reformers engaged in what historians call
"social housekeeping." Their efforts to apply domestic values to
their communities brought them far outside the walls of their
homes and made many of them quite visible in the public realm
as reformers committed to social change. Activities that began in
settlement houses and women's clubs brought women deep into
political life at the local, state, and national levels.*

*Women progressive reformers tended to bring a particular
understanding of gender to their activities. Because they believed
that social improvement in all of its forms was an extension of
women's domestic responsibilities and used this belief to justify
their own public participation, they tended not to challenge traditional gender conventions out loud, although some ignored them
in their personal lives. To do so would have left them vulnerable to
criticism not only from their husbands, but also from the very*

civic and business leaders whose behavior they sought to influence. As a result, progressive women rarely demanded equal participation or recognition; doing so would threaten their effectiveness in accomplishing the goals nearest to their hearts.

At the same time, by claiming the right to extend the domestic sphere deep into the public world, progressive women successfully claimed new arenas of influence for themselves. Men found it hard to argue with women's domestic claims and so had little choice but to grant women at least a hearing, if not always what they wanted. In the process some women carved new public careers for themselves, moving from voluntary organizations to government agencies and a host of official positions with reform groups, colleges and universities, and social welfare institutions.

Most of the women who engaged in progressive reform were educated, middle-class, and native-born, and their beliefs reflected their background. They thought they understood how best to live far better than the poor and immigrants they sought to help, not realizing that in the process they imposed their own cultural values on people often reluctant to accept them. Nevertheless, these women were at the forefront of significant social change in the early twentieth century, championing causes and demanding solutions to problems that were unpopular with powerful men. That they did so in sometimes problematic ways should not blind us to their accomplishments. Tina Roberts provides an introduction to one such group of progressive women in Maine who claimed responsibility for the environment.

BIRD LOVERS, TREE KEEPERS, AND PARK PROTECTORS: THE MAINE FEDERATION OF WOMEN'S CLUBS AND RURAL CONSERVATION, 1897 – 1932

Tina Roberts

On the morning of October 7, 1897, President Alice Frye Briggs of Auburn, Maine, struck the gavel and called to order the fifth annual meeting of the Maine Federation of Women's Clubs (MFWC). Convened in Bangor, the meeting drew women from across the state: from the western mountains, the northern tip of Aroostook County, the communities of the eastern coast, and the state's population centers of Portland, Augusta, and Lewiston. United by their desire to improve both their own lives and those of their fellow Maine citizens, the Clubwomen gathered for two days of lively debate, stimulating lectures, rekindling of old friendships, and a festive celebration of the previous year's accomplishments.

In the midst of the commemoration and remembrances, the 1897 meeting was also a time to look ahead. Engaging in the first act of what would be a long history of commitment to the Maine environment, the meeting delegates, on the motion of Mrs. H. B. C. Beede, adopted the following resolution:

Whereas the glory of Maine has been its forests, and whereas from its millions of acres of rich timberland only a few thousand now remain in possession of the state, and, Whereas, it is important that the natural resources of the state be preserved that the pine tree state may not be an empty name, therefore;

Resolved, that the Maine Federation of Women's Clubs, as far as possible, pledge ourselves to take up the study of forest conditions and resources and to further the highest interests of our state in these respects.[1]

Coming at a time of heightened political awareness of the threats posed by the pulp and paper industry to Maine's forest resources, and when women's participation in the public and political sphere was burgeoning, the motion established forestry as the foundation of the MFWC's new conservation agenda. Although the women soon added a vast array of other issues to their list of conservation priorities, the trees of Maine remained their greatest passion for several decades.

The MFWC organized in 1892 "to bring together the several Women's Literary and Educational Clubs of the state for mutual benefit."[2] For many women, the MFWC provided an outlet for their creative and philanthropic energies, a counter to the potential isolation of rural living. The MFWC's membership consisted largely of educated women whose economic status allowed them the leisure time necessary to pursue the club's activities, although the Clubs' outreach programs sought to include women of varying means and backgrounds. Geographically, the MFWC women hailed from all over the state. But no matter what their town of origin, the particulars of their economic background, or their connection to Maine's environment, the women shared an ideal of Maine life that they believed its natural environment embodied. Club records show that as they developed social outreach programs, the Clubwomen never lost sight of their rural environment and the needs of rural women. This same sentiment guided their conservation interests.

During the progressive era, Clubwomen in nearly every state played a vital role in the development of conservation policies and in creating a widespread concern for the condition of the land and its resources. What was unique in Maine was the rural orientation of the women involved. They reinforced the rural ethic that stood behind progressive era conservation in Maine, while at the same time defining their commitment as stewards of rural values in terms of their roles as wives and mothers. By interweaving ruralness and gender, the women of the MFWC developed a viable strategy to achieve their conservation goals. While hardly a daring or innovative tactic for the time, the MFWC utilized their gendered roles to gain respect in an arena where without it they would have had none. Such an approach gained them a level of respect that they would not have been afforded had they chosen another, less cautious approach. The strategy proved very effective.

The women of the MFWC saw themselves as the guardians of the home and family and assumed responsibility for their children's futures. Conservation played a part in that responsibility. "Women are interested in their homes," Conservation Committee chair Grace H. Thompson wrote in 1911, "and forestry and water touch the home intimately."[3] And, at a time when the state annually suffered significant population losses, conservation to Maine women included stimulating growth in the economy and slowing the overwhelming exodus of young people.

Beyond this commitment to their domestic roles, the women of the MFWC shared a sense of the superiority of rural life and of its unique value to society. They yearned to preserve it from the encroachment of cities and accompanying urban ideals. Maine women prided themselves on raising children who became leaders of wisdom and virtue for the nation, a result of Maine's rural nature and deep ties to the land. "Maine does not gather the richest harvest from her soils," Thompson boasted in 1911, "but she has furnished men who have made their vigorous strength felt wherever they have located over our broad land. She will conserve and develop her own resources, and will teach her children to guard their heritage with wisdom in just proportion as she senses the need of fostering public intelligence and of converting ideas into righteous action for the good of mankind."[4]

Because they saw themselves as conservators of rural life and values, the MFWC defined conservation very broadly. They assigned such traditional conservation issues as forestry, wildlife protection, and parks and preserves to their respective conservation committees, but they also placed such areas as health and sanitation, nature study, and beautification under the umbrella of conservation as well. This is not simply because these areas were women's issues but because the Clubwomen were trying to conserve both the land and its resources, along with a rural way of life. Each of these environmental factors contributed to the quality and continuation of that rural life and hence fell within the realm of women's influence.

Since the Maine economy depended so heavily on its trees, forestry was the MFWC's most prominent conservation issue. They demanded early on that officials enact a strategy of scientific management of forest resources. When the state legislature met in the summer of 1902, it acted on one of the Clubwomen's first forestry-related demands: establishment of a school of forestry at the University of Maine. The University received an appropriation of $2,500 to create the College of Forestry and hire its first professor. Applauding its own efforts, the MFWC Forestry Committee encouraged the individual clubs to "use their influence to make certain a repetition of the appropriation for it by the legislature," and to "continue to be interested in the forestry school, which truly is a child of the Federation."[5]

Much of the MFWC's early work in forestry happened at the local level, and it used the celebration of Arbor Day as a rallying point. The first call for MFWC recognition of Arbor Day went out in 1905 and met with limited, but enthusiastic, response. Forestry Chair Ada A. Viles noted that "six clubs reported splendid work done." They included the Pierian Club of Presque Isle which, with the assistance of local schoolchildren, planted thirty-one elm trees on Main Street, and the Town Improvement Society of Skowhegan, which distributed flower seeds to all the rural schools of the town.[6] In 1912, the Conservation Committee proudly announced that 182 cities and towns and 1,596 schools observed Arbor Day.[7] After World War I, Arbor Day took on special meaning as the clubs honored fallen soldiers with memorial tree plantings.

Many of the individual clubs answered the Arbor Day call by placing forestry speakers and programs on their yearly schedules. These were significant acts in that the MFWC considered education a vital component of their conservation efforts. The Clubwomen knew that their knowledge of the given subject had to be impeccable—at least equal, if not superior to any man's—if their voices were to be respected in conservation debates. While their roles as wives and mothers could get them in the doors of conservation debates, once there they needed knowledge in order to participate fully. The MFWC prioritized efforts to read, study, discuss, and thoroughly understand all the implications of important issues. It expected its local clubs to schedule regular lessons and discussions of forestry and conservation at their meetings.

One of the MFWC's most knowledgeable speakers on forestry was Louise Coburn of Skowhegan, who chaired the first committee on forestry. A member of one of Maine's most prominent families, Coburn was Colby College's second female graduate, its first female trustee, and a tireless worker for equality for women students and alumnae there. She spent summers studying botany at Harvard and collected a carefully checked and analyzed herbarium of more than three thousand mounted specimens. A prolific writer, Coburn authored several books.

Coburn devoted much of her time, energy, and family wealth to the betterment of her community. While active in many causes, Coburn's particular affinity was nature and its preservation for future generations. In 1927, she initiated the Somerset Woods Land Trust to acquire and hold land in Somerset County for the benefit of its citizens. Some of the land became playgrounds and parks, some arboretums, and some remained in its natural state. In 1941, Coburn reported that the trust held 545 acres.[8] Praising Coburn's generous acts, one local paper wrote: "The forests of the future will be conserved and cultured as a priceless possession. He who provides for the preservation or culture of a tree is a friend to man, he or she who is able to perpetuate large areas of forest verdue for future generations confers a blessing which transcends the limits of commercial value and extent of time."[9]

Not all of Maine's women conservationists had Coburn's resources. As citizens without the power of suffrage or independent incomes, they instead relied on other means of influence. These could include letter writing campaigns, visits to legislators, contests for schoolchildren, and lobbying their husbands, sons, brothers, and male friends who could vote. A few passionately committed women achieved particularly great successes. Such a woman was Grace Thompson of Bangor, who spearheaded one of the MFWC's most important forestry efforts.

As the 1908 and 1911 MFWC Forestry Committee chair, Thompson promoted many conservation causes and wrote articulately on the connections among land, home, and life. Her greatest accomplishment, however, earned her only limited recognition, despite a commitment lasting over a decade. "When the rugged region round Mt. Katahdin . . . has been set aside as a National reservation and tourists from all corners of the country are flocking to it," the *Lewiston Evening Journal* reported in 1914, "credit for its 'coming to pass' must be laid at the door of the Maine Federation of Women's Clubs. And special thanks must be given to one woman in particular . . . Mrs. Joseph A. Thompson of Bangor."[10]

Thompson was among the first to conceive of a state reserve in the region and to lobby the legislature to protect Katahdin and its environs. She suggested the idea of preserving the Katahdin region as one of the MFWC's forestry projects for the year 1905 and gained enthusiastic support for taking the plan before the 1908–1909 state legislature. Thompson and the MFWC argued for the reserve on two primary fronts. First, the Committee appealed to people's economic sensitivities. "Soon the state of Maine might join the ranks of those states which find it important to keep some of the poorer land for the purpose of growing trees," they noted, warning, "when we consider the value to Maine of her forest resources, we see that we can not afford to neglect them."[11]

Aware of the MFWC members' concern with the health and livelihood of their families and their perceived role as guardians of future generations, the Committee tied a second of the Federation's yearly goals to the state reserve issue. "This Federation has on its program the question of wiping out the Tuberculosis plague," they reported, and "this creation of state forest reserves ought to appeal for that reason. One of Pennsylvania's forest reserves, of about 45,000 acres, is the seat of the state sanatorium or tuberculosis camp."[12] Such efforts to promote the health benefits of the woods were not unusual; Maine's tourist literature routinely noted the significant health benefits that clean, pine-scented air, fresh water, and vigorous exercise provided.

At roughly the same time, the United States Congress was considering the Weeks Bill, an act to expand national forests by including land at the headwaters of navigable streams. Thompson wrote a resolution on behalf of the MFWC which described the value of the Katahdin region and called for the establishment of Mount Katahdin National Park. The MFWC worked hard to pass the Weeks Bill, and when it did pass claimed much of the credit. Conservation Chair Mrs. Joseph P. Strout proclaimed that "Clubwomen should be proud of their efforts on its behalf, especially the women of Maine who did the first active work towards the results, which now bring people of the Eastern States advantages long desired." Among the advantages, she noted, were that "the Appalachian forest is secured. This includes the White Mountains and forest watersheds of navigable rivers in New England."[13] The Weeks Act, however, did not include the creation of Katahdin as a national park. As the debate returned to the state level, Thompson's interest waned and the MFWC turned its attention elsewhere.

Some of the Clubwomen's energy went toward another critical issue of progressive era conservation, the protection of birds. Along with forestry, the MFWC took up birds as one of their earliest and most passionate conservation causes. They tied it, as they did the forestry issue, to the futures of their homes and families. "While we realize that forestry is the very foundation of Conservation of all natural resources," wrote Clara Powers in closing her 1913 Conservation Committee report, "birdlife is closely related to forestry, because birds are natural protectors of the trees as well as other vegetation. One writer has said, 'no birds, no trees; no trees, no birds.'"[14]

Audubon societies sprang up in many states during the progressive era, especially those on the East coast. *Bird Lore,* the official journal of the Audubon Society, began publication in 1899 and set the parameters for bird conservation efforts of the time. Two gender-based concerns dominated the magazine's early issues: protecting game birds from male hunters and their nests from egg-stealing boys, and protesting the fashionable use of bird feathers on ladies' hats. These two concerns united bird conservationists across the country and became the cornerstone of the effort nationwide.[15]

This was not entirely true in Maine, however. Maine Clubwomen recognized the importance of both concerns, but afforded them only limited attention. Mrs. J. M. Strout reported in 1912 that her Conservation Committee received flyers which asked Clubwomen to eschew bird plumage as a fashion statement. "This is a question," she wrote, "on which we hold the right of suffrage and in which the voice of women carries even more weight than that of men, for the sole reason that women create the market for these goods."[16] The Conservation Committee sent each club a poem, "Dead Birds," to be read to members with the idea that "no woman who reads or hears it can again wear bird plumage as a decoration."[17]

These small occurrences, however, were the only real acknowledgment of the plumage concerns, and little was said about them in subsequent years. In general, efforts focused much more on addressing specific local needs and appealing to rural sensibilities. Along these lines, bird hunting attracted slightly more attention. Strout noted it in her 1913 report, lamenting "the thoughtless boy with the new gun who shoots birds indiscriminately, while men prey on the larger useful birds for game."[18] Her successors encouraged lessons in schools against stoning and shooting the birds.

Taking a cue from their forestry efforts, the women approached bird conservation first from an economic standpoint and second from a maternal one. "The boy or girl who learns to feed birds and treat them kindly and protectingly will always be their friends and will realize and appreciate their esthetic as well as their economic value," noted the

1923 Conservation Committee.[19] Economic value was expressed in terms of benefit to the farmer. "Birds of at least four faunal zones breed in Maine," proclaimed Mrs. J. H. Knowles, "these are among our best friends and the insect eating and weed seed eating birds are the farmers best servants."[20]

Clubwomen emphasized instruction on birds and plants in the rural school curriculum and framed the need for such lessons in humanistic terms: "to help train the heart and hand of the coming citizen to learn how to attract and protect these people of the underbrush, the tree-top, and the fresh air."[21] In fact, schools were the location for most of the Federation's significant bird conservation work. Children built birdhouses, participated in contests, and planted trees, vines, and shrubs with materials supplied by the MFWC, and local Clubwomen sponsored essay contests in several high schools. Knowles, chair of the 1918 Conservation Committee, noted that they had expanded the school contests by that time to include prizes in elementary schools for birdhouses and vegetable gardens.[22]

From the onset of their interest in conservation, Maine women claimed authority on the subject based on their guardianship of the home and their roles as stewards of their children's futures and guarantors of their moral upbringing. As such, Maine's women conservationists claimed a wide purview; they accepted as a matter of course that conservation not only encompassed trees and birds, but also good roads, better food production, expanded water power, and the development of school and community gardens. Belle Smallidge Knowles, 1919 Conservation Committee chair, summarized the changes brought upon Clubwomen by World War I and charted a brief history of her committee. Her words offer insight into the MFWC's ultimate conservation mission:

When this department was first organized it was concerned only with the conservation of forests. Gradually the scope enlarged to include all natural resources. Later roads, although not a natural resource, were added, then roadside planting and beautifying. Food production, because of its relation to soil, was assigned to this department as special war work, and since production involves transportation, that, too, was given us. Last, but not least, with all the other departments of work, we are pledged "To concentrate on human efficiency," hence this department will hereafter include the conservation of human beings, the ultimate aim of conservation.[23]

Buoyed by the leadership and vision of Mrs. George F. French, the MFWC brought these multiple issues under the conservation umbrella and followed several paths that would not be forged again by conservationists until the 1960s. Along with commitment to particular issues, the fledgling Conservation Committee shared French's values and motivation. She took great pride in Maine's agricultural heritage and in its ability to support its families through hard work and tilling of the soil. French urged her fellow citizens to resist the negative influence of western speculation and instead to support each other through home investment in Maine industry. Moreover, she feared the extinction of Maine's way of life as its young people fled the state. French had a long history of conservation activism within the MFWC. In 1908 she pointed out the need for civic beauty, control of pollution, and an appreciation for natural advantages such as water power. In doing so, French reminded Clubwomen that gains in these areas would increase tourism, improve the economy, and most important, would assure that "the old saying 'Maine is a great state from which to emigrate' would lose its force and cease to be heard."[24]

As a state, Maine struggled to accommodate and promote agriculture, lumbering, fishing, and tourism, and water was a divisive yet critical issue. In fact, next to forestry and birds, water was perhaps the most widely debated resource issue for progressive era women conservationists all over the country. In Maine, the water question broke down into several sub-issues, including the development of waterpower, the maintenance of a clean and healthy water supply, and the proper balance between recreational use and preserving the aesthetic value of the state's rivers, lakes, ponds, and streams. The MFWC sought to forge an acceptable middle path between development of the resource and protection of local interests. In doing so, the organization placed itself at the forefront of developing Maine's burgeoning water conservation ethic.

Some of the MFWC's earliest work on water issues occurred as by-products of their forestry work. Better forestry laws, the women argued, would safeguard the watersheds of the region. In lobbying for the Weeks Act in 1911, the women highlighted the protection it afforded the headwaters of Maine and New Hampshire rivers. Those who advocated the preservation of the Katahdin area regularly pointed out that the great natural forest reserve in the area protected the streams that supply the Kennebec and Penobscot rivers as well as the beautiful lakes on which many Maine people depended for recreation and employment.

Most of the MFWC's water conservation energy went toward the development of Maine's waterpower sources. It was here that the women sought balance between the need to develop water resources and to maintain the integrity of their rural lives and livelihoods. The MFWC pointed out that no other state enjoyed Maine's potential for water supply and distribution; the state claimed 1,700 lakes and ponds and 5,000 rivers and streams. But, they noted at the same time, Maine had more undeveloped waterpower than any state in the Union.

The women actively sought to encourage expansion of Maine's hydropower sites, but not at the expense of local control. Noting that out-of-state interests were poised to wrestle an important resource from local hands, the MFWC embarked on an education campaign. They professed amazement at how little Maine people actually knew of the possible takeover: "When the monopolistic interests were brought into the limelight," reported the 1911 Conservation Committee, "great surprise was manifested that things of this order prevailed." In addition to public education, the women continued lobbying for secure local control of water resources.[25]

The legislature had enacted the "Fernald Law" in 1909, which said that no power developed from water could be conducted from the state, but the battle for local control did not end there. The out-of-state developers continued to infiltrate through consolidations and expansion into undeveloped territory. Recalling earlier struggles, Mrs. J. M. Strout issued a call to arms in 1916. "For some time this great natural resource has been the envy of outside capital," she reminded Clubwomen, warning, "Don't deceive yourself with the thought that these investors are seeking this privilege for the convenience of the people of Maine."[26]

Strout challenged the MFWC to act as a watchdog to prevent concessions to these powerful interests. She reminded Clubwomen that harnessing waterpower meant "double conservation," in that a currently idle source of power (water) would become available, and the stress on other resources to provide power would be relieved. She cautioned them to be awake to the sneaky tactics of the power companies and to be prepared to combat the "secret resources" that the companies no doubt had. The 1921 Conservation Committee claimed partial credit for the creation of the Water Powers commission the year before, as they had long agitated for state ownership and development of waterpower.[27]

The MFWC also paid attention to the condition of Maine's roads. They particularly disliked roadside billboards and took up their abatement with vengeance and foresight. "Civic beauty can be enhanced," Mrs. French wrote in 1914, "by doing away with all billboards which are, at best, unsightly, hideous, and an offense to the eye, disfiguring roadways, public grounds, and even the beautiful in architecture."[28]

French detailed a three-part plan by which MFWC members could influence the issue. First, she suggested that women lobby to enact local ordinances banning the posting of advertising signs on public property. Second, she suggested that a toll be implemented so that "billboards upon private property may be taxed out of existence." Finally, she appealed to the role of women as decision-makers within their homes. "If you are annoyed by billboard advertising of an article," she suggested, "when in need of it, remember there are others just as good and buy accordingly."[29]

In 1930, the MFWC established a Committee on Roads Beautification to deal with the natural beauty along Maine's highways. The billboard issue remained; among its many goals, the Committee worked to convince farmers "that it is not good business to PLANT HIS FIELDS TO BILLBOARDS!" Members combed the state for illegally placed signs and instructed the Highway Department to remove them. It rallied every club in the Federation to provide a delegate in Augusta when the legislature considered a bill to tax billboards. "We spend thousands of dollars advertising the state," the Committee complained, "describing its beauty, inviting [tourists] to come here. As they cross the New Hampshire line what greets them? Twenty-one billboards. Let there be no doubt where we stand."[30] In the 1950s, Maine would become one of the first states in the nation to regulate billboards.

World War I and its aftermath forced new issues onto the MFWC's conservation docket. Mrs. J. H. Knowles, Conservation Chair in 1919, emphasized that War Emergency Work took up most of her and her colleagues' time.[31] Food production took top billing as it provided a vital means for women to contribute to post-war reconstruction and to enhance the spirit of the age. Knowles encouraged members to make good use of government bulletins on gardening and raising live-stock, poultry, and fish, and to utilize county extension agents to help them produce healthy food for the war effort.

Thrift was the key word during and after the war years. Recognizing this, the MFWC changed the name of its Conser-vation Committee to the Committee on Conservation and Thrift in 1921, and again branched into several new conserva-tion directions. Chair Ivanella Palmer listed the Committee's many accomplishments over the previous year: "Canning of fruits and vegetables has been emphasized, talks on child wel-fare welcomed, playgrounds improved, seeds sent to country schools, clean and well ventilated school rooms emphasized, and an active interest aroused in 'Clean-up Week.'" She noted that the most important work done by her committee that year was aimed at the "Conservation of Humanity."[32]

Just as the women assumed responsibility for increasing their own knowledge of birds, trees, water power, roads, food, and civic beauty as part of their conservation agenda, so did they believe that children should do the same. One of the most important ways that women brought nature study into the lives of children was through the planting of school gar-dens. "In their establishment," wrote the 1913 Conservation Committee, "we have a fund of great sociological value as well as exciting a love for agricultural clubs among the young." The MFWC provided vegetable and flower seeds to many schools, and at least two clubs, the Old Neighborhood Club of Old Town and the Berwick Women's Club, offered prizes for the finest gardens. Outside of the schools, women mobilized children to form Garden Clubs.[33]

While supporting school gardens advanced the MFWC's goals of teaching children about the environment and having pride in their home state, its garden work certainly did not stop there. The Garden Club movement was taking hold across the nation and Maine women jumped in at both the personal and the public level. An activity that rural women had long engaged in for subsistence as well as for pleasure, among the affluent gardening was coming into favor as a hobby. It also drew praise as a new means by which to practice conservation in local areas. By the late 1920s gardening became such an important part of its conservation agenda that the Committee's name changed yet again, this time to Conservation of Natural Resources and Gardens. "The division of gardens was added," wrote MFWC President Edna Hutchins, "because we realize the value of outdoor beauty and that all people in America believe today that this beauty is being sacrificed. It is hoped that our women's clubs may be instrumental in securing legislation that will preserve the beauty of Maine."[34]

Edith Pratt Brown of Waterville led the MFWC into this new era of conservation activism. A graduate of Colby College, Brown was an active member of her community and "an enthusiastic conservationist, having the true nature lovers desire to conserve all Maine's natural resources with special desire to make and keep the state beautiful."[35] Under her direction, the new Conservation Committee became even more active than any other in the past. Promoting gardens, for aesthetic and spiritual reasons as well as for the conservation of trees and plants, consumed the Committee. "Our sincere hope is that the clubs of the state may continue in this work," Brown explained, "until there shall be a veritable epidemic of planting!"[36]

To forward her cause, Brown hosted a weekly radio show on WLBZ on the topic "Maine Beautiful" and regularly submitted articles and editorials on conservation to Maine newspapers. She visited local high schools to lecture and distribute conservation literature. Her Committee cooperated with the National Wildflower Preservation Society to document specific flowers in Maine and with groups interested in constructing an International Peace Garden between Canada and the United States. They prepared slide shows to be used by individual clubs and stressed tree plantings and the development of Christmas tree farms. All over the state, the MFWC worked tirelessly to make the Pine Tree State "garden-minded."[37]

Approaching gardens from their rural perspective, Maine women recognized the value of gardening to moral and spiritual health. They understood the value of the science of botany and the need to protect indigenous or endangered flora. But while many MFWC women no doubt tended spectacular gardens of their own, within the parameters of conservation they focused more precisely on public gardening. They pursued the creation, maintenance, and harvesting of gardens as a means to better the community as a whole. As such, the focus of their efforts was not solely on flower gardens, but on vegetable production and tree planting as well. Both, after all, were vital components of most Maine people's lives. Both contributed to the conservation of their rural way of life.

The women of the MFWC were not different from women elsewhere in the country in approaching conservation through the lens of their gendered roles as wives and mothers. What does differentiate the women of Maine from their progressive era colleagues is their linking gender and ruralness to form a solid basis for their conservation activism. Their approach was not risky, nor did it do anything to promote the position of women in general within political and social arenas. It kept them out of certain progressive conservation debates, notably wildlife preservation, but on the other hand it allowed them to expand conservation beyond the usual definition to include civic improvement and health-related concerns. In short, there were tradeoffs for maintaining a gendered stance, but in the end the MFWC achieved many of its goals. While their male counterparts argued over scientific justifications for resource conservation, or jockeyed for political and economic power, the MFWC pursued conservation as a practical effort aimed at preserving their rural lifestyles and safeguarding the futures of their families. The legacy of these women conservationists is evident in the rural values which Maine people still hold dear. Maine people still pride themselves on the beauty of their natural environment and thrive on many of the resources that these women worked so hard to protect.

1. *Yearbook of the Maine Federation of Women's Clubs* (hereafter cited as *Yearbook*), 1897, 21.

2. Maine Federation of Women's Clubs By-Laws, in Georgia Pulsifer Porter, *Maine Federation of Women's Clubs Historical Sketches, 1892–1924* (Lewiston, Maine: Lewiston Journal Printshop, 1925), 11.

3. Records of the Annual Meeting, MFWC, 1910–1911, 19.

4. Ibid., 25.

5. *Yearbook*, 1903, 17.

6. *Yearbook*, 1905, 20.

7. *Yearbook*, 1912, 24.

8. Louise Coburn, *Skowhegan on the Kennebec* (Skowhegan, Maine: The Independent Reporter Press, 1941), 971.

9. Unidentified newspaper clipping, 17 May 1928, Josselyn Botanical Society, Box 1334, Folder 8, Special Collections, Fogler Library, University of Maine, Orono, Maine.

10. *Lewiston (Maine) Evening Journal*, 24 October 1914.

11. *Yearbook*, 1908, 20–21.

12. Ibid.

13. Ibid., 22–28.

14. *Yearbook*, 1914, 44–45.

15. Carolyn Merchant, *Earthcare: Women and the Environment* (New York: Routledge, 1995), 132–36.

16. *Yearbook*, 1912, 23.
17. *Yearbook*, 1914, 36.
18. Ibid.
19. *Yearbook*, 1924, 46.
20. *Yearbook*, 1919, 28–29.
21. *Yearbook*, 1912, 25.
22. *Yearbook*, 1919, 30.
23. *Yearbook*, 1920, 28–29.
24. *Yearbook*, 1908, 26–27.
25. *Yearbook*, 1912, 27.
26. *Yearbook*, 1916, 45–47.
27. *Yearbook*, 1921, 30.
28. *Yearbook*, 1914, 36.
29. Ibid.
30. *Yearbook*, 1930, 49–50.
31. *Yearbook*, 1919, 29–30.
32. *Yearbook*, 1921, 22–24.
33. *Yearbook*, 1913, 39–40.
34. *Yearbook*, 1930, 23.
35. *Bangor Daily News*, 12 April 1931.
36. *Yearbook*, 1930, 41.
37. *Yearbook*, 1931, 54.

Early-twentieth-century women could confront the tensions between traditional roles and rising expectations in any number of complex ways. While some sought to hold on to tradition and only reluctantly allowed modernity to gain entrance into their lives, others embraced new opportunities without a backwards glance. Their efforts to do so, however, were often limited by the strong lock tradition held on opportunity, thus denying women access to education and jobs deemed inappropriate for them.

These concerns confronted women throughout the country. But opportunity had a spatial as well as an occupational dimension, and particularly in rural areas ambitious women had to find ways to reconcile their career goals with the limits of their locations. One way to respond was by migration, and in the first three decades of the twentieth century, many women fled the countryside—in this country and abroad—for the opportunities of big cities.

Another way to respond was to try to transform obstacles by organizing with others facing similar predicaments. Americans had a long history of forming voluntary societies devoted to collective improvement; women were avid participants. Pleas for widened occupational choices for women were familiar long before the turn of the century. New, however, was the self-consciousness with which women demanded increased opportunity—and without being willing to leave home to get it. Earlier, ambitious women who sought careers and economic advancement generally had to travel to cities to escape the limits posed by traditional roles. But as the cracks in tradition deepened and spread as part of the transformations associated with modernity, women expanded the pressure by demanding access in small cities as well as large, and in groups as well as individually. In doing so, they extended the cracks in tradition to even more remote locations—along with the tensions the cracks caused.

Nowhere were these cracks more threatening than where women sought to compete directly with men. Women who wished to enter high-status professions like medicine, law, and the ministry found their way blocked by men determined to preserve these areas for themselves. Women faced similar difficulties wherever licensing or educational restrictions could keep them out. However, in the early decades of the twentieth century, women began to make inroads into these fields, and even more progress in those areas where the restrictions against them were more informal. Candace Kanes offers insight into the experiences of a group of Portland women who organized to improve their own economic opportunities.

SERIOUS AND AMBITIOUS CAREER WOMEN:
THE PORTLAND BUSINESS AND PROFESSIONAL
WOMEN'S CLUB IN THE 1920S

Candace A. Kanes

Mary Clarity's early working life resembles that of many women born in the 1870s to Irish immigrants. By 1890, Clarity was a sales clerk in a Portland department store and lived at home with her parents and two sisters. Her father was a laborer. Unlike most young Irish-Americans who married after working several years in low-skill, low-paying jobs, however, Mary Clarity remained single—and got promoted.[1] In 1900, she was the buyer in the department store's corset department. Her sister Nellie, ten years her junior, was her assistant. In 1906, the sisters opened their own corset shop. By all accounts, the shop did very well, attracting customers from throughout Maine and other states, and prospering enough to allow the sisters to purchase their own home in 1922.

The Claritys also were among more than two hundred charter members of the Portland Business and Professional Women's Club, a local chapter of a national organization that began in 1919. Members of the BPW clubs locally and nationally were serious and ambitious career women who helped to create the identity of the "business woman." Examining the first decade of the Portland BPW club and some of its members provides several important insights about self-defined business women. First, they considered themselves career women, not temporary or marginal workers. Many people at the time, as well as later historians, have viewed women in the types of jobs most of these club members held as lacking in ambition and their opportunities as limited. Yet, regardless of the nature of their jobs, BPW members were committed to working efficiently, and rising in job responsibility and skill. Second, whether they were bookkeepers or physicians, they considered themselves successful, prompting us to re-evaluate the term "success." Often, our understanding of success is based on men's experiences; BPW members defined it in terms more appropriate to women. An examination of BPW further reveals some of the limits of the census, one of our most common sources of information about women and work. Finally, many business women thrived and succeeded because of the professional support and advocacy provided by groups like the Business and Professional Women's Club, which provided much needed social and emotional support as well.

Portland, Maine, women were not unique in their enthusiasm for organizing as business women. As World War I ended, women formed three national groups of business and professional women: the National Federation of Business and Professional Women's Clubs, the Quota Club, and the Confederation of Zonta Clubs. Altrusa, organized several years earlier, reconstituted itself and began growing after the war. Several other national groups began within a few years. The National Federation of BPW Clubs was the largest of these groups, and the one with the least restrictive membership policies.[2] Despite the proliferation of clubs, all the groups grew during the 1920s, and all remain active at the turn of the twenty-first century.

The women who formed the postwar business women's groups were excited that their wartime efforts and society's emphasis on the valuable role women had in assuring victory might mean increased opportunities for women.[3] In addition, the long struggle to gain the vote was nearly over and many

women thought their newfound political voice would contribute to their efforts in the business world. The 1920s was a
unique era for women, contrasting increased personal free-
doms with less emphasis on feminism and women working
together.[4] A number of observers of the era have noted that
heterosexual support and relationships began to take the place
of the nineteenth-century "separate sphere" in which women
supported and nurtured one another on a personal level and in
same-sex organizations.[5] Business women's groups were an
exception to the new trends of the 1920s; they were single-sex
groups that stressed the importance of women's emotional
and social as well as professional support of one another, even
while adopting a version of 1920s individualism. In addition,
it is important to note that business women's groups had
existed since the end of the nineteenth century, as had publications aimed at business women. It was neither World War I
nor the imminent passage of the Nineteenth Amendment
that brought women to business or to organizing as business
women. Most of the organizers of the new groups had themselves been business women for many years. What the war
provided was an additional boost and a renewed sense among
women that old barriers were about to fall.[6]

While this study focuses on Portland, its conclusions resonate with other Business and Professional Women's clubs,
and with similar organizations in other cities. In various
ways, each of these groups sought to improve the status of
business women, gain recognition for their achievements, create more opportunities for women, especially those involved
in business and professions, and in general, provide support
and encouragement for self-identified business women.

While clubs across the country shared similar goals and
resembled one another in many ways, each group had its own
personality. Portland's size was one of its identifying charac-

teristics. The club averaged about five hundred members during the 1920s. Those numbers, along with the strength of the Maine Federation of Business and Professional Women's Clubs, helped Portland host a successful national convention in 1925. The club also boasted the first-in-the-country all-BPW orchestra, won the national competition for most publicity garnered in 1928, and sent one of its members, Helen Havener, to New York to edit the national BPW magazine in 1927. In addition, it had several nationally known members such as Pinckney Estes Glantzberg, a New York lawyer who was active in the early stages of BPW, and Maud Wood Park, head of the national League of Women Voters. Both women lived in Maine in the summer and joined the Portland group in the 1920s. These national connections helped give the Portland club a sense of the importance of BPW and the possibilities for individuals within the club.

The Portland Business and Professional Women's club began in 1920, about six months after the formation of the National Federation of Business and Professional Women's Clubs. Among the Maine women who had attended the July 1919 convention in St. Louis, Missouri, at which the national federation began, was Ina McCausland of Portland, a member of the YWCA Business Women's Club and a teacher. She came back from the convention and helped organize the local group, attracting many teachers in the process. By the fall of 1920, the Portland club was growing rapidly. Like the national organization, the local and state groups did not specify who qualified as "business and professional" women. Clubs' personalities grew, in part, out of the mix of members the group attracted. In the Portland club's first year, at least eight members taught at the Maine School for the Deaf, and a total of 13 percent were school teachers. The club's first president, Helen M. King, was principal of a Portland school and active in the Portland Teachers' Association.

Members of the Portland club were clustered in several other occupations as well. Statistics from individual entries in the 1920 census show that about 40 percent were clerical workers and 5 percent each nurses and sales clerks, in addition to the 13 percent teachers (see table 1). Despite the clustering in a few jobs, club statistics in 1921 indicated that members represented sixty-five different occupations. The club announced in its newspaper column that it "proudly cherishes the theory that there are few business and professional women's clubs throughout the United States in cities the size of Portland which can boast of so wide a range of occupations among the membership."[7] The members of the club enjoyed both its diversity and its large membership.

The fact that about two-thirds of the Portland BPW members held women-dominated jobs is not surprising, given occupational trends for women following World War I. A number of historians have commented on the increasing sex segregation of jobs in the 1920s. As clerical job openings steadily increased, for instance, more and more such jobs went to women, with most supervisory positions reserved for men. The pay and status of the remaining women's jobs were limited. Still, for many decades, clerical work offered considerable promise to women.[8]

Even though many Portland BPW members were clustered into clerical, teaching, nursing, and store sales jobs, they were neither temporary workers nor women without opportunity for advancement, as is often the description of such jobs. Club members were career women who believed they could rise up through whatever ranks they could get into, and who would devote themselves to their work. They valued success. Similar qualities might describe many men and women excited about business opportunities in the 1920s, the decade in which President Calvin Coolidge declared that the "chief business of the American people is business."[9] Yet,

TABLE I

Percentages of Portland working women
in various occupations, 1920

Occupational group	BPW N=188*	All Port. N=579
Clerical	38%	27%
Bookkeepers	15	6
Clerks	6	9
Stenographers	17	12
Trade, professional	28	31
Teachers	13	8
Nurses	5	4
Non-factory manual trades	5	7
Arts	0	2
Commerce	5	10
Higher-level white collar	10	1
Office workers	3	<1
Social workers, etc.[1]	4	<1
Upper professionals[2]	3	<1
Proprietors	2	1
Managerial	2	1
Managers	1	<1
Corporate officers	0	0
Commercial supervisors[3]	1	<1
Factory	<1	11
Domestic service	0	16
Not working	6	0
Other	20	12
TOTAL	100%	100%

*This is number of members located in census. Total 1920 member-
ship was approximately 231.
1. Includes agency directors, journalists, librarians, women in advertising, public relations.
2. Includes doctors, lawyers, judges, architects, dentists.
3. Includes managers of retail stores or large departments of commercial businesses.
Sources: Portland BPW membership lists, Fourteenth Census of
Population, Cumberland County, Portland, Maine.

despite their ambitions and achievements, BPW members cannot simply be compared to business men if we want to understand what they accomplished and what they strived for. Because of the sex-segregated nature of the work force, and because of gender expectations of both men and women, comparing the two often erases the real experiences and the real achievements of women. Men's accomplishments often seem more valuable. But much of what men achieved was not available to women, even the most ambitious and unusual among them. For instance, women were barred from many professional schools. The few who got into medical school often were prohibited from serving residencies that would have allowed them to practice.[10] Since many women were denied credit in their own names, their economic opportunities were often limited.

When these self-proclaimed business women are compared to other working women, however, they stand out in a number of ways (see table 1). They were rarely factory workers or domestic workers; they held white collar and supervisory jobs in much higher numbers than did other working women in Portland; and, within clerical work, were more likely to hold prestigious bookkeeping jobs than were other working women. It is in these comparisons that their achievements begin to become visible.

A few brief biographies of club members show the particular ways in which these women advanced and succeeded. Lena M. Payson Dickey, who was forty years old, was a widow who sold life insurance, compiling more than a quarter million dollars in sales in 1920.[11] She had previously been a teacher, but after her husband died, did not think she could support her children on that salary. Another insurance saleswoman, Mabel Lord, 43, had been head bookkeeper for a Portland firm in 1920. Early the next year, she decided to attend an insurance school in Pittsburgh for three months and work for Phoenix Mutual, a company that employed her brother.[12] She, too, sold notable amounts of insurance.

Abba Harris, 38, and Ruby Jackson, 33, were former stenographers who, in 1910, purchased a business that offered stenography, multigraphing, and mail services. They took out small loans and, despite the fact that they had no experience running a business, increased the firm's output five-fold in ten years. They employed six women.[13]

Jane Merrill Hayes had been in charge of gloves at Smiley's department store, but lost her job there when the department was discontinued. Shortly thereafter, she became manager of the Women's Employment Bureau of the YWCA, a service started by the Chamber of Commerce and YWCA, with the support of BPW.[14]

Helen M. Robinson, 41, had been deputy superintendent of the Portland Public Schools since 1913. She began as a clerk in the superintendent's office in about 1906. When the superintendent became ill, Robinson took over many of his duties and was subsequently named deputy. She was in charge of the payroll, the district's budget, statistics, monthly reports, and other business tasks, and supervised one full-time and several part-time clerks, as well as continuing to fill in for the superintendent when he was out of the office.[15]

Anita S. Files had spent two seasons when she was younger as a millinery apprentice, then took up sales work in a jewelry store about 1911. She was enticed away by a job as an assistant buyer at a store in St. Louis, but did not like living there. She returned to Portland as head of J. R. Libby's millinery department, where she supervised ten saleswomen and went on trips to New York every three weeks to keep up with the trade. By 1927, she had opened her own millinery shop.[16] Another milliner, Sarah J. Blair, 59, a daughter of Irish immigrants, owned her own business and her own home, where she lived with her maid. Blair, who began her shop in partnership with another woman in 1907 and had run it alone since about 1917, also made frequent trips to New York to keep up with the latest styles.[17]

Another success story was Margaret Chase Smith, a member of the Skowhegan BPW. Smith was president of the Maine Federation of BPW Clubs in 1925, the year the national BPW convention was held in Portland. At the time, there were twenty-four BPW chapters in the state with a total membership of some fifteen hundred. Smith, single at the time, joined the Skowhegan Club when it was formed in 1922, served as state president, and produced the statewide BPW newsletter. She married at age thirty-two and her husband was later elected to Congress. Smith herself was elected to the House of Representatives after his death in 1940 and to the Senate in 1948. She had been a teacher briefly after graduating from high school, then turned to clerical work, where she rose to positions of responsibility. Her ultimate success in Congress was due as much to her BPW training and connections as to her marriage.[18]

While advancement, or climbing job ladders, clearly was important to BPW members, they also recognized that all achievement was not tied to one's job title. Jeannette Craig, a stenographer at an architect's office, is a good example. A club newspaper column said about her: "Everyone knows that she is a great deal more important to the establishment than any mere stenographer would be." She was credited with knowing more than anyone in the firm except the partners. She learned so much about architecture from her work that she designed the house in which she and her mother lived.[19] Her achievement came in the amount of knowledge she acquired and what she was able to do with it at work and outside of the office.

What is apparent from these few brief stories about BPW club members is that seemingly ordinary clerical workers, women in stores, and tradeswomen thrived in unexpected or previously unnoticed ways. Clerical workers regularly moved into other, often "better" jobs, and many of those who remained as clerical workers did not experience their jobs as ordinary or dead-end. Women who worked as milliners or corsetieres moved from employee to employer status, doing well enough to stay in business for many years and to live comfortably, or remained as employees in positions that allowed them considerable independence to travel, to supervise others, and to make decisions. Sales clerks could become buyers, a "glamorous and responsible" position.[20] Not every club member experienced equal attainments, but as members of the BPW club, all announced themselves as aspiring and career-oriented and sought success in the business world.

We have failed to recognize these women's achievements for several reasons. Among them is that the U.S. Census, upon which we rely to gain information about the types of jobs people held, often misrepresented women's work. Other scholars have demonstrated some of the shortcomings of the census in relation to women.[21] Examining individual entries in one city reveals a variety of problems. Among the 1920 members of the Portland BPW Club, for instance, six percent were listed in the census as having no occupations, when club records indicated that all those women worked for pay; approximately fifteen percent were listed with incorrect or misleading occupations. These misrepresentations can be found both in the jobs the enumerators wrote on the forms and in the codes the census office in Washington subsequently added. Those codes were used to compile summary statistics, which are often the major source of information about women and work.

For example, the Claritys, who owned the corset shop, were enumerated correctly, but coded in a category of semi-skilled operatives in corset factories, a designation that misrepresented their experiences as owners and operators of an independent business. They did make corsets, but more accurately, were business proprietors. It is the census codes that have lived on in the summary statistics, not the enumerator's designations. Harris and Jackson, owners of the stenography and mailing business, were coded as stenographer and clerk, respectively, rather than as business proprietors. Lena Dickey, the insurance saleswoman, was enumerated and coded as a bookkeeper.

In other instances, the census statistical groupings, based on the codes that were assigned in Washington, led to misrepresentations. Women were coded as teachers, regardless of whether they taught in a classroom, taught sewing, worked as governesses, or were principals, school managers, or assistant superintendents. Helen M. King, the first club president and supervising principal of the Portland Schools, was coded as a teacher, as was Helen M. Robinson, deputy superintendent. Both had risen to supervisory positions. King had begun as a teacher and Robinson as a clerk. Those advancements were significant in the eyes of BPW and its members, but were not reflected in codes used for summary statistics.

Also coded together were store saleswomen and buyers, and nurses and nursing supervisors. A similar collapsing of categories occurred in some jobs held predominantly by men. For women, and for reconstructing the experiences of these 1920s business women, the coding scheme is more critical. Men generally had many more chances for advancement and as a whole appeared in the census in higher-level occupations than did women. In many cases, especially sex-segregated jobs, when women moved upward, they were often categorized with those in the jobs they had left. With fewer supervisory or management opportunities for women, these category erasures are especially significant.

Our views about "success" also have led us to miss the achievements of these self-defined business women. The common American notion of success includes gaining autonomy or increased responsibility in a job, supervising others, perhaps owning one's own business, or rising to the uppermost levels of management; material gains beyond "comfort"; and recognized power or influence in the larger community. Many of those elements of success come from men's experiences and from cultural myths about success, such as the Horatio Alger stories. BPW members may have attained many of those attributes of success, and they certainly did not reject them. Yet jobs in upper management, great wealth, and widespread influence were available to few women in the 1920s, regardless of talent or ambition. The Horatio Alger ideal applied, if at all, to men. For women, the more common cultural myths of success were fairy tales or novels and short stories that saw the ultimate goal for women as a good marriage, that is, marriage to a man of some means.[22] Trying to fit women into the male ideal of success usually is a disappointing experience. Women just do not measure up.

These business women understood, even though they did not necessarily accept, the limits they faced. Attaining or even aspiring to the same heights as some men was not necessary for these women to consider themselves successful. Instead, they needed to apply a serious work ethic, be ambitious, climb whatever ladders were available to whatever rungs were open (and push those limits), gain responsibility, and adopt other ideals important to *women's* notions of success. These included economic independence, ethical behavior, and cooperation. It was clear to 1920s business women that men and women had different opportunities and barriers and, therefore, "success" defined by male experience was not appropriate for judging women. Understanding how the women saw "success" can help in understanding their occupational experiences and their descriptions of themselves.

Economic independence was an especially important aspect of "success" for business women. Since women had entered the work force in large numbers beginning in the late nineteenth century, their wages often had not been sufficient to operate a household or support others. Women generally were paid less than men, even for comparable work.[23] The Portland club described itself as being composed of "self-supporting women," a fact of which they were proud.[24] One indication that they were self-supporting is that a quarter of the members were listed in the census as heads of the household, with another quarter living as boarders, suggesting that at least half of the club members were not dependent on someone else for financial support. While a fifth of the members were listed in the census as "daughters," one in three of those daughters was the only person employed in the household. The club members were much more likely to live apart from family members than other working women in Portland, nearly two-thirds of whom lived with family members (see table 2).

In addition, club members were predominantly single, which contributed to their need to be self-supporting. In 1920, 82 percent were either single or married with no spouse present. Their median age was forty-three, long past the usual age of marriage. Many were socially as well as economically independent, which made the business women's club vital for providing more than business information and contacts. A national survey of all Business and Professional Women's clubs in 1927 indicated that the "great majority" of the 14,000 women who responded were economically independent and that many of those club members were totally or partially responsible for the support of others as well.[25]

Being independent was so important to Portland's club members that the concept appeared prominently in a proposed club cheer early in 1921. Clubs used such cheers to identify themselves at conventions and other meetings. The suggestion was:

Business, Business
Rah! Rah! Rah!
Professional, Professional
Rah! Rah! Rah!
I-n-d-e-p-e-n-d-e-n-t
That's us![26]

Beyond economic independence, other aspects of "success" for business women included cooperation, consideration of customers and others, and generally ethical behavior. For example, a newspaper article praised Leonie Landry and Lula Bowman, operators of a lunch room, as "the type of women who give a hundred cents' value on the dollar" and as

TABLE 2

Relationships to head of household
of working women in Portland, 1920
(percentages)

Relationship to head	Portland BPW N=188	All Portland N=579
%		
Head	25%	15
Wife	6	15
Friend	1	0
Daughter	20	35
Sister*	13	9
Mother*	1	1
Other relative	4	4
Boarder	26	13
Other	4	8
TOTAL	100%	100%

*Or in-law.
Source: Manuscript Fourteenth Census of Population for Cumberland County, Portland City, Maine; membership list of Portland Business and Professional Women's Club, 1920.

having achieved "the kind of success that really counts—promptly paid bills and satisfied customers." These proprietors were "not making themselves wealthy at the expense of customers."[27] The club described the keys to Sarah Blair's success as her being "a diligent worker, a shrewd buyer, a keen judge of the styles—and she believes in giving a 100-cents value on the dollar."[28] What mattered to business women was being honest and honorable, treating others with respect, working hard, and being solvent and responsible.

In addition, many of the independent business women kept their businesses going for many years. The survival rate of small business, in the 1920s and through most of the twentieth century, was low. Five years was considered a long time for a small business to last. Many BPW members remained in business for 30 or 40 years, and managed to stay afloat during the Depression years of the 1930s.[29] For instance, the Claritys continued in the corset business from 1906 until the early 1940s. Mary Clarity died in January 1945. Sarah Blair continued her millinery shop from 1907 through 1945; she died in November 1946. Leonie Landry of the lunch room that began in 1914 died in 1923, but Lula Bowman continued in the restaurant business until the 1960s. Mabel Lord kept her insurance business active until her death in 1951. Harris and Jackson, stenographers and multigraphers, stayed in business from 1910 until the mid-1940s. Harris had married in the 1920s, but Jackson kept the business going under the same name by herself.

Even though success in business generally equates with individualism, BPW members favored individual achievement gained not through selfishness or greed, but through cooperation. At the national convention held in Portland in 1925, the national president urged members to leave behind "personal ambition, petty spite and jealousy," and instead embrace "friendship, love, cooperation, faith, goodwill and opportunity."[30] The theme of cooperation, of helping other women to succeed and to gain opportunities, and putting aside any personal ambition that would harm others was a continuing one for BPW, locally and nationally. As the earlier quote about the lunch room proprietors suggests, individualism, which might mean gaining wealth at any expense, was put aside for adequate financial reward, without taking unfair advantage of customers. Selflessness, long an admired trait in women, now was being equated with success in business.[31]

A number of the women who joined the Portland BPW Club when it began in 1920 already had been in independent businesses or had been serious about their occupations for a number of years. The group, however, gave form to their perceptions of themselves as ambitious business women, and brought them into contact with hundreds of other women of similar ambitions. The "cooperation" element so stressed by the organization was fostered through personal contact and friendships that developed within clubs. These predominantly single, often socially independent women relished the friendship and encouragement club membership offered.

Mabel M. Spear, Portland's second president, captured the club's dual nature of serving both professional and personal needs when she spoke at her installation as president. She said her goal for the year was to help the club "grow big in business ways and social ways." Her remarks had followed those of the club's first president, Helen M. King, who said the efforts to organize a BPW club initially were sluggish because potential members did not know one another well and were, therefore, unsure of whether they should commit to the new group. To gain "solidity," the executive board had "catered to the social element" during the club's first year. The effort was successful, but King told members it was time to "function in the world's work and in the work of the city."[32] Spear's "business ways and social ways" were crucial both to the success of the club and of individual members. In a variety of ways, the club strived for both goals.

BPW members knew that success usually did not come from business activity alone. The woman who did not take time for the more "social ways" probably could not sustain a strenuous business life. Mary Stewart of Washington, D.C., the national legislative chairman for BPW, told the 1923 national convention that one of the best things about the organizations was the friendships that members made across the country.

> You know how we can work alone and fight alone the way we are meant to do. Why? Because we can play together, that is why. And so what business women have needed more than anything else is to learn to have a good time together, and it is a mark of civilization that our women can play.[33]

The Portland women took those remarks to heart. The club had a sports committee that sponsored events and provided numerous types of instruction. The committee reflected the local and national emphasis on recreation, fresh air, exercise, reading for business and for pleasure, and leisure. During the 1922–23 year, for example, it organized weekly bowling parties, a Memorial Day picnic and a weekend outing with sports events, other seasonal picnics and outings, dance lessons, dances, and winter snowshoe hikes. In 1924, the club had two bowling teams. By 1927, bowling was so popular that the club had its own league, with ten teams that bowled weekly for thirty weeks of the year. Some years, there were weekly hikes, horseback riding, and swimming lessons, sports nights with many children's games (played by the adult women), and regular card parties, which served for both recreation and fund-raising.

The club started an orchestra about 1922, with some thirteen members at its outset. It was said to be the only club in the country with an orchestra composed entirely of club members.[34] It also formed a glee club in the late 1920s. In 1921, the group began a drama club, with a young member as director. They produced plays every year, some for the public, others for club members only. Sometimes professional actresses in touring companies that stopped in Portland participated in the plays and other club activities.

Social meetings alternated with business-oriented meetings. At the socials, members listened to music or performed for other members, played bridge and other card games, sewed, and chatted with one another.

Equally important as the organized activities were the informal contacts and friendships among these predominantly single and middle-aged members of the Portland BPW. These were women leading non-traditional lives by virtue of their being single, and their focus on occupations over domestic pursuits. In 1920, when about 80 percent of the Portland BPW members were single, a nearly equal percentage of women over age twenty in the U.S. were married, or had been married.[35] Friendships and relationships among BPW members, in many cases, provided the types of support and social activities married couples might have shared, or those in which young women and their families engaged.

The bowling parties, card parties, organized hikes, and other recreations the club offered were the starting point. Beyond those, club members entertained one another at dinners, picnics, and get-aways to beach houses, family homes in other cities, or similar retreats. These activities were so important to club members that they often were detailed in the club's weekly newspaper column. The announcements frequently supported the importance of independence, especially by the emphasis on automobiles and auto trips. Business women's clubs throughout the country bragged about members who were the first—or among the first—

women in the city to drive an automobile. Portland's newspaper column in 1922 noted that "the number of club members who own their own cars is rapidly increasing."[36] Items about autos were common. Members took club visitors from out of town on motor tours of Portland and went on motor tours when they attended national conventions. But most importantly, pairs or groups of club members "motored" to the shore, to weekend outings, or on longer vacations.

Their more business-oriented club activities included lectures at club meetings and organized classes that focused on business topics. Lecturers spoke about current events; local, state, and national political issues; banking and credit; business law; and other related topics. Classes included business English, parliamentary law, income management, French, public speaking, and current events. Club members also divided into vocational groups of stenographers, store clerks, proprietors, teachers, journalists, nurses, and doctors to discuss common concerns and issues and to share advice.

Members of the Portland BPW Club used both "business ways and social ways" to achieve their many successes. They reflected these successes not only in their activities, but in their newspaper columns where they let the larger community know what they were doing and accomplishing. One national official said BPW "seeks to show the real, human qualities of the constructively successful women of the day, and to present portraits of them that engage the imagination, stir the impulses and inspire the mind and soul of those who look upon them."[37] Those goals were clear in the Portland club's activities and publicity.

Members of the Portland Business and Professional Women's Club through both words and deeds provide a challenge to many commonly held notions about women and work. They were career women, many of whom remained single and devoted their lives to their jobs. They were ambitious. They climbed job ladders. Their experiences help demonstrate the ways in which our ideas about success are gendered. Women did not necessarily reject "male" success, but neither did they judge their own lives and achievements by standards that were based on experiences they could not have. These business women were economically and socially independent, using the club as social and business support. They believed they were successful and provided evidence of it through the Business and Professional Women's Club activities, newsletters, publicity, and records.

1. See, for example, Alice Kessler-Harris, *Out to Work: A History of Wage-Earning Women in the United States* (New York: Oxford University Press, 1982), 123–28.

2. Quota, Zonta, and Altrusa all were classification organizations. They limited membership to a certain number of women in each category, based on the type of business in which the woman was engaged. Classifications were based on business activity, not the woman's specific job title. BPW did not have such membership restrictions.

3. These comments are frequent in records of the National Federation of Business and Professional Women's Clubs and its predecessors, the Woman's Association of Commerce and the Business Women's Committee. All such records relating to the war and the immediate post-war periods can be found at the Marguerite Rawalt Resource Center, BPW/USA, Washington, D.C.

4. See, for example, Nancy Cott, *The Grounding of Modern Feminism* (New Haven: Yale University Press, 1987), 147–60; and Dorothy M. Brown, *Setting a Course: American Women in the 1920s* (Boston: Twayne Publishers, 1987), 101–5.

5. Carroll Smith-Rosenberg's "The Female World of Love and Ritual" in *Disorderly Conduct: Visions of Gender in Victorian America* (New York: Oxford University Press, 1985), 53–76, best describes the earlier conditions for white, native-born women.

6. Among the national post-war groups were the National Federation of Business and Professional Women's Clubs, founded in July 1919; the Quota Club, founded in February 1919; the Confederation of Zonta Clubs, found-

ed in November 1919; Soroptimist and Pilot, both founded in 1923; and Altrusa, founded in 1917, but reorganized to allow its spread in 1924.

7. "Many Occupations Slate For Officers For Business Women," *Portland Daily Press*, 26 February 1921, 11.

8. See, for example, Kessler-Harris, *Out to Work*, 217–49; Brown, *Setting a Course*, 97–99; Margery W. Davies, *Woman's Place Is at the Typewriter: Office Work and Office Workers, 1870–1930* (Philadelphia: Temple University Press, 1982), 161–74.

9. Keith L. Bryant Jr. and Henry C. Dethloff, *A History of American Business* (Englewood Cliffs, N.J.: Prentice-Hall, 1983), 1.

10. See Barbara Miller Solomon, *In the Company of Educated Women: A History of Women in Higher Education in America* (New Haven: Yale University Press, 1985), 115–40.

11. "Prosperous Business Woman, Member of Local Club Whose Earnings Were $8000 Last Year," *Portland Daily Press*, 12 March 1921, 3.

12. "Has Seen Much Service As War Nurse," *Portland Daily Press*, 26 March 1921, 3. All ages reflect those listed in the 1920 census.

13. "Business Women's Club Has Firm in Its Membership," *Portland Daily Press*, 2 April 1921, 9.

14. "Take Pride in Work of Miss Hayes," *Portland Daily Press*, 16 April 1921, 4.

15. "Eight Years Deputy Superintendent City School," *Portland Daily Press*, 23 April 1921, 9.

16. "Looking for Expert on Millinery?" *Portland Daily Press*, 28 May 1921, 4.

17. "Pioneer in Movement Start Club," *Portland Daily Press*, 2 July 1921, 5.

18. Patricia Schmidt, *Margaret Chase Smith: Beyond Convention* (Orono: University of Maine Press, 1996), 66, 73 ff.; and Patricia Ward Wallace, *Politics of Conscience: A Biography of Margaret Chase Smith* (Westport, Conn.: Praeger, 1995), 23–24.

19. "Efficiency Plus, All Time . . . That Describes Jeannette Craig, Stenographer and Member of Business Women's Club," *Portland Daily Press*, 3 September 1921, 5.

20. Susan Porter Benson, *Counter Cultures: Saleswomen, Managers, and Customers in American Department Stores, 1890–1940* (Urbana: University of Illinois Press, 1986), 25.

21. For other examples of how the census has misrepresented women's experiences, see Margo Anderson Conk, *The United States Census and Labor Force Change: A History of Occupational Statistics, 1870–1940*

(Ann Arbor, Mich.: UMI Research Press, 1978, 1980); Nancy Folbre and Marjorie Abel, "Women's Work and Women's Households: Gender Bias in the U.S. Census," *Social Research* 46, 3 (Autumn 1989): 545–69; and Claudia Goldin, *Understanding the Gender Gap: An Economic History of American Women* (New York: Oxford University Press, 1990).

22. Among the many examples of this phenomenon, see Edith Wharton, *The House of Mirth* (New York: Scribner's, 1905); any of the works of Jane Austen; the stories in Maureen Honey, ed., *Breaking the Ties That Bind: Popular Stories of the New Woman, 1915–1930* (Norman: University of Oklahoma Press, 1992); and tales such as "Cinderella."

23. See, for example, Brown, *Setting a Course*, 85; and Goldin, *Understanding the Gender Gap*, 68–73, 89–90.

24. "Making Plans for Big Bazaar," *Portland Daily Press*, 27 August 1921, 3.

25. Margaret Elliott and Grace E. Manson, "Earnings of Women in Business and the Professions," *Michigan Business Studies* 3, 1 (September 1930): 108. The National Federation of BPW Clubs commissioned the survey, which was sent to all fifty-three thousand members.

26. "President's Night Will Be Observed," *Portland Daily Press*, 7 May 1921, 3.

27. "Lunch Room Proprietor One Members; Another Many Occupations Represented in Business Women's Club," *Portland Daily Press*, 14 May 1921, 3.

28. "Pioneer in Movement Start Club."

29. Wendy Gamber, *The Female Economy: The Millinery and Dressmaking Trades, 1860–1930* (Urbana: University of Illinois Press, 1997), 36; and Mansel Blackford, *A History of Small Business in America* (New York: Twayne Publishers, 1991), 58.

30. "History of the Federation of Business and Professional Women's Clubs of Maine," 16, Maine Federation of Business and Professional Women's Clubs collection, Special Collections, Fogler Library, University of Maine, Orono.

31. Selflessness was especially well expressed as an important trait for women by Catharine Beecher. See Kathryn Kish Sklar, *Catharine Beecher: A Study in American Domesticity* (New York: W. W. Norton, 1973), xiv.

32. "Up to Women to Prevent War Threatening in Europe," *Portland Daily Press*, 10 May 1921, 1, 6.

33. "Fifth Annual Convention, Portland, Ore., July 1923, vol. 1 of 2, NFBP-WC, Inc.," 11 July 1923, 231, Marguerite Rawalt Resource Center, BPW/USA, Washington, D.C.

34. *Independent Woman* 5, 4 (October 1922): 17.

35. According to the 1920 census, 70 percent of the women ages twenty and older were married, with another 14 percent divorced or widowed. Only 10 percent of women over age thirty had never been married. *Fourteenth Census of the United States, Taken in the Year 1920, Vol. II, Population* (Washington, D.C.: Bureau of the Census, 1922), 388.

36. "Business Women's Club Notes," *Portland Evening Express & Advertiser*, 20 March 1922, 9.

37. "Is the Able Woman a Freak?" *Independent Woman* 2, 4 (March 1921): 7.

For many ethnic groups at the turn of the century, immigration and industrialization were intertwined experiences. While not all immigrants came from agricultural backgrounds, and not all ended up working in the factories and living in the tenements of America's growing cities, enough did to create a dilemma for historians. Can we best understand their experiences in the aggregate, ignoring their differences of religion, language, culture, and the like in favor of their shared difficulties and adjustments as immigrants? Or are we better off focusing on the particular, examining each group's reasons for leaving and adaptations to their new environment without reference to the others? At the same time, historians must ask how we can best understand women's experiences. How do we explain and compare groups that sent mostly daughters across the ocean to work, like the Irish, or mostly sons, like the Chinese? How do women's experiences in these groups compare with those from groups that came to the United States primarily as families? Why did some family-centered groups encourage daughters to work for wages outside the home (eastern European Jews) while others did not (Italians)?

In addition to grappling with similarities and differences of ethnicity and gender, historians must also consider what immigrants found when they arrived here. Those who moved to large industrial cities with high concentrations of newcomers could live in ethnic enclaves so large that sights and sounds, language and food remained reassuringly familiar. Those in smaller cities and towns faced a more diverse environment that raised new kinds of concerns. How could ethnic and gender identity be preserved in the face of forces that diluted ethnic life? How could mothers protect their daughters while encouraging them to take advantage of the opportunities implicit in the decision to come to this country?

All immigrants and their children needed protection from widespread limits to opportunity. Not only were living and working conditions often harsh, but ethnic and gender prejudice were rampant. Opportunity may have been greater than at home, but the realities of factory and tenement forced immigrants to develop practical and creative ways to adapt to new surroundings. Each immigrant group did so in a characteristic manner while simultaneously struggling with the complexities of what it meant to be American. Women faced an additional layer of difficulty as they struggled to come to terms with the differences between the views of womanhood they brought with them and those they found current in the United States. Eileen Eagan and Patricia Finn offer a picture of the ways in which Irish women in Portland struggled with these issues and the solutions they devised.

Eileen Eagan and Patricia Finn

In February 1864 the steamship *Bohemia*, sailing from Liverpool, England to Portland, Maine with cargo and passengers, ran into Alden's Rock off Cape Elizabeth, Maine and sank; of the 218 passengers, forty-two, mostly Irish immigrants in steerage, drowned. Twelve were unclaimed and were buried in an unmarked grave in Calvary Cemetery in South Portland. The event, the worst loss of life in Casco Bay up to that time, attracted considerable attention in the local press, partly because of the loss of many expensive goods.[1] Seventy-five years later, Alzira Peirce painted a Works Progress Administration mural of the shipwreck for the South Portland Post Office.

Figure 1. Alzira Peirce mural of the wreck of the steamship
Bohemia in 1864, at the South Portland Post Office.
Photo courtesy of the *Portland Press Herald*.

In 1980 Bartley Conley, a postal worker of Irish descent, looked into the story behind the painting. Touched by the history, of which he had been unaware, Conley proceeded to raise funds from local Irish groups for a monument to those who lay neglected in the cemetery. Four years later, the group erected a Celtic cross with the names of those who lay buried and in honor of all whose lives were lost in the wreck.[2]

The wreck of the *Bohemia* and the mural were brought to renewed attention as an aspect of ethnic and religious identity. However, the shipwreck also represents the irony of people leaving one disaster only to find themselves facing new difficulties. The story of Irish women in Portland is the story of the interaction of the culture that they brought with them with the circumstances of their new land. The history of Irish women in Portland reveals the importance of physical environment and space in shaping gender roles and the importance of gender roles in shaping a community's development. This is the story of the ways in which Irish women, individually and collectively, made use of old traditions and new institutions to overcome disaster and make new lives.

Gorham's Corner, close to Portland Harbor on Casco Bay, is the intersection of Center, Fore and Pleasant Streets. To that area from the early nineteenth century onward came Irish immigrants looking for shelter, work, and a new life. By 1828 St. Dominic's Roman Catholic Church had been built, bringing a traditional center of Irish life to the neighborhood. In the aftermath of the famine in Ireland, an increasing number of migrants came directly to Portland, or indirectly, frequently from Boston or Canada, having landed first in Halifax or St. John or Quebec City.[3] By 1860 the Irish were the largest non-English immigrant group in Portland. They settled along the waterfront and formed distinctive neighborhoods to the east on Munjoy Hill and to the west in Gorham's Corner. These locations reflected the availability of work for men on the docks and for women in packing and canning factories. In the nineteenth century Gorham's Corner in particular had the reputation of a tough neighborhood, generally defined by the behavior of the men and shocking to the native-born. Portland's chronicler Edward Elwell described it as "an unsavory locality of the town, in bad repute because of the turbulent character of its inhabitants, the center of sailor boarding houses, the scene of street brawls and drunken rows."[4]

The experience of Irish women in Portland was shaped by the specific characteristics of Irish immigration to Maine and to the United States. A large percentage of Irish immigrants were single women. Many took part in chain migration, in which one member of an extended family, typically a woman among the Irish, would migrate, save money to bring over her relatives, then help them find jobs.[5]

Irish cultural traditions had both negative and positive aspects for Irish women in Portland in the late nineteenth century. While the family and regional connections fostered a sense of community, some characteristics of the group limited their job opportunities. Gaelic was the first language of many; some did not speak English. As late as 1900, about 30 percent of women in Gorham's Corner could not read or write in either language.[6] While most Irish men became general laborers or longshoreman, most women were employed as domestics or factory workers. For women language and literacy could determine what kinds of domestic work were offered. In 1900 the United States Hotel at Monument Square in Portland employed a predominantly Irish female servant staff who lived in the hotel. The head housekeeper, Elizabeth Powers, was born in Maine of Irish parents and was literate. However, most of the chambermaids were illiterate immigrants.[7] Other English-speaking Irish women got jobs in the growing number of upper-middle-class households on Congress Street, near the Western Promenade area or Deering

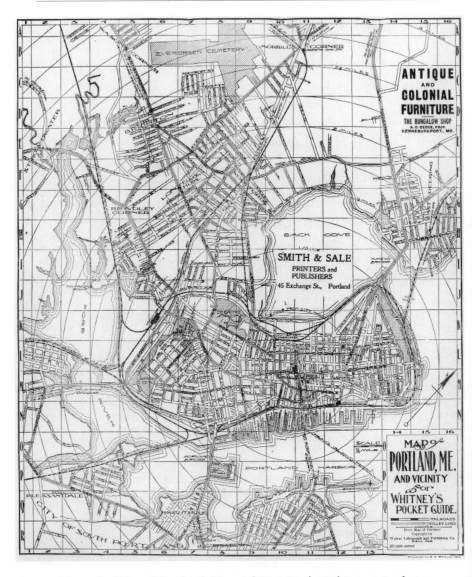

Figure 2. "Map of Portland, Me. and Vicinity for Whitney's Pocket Guide" (Portland, Maine: Smith & Sale Printers and Publishers, 1910). This map shows a general view of Portland with surrounding bodies of water. Munjoy Hill is located approximately at sections 12--15L and 12–14M; Gorham's Corner is at 10M.

section as streetcars allowed the wealthy and middle classes to move out from the city center.[8]

Servants' jobs reflected the positive aspects of Irish cultural patterns. Some of the women had experience working as domestics in Ireland. Family ties were frequently the means of obtaining employment, and ethnic ties resulted in the concentration of Irish women in certain workplaces. An Irish owner of a hotel, or Elizabeth Powers as head housekeeper, surely provided employment for newcomers, easing the transition to life in Portland.

While service was the major area of employment, other occupations also drew a relatively high percentage of Irish women. The 1892 *Report of the [Maine] Bureau of Industrial and Labor Statistics* reported that rag sorters (many of whom did not speak English) were almost all born in Ireland or of Irish parents, especially those employed at junk shops in Portland, and all were women.[9] An unnamed rag sorter was quoted in the report: "It is hard work to clothe a body and be a decent woman, but the work is healthy. Not many of us have any education, but we live and die about the same as better folks."[10]

In 1888 the Portland Star Match Factory on West Commercial Street was the largest match manufacturer in the state and the second largest in New England. Along with perhaps forty men, the company had thirty-nine female employees— twenty-eight Irish-Americans and the rest, as the labor report informs us, "Americans." The women workers' job was to sort, count, and wrap the matches, putting them up into small bunches. Paid on a piecework basis, they made around five dollars a week. This was not healthy work. The phosphorus used on the matches had negative effects on the workers' teeth and jaws, creating a condition called "phossy jaw" that damaged the bone.[11]

Before 1900, few Irish women in Portland were employed in white-collar positions—in office work, in sales, or in the emerging occupation of telephone operator. Teaching was the primary professional position. In Catholic schools these jobs were filled by women religious, including many Irish-born and Irish-American women.[12] By 1880 a handful of Irish teachers were in the public schools, especially in the Irish parts of the city. Their numbers increased partly because of the support of Irish men such as Daniel O'Connell O'Donoghue and Patrick McGowan, who were elected to the Portland school committee. By 1900 Irish women were a substantial presence in the schools in Irish neighborhoods. Between 1900 and 1910, the number of Irish women teachers in the schools doubled to about 13 percent of the total Portland teaching staff. However, none were high school teachers and only two were principals, both of kindergarten schools.[13]

Changes in economic conditions affected changes in Irish women's labor. Portland's work opportunities were shaped by its history as a port rather than as an industrial center. Whereas by the turn of the century women in cities like Boston or New York—or Saco-Biddeford or Lewiston-Auburn —were increasingly employed in the textile and shoe industries and often unionized, in Portland few such jobs existed. Instead, most factory jobs were in packing, canning, and food processing. Even these jobs were not reliable over time. Portland's strength as a port began to decline when its civic leaders turned away from developing port facilities and toward tourism as a basis of the city's economy, although fishing continued to be the city's mainstay.[14] Thus, employment for Portland's Irish women was concentrated in non-unionized factories or in domestic work. Some of it was seasonal, dependent on the fish catch or the agricultural harvest, or related to the summer tourist industry.[15]

DEMOGRAPHIC AND LIVING PATTERNS

Still, for immigrants Portland remained a place of promise. Another wave of Irish came to America in the 1880s, and single Irish women continued to come in large numbers. By 1900 the Irish were about 40 percent of the first and second generation immigrants to Portland, or about 15 percent of the city's total population of just over fifty thousand. Although this was a small percentage compared to the Irish presence in places like Boston, Lowell, or Philadelphia, in certain parts of Portland, the Irish were quite visible.[16]

At the turn of the century the Irish were still concentrated in the areas along the waterfront. Gorham's Corner had a large number of Gaelic speakers and a religious center close by at St. Dominic's Church. The community was tied to the waterfront for jobs. It maintained a distinctive, if changing, culture. As late as 1940, the Works Progress Administration's *Portland City Guide* offered a nostalgic stereotype of the area, noting that Gorham's "corner had many a kitchen barroom where beer and ale could be purchased for five and ten cents a pail and carried out for consumption."[17]

Work requirements shaped single women's housing choices. In Gorham's Corner, women who worked on their own lived with relatives or in boarding houses with relatives nearby. Katharine McCarty, who worked at the match factory, lived with her parents (her father was a laborer) and four brothers and a sister, Johanna, twenty-eight and single, who was employed in a factory as a shoe stitcher.[18]

While the port area offered factory jobs, Portland's commercial development at the turn of the century also created employment for women in the hotels in the center of town that served business travelers and tourists. Most of the hotels had dining rooms that also provided employment. Although hiring practices varied, most of the women employees in the hotels were Irish and many were recent arrivals. They are listed in the census as servants who boarded at the hotel. At the Preble House on Congress Street, for example, of eleven Irish servants employed in 1900, four had immigrated to Portland in 1899.[19] Elizabeth Powers lived at the U.S. Hotel at Monument Square. Her status as a "renter" put her closer to the position of upper level employees and residents. Boarding houses in the downtown area also provided jobs for Irish women as servants, cooks, and in some cases as managers. Women who worked as live-in servants for families could find themselves more isolated, in middle-class neighborhoods with fewer Irish people.

Other women lived with their families in the Gorham's Corner area and worked downtown. Alice Welch, Maine-born, twenty-six and single, worked for the *Portland Evening Express* as a compositor and lived with her Irish-born parents, brother and two younger sisters, Margaret and Clara.[20] By 1920, Alice had become the head of the household. She lived with Clara, a matron at the phone company,[21] and Margaret, a telephone operator supervisor. By the mid-1920s they had moved to an area of upwardly-mobile families. These jobs represented the upper level of Irish working women's success. The Welch sisters' move out of the Gorham's Corner area shows the connection between economic mobility and physical mobility. It shows how the family structure of the Irish adapted to the economic opportunities of the place and time, and helped to provide increased opportunity for single Irish women.[22]

Most Irish women heads of households were concentrated into the ward that included Gorham's Corner, clustering on particular streets and even tenement buildings. In 1900, Ward Four included 433 heads of household, of whom 53 (12.2%) were women; about 42 (80%) of these were widows. Irish mothers assumed tremendous responsibility for their families, even when their children were grown.

Women's employment outside the home was determined by their marital status and by the Irish (and American) ideology about marriage and motherhood. Beliefs about the significance of marriage and motherhood contrasted with the economic independence and public lives of single Irish women who were expected to work for wages.[23] Virtually no married Irish woman was listed in the 1900 census as having gainful employment. Irish women followed and indeed exceeded the American woman's pattern of (apparently) abandoning paid employment at marriage.[24] This was partly because of the large number of Irish children. However, married women made important economic contributions to their families as well as engaging in more informal sorts of paid labor.

Reality often clashed with prescriptive ideals. Since many husbands did not make enough money to support their families, or died or abandoned their wives, children's income became important in supporting the family. Whenever supplementing the family income became necessary, the Irish demonstrated a clear preference for sending children to work, rather than married women. Sometimes widows lived with their married children; more often a household consisted of a woman and one or more single adult children who were in the work force. A woman whose children were too young to work or who did not have children to support her had to find employment. Mary Milan, for example, a thirty-seven-year-old widow, worked as a hotel scrubwoman to support herself and her five children—aged thirteen, twelve, ten, eight, and six years. Bessie Maynard, at seventy, supported herself as a rag picker.[25]

In religion and popular culture, including such sentimental turn-of-the-century songs as "Mother Machree," respect for motherhood was an important component of Irish and Irish-American culture.[26] In spite of the public images celebrating maternity, including the statues of Mary attached to churches, Irish motherhood had a grim side. Even though they married later, Irish-born and first-generation Irish-American women had substantially more children than other women; the Irish also had a higher rate of infant mortality.[27]

Poorer, more densely populated neighborhoods such as Gorham's Corner suffered disproportionately from death by accident and disease; infant mortality and death in childbirth were common. For example, Margaret Hamel, a fifty-year-old widow, had given birth to twelve children, of whom only one was living in 1900.[28] Most women were more fortunate in terms of family survival, but few women of that time and place saw all their children outlive them.

The difficulties mothers faced were ongoing, and institutions developed to help them. Funded by the local Women's Christian Temperance Union, the Temporary Home for Women was established in 1882 to house unwed women during pregnancy and childbirth.[29] About the same time, a settlement called Fraternity House was established for immigrants and working-class people in the Gorham's Corner neighborhood. Created by Protestant, middle-class women, the Fraternity House nonetheless became an important part of the community.

The women who founded Fraternity House quickly learned how fragile were the lives of local residents. In 1913, the resident head worker, Elsie Nutt, recognized the reality that poverty, as well as maternity, was a major influence on the lives of Irish women. Nutt observed that a meat dish would be cost-efficient and tastier if it were prepared over heat for the better part of the day. However, since the bulk of the fuel was gathered by children on an as-needed basis, the slow-cooking method was impossible.[30]

In another Portland neighborhood at the foot of Munjoy Hill, Lillian O'Donohue, the unmarried daughter of an Irish immigrant, operated the Portland Milk Station beginning in 1911. The dispensary was established as one of the local answers to the serious national public health concerns regarding contagious diseases. O'Donohue would be the only "milk nurse" credited with dispensing "certified" (clean) milk to poor and often immigrant mothers on a weekly basis. By 1921 this progressive era public health movement expanded its services to include the Portland Baby Hygiene and Welfare Association in the neighborhood near Gorham's Corner.[31]

RELIGIOUS ORDERS AND CATHOLIC INSTITUTIONS

Another opportunity for Irish women was presented by the religious life. In Portland's Irish community, Catholic women's religious orders played important economic and social roles. They provided many educational and social services for the community, running schools, hospitals, and orphanages. They also offered individual women employment and security within the religious order, and, within a set framework, opportunities for professional careers.[32] The first order of nuns to come to Portland to teach in parochial schools was the Sisters of the Congregation of Notre Dame, a French-speaking order from Canada. In the 1870s they were succeeded by the Sisters of Mercy, an English-speaking, predominantly Irish order, who arrived in Portland at the invitation of the Bishop James Healy, the Maine Catholic diocesan prelate. By 1900 these nuns ran the parochial schools, an academy for female students, a home for aged women and two orphanages.[33] Their convent was in a diverse downtown neighborhood where the nuns taught at St. Elizabeth's Academy for Girls.

Since there would not be a Catholic women's college in Portland until 1915, the academy offered access to the highest possible level of education for Irish-Catholic women in the area. The lack of higher education in Portland was a clear limitation for women unable to afford going away to school. Business schools, such as Gray's Business College, were one option.[34] The closest public teacher's college was in Gorham —an area quite distant culturally from Gorham's Corner. St. Elizabeth's offered an education designed to perpetuate traditional values and to teach some of the skills necessary in a changing environment. Katharine Quinn graduated from St. Elizabeth's Academy, then went to New York for nursing training and to Boston for graduate work. She became Portland's first Public Health Supervisor of Nurses in 1918, later becoming the superintendent of the expanded staff of public health nurses. Like other Irish women with good jobs, she remained single.[35]

The schools are an example of Irish women creating institutions that helped Irish and other Catholic women succeed. Winifred Kavanagh, single and Irish-Catholic, from an upper-class family, contributed the money and land to open the first Catholic orphanage in Maine in North Whitefield. Not long after making this generous gift, she gave $25,000 to build the Kavanagh School for Girls, kindergarten to grade nine. It opened in 1879 with forty-five pupils and included a teaching staff of eight Sisters of Mercy.[36]

Another institution staffed by the Sisters of Mercy would play a double role for Irish women. St. Elizabeth's Orphan Asylum provided shelter for orphans of Catholic families. It also took in children of single mothers who needed assistance. While the grim economic reality of working-class life is reflected in the history of St. Elizabeth's, which took in children whose mothers could not afford to keep them, its history also shows how Irish women used institutions that helped them survive hard times. In 1900 the director was Sister Mary Margaret, forty years old, born in Canada of Irish parents, who had come to the United States in 1862. Seventy-three children, fifty-eight female and fifteen male, were listed as "inmates." Of these, 40 percent were Irish—that is, they had mothers who had been born in Ireland. The girls ranged in age from one to eighteen years. In many cases there were two children from the same family; in one case five, ranging from five years of age to nineteen, including one boy.[37] Later, more in keeping with the Irish Catholic ideology of gender segregation, a separate orphan asylum, St. Louis's Home and School, was created for boys.[38]

Irish Catholics believed they needed their own schools and orphanages. In 1900, only a small number of the children at the non-Catholic Female Orphan Asylum had Irish parents. None of its workers was Irish even though it was in an Irish neighborhood.[39] Whether the community distrusted it or faced discrimination, they preferred to create their own support institutions. St. Elizabeth's filled this need.

INCREASED OPPORTUNITY AND ITS LIMITS AFTER 1920

Women's lives continued to change in the 1920s as national and international events shaped Portland's economic development and the nature of the neighborhoods. One important factor was changes in immigration. In 1920 the foreign-born were about 20 percent of Portland's total population of slightly over seventy thousand. While Irish people continued to immigrate and settle in Portland, they accounted for a smaller percentage of immigrants than they had in the past. As was true elsewhere, between 1900 and World War I new immigrants arrived—Greeks, Italians, Russians, eastern European Jews, and Armenians. Many settled in neighborhoods close to the Irish.[40] Despite the physical proximity, one major difference between the Irish and the newer groups was that while single Irish women continued to comprise a large proportion of Irish immigration, Italian and Armenian immigrants were mostly single men, and Jewish immigrants largely came as families.[41] Although some Irish were moving out of their original neighborhoods, Gorham's Corner remained overwhelmingly Irish, and Gaelic continued to be heard on the street.[42]

Irish women continued to be disproportionately unmarried and active in the labor force. Nationally, in 1920 about a quarter of all women were employed outside the home; in Portland a third of the Irish women were so employed. Concentrated at the lower end of the economic scale, they had begun to expand into some better-paying occupations. Although many women, especially recent immigrants, continued to find work as domestics, some second-generation Irish women began to move into white-collar jobs and professional occupations, particularly nursing and teaching. This, however, tended to be less true of women in the Gorham's Corner neighborhood than in other areas.[43]

Irish women's occupations had become more diverse since 1900. Three women in Ward Four were telephone operators, two were nurses, and two were teachers. The small number of professionals may reflect two issues: women moved out of the area when they made more money, and Irish women in this ward were less likely to have professional opportunities than Irish women (and others) living in other parts of the city.[44]

Domestic service remained important, although it was changing in response to increasing options for women and their desire for independence. Many servants continued to live in private residences, but there was an increasing tendency toward day work. This may be reflected in the larger number of women living at home listed in the census as housekeepers. In another change since 1900, women who did domestic work in hotels no longer lived at their workplace. Some lived at home and commuted; others lived in boarding houses near the hotels. This may have been more expensive, but offered the women much more autonomy.[45]

There was more opportunity outside of Gorham's Corner. Despite the few telephone workers in Ward Four, Irish women comprised an increasing percentage of workers for the phone company. Many of them, like Cora Smith, president of the International Brotherhood of Electrical Workers Local, which represented telephone operators, were leaders of the Union during their successful strike in 1919. Along with workers throughout New England, they won a pay increase setting a minimum weekly wage at $10 a week, with the possibility of $19 a week after seven years.[46] Unions made inroads into other areas employing large numbers of women. Hotel and Restaurant Employees Local Union No. 308 had some success in Portland in the early 1920s.[47]

Teaching continued to employ Irish women, particularly those of the second and third generations. As with other jobs, teaching sometimes was a family occupation—sisters, or mothers and daughters followed the same career. Elizabeth (Lizzie) and Katie Walsh were among the first Irish-Catholic teachers in the public schools. They were the children of Mary and Thomas, a laborer—both from Ireland. Katie taught for a short period of time in the late 1870s and 1880s. Lizzie graduated from Portland High School and began teaching in 1878. She received her training at the Portland Teacher Training School and was assigned permanently to Staples School, Gorham's Corner, where she worked for fifty-seven years. She eventually became principal of the Staples school district and owned a home nearby.[48]

As the training requirements for teaching increased, the normal schools became the avenue to work in the public schools. The closest state normal school was in Gorham, twenty miles away. Despite the physical and cultural distance, after 1900 an increasing number of young Irish women from Portland went there for two- or three-year programs.[49] Students enjoyed free tuition and books and only had to pay for room and board. However, although nominally secular, Gorham Normal School was run as a Protestant institution. Chapel was required, and while the students could choose what church to attend on Sunday, there were only Protestant churches in town.[50] Parts of the graduation ceremonies were held in the nearby Methodist and Congregational churches. For Irish women looking for economic mobility, this amounted to enforced assimilation.[51]

In response, the Catholic Church set up its own teacher training program to prepare students for the examination to receive a state teaching certificate. Once again the Sisters of Mercy were in charge. St Joseph's Academy in Portland began teacher training and in 1915 received a charter from the state to found a college for women.[52]

While the Catholic schools for girls certainly offered educational opportunity, they also embodied the contradictions of the Irish Catholic view of women—valuing the economic role of single women, but defining women's major role as motherhood and the family. At a graduation ceremony at St. Joseph's, a student, Dorothy Day, spoke about "A Women's Sphere in Life." She noted that women should look first to their domestic roles, seeking to make the home atmosphere happy and pleasant. At the same time, she won a Gold Medal for Latin. Bishop Walsh, in a 1915 graduation address at St. Joseph's, expressed the church's attitude toward women and coeducation. He warned that "any Catholic who sends her daughter to an institution where there is coeducation, is responsible for the very worst possibilities that can be imagined."[53]

Just as the Catholic students in the normal schools encountered a dominant Protestant culture and hegemony, potential teachers in the public schools were subject to the "Americanization" movement after World War I. As part of an attack on Catholics, Jews, and immigrants, Eugene Farnsworth, the Grand Kleagle of the Portland Ku Klux Klan, fulminated against the presence of Catholics as teachers and members of the school board. He declared, "The schools need to have no more Catholic teachers until they become Americans."[54] An alliance of the Klan with the Yankee elite in 1923 led to the complete restructuring of the district election of the school board, as well as the city council. The creation of an at-large system of election, as opposed to electing school board and city council members from specific districts, served to eliminate representation of minority groups. The result was that in the next, at-large, election, no Catholic or Jew was elected to the school board.

As in education, Irish Catholics in Portland created hospitals to serve their community. While some of this may have been their own choice, reflecting Irish traditions and institutions, it was also clearly a response to anti-Irish discrimination in existing medical institutions. In the early 1900s, two major hospitals and nursing training institutions in Portland were Maine General Hospital and the Maine Eye and Ear Infirmary. At Maine General Hospital only one nurse had been born in Ireland (of Danish and English parents); two had Irish parents. None of the physicians was Irish or female. On the other hand, the hospital did employ Irish women to work as live-in maids, cooks, and laundresses.[55] The situation was similar at the Maine Eye and Ear Infirmary. Of twenty-two nurses, none was Irish. None of the three students listed was Irish. Of other employees, one of the four "ward maids," one of the three scrub women, and both laundresses were Irish.[56]

In 1918 the Sisters of Mercy opened the Queen's Hospital, which initially only served women. Its mission was to serve the medical needs of Catholics and provide employment for Catholic nurses and other health care workers (including physicians). In 1920 the hospital established a training school for nurses. The superintendent of nurses was Sister Mary Constance McCarron. Born in Canada to a Canadian mother and an Irish father, she was a graduate of Catholic University in Washington, D.C. In 1923 she instituted a three-year diploma nursing program at Queen's Hospital. Two other nuns on the hospital staff in 1920 were also of Irish parentage, and Sister Mary Barbara Foley served as head cook from 1925–1937.[57]

Queen's Hospital also hired nurses from outside the order. Josephine McLaughlin, born in Maine of Irish descent, was fifty-two years old and single when, in 1925, she moved into the nurses' residence next to the hospital.[58] Other nurses continued to live with their families. In 1920 the O'Neil family, for example, lived in a home owned by Mary O'Neil, a widow and the head of household. She had no listed occupation, but the household included her daughters, Margaret and Mary, both nurses; another daughter, Helen, an elementary school teacher; and yet another daughter and her husband and four children.[59]

Family collaboration allowed some women to go into business. The Sheehan sisters—Agnes, Alice, and Lauretta—ran the Misses Sheehan Millinery on Congress Street in the downtown department store district. In 1925 they were successful enough that Alice paid almost $240 in taxes and Lauretta $166.[60] Mollie Flaherty and Katherine Mitchell had a business in stitching and plaiting. Mollie Flaherty's mother did day work as a housekeeper after her father died. Mary and Nellie Clarity operated a successful corset shop near the major department stores.[61] The Clarity sisters and Sarah Blair, who ran a millinery business, belonged to the Business and Professional Women's Club in Portland.[62]

These women and others like them combined distinctive family patterns—remaining single, delaying marriage, living with siblings—with new economic opportunities for women in the 1920s. Their lives and work were shaped by the interplay of their household structure, physical environment, cultural background, and cultural changes. Their lives also were shaped by economic and social developments in Portland and the United States.

The written record, especially the census data, leaves many questions unanswered. Did married Irish and Irish-American women really not participate in paid labor? What was the relative impact of ideology versus economic necessity? Why did Irish women work in particular jobs? How long did these patterns persist? How did they think about their lives? Looking at some individual examples drawn from an oral history project sheds some light on these questions.

THE INDIVIDUAL STORY

Irish culture and Catholic ideology about sexuality and motherhood certainly shaped the roles of Irish women in Portland. However, the crises of the Great Depression and World War II show how immediate needs and women's response to them overcame theoretical dictates. Both events highlighted the contradictory views implicit in the Irish Catholic definition of women's roles. When male breadwinners could not or would not support their families, it was impossible to sustain the idea that work outside the home was good for single women but bad for married women. Like other women, Irish women in Portland in the 1930s and 1940s abandoned the ideal of a married woman's place being in the home when faced with the need to support themselves and their families.

An oral history project about women in Portland's West End, including Gorham's Corner, focused on the ways in which women and their families struggled in the 1930s and their strategies for survival.[63] These reflected their own work, community resources, and a willingness to go beyond prescriptions about married women's roles. Single, married, divorced, or widowed women worked packing fish, doing laundry, scrubbing floors, clerking in department stores, cleaning in hotels, waitressing, teaching, and sometimes several of these occupations at once.

Helen York, like many of the women in the area, worked at the Portland Fish Factory, not far from Gorham's Corner. Seasonal work, canning was often not considered full-time employment by census-takers, and therefore was not recorded for married women, but for many people it meant survival. When the fishing vessel coming into the docks blew its horn, women would gather their children and go down to the factory and pack sardines. "The fish smelled but the money didn't," York noted.[64]

Other Irish women continued in domestic work. Margaret Coyne, for example, immigrated from Galway in 1929 and moved into the Gorham's Corner area. After working as a housekeeper for private families, she became a housemother at the student residences for the Mercy School of Nursing.[65]

Whatever the census may have indicated, many, if not most married women worked outside the home all through the Depression. For some of them, World War II brought better-paying jobs.

Mary McDermott Walsh immigrated to Portland in 1923, following two sisters who were working as domestics. She married Philip Foley, whose parents were from Ireland. When he died, leaving her with two children, she went back into domestic work as a cook for private families and in seasonal restaurants in resort areas in Maine. The war, however, brought her, like other women, new employment and better pay. She became a welder at the New England Shipbuilding Company in South Portland.[66]

In the recollections of those who looked back on a difficult period, mothers played a key role. Julia Foley, for example, recalled at length the doll her mother had painstakingly made for her, one of the few toys she had as a child.[67]

The story of Barbara Carey Joyce illustrates changing aspects in the lives of Irish women in that period. It is also a good example of the ways individuals and families dealt with social and personal crises. A second generation Irish American, Joyce was born in Massachusetts but raised in Gorham's Corner in the 1930s. Married at sixteen, she had seven children by the time she was twenty-five, and eventually had eleven. In an interview she revealed that her first husband, like her stepfather, was abusive. Once, when she was in labor, he made her walk to Mercy Hospital through a snowstorm. Barbara Joyce noted that she left her husband three times, but, she added, "I was a very good Catholic then," and in accordance with the ideology of married women's role, she went back to "do her duty." Finally, however, she left for good, divorced him and eventually remarried.

In the meantime she needed to raise her children. She received support from her mother ("who was always there" for her), her brother, and friends. She worked as a waitress or at the sardine factory. Two institutions—one secular and one Catholic—provided important assistance: the Fraternity House, Portland's settlement house; and St. Elizabeth's Orphan Asylum. When she was growing up and after she was married, she participated in the activities at the Fraternity House. The director was Hazel Tapley and the programs included variety shows, children's clubs, a toy lending library, classes, and mother's clubs. Unlike some other institutions where the middle class Yankee women were patronizing and hostile to immigrant culture, at the Fraternity House there was a real sense of community, and Tapley, like her predecessor, Elsie Nutt, was an important part of the community.

St. Elizabeth's played a role for Barbara Joyce and her family similar to that which it had played for others since its founding. Faced with economic difficulty, she placed some of her daughters at St. Elizabeth's and the boys at St. Louis.

Although she knew it had been necessary, years later she was reluctant to discuss it.[68] One daughter, Judy Smith, remembers being there for six years, then finally being reunited with her mother and her new family. Despite experiencing some loneliness there, she has positive memories of St. Elizabeth's and of the nuns who ran it, and especially of the summers on Little Diamond Island. She also understood her mother's need to place her at St. Elizabeth's. Barbara Joyce's daughters were not alone in finding temporary refuge there. Smith describes three groups at St. Elizabeth's: children from homes "broken" by abandonment or divorce, "real" orphans who had lost both parents, and children of affluent parents who used St. Elizabeth's as a day school.[69]

Later, drawing on her own experiences with poverty and domestic violence, Barbara Joyce became a community activist, working with neighborhood groups on the West End and with Planned Parenthood. In her interview, she noted that she, like many of her friends, had moved out of the Gorham's Corner neighborhood. Still, they came back, some to the People's Building,[70] some to St. Dominic's, the religious center of the community. In 1999 St. Dominic's was closed by the diocese because of a declining congregation. The Fraternity House is now lawyer's offices and Staples School apartments. The cannery is a microbrewery and some neighborhood streets are dominated by parking lots. Yet the history of Gorham's Corner and of the Irish women who lived there persists. Some of it has been recounted in a play based on oral histories: *All My Life* by Nance Parker.[71] Some is kept alive in family stories and interviews. Some was salvaged in the struggle by many in Portland's Irish community to save St. Dominic's.

The impact of Irish culture on Portland's Irish women declined over the years as economic and social changes occurred. World War II was a pivotal moment in the history of Gorham's Corner, as economic and social changes led many of the residents to move elsewhere. However, ideas about women's role as mothers, and the value placed on work for single women, continued to shape the lives of women and their community. The religious and social institutions that Irish women created and those like the Fraternity House that they adopted helped them play an active role in shaping their lives and the community in which they lived. One image of the sinking of the *Bohemia* is of a young Irish woman who strapped her baby to her back and successfully swam to shore. It is a romantic and perhaps sentimental image, but, in the end, an apt one to represent the experiences of Irish women in overcoming disaster to find life in a new land.

1. William B. Jordan, *A History of Cape Elizabeth, Maine* (Portland, Maine: House of Falmouth, 1985), 246–49; "Serious Marine Disaster, Wreck of the Steamship Bohemian," *New York Times*, 24 February 1864, 5; 26 February 1864, 1. See also Coroner's Report, "Bohemia" files, Box 1, Maine Historical Society, Portland, Maine.

2. Abby Zimet, "Shipwrecked at Liberty's Doorstep," *Maine Sunday Telegram*, 4 November 1984. This mural is still in the post office. Tess Naclewicz, "Shipwrecked," http://www.cascobay.com/history/shipwrek/shipwrek.htm.

3. Michael Coleman Connolly, "The Irish Longshoremen of Portland, Maine, 1880–1923" (Ph.D. diss., Boston College, 1988), 106. The Irish comprised two-thirds of the 3,900 immigrants at that time, and 10% of the city's population.

4. Edward Elwell, *Boys of '35*, cited in *Portland City Guide* (Portland: Forest City Printing Company, 1940), 213–14.

5. Hasia Diner, *Erin's Daughters in America: Irish Immigrant Women in the Nineteenth Century* (Baltimore: Johns Hopkins University Press, 1984), 34.

6. United States Bureau of the Census, *Census of the United States*. Town of Portland, Maine. (Washington: Government Printing Office.) (Hereafter: *Manuscript Census*), 1900, Ward 4. The situation changed after 1900 when Ireland began improving education. Kenneth E. Nilson, "Thinking of Monday: The Irish Speakers of Portland, Maine," *Eire-Ireland* 25, 1 (1989): 6–19.

7. Eleven women listed in the 1900 census as servants were recent immigrants from Ireland (many within the year); six could not read or write and three of these did not speak English. Of these, two were recent arrivals, but one had been in the United States for fifteen years.

8. Connolly, "Longshoremen," 122; Mona Hearns, *Below Stairs: Domestic Service Remembered, 1880–1920* (Dublin: Dufour Editions, 1993), 104–5. The situation of women in Portland paralleled the experience of Irish women elsewhere in the United States. As late as 1900, 54 percent of Irish-born women (and 19 percent of second generation) were house servants, and another 6.5 percent were laundresses. In the South, African American women were the major group in domestic work; in New England, Irish women were the majority. For women in general (in nonagricultural jobs) the percentage was about 30 percent.

9. Of thirty-two listed, all except two were Irish. Those two were from Nova Scotia. *Sixth Annual Report of the Bureau of Industrial and Labor Statistics for the State of Maine* (Augusta, Maine: Burleigh & Flynt, 1893), 98–99. English-speaking Canadian women who came to Maine from the Maritimes were quite similar to the Irish in their choice of employment in domestic work.

10. *Sixth Annual Report,* 154.

11. *Second Annual Report of the Bureau of Industrial and Labor Statistics for the State of Maine* (Augusta, Maine: Burleigh & Flynt, 1889), 138. The statistics in these reports should be used cautiously, since the methodology was primitive and the returns erratic. However, the investigators did provide first-hand reports on some specific workplaces, including the Portland Star Match Factory.

12. See below for a discussion of the role of women religious.

13. City directories list all the teachers each year. *Directory of the City of Portland* (Portland, Maine: Dresser McLellan & Co., 1882–).

14. Robert Babcock, "The Rise and Fall of Portland's Waterfront, 1850–1920," *Maine Historical Society Quarterly* 12 (Fall 1982): 82–83.

15. The manuscript census of 1900 gives a collective picture of Irish women's position in Portland. It also allows us a glimpse of individual lives. There are some problems involved in using census data, especially with information relating to women. In his 1929 report on women in gainful occupations in the United States Joseph Hill notes discrepancies in reporting women's employment that may be based on the assumptions of the census-takers. Joseph A. Hill, *Women in Gainful Occupations, 1870–1920: Census Monographs IX* (Washington, D.C.: Government

Printing Office, 1929). Discussing reasons for the apparent slowdown between 1910 and 1920 in the increase in married women employed outside the home (or for wages), Hill notes the changes in census wording and instructions. He notes, for example, that in 1910 the instructions to the census-takers explicitly directed them to include occupations for women and children. The occupation, if any, followed by a child of any age or by a woman was just as important, for census purposes, as the occupation followed by a man. Therefore it must never be taken for granted, without inquiry, that a woman, or child, was listed as having no occupation. This instruction was omitted from the 1920 census instructions. According to Hill, this may not have made much difference since the statement, in his words, expressed a more or less obvious truth and the enumerator had to fill in an entry for all women anyway. His faith in the enumerators may be somewhat misplaced, however, for there is evidence that individual census-takers did not always follow instructions. An example of this in the enumeration in Portland adds to the difficulty in tracking women's immigration. In the 1900 census, one of the enumerators, Arthur Leach, ignored the instructions to include date of immigration for all immigrants and only included immigration dates for men. The instructions said: "The question of immigration . . . applies to all foreign-born persons, male and female, of whatever age." In the Fourth Ward, however, we only have the dates of immigration for Irish women in three of the four districts. To add to the problem, they were omitted from the sixty-fourth enumeration district of the 1900 census, the district with the largest number of Irish immigrants. This is a visible example of data affected by the census-taker's bias.

16. For two somewhat different views on the Irish in Portland at the turn of the century, see Connolly, "Longshoremen," 106–48, and Deborah Tracy Krichels, "Reaction and Reform: The Political Career of James Phinney Baxter" (MA thesis, University of Maine, Orono, 1986), 26–39.

17. *Portland City Guide*, 213–14.

18. *Manuscript Census*, 1900, Ward 4, Enumeration District 37.

19. *Manuscript Census*, 1900, Ward 4, Enumeration District 63. All eleven were single, ranging in age from eighteen to forty-two, with most in their twenties; all of them could speak English, but five could not read or write. All were born in Ireland except Alice Egan, thirty, whose parents were Irish.

20. *Manuscript Census*, 1900, Ward 4, Enumeration District 63. Her father, William, was a longshoreman, and Maria, her mother, had given birth to nine children, of whom four survived. In 1900 their household included three wage earners, William, Alice, and Clara; two younger children were in school.

21. A matron in a telephone company was a woman older than the opera-tors, who supervised the break room and dispensed advice about health and hygiene. Stephen H. Norwood, *Labor's Flaming Youth: Telephone Operators and Worker Militancy, 1878–1923* (Urbana: University of Illinois Press, 1990): 49–50.

22. *Portland Directory,* 1913–39.

23. Timothy J. Meagher, "Sweet Good Mothers and Young Women Out in the World: The Roles of Irish American Women in Late Nineteenth and Early Twentieth Century Worcester, Massachusetts," *U.S. Catholic Historian* 5, 4 (1986): 342. The "widows" as reported in the *Directory of Portland,* 1900–1920, were frequently running boarding houses to supple-ment their income enough to stay alive.

24. Diner, *Erin's Daughters,* 52–53.

25. This was a pattern for the Irish elsewhere too. See Greg A. Hoover, "Supplemental Family Income Sources: Ethnic Differences in Nineteenth-Century Industrial America," *Social Science History* 9, 3 (Summer 1985): 303. *Manuscript Census,* 1900, Ward 4, Enumeration District 37.

26. William H. A. Williams, *'Twas Only an Irishman's Dream: The Image of Ireland and the Irish in American Popular Song Lyrics, 1800–1920* (Chicago: University of Illinois Press, 1986), 45.

27. Diner, *Erin's Daughters,* 54; Meagher, "Sweet Good Mothers and Young Women Out in the World," 325–44; "Birth and Death Rate of Children," *Manuscript Census,* 1900, Ward 4.

28. *Manuscript Census,* 1900.

29. *Temporary Home for Women Annual Report, 1882* (Portland, Maine: The Home, 1882). The Temporary Home for Women was established by Lillian Ames Stevens, second president of the national Women's Christian Temperance Union. It was located in the Libby's Corner section of Portland on the outskirts of Portland's west side, in a large home on Powsland Street with adequate provisions for the unmarried pregnant young women and the babies born there.

30. *Annual Report of Resident and Head Worker Fraternity House,* 1912–1913, Maine Historical Society, Portland, Maine.

31. Annette Vance Dorey, "The Milk Connection: Portland's Infant Milk Station and Public Health Education," *Maine History* 38, 2 (Fall 1998), 129--33.

32. See Diner, *Erin's Daughters,* 130–38. On the role of women's religious orders in Maine, see Mary Raymond Higgins, R.S.M., *For Love of Mercy* (Portland, Maine: Sisters of Mercy, 1995).

33. Higgins, *For Love of Mercy*, 333.

34. *Directory of Portland*, 1915.

35. "Miss Quinn, 91, Public Health Pioneer Dies," *Portland (Maine) Evening Express*, 17 May 1967, 2. She lived with her widowed mother on Montgomery Street during the 1920s and 1930s, but moved to a very large home at 166 Eastern Promenade with her brother in 1936. However, she died in a nursing home in Massachusetts.

36. To commemorate Kavanagh's philanthropy, the girls' high school located on the property of the Immaculate Conception Church on Congress Street was named for her. Higgins, *For Love of Mercy*, 305. Also see Polly Welts Kaufman, *A Women's History Walking Trail in Portland, Maine* (Portland: Maine Humanities Council, 1997), 36.

37. Of the other eight nuns who worked at St. Elizabeth's, five were born in Ireland, two were born in the U.S. of Irish parents, and one was from French-speaking Canada. *Manuscript Census*, 1900, Ward 4, Enumeration District 65.

38. This was located at Dunstan Corner in Scarborough, Maine.

39. *Manuscript Census*, 1900, Ward 6, Enumeration District 69.

40. *Manuscript Census*, 1900.

41. *Manuscript Census*, 1920.

42. Josephine O'Hare, interview by Ann Munch, Portland, Maine, 29 March 1984, "Victoria Society Oral History Project," Maine Historical Society, Portland, Maine. O'Hare grew up on Munjoy Hill. When asked if she learned Gaelic, she responded that she did not hear Gaelic in her neighborhood, but "I heard it, you know, down around Center Street, that area."

43. *Manuscript Census*, 1920; for national figures, see Hill, *Women in Gainful Occupations*, 76.

44. *Manuscript Census*, 1920, Ward 4. The nuns who were teachers no longer lived in that district.

45. Diner, *Erin's Daughters in America*, 55; *Manuscript Census*, 1920, Ward 4.

46. *Portland Evening Express*, 15–16 April 1919.

47. *Directory of Portland*, 1923–1925.

48. "Veteran Teacher Dies Here at 81," *Portland Evening Express*, 18 August 1942; *Manuscript Census*, 1880, Ward 1; *Directory of Portland*, 1927, 1943.

49. Mary Ellen Sullivan, for example, was in the graduating class of 1915, along with Mary Elizabeth Curran, Catharine Anna Foley, and others of apparently Irish background. Whereas before 1900 graduation lists consist

almost entirely of Yankee names, the 1915 roster was about 10 percent Irish. *Graduation Exercises, Class of 1915, Western Normal School*, Gorham, Maine, pamphlet, University of Southern Maine Archives, Portland, Maine, cited in the *Alumni Directory*, Gorham State College of the University of Maine (1969). For a discussion of Irish teachers in Boston, see Polly Welts Kaufman, "Julia Harrington Duff and the Political Awakening of Irish-American Women in Boston, 1888–1905," in *Women of the Common-wealth: Work, Family and Social Change in Nineteenth-Century Massachusetts*, ed. Susan L. Porter (Amherst: University of Massachusetts Press, 1996).

50. Father Joseph Landry, telephone interview by Patricia Finn, Gorham, Maine, 11 October 1997. According to Father Landry, St. Ann's Mission was established in 1941 in Gorham close to the Normal School campus for the benefit of Catholic students.

51. These practices continued into the 1950s. See graduation programs, Western Normal School (with various name changes), University of Southern Maine Archives, Portland, Maine.

52. S.L.J., "St. Joseph's Academy," *Maine Catholic Historical Magazine* 4 (April 1914): 5–6; William Leo Lucey, *The Catholic Church in Maine* (Francestown, N.H.: M. Jones Co., 1957), 336.

53. *Maine Catholic Historical Magazine* 5, 1 (1915); reprint of talk in *Daily Eastern Argus*, 21 June 1915.

54. *Portland Press Herald*, 12 August 1923.

55. *Manuscript Census*, 1920, Ward 7, Enumeration District 50. Unlike the hotels, the hospitals continued to board their staff and employees.

56. *Manuscript Census*, 1920, Ward 7, Enumeration District 50.

57. Patricia Finn, "The Establishment of the Queen's Hospital," manuscript, Portland, Maine, 14 July 1996; Higgins, *For Love of Mercy; Manuscript Census*, 1920, Ward 4, Enumeration District 45.

58. *Manuscript Census*, 1920, Ward 7; *Directory of Portland*, 1915, 1925.

59. *Manuscript Census*, 1920, Ward 7, Enumeration District 7.

60. Agnes apparently paid less than $100 in taxes. They were able to afford a summer home on Long Island. *Manuscript Census*, 1920, Ward 4, Enumeration District 37; *Directory of Portland*, 1925.

61. *Manuscript Census*, 1920, Ward 7; *Manuscript Census*, 1920, Ward 4, Enumeration District 37; *Directory of Portland*, 1923, 1925.

62. See Candace Kanes' study of the Business and Professional Women's Club in Portland in this volume.

63. Portland West End Working Class Women's History Project, 1988, University of Southern Maine.

64. Helen York, tape recording, Portland West End Working Class Women's History Project.

65. "Margaret A. Coyne, housemother at nursing school," *Portland Press Herald*, 25 October 1995.

66. "Nora McDermott Walsh, enjoyed bridge, scrabble; was Celtics fan," *Portland Press Herald*, 23 June 1996.

67. Julia Foley, tape recording, Portland West End Working Class Women's History Project.

68. Barbara Carey Joyce, tape recording, Portland West End Working Class Women's History Project; "The Lost Heart of the Maine Irish," *Maine Sunday Telegram*, 16 March 1986.

69. Judy Smith, interview by Eileen Eagan, Portland, Maine, May 1997.

70. Kaufman, *A Women's History Walking Trail*, 39. The People's Building at 155 Brackett Street began as a primary school in 1852, then was occupied for many years by various manufacturing firms. When it faced demolition in the early 1960s, community advocates kept it open and restored it as a community center housing several groups, including Portland West Neighborhood Planning Council.

71. Nance Parker, "All My Life," performed at Reiche School, Portland, Maine, 1991. Some of the players were the children and grandchildren of the women who participated n the Portland West End Working Class Women's History Project. Jane Lamb, "Puppets Tell West End's Vibrant History," *Portland Press Herald*, 10 May 1991.

Maine resonated with meaning for temporary visitors as well as immigrants and those with longer connections to the state. Beginning in the late nineteenth century, Maine self-consciously began to market itself as a site for tourism. Railroads, resorts, and manufacturers of wilderness gear worked together to encourage city dwellers to take advantage of the opportunities for recreation and relaxation offered by the Maine experience. In many respects, this tourism was a highly gendered affair, designed to lure men into adventures that would counter the feminized refinement of urban life. The woods were masculine and would reinvigorate and energize the men who pushed their physical limits and conquered the wilderness. Yet Maine tourism could also be domestic, as families were encouraged to get away from urban crowding and contagion for the sake of healthy children. This tourism was genteel and refined, offering wholesome pleasures centered around family activities.

Whether aimed at offering men a chance for masculine adventure or families a domestic retreat, Maine's tourist industry did little to challenge traditional notions of appropriate behavior for men and women. Instead, it sought to reinforce middle class ideals that were increasingly being threatened by the pressures of city life;

tourism offered the urban middle class a way to return to its figurative roots, where the roles of men and women seemingly remained unchanged. A vacation in the wilderness, or in one of the increasingly comfortable tourist destinations that claimed to be rustic, offered weary urban-dwellers a respite from the uncertainties created by class tensions, competitive capitalism, and challenges to gender conventions.

At the same time, the purveyors of tourism hoped to sell the Maine experience as a commodity to the largest number of people. Nan Cumming offers yet another trope of tourism at the turn of the century, this one aimed at women without being centered around familial roles. This was a view of wilderness activity neither built on the masculine imagery of conquering nature nor the sentimental domestic purity of rural life, but rather built around expanding ideas of women's roles. The marketing of Maine's tourist activities became part of an ongoing debate about the meaning of the wilderness as well as women's roles.

FOLLOWING DIANA: THE NEW WOMAN IN THE MAINE WOODS

Nan Cumming

Diana, savage Roman Goddess of the hunt, was a beloved figure in nineteenth-century art and literature. As Victorian artists romanticized the goddess, they made her a more palatable and less intimidating female figure, taming her original uncivilized, wild, and violent nature in highly idealized portrayals. By 1900, many American women suffered the same fate—their true human natures were stifled by social critics who tried to confine upper- and middle-class women in rigid social roles. Throughout much of the nineteenth century, women had been cast as the managers of the domestic realm, while their husbands braved the public sphere and did business in town. This ideal for upper- and middle-class women was known as "True Womanhood," a moral femininity whose care of family, virtue, and respectability were of foremost importance. By the 1880s, however, the reality of middle-class women's lives began to tear the ideal apart in a very public way. Women who sought change and equality with men were labeled "New Women" by the press. Many women began to work for wages outside the home, while others rallied for voting rights, education for women, temperance, clothing reform, and a variety of programs aimed at curing the social ills of their communities.

Of all their causes, upper- and middle-class women worried most about the problems rapid growth had brought their cities. Young men and women from the country and immigrants from around the world poured into urban areas looking for jobs in the United States' new factories. These populations crowded the cities, pressuring municipal services and shifting the demographics of many towns from primarily Anglo-Saxon Protestant to Irish or southern European. Upper- and middle-class residents worried about the overcrowding, pollution, noise, and disease which the newcomers seemed to bring with them. Like other reformers of the time, New Women considered nature a potent antidote for the problems of urban civilization. Following Diana's lead, they sought sublimity and experience outside the artificial boundaries of their lives. So, men and women with sufficient leisure time, along with the means to travel, escaped from the pressures of turn-of-the-century city life by vacationing in the wilderness for at least a few weeks a year. The Adirondacks of New York State, the Canadian Rockies, Yellowstone, the Upper Peninsula of Michigan, and other rustic, untamed places became popular destinations for a cadre of "Back-to-Nature" tourists.

Maine soon became a favorite destination among travelers from the eastern United States. Upper-class men began journeying to Maine for outdoor recreation in the middle of the nineteenth century, establishing a tradition that quickly came to include women. Between 1880 and 1910 most of these hunting, fishing, and camping enthusiasts known as "sports" traveled via a series of trains that took them from their own downtowns through Portland and into northern Maine. They spread the word about the great wilderness of the "Pine Tree State" and Maine's residents encouraged their perception, acknowledging tourism's boost to the state's economy. Thus, Maine's reputation as a healthy, wild, wooded area was established at this time.

Throughout the second half of the nineteenth century, Maine people prepared for the arrival of these city-weary tourists by converting logging camps into sporting camps and offering their services as hunting and fishing guides. Although these camps may have been designed, in part, to help jaded urban men relearn unadulterated "masculine" traits, such as strength, toughness, and daring, the camps were not exclusively male enclaves. Women shared many of the same reasons for seeking a place in nature. After decades of supposed inactivity, women began taking doctors' advice to exercise in the fresh air. In addition to their anti-urban sentiments, many upper- and middle-class women also journeyed to the woods to seek physical and spiritual wellness. Turn-of-the-century magazines, books, and newspapers encouraged women to venture into the wilderness.

An important columnist and role model was "Fly Rod" Crosby. Cornelia Crosby, known as "Fly Rod" to her fans across the United States, was Maine's most famous "sport" of either sex (figure 1). Born in Phillips, Maine, Crosby

Figure 1. "In the Shadow of Mt. Kineo," "Fly Rod" Crosby, postcard (ca. 1906). Author's collection.

worked as a bank teller in Farmington before her doctor induced her to try outdoor recreation in order to help cure her consumption. Soon, Crosby became an experienced hunter and fisher in the Rangeley area, and, because she was one of the first sports to employ a bamboo fly-fishing rod, she wrote about her experiences using "Fly Rod" as her pen name. "Fly Rod's Notebook" was originally published in the *Phillips Phonograph* but was later picked up by state and national newspapers. In 1895, she convinced the Maine Central Railroad to sponsor an exhibit on the sporting regions of the state at the first Sportsman's Show in New York City. Right in the middle of Madison Square Garden she erected a log cabin, complete with Maine guides and stuffed game. She was the hit of the show. Tourism to the Maine woods increased so dramatically the following year that the railroad hired her in its publicity department. From that office she coined the phrase "Maine: The Nation's Playground" and planned her exhibit for the 1896 show, an even more impressive success which earned worldwide attention for Crosby and the state of Maine.

Until that time, Maine guides had been completely unregulated. When the state's Commissioners of Fisheries and Game began lobbying the state legislature for professional registration, Crosby was one of the most vocal advocates. After the law passed in 1897, she became Maine's first licensed guide. Throughout her career, "Fly Rod" promoted hunting and fishing in Maine and pioneered a new role for women by encouraging their participation in outdoor activities traditionally reserved for men. She inspired other women; within the next few years, the state also registered Mrs. Mabel Harlow and daughter Ethel Harlow as sporting guides.[1]

G. Smith Stanton described women's participation in sports in his 1905 travelogue, *Where the Sportsman Loves to Linger*: "The ladies seem inclined to follow the men to the woods, as they have on bicycle and golf grounds."[2] His publication was not the first to encourage women to visit Maine. Since 1895 travel magazines actively marketed—and sold—the Maine woods to women across the country.

Two Maine publications helped create the sporting industry that targeted New Women. Taking advantage of women's increased activity and quest for leisure outside the home, these magazines encouraged women to adopt field sports—hunting, fishing, hiking, and camping—as part of their new regimen of physical activity. *Maine Outings*, published in Portland from 1895 to 1896, tied bicycle-riding and women's collegiate athletics directly to field sports in its editorials about female athleticism. Yearly volumes of the Bangor and Aroostook Railway's *In the Maine Woods*, published between 1900 and 1910, also encouraged female tourists to hunt and fish, but related the experience less to general athletics.

Maine Outings articulated its plan to create a new leisure industry in its first issue. The editors intended "to not only foster and advance those interests . . . but to *create* the interest where it is not." They also hoped to "number many of the fair sex among our contributors, for we do not see why they should not be interested, and they can not fail to see that *Maine Outings* is a useful and practical friend."[3]

Followers of *Maine Outings* were interested. Within the magazine's first year the editors introduced a section written by women specifically for its female readers. Entitled "Fin de Siecle Diana," this section included sporting advice, reports from the field, and fiction based on sports. Although the magazine was illustrated with both photographs and simple line drawings, the masthead for "Fin de Siecle Diana" revealed the philosophy of the magazine most succinctly. In the center frolics Diana; with bears and rabbits dancing around her, she raises her bow and arrow in the air. To either side of her image are contemporary sportswomen: a cyclist in bloomers riding a solitary road, a "gunner" in a hunting suit taking aim

Figure 2. Masthead for "Fin de Siecle Diana."

at a bird, a fisherwoman in short skirt angling on the bank of a river, and a sailor in a fashionable sailor suit at the wheel of a yacht (figure 2). These new Dianas participated in a variety of sports, wore the latest sporting fashions and, according to the illustrations, pursued these activities independently. Not all articles of interest to women were relegated to this section; this space was simply for those columns directly aimed at them, such as the continuous and heated debate over the appropriate apparel for cycling and other sports. In every issue writers and readers discussed bloomers, the loosely cut pants advocated for women since the 1850s.

Although *In the Maine Woods* (titled *In Pine Tree Jungles* in 1902 and *Haunts of the Hunted* in 1903) also promoted opportunities for women in field sports, the magazine was published as a yearly advertisement for the Bangor and Aroostook Railroad Company, and its objective was to promote rail travel in Maine. As an advertising tool of the railroad, the magazine marketed outdoor recreation to women as potential customers, without becoming overtly political or focusing more than one article each year on specifically female experience. All other articles were directed at the male audience, mentioning women's participation only marginally. The magazine was heavily illustrated with photographs of both men and women, however, clearly presenting the Railroad's own image of female "sports."

In a time of controversy over changing roles for women, both publications sought to affirm the respectability of women engaging in field sports. They attempted to sell their product to the "New" active woman without alienating the "True" woman and her values. The magazines encouraged women's participation by appealing to the benefits they would garner: improvements to their health and physical strength, spiritual enrichment in discovering nature, and the freedom of wearing comfortable athletic clothing.

The magazines sold the outdoor experience well. *In the Maine Woods* noted its own success: "A lady may make any of these canoe trips. . . . The number of ladies taking these trips is increasing each year."[4] Although the exact number of women who vacationed in the woods is difficult to determine, guest registers of Rangeley's Pleasant Island Camps give an impression of the composition of guests at one sporting camp in 1884. Visitors arrived from Boston, Providence, Philadelphia, and Brooklyn, and approximately one in ten was female. Most often, women traveled with their husbands, but the names of a few single women also showed up in the register that year.[5] Guest registers from nearby Pickford's Camps show that female guests made up almost two-thirds of the visitors from 1900 through 1902. Female tourism had probably increased, although this camp may have been particularly welcoming to female guests. Records show groups of unmarried women registering together and even mothers arriving with their daughters. Like other "back-to-nature" tourists, they traveled from urban areas like New Haven, Worcester, and Buffalo.[6]

The editors of *Maine Outings* and *In the Maine Woods* placed very few restrictions upon women's activities once they arrived in Maine. Both magazines marketed Maine tourism and, therefore, emphasized the options open to women in the woods. Women were encouraged to try all the activities the outdoors offered, including hunting, fishing, canoeing, and simply enjoying nature. While *In the Maine Woods* showed respect for its female readers and passengers regardless of their preferred level of activity, *Maine Outings* was somewhat more critical. As a magazine aimed at active women, it often poked fun at those who lazed around camp working on their embroidery.

The editor's scorn is clear in a fictional piece entitled "A Romance of the Maine Woods," which contrasts young Alice Reid, a thoroughly "New" woman, with Mrs. Dent, an older relative whose family Alice joined on a hunting excursion. While Alice was described as "healthy" and "elastic," Mrs. Dent felt it a privilege to continue to wear her corsets in the woods and attended the trip only as a "wifely duty." Likewise, as Alice hiked, fished, and paddled, Mrs. Dent embroidered and read romantic novels in her tent. Mrs. Dent's ladylike behavior was censured by the author. One of the male hunters in the party even claimed she had no soul.[7] In this fictional juxtaposition between new and old notions of femininity, the "New Woman" triumphed over the "True Woman."[8]

Most women reported their experiences of hunting in Maine with relatively few comments reflecting the timidity or squeamishness that might have been expected from urban women unused to killing; indeed, learning to hunt and kill was an important part of their back-to-nature experience. Several articles in *In the Maine Woods* recognized urban women's lack of experience with firearms by describing their progress in learning to handle a gun. The satisfaction women gained from shooting is evident. A pair of photographs captioned "There He Is" and "Steady Now" show Ella S. Williams learning to shoot. The hearty woman from Worcester, Massachusetts, stood a head taller than the guide who directed her aim and fire. She explained the pleasure she derived from a hunting trip: "I am sure that I am as anxious as my husband for the day starting to arrive."[9] Another correspondent, intent on bagging a moose, recorded his encounter with a man who was bleeding one of the largest bull moose he had ever seen. Upon congratulating the hunter, he was directed to the lady perched on a nearby log. "She's the one to talk to! My wife did the shooting!" After recovering from his initial shock, the writer listened to Mrs. Worster's story about the moose:

> "He was partly hidden behind a fallen tree. . . . My husband told me to take careful aim and shoot. I did so and down he went with a crash. But he wasn't dead and my husband told me to go up close and finish him with a bullet through the neck. Yes, that's where I was a little timid, but I crept up and shot him all right and that finished him. Isn't he a big fellow?"[10]

Mrs. Worster proved her worth that day in the woods. The author (or his editor) begrudgingly titled that episode "Beaten By the Fair Sex," yet he praised her accomplishment.

> It is a wholesome sign of the times that women are more and more becoming the companions of their fathers, husbands, and brothers in the open, be it hunting, fishing or canoeing. The fragile young lady of our great-grandmother's day, who was timid and sweet and unutterably inane, and who fainted on every occasion, is fortunately a feature of the early period only. Our modern girls are of different calibre and metal [sic].[11]

After learning to shoot and overcoming her timidity, Mrs. Worster vanquished a large and powerful animal, a moose that this author had been respectfully calling "His Lordship."

Traditionally, men claimed power through bloody, violent victory over a foe. Through hunting, Mrs. Worster and other women showed themselves as victors, demonstrating their own power. In doing so, they not only gained the respect of men, but also helped shape perceptions about their role and position in society. After admitting his surprise at meeting Mrs. Worster, the author's view of women changed; he made the older ideal of womanhood seem ridiculous compared with the stronger, braver, more powerful kind of woman he had just met.

In the Maine Woods recognized the social progress women gained by their actions in Maine. A photograph of a confident hunter gazing down at her freshly killed buck was captioned, "Women's Nerves are Steady Nowadays." By demonstrating that she had the composure needed to shoot and kill the animal, she triumphed not only over the deer, but also over traditional Victorian notions of feminine indecisiveness and excitability. In 1906, *In the Maine Woods* stated that "The 'Gentler Sex' can Hunt, Too" (figure 3). The woman in the accompanying photograph leans against a tree trunk dressed in men's clothing for the picture, comfortable with nature, a rifle in her hand, and with her victim stretched out beside her. While little about this woman makes her appear "gentle" in a stereotypical sense, by titling the picture this, *In the Maine Woods* redefined the "Gentler Sex." In learning about the natural world, women could create for themselves a new, stronger kind of femininity. They could hunt and still remain ladies.

For many women, playing Diana in the woods may not have been enough to satisfy their new self-perception. They wanted to share their new identity with their family and friends once they returned home from Maine. *In the Maine Woods* claimed: "The number [of women] who distribute venison of their own shooting among their friends at home is increasing each year."[12] The gift may have alarmed those

Figure 3. "'The Gentler Sex' can Hunt, Too," *In the Maine Woods*, 1906. Collections of Maine Historical Society.

acquaintances who still believed femininity rested with passivity, but did not stop women like Boston resident Mildred Howes, who recorded her adventures in a camp journal. She kept careful track of her catches, updating her record almost daily and totaling her prey at the end of each trip. She registered her total kills from year to year on the inside cover of the volume:

1910	20 fish, 16 partridge, 1 black duck
1913	93 trout, 37 partridge, 1 deer
1915	41 fish, 34 partridge, 1 deer
1917	32 fish, 17 partridge, 2 deer, 1 duck[13]

Other huntswomen settled for photographs of their accomplishments. They posed beside their bloody trophies with proud smiles or looks of stoic determination. Traditionally, men and women stood next to the wooden stakes on which their deer or moose were hung to drain at camp. Such posed shots of a woman and her quarry proved that she had visited Maine, vanquished her prey, and returned home changed, quite possibly with a new self-perception, confidence, and awareness of her potential.

Yet the "New Woman" would need more than Diana's bows and arrows for her hunt. By the end of the nineteenth century, the sporting goods industry was ready to provide new equipment for a variety of developing pastimes, including hunting. A female writer for the New York magazine *Ladies' World* reported in the late 1880s that "the makers and dealers in sporting goods say that there has never been such a demand for rifles by women." *Ladies' World* explained the importance of having the correct equipment:

If a woman is not very strong she can handle a light weapon. The fact that she can do as much hard shooting with her dainty rifle as can the guide with a gun she can hardly lift, gives her confidence, and she soon becomes as expert, sometimes turning out to be a better shot than the average man.

The magazine recommended a 30-calibre rifle weighing less than seven pounds.[14] J. Stevens Arms and Tool Co. appeared ready to oblige. In 1906, the inside back cover of *In the Maine Woods* featured a full-page advertisement for Stevens Rifles intended to appeal to women. The text did not claim that the rifle was made exclusively for women, but a huntswoman, rather than a man, demonstrated successful bird hunting using the straight shooting rifle. The potential for female customers must have been great enough to warrant Stevens' directing its one advertisement in this yearly magazine specifically at Diana and her followers.

Although many of the same women who hunted also enjoyed fishing, the sport offered an alternative appeal for some women. Unlike the hunter who tracks down a live animal, shooting it once or more until it dies, the fisher does not witness the life of the fish before pulling it from the water on her hook. In fact, she may not even know the prey is nearby until it is caught. After landing her catch, a fainthearted or sensitive woman still had the option to throw it back, letting it live. Even in the late nineteenth century, conserving resources by returning unwanted fish to the water was a popular idea, so women did not have to take a life if killing contradicted their moral sensibilities.

Yet the struggle for life and death, and the excitement it generated, remained a powerful attraction for some women. After hooking her first fish and showing off her prize, novice fisher Ida May returned to her room at camp and then felt "a pang of regret for the gallant life I had taken." Self-recriminations flew through her head: "How the cruel hook must have hurt. Did not those frantic leaps and rushes eloquently tell? And how he gasped and struggled." Sounding like a nurturing "True" woman, May scolded herself reproachfully until her earlier exhilaration returned. "Then there stole over me again something of the same sensation that came as I felt his first wild burst," she confessed, "and my brief pity was stifled in the more human, though perhaps less merciful, exultation of the victor."[15]

Not only did some women prefer fishing, some experts believed that women were particularly well suited for the endeavor. "Fly Rod" Crosby herself expressed her preference: "I really doubt whether there is any sport in the world half so delightful as angling, or half as graceful and healthful for our sex."[16] The graceful sport also required great patience, a characteristic traditionally attributed to women. Whether trolling slowly around a pond or standing still for hours, the quiet persistence of the ideal woman made the recreation seem like a perfect choice for her. D. C. Farrington furthered the argument in his article "Ladies in Camp," asserting that women made better fishers than men because "They are not fish-hogs." Assuming her softhearted nature, he claimed that a lady would not kill a trout unless she wanted one for dinner. Perhaps women did understand the necessity of preserving trout in Maine waters better than men, but Farrington's reasoning was so completely immersed in female stereotypes that his argument became humorous. He described how women's experience handling multiple suitors made them better anglers:

> A trout is a gentleman and should be treated as such, and no one knows how to treat or manoeuver a gentlemen or a trout so well as a lady. If a girl can have two or three fellows on the string why can she not manage two or three trout on the line?[17]

His comic exaggeration fostered the notion that the virtues of the "True Woman" made the "New Woman" a superior fisher.

Despite continued stereotyping, women could gain a certain independence in fishing that was not possible in other field sports. Mildred Howes recorded in her diary that when she wanted to spend her day trout fishing, she left with one of her guides while her husband stayed near the camp and entertained friends. At the end of her day she proudly recorded 13 solo catches. However, if a woman knew the region well, she could paddle her own canoe without even requiring the assistance of a guide and thus exercise another trait she might not practice at home—self-reliance.

In the years after her first emotional confrontation with a trout, Ida May took up fishing seriously, enjoying the individualism of the sport and stressing the possession of her own equipment as she described selecting "*my* tackle, *my* rods, *my et coetrera*" as carefully as her husband chose his. Married women like May might have enjoyed joining in outdoors adventures with their husbands rather than staying home as their mothers had done. Furthermore, as with hunting, women could improve their status by participating in a sport with men on equal terms. If the Maine woods were as much of an equalizer of men as male sportsmen loved to boast, surely any woman who joined with men in a sporting party must have earned new respect. Although Ida May concluded that "we are re-created by such experiences" in the outdoors and felt "of infinitely greater value to myself and to all who have to do with me" after she took up fishing, she did not claim to have been improved so much as transformed by learning to kill. In allowing herself to experience "exultation" and other traditionally male responses like domination along with her "feminine" reactions, May learned from nature how to explore more complex aspects of her personality.[18]

For many women even fishing contradicted their peaceful quest for nature. But the Maine woods still offered them wilderness riches. Even without joining in hunting and fishing sports, a woman could enjoy Maine's lakes and rivers, and tackle water sports not available at home. Paddling was an option. *In the Maine Woods* cited this sport as one of women's favorites in an illustration captioned "Canoeing is a Woman's Delight."[19] Paddling a canoe offered women both good exercise and an opportunity to explore distant reaches of the wilderness. Yet swimming—actually submerging one-self in the depths of unknown waters—must have been equal-ly exhilarating. Over the course of four trips to Maine, Mildred Howes remembered both swimming and bathing in a "secluded spot" when the weather was warm enough. That she cited both swimming and bathing in her memoirs sug-gests that she used the word "bathing" to mean washing her-self, rather than the judicious wading which women in cum-bersome wool dresses undertook at seaside communities. Her care to find seclusion implies that she reposed naked as she washed in a lake or stream. Indeed, no swimming cos-tume appears in her meticulously recorded "Clothes Taken" lists.[20] For ladies accustomed to indoor plumbing, taking a bath in a lake or river must have seemed like a genuine bap-tism in the back-to-nature movement.

Other women studied nature more academically. Cap-turing the wilderness in a pencil sketch or painting allowed them to retain their traditional gender roles while closely surveying their surroundings. Nature's students collected wildflowers or mineral specimens. Likewise, meeting the local fauna could also be done peacefully, as demonstrated by an *In the Maine Woods* photograph of a female vacationer petting two deer, a highly idealized portrayal of a gentle woman's discovery of the wonders of the forest.

Women from cities across New England saw Maine as an old-fashioned, safe haven from the challenges of modern liv-ing. The women's elite status reinforced the profound effect a Maine woods vacation must have had on their lives. The wilderness provided an arena where men and women could share sporting pleasures and learn about nature, enriching their lives with its lessons. Camping in the wilds, away from predetermined expectations of their behavior, freed women to experiment with new activities, new roles, and new equality with their male companions. Their mementos—a painting of the area, a deer head mounted on a wall, or a photograph of a day's catch—proved that they returned to the city changed, holding evidence that they were part of the back-to-nature movement. And whether they defined themselves that way or not, in society's eyes they returned home as "New Women."

1. Fly Rod Scrapbook, compiled by Kathleen Toothakers, Phillips Historical Society, Phillips, Maine.

2. G. Smith Stanton, *Where the Sportsman Loves to Linger: A Narrative of the Most Popular Canoe Trips in Maine, The Allagash, the East and West Branches of the Penobscot* (New York: J. S. Ogilvie, 1905), 101.

3. *Maine Outings*, March 1895: 48, 49.

4. "Enjoying Maine's Waterways," *In the Maine Woods* (Bangor, Maine: Bangor and Aroostook Railway, 1907), 43.

5. Guest Register of Pleasant Island Camps, 1884, Rangeley Lake Region Historical Society, Rangeley, Maine. These statistics are based on the names of the guests in the registers. Because many guests registered using only first initials, hard statistics are difficult to determine. The number of women staying at Pleasant Island Camps may actually have been much greater.

6. Guest registers of Pickford's Camps, Rangeley, Maine, 1900–1902, Rangeley Historical Society.

7. *Maine Outings*, February 1896: 3–14.

8. For a discussion of women and the tension between domesticity and hunting in Africa, see Vera Norwood, "Women and Wildlife," in *Made From This Earth: American Women and Nature* (Chapel Hill: University of North Carolina Press, 1993), 203–60.

9. Ella S. Williams, "Outing Hints By a Lady who has 'Been There'," *In the Maine Woods*, 1910, 84.

10. Edward Breck, "A Sporting Pilgrimage," *In the Maine Woods*, 1910, 93.

11. Ibid.

12. Winifred M. Thompson, "Big Game in the Maine Woods," *In the Maine Woods*, 1900, 123.

13. Diary of Mildred Cox Howes, 1910–1917, Mildred Cox Howes Papers, Massachusetts Historical Society, Boston, Massachusetts.

14. Clipping from *Ladies' World*, Fly Rod Crosby Collection, Phillips Historical Society.

15. Ida May, "My First Trout," *Maine Outings*, May 1895: 67–68.

16. *Washington Times*, 19 April 1896.

17. D. C. Farrington, "Ladies in Camp," *Maine Outings*, November 1895: 273.

18. May, "My First Trout," 68.

19. *In the Maine Woods*, 1906.

20. Mildred Cox Howes, "Camping Trips" [n. d.], Mildred Cox Howes Papers, Massachusetts Historical Society, 8.

While women "from away" were flocking to the state as immigrants and as tourists, many Maine women felt compelled to leave the state in pursuit of opportunity. Some were pulled by their desire for education or the promise of better jobs. Some sought the excitement of bigger cities than those found in the state. A very few sought fame and fortune as artists.

In all of these goals, Maine women who left the state were not unlike rural women elsewhere in the nation who hoped to improve their prospects by leaving farms and villages for the enticements of the city. In fact, tensions between rural and urban places became a significant part of the national debate between traditional and modern values in the early twentieth century. Opponents of urban life characterized the city as corrupt and dangerous, filled with temptations and immorality. Rural areas, by contrast, were portrayed as idyllic strongholds of tradition where hard work and wholesome amusements created virtuous citizens. Proponents of the city countered by celebrating, among other qualities, the cultural possibilities inherent in urban life. Freed from the bleak drudgery of the countryside, city dwellers could enjoy access to libraries, theaters, museums, and other places of cultural enlightenment.

The ways in which turn-of-the-century Mainers, especially women, participated in cultural activities can be perplexing for historians to comprehend. Should we divide culture into "high," "middlebrow," and "folk" and look for the ways Maine women participated in each? Certainly women participated in informal cultural activities in their homes, churches, and communities, singing with their families on winter evenings, performing in community theatricals, or writing for community newspapers, as Joan Radner described. But cultural expression was becoming increasingly self-conscious and innovative around the turn of the century, inspired in part by Europeans. What opportunities were available to enjoy and participate in innovative art, music, theater, dance, and the like in areas far removed even from major cultural centers in this country, like New York and Boston? To what extent was participation in these activities encouraged in a culture whose dominant imagery extolled practicality and thrift and frowned on the free expression of emotion?

Maine was hardly the cultural backwater its rural location might imply. Maine communities were home to theater companies, orchestras, galleries, and other groups devoted to the performance and display of both familiar and avant-garde art. Traveling companies of professional performers routinely visited Maine, especially during the summer. Creative people "from away" visited Maine; some became entranced and stayed. Still, women like the divas who are the subjects of Norma Johnsen and Allison Hepler's essay routinely left Maine to pursue creative training and opportunity, raising questions about the tensions between cultural expression and rural isolation.

LILLIAN NORDICA AND EMMA EAMES, DOWNEAST DIVAS

Norma Johnsen and Allison L. Hepler

Those who imagine American women before 1920 as voiceless should consider the opera singers. Two divas with deep roots in Maine were outspoken, independent, emancipated professionals at the turn of the century. Lillian Norton—stage name Nordica—of Farmington and Emma Eames of Bath lived out true American success stories. From obscure backgrounds, these Maine women became glamorous international stars, shone for a decade, then disappeared from all but the most esoteric pages of cultural history. Their accomplishments as successful women artists and public figures are today forgotten, yet their careers were remarkable. Eames admitted that her "greatest joys" came from her work; Nordica aspired to become "a really great American artist," and she reached her goal.[1]

Nordica and Eames were the "New Women" described by early twentieth-century novelists, journalists, and social observers. Self-identified as artists, both nevertheless attempted to combine careers with marriage, and thus were among the first public figures to expose the difficulties of negotiating new marital roles. These negotiations exemplify the larger cultural significance of the divas. Their struggles for voice and power in the patriarchal world of opera emboldened ordinary women and inspired novelists from George Eliot to Willa Cather. Not only were Eames and Nordica musical pioneers breaking ground for Wagnerian singers,[2] they were role models, leading the way for a new generation of women who sought more public lives.

Maine divas claimed public space far beyond family circles and music societies. A 1911 photo of Nordica epitomizes the confidence and range of these nineteenth-century vocalists. At ground-breaking ceremonies for the Panama-Pacific Exposition in San Francisco, Nordica emotes in public—a big, expressive woman, arm outstretched in dynamic motion in contrast to passive, dark men, including President Taft (figure 1). In the picture, Nordica dominates space, public space, belying the conventional wisdom that before women got the vote in 1920, this environment belonged to men. At a time when few women had public presence, public identity, role or

Figure 1. Lillian Nordica at the ground-breaking ceremonies for the Panama-Pacific Exposition in San Francisco in 1911. President Taft is on her right.

voice, divas were in the vanguard. They spoke out. They gave voice. They were loud and emotional on stage and in public arenas. Contrary to stereotypes of late nineteenth-century middle-class womanhood, these women did not faint and they were not anorexic. They were large, regal, determined, and powerful.[3]

While Maine is not ordinarily viewed as being at the center of American culture, the experiences of these divas remind us that neither Maine nor Mainers were culturally deprived. Although Hallowell and Portland were the state's centers of music in the nineteenth century, music, according to historian William Barry, was "one of the first endeavors to link citizens across the district of Maine."[4] Moreover, coastal towns often served as the connector between the wider world and the inland communities.[5] Emma Eames grew up in nineteenth-century Bath where musical societies flourished.[6] Lillian Norton was born in Farmington into a family of amateur musicians whose ancestors brought their love of music from coastal Massachusetts to the mountains of western Maine.[7]

Although Eames and Norton grew up in a culture that did not always support artistic women, they were not the first prominent Maine singers. Annie Louise Cary of Wayne predated them by nearly twenty years and began serious training in oratorio music in pre-Civil War Portland. Born in 1841, Cary preferred the more "moral" singing roles found in oratorios and concerts. For most of her professional life she specialized in religious music, but financial concerns periodically compelled her to sing operatic roles, which she had been brought up to think of as "dangerous, if not positively sinful." Even though her singing career reflected more traditional roles for public women, in 1874 Cary became the first American woman to sing a Wagnerian role in the United

States.[8] Cary retired from her career after she married, however, following the accepted pattern for women artists.

Unlike Cary, Emma Eames would eventually depart from the traditional gender norms, although in her early years her needs were subordinated to those of her brother. Born in 1865 in Shanghai, China, where her father was a lawyer, Eames and her mother and brother came to Portland, Maine, in 1870. Five years later, Eames was sent to live with her maternal grandparents in Bath while her mother remained with her brother in Portland "where he might continue the education to prepare him for the Navy." Eames did not graduate from Bath High School because she was expected to attend her brother's graduation from the Naval Academy, missing her own final exams.[9] Clearly, Emma Eames was the least important sibling in the family.

There was some question as to her singing ability as a child—a classmate reported that Eames showed "little ability or inclination to sing during her school days"—but a Bath expatriate living in France, a subscriber to the Paris Opera, heard Eames sing at the Bath Swedenborgian Church and encouraged her musical training.[10] Thanks to the largesse of an uncle, Bath Iron Works founder Thomas W. Hyde, Eames took singing lessons in Portland, then in Boston. Studying music under Clara Munger, also from Maine, and acting with Annie Payson Call, Eames made professional appearances in churches and with the Boston Symphony Orchestra, with whom she made her Maine debut in 1885.[11] Thus began Maine media coverage of this home-grown diva, the Bath papers calling Eames one of the most "satisfactory and delightful" soloists heard in the city.[12]

Even as these artists became role models for the next generation, they themselves had few guides or mentors and limited encouragement. Eames lived with her grandparents, strict Congregationalists she described as people for whom

Figure 2. Emma Eames in her operatic debut as Juliette in Gounod's
Romeo and Juliette, Paris, 1889.

"love and happiness and amusement were among the least of
the necessities of life." From her grandmother she learned to
believe that nothing she ever did "could possibly be correct

or free from sin."[13] Such severe attitudes, according to Eames, created "much unnecessary self-condemnation." The repercussions over her lifetime were painful. She stopped reading reviews after the first few and was extremely hard on herself.[14] Even though she received numerous favorable reviews, Eames ignored them and often recalled her grandmother's description of her: "eyes like a pig's, a nose like a prow of a ship and a receding chin."[15]

Despite early discouragements, Eames continued her studies. On borrowed money, Eames and her mother sailed for Europe in 1886 to continue her voice studies with Madame Mathilde Marchesi, who has been described as a "martinet and vocal drill master."[16] Eames's decision to train in Europe was greeted with pride at home; Bath newspapers enthusiastically followed the activities of "one of the most fascinating women that Maine ever sent out to the world."[17] When Eames made her operatic debut as the soprano Juliette in Charles Gounod's *Romeo and Juliette* in Paris in 1889 (figure 2), the well-known political leader Harold M. Sewall of Bath was in the audience, and later declared to his neighbors that Eames was successful "as much for her beauty, her svelte figure, and her graceful acting as for the clarity and perfection of her voice."[18] Eames debuted in London in 1891 in another Gounod opera, *Faust,* and later that same year in the New York City Metropolitan Opera's version of *Romeo and Juliette.* Eames would continue at the Metropolitan for eighteen years, retiring in 1909 ostensibly due to her desire to leave while at the top of her career, although artistic clashes with Arturo Toscanini and Giulio Gaiti-Casazza, the Metropolitan's two new directors, also played a role in her decision to leave.[19]

Lillian Nordica's career was described by writer Willa Cather as "one long conquest of difficulties."[20] When asked what professional success for a woman entailed, Nordica replied, "Work, work, and more work," and with work, she included "loss of friends, money and pride."[21] Born in Farmington, Maine, in 1857, Lillian Norton was the ignored child; according to her biographer Ira Glackens, her parents, Edwin and Amanda Norton, paid her not to sing. Poor to begin with, they sacrificed everything to educate their children, particularly their talented older daughter Wilhelmina. Edwin, an unsuccessful farmer, never seemed to find the right job. After the Nortons moved to Boston to be near good musical training, Amanda worked at Jordan Marsh department store to support the family while Wilhelmina studied at the New England Conservatory of Music and began singing professionally. Lillian's voice went unnoticed until her sister "Willy's" tragic death at sixteen from typhoid fever. Then, finally, Amanda turned her attention and ambition to Lillian. When Lillian was fourteen, she began studying at the New England Conservatory with John O'Neill, Wilhelmina's former teacher.

After her early training with O'Neill, Lillian sang in churches and with Gilmore's Brass Band, not an auspicious beginning for a serious musical career. Like Eames, young Lillian Norton was accompanied by her mother as chaperone, coach, and companion. During an 1878 European tour, Lillian and Amanda left the band in France for one last sustained attempt to prepare Lillian for opera. After months of study and practice, supporting herself and her mother by giving music lessons, Lillian debuted in Milan, Italy, playing Elvira in Mozart's *Don Giovanni*. She was dubbed "Nordica" by her Italian voice teacher, who claimed Italians would never be able to pronounce the name Lillian Norton. After Italy in 1880, Nordica subsequently sang for the Czar and Czarina in St. Petersburg, Russia, and after that, like Eames, she sang all over Europe. In Italy, she performed Gilda in *Rigoletto* to great critical acclaim. From Italy, she moved to France, creating a sensation as Marguerite in *Faust* at the Paris Opera. A fashionable new cloak was named "La Nordica" and the season's new color, a pinkish mauve called "nordica," was all the rage. Reportedly, during one of her performances at the Paris Opera, an American stood up and shouted, "She's there, she's there, she's there!" Her career was launched. But perhaps her greatest triumph came when she was the first American singer to perform Wagner at Bayreuth, Germany, the site of yearly Wagner extravaganzas. Invited and coached by Cosima Wagner, the composer's widow, Nordica sang Elsa in *Lohengrin* there in 1893 (figure 3).[22]

These divas had come a long way from rural Maine. Their full participation in the Golden Age of Opera testifies to their artistic talent and personal determination, especially given the patriarchal history of opera from its origins in the courts of Renaissance Italy. For generations, composers, musicians, and singers were exclusively male. Female roles were acted and sung by men—castrati with three-octave voices. Although men continued to perform female roles throughout the nineteenth century, women gradually replaced them. Eventually, operas were written to showcase the soprano voice. In fact, the gender reversal reversed, and women often sang parts written originally for castrati voices, "trouser roles" such as Orfeo, the male lead in Gluck's *Orfeo*. As Rebecca A. Pope writes, "With [the] decline [of castrati] came the rise of the female singer, who took over roles previously sung by men and ultimately made the upper registers her own."[23] The heady ownership of voice to which Pope refers to is evident in a passage from Willa Cather's novel about an opera singer, *The Song of the Lark*:

> The soprano voice, like a fountain jet, shot up into the light! . . . How it leaped from among those dusky male voices! How it played in and about and around and over them, like a goldfish darting among creek

Figure 3. (left) Lillian Nordica as Elsa in Wagner's *Lohengrin*.
Figure 4. (right) Emma Eames in the same role.

minnows, like a yellow butterfly soaring above a swarm of dark
ones.[24]

Although recognition of the woman's voice indicated
increased power and respect for singers, divas, according to
John Dizikes, often "fulfilled the archtypical male image of
the emotional and hysterical woman."[25] Opera roles for
females during this period ranged from the innocent wronged
woman to the scheming jealous wife. In *Iris* by Pietro
Mascagni, Eames played a Japanese female lead, Iris, who is
kidnapped and set free, and rejected by her father; she eventually tries to commit suicide. In the end, she weighs her
choices between the man who kidnapped her and the father
who rejected her, and chooses neither, preferring to become

one with the Sun God. Eames and Nordica both portrayed Elsa in Richard Wagner's *Lohengrin*, a character who is undone by her curiosity and lack of trust in the man of her dreams (figures 3 and 4). Later in their careers, they both performed Aida in Guiseppe Verdi's opera of the same name (figure 5). Aida is an Ethiopian slave who chooses to die with her Egyptian lover after he first captures her father, then shifts his allegiance to Aida.[26]

Stereotypes about women were reinforced by critics who objectified women in their reviews. Indeed, here is how one described Emma Eames as Juliette:

> Twenty years old, tall, svelte, the figure and the profile of Diana, the nose fine and the nostrils quivering, the carmine mouth exhaling the breath of life, the face a pure oval lit by big blue eyes full of impudence and candor at the same time, the expression astonishingly mobile, the forehead high and crowned by a mass of blonde fleece, the arms superb, attached to the charming shoulders—such is Mlle. Emma Hayden Eames—such is the new Juliette.[27]

Writers focused on Nordica's body also, describing her low-cut gown revealing "magnificent shoulders."[28] They lingered over her "magnetic womanliness," and praised the "richness and roundness of her upper register."[29]

Even viewed through such diminishing rhetoric, we glimpse the genuine power of these singers. For audiences of the period, the very voices of divas were erotic. Wayne Koestenbaum calls the voice of the diva "the sound of nineteenth-century sexuality."[30] Confirming the truth of his remark, writers of the period used voice to hint at sexual passion, to insert into their texts "unmentionable" sexuality. In *The Lady of the Aroostook*, for example, William Dean Howells describes a man so thrilled by the "quality of latent passion" in a young singer's voice that he falls in love with her.[31] Similarly, George Eliot's diva heroine, Armgart,

Figure 5: Eames in the role of Aida in Verdi's opera of the same name.

describes singing as "pouring [my] passion on the air."[32] Armgart's speech suggests that the opera singer was more than a passive performer of masculine texts. As Koestenbaum writes, "The diva exposes her capacity for independent pleasure: her joy comes from the body, the throat; she presents the . . . antipatriarchal spectacle of a woman taking her body seriously—channeling, enjoying, and nourishing it."[33] Freedom was implicit in turn-of-the-century voice education as well. According to Debra Cumberland, divas trained by Lily Lehmann in the early twentieth century were encouraged to understand and enjoy the sensuality of singing, and contemporary theories of vocal training encouraged women to experience voice as rooted in body, as pleasurable.[34] If sexuality is broadly defined as the enjoyment of one's own physical being, Koestenbaum's provocative identification of voice with sexuality goes beyond masculinist objectification to underline the essential emancipation of singers like Nordica and Eames.

Reviews by Willa Cather, then a young midwestern journalist, illustrate the influence of these great opera singers. For Cather, Nordica and other divas represented a new tradition of female authority and power. Few female opera roles convey this power as much as does Brunnehilde in Richard Wagner's Ring Cycle operas. A powerful supernatural force,

Brunnehilde is very different from opera's romantic ingenues and scheming wives. Nordica is especially remembered for her performances of the heroic Brunnehilde, the chief maiden of the Valkyries—winged mythic creatures who swoop down to take heroes up to Valhalla in the Ring Cycle (figure 6). Observing Pittsburgh's Metropolitan Opera season, Cather found Wagner's Valkyrie an appropriate role for Nordica: "She had much of the Valkyr in her before she ever sang Brunnehilde."[35]

Cather and many other critics applauded the two Maine divas when they performed together during the "legendary" 1893 Metropolitan season in New York. Their performance of the famous "letter" duet in Mozart's *The Marriage of Figaro*—with Nordica as Susanna and Eames as the Countess—was considered "remarkable."[36] When Nordica sang Elsa yet again in 1897 with the Metropolitan Company in Pittsburgh, Willa Cather was in the audience. She wrote:

> I never saw her give herself out to her audience as she did that night. She is becoming a proficient actress, that determined woman from Maine with the strong chin and the big, firm hands, like a man's. . . . She comes in regally, confident, fearlessly, . . . her face is shining with the fullness of her faith.[37]

In 1898, in London, Eames and Nordica sang together again in Wagner's Ring Cycle, again with great success.[38]

Critical acclaim brought other rewards. Queen Victoria gave Eames "many rare and beautiful gifts" and Nordica a pearl brooch. The Czar of Russia presented Nordica with a jeweled bracelet, and in 1896 her admirers gave her a tiara of diamonds set in platinum.[39] But even with the professional achievement, the jewels, and the glamour, for both divas this was "success at a price." Neither woman had a satisfying personal life. Newspaper headlines gave only the sensationalized

Figure 6. Lillian Nordica as Brunnehilde in Wagner's *Ring Cycle*.

details, but turn-of-the-century fiction provided a more in-depth glimpse of the kind of conflicts they faced. George Eliot's *Armgart*, Rebecca Harding Davis's *The Wife's Story*, and Elizabeth Stuart Phelps's *The Story of Avis* all dramatize the difficulties of combining a musical or artistic career with a woman's traditional roles—especially the role of wife. These works all address the question: Can a woman be an artist and remain a woman? In Eliot's verse drama, the singer's lover calls her "unwomaned" by her ambition.[40] In Davis's story, the singer/composer has a nightmare vision of losing her voice, and of her "selfish" ambition causing the death of her husband.[41] In Phelps's novel, the artist must give up her work, realizing that "[God] has set two natures in me, warring against each other."[42] In these fictional representations, the singer loses either her voice, her career, her love, or her life. Obviously, writers were well aware of the painful conflicts faced by woman artists. Recognizing this, Willa Cather observed, "Married nightingales seldom sing."[43]

This was certainly true of Nordica. Feeling she could not be both singer and wife, she announced her retirement—temporarily—each time she married. But her marriages—three of them—faltered anyway. Her first husband, Fred Gower, ruined her early career by whisking her away from two important engagements, one in Paris and one in Chicago. He forbade her to sing, burned her music and gowns and—after Nordica obtained a separation on grounds of abuse—disappeared in a balloon over the English Channel, never to be seen again.[44] Nordica's second husband, the Hungarian opera singer Zoltan Döme, was unfaithful; when she left him he threatened to murder her.[45] Her third husband, George Washington Young, spent all her money on wild financial schemes. Newspapers and tabloids found the details exciting and titillating, but Cather's story "The Diamond Mine," based on Nordica's life, shows a lonely woman who struggles to support a group of parasites—family members, husband and ex-husbands, and other hangers-on.[46] Nordica herself said she was "a poor picker of husbands," but the situation was more complex than that.[47] The novels had it right. Artists—if they were women—had to choose between love and art. They could not have both.

Emma Eames also had troubled relationships. Eames married twice, divorced one husband and separated from the second, and had no children. Her friend, novelist Alexandre Dumas, predicted that Eames would never be satisfied with the love she inspired, but it seems clear that, like Nordica, she continued to seek it.[48] In many ways these divas resembled other public women of the period. Many professional women during this time felt they could not marry and keep a career; those who married tended to leave their careers, as Nordica and Annie Louise Cary did. At the turn of this century, the birth rate was the lowest it had ever been for white middle-class women. In part, this decline in fertility was due to the first generation of white women who completed college and carved out careers for themselves. They tended not to marry because marriage inevitably led to expectations of full-time attention to household and family.[49]

Eames and Nordica fit into the cohort of women born between the late 1850s and 1900 who, according to historian Carroll Smith-Rosenberg, got caught in the crossfire between the traditional societal expectations of their mothers and their own growing need for an independent, professional identity. Popularized by novelists such as Elizabeth Stuart Phelps, Sinclair Lewis, and Henry James, these "New Women" tried to live economically and socially autonomous lives. In their rejection of bourgeois conventions, writes Smith-Rosenberg, many New Women moved into creative and artistic fields and became comfortable in the public spotlight. While this autonomy proved exhilarating to women, it also fostered anxiety and tension from more traditional elements of society that were more comfortable with familiar traditional women than with assertively independent "public" women.[50]

Indeed, there were risks associated with being a "public" woman. Just as tabloids ran blow-by-blow headlines of Nordica's messy divorces, Maine newspapers exposed the private life of Emma Eames, including her marriage to her first husband, Julian Story, and their subsequent divorce, which followed Eames's discovery of his extra-marital affair.[51] Her second marriage, to Emilio DeGogorza, received even more publicity, following as it did a "scandal-ridden suit for alienation of affection" brought by DeGogorza's first wife.[52] The first Mrs. DeGogorza charged Eames with "holding her husband under a spell."[53]

This exposure reflects the two-edged sword of being a woman in public. According to historian Mary P. Ryan, nineteenth-century women who stayed at home were supposedly protected by the ideals of domesticity and endangered by the hazards of urban life. Their public space was restricted. In exchange for living a more public life and claiming more public space, independent women were perceived as less worthy of protection and also more dangerous, not unlike prostitutes.[54] Female artists straddled both public and private realms, and were considered both "in danger" and "dangerous." Nordica's troubled marriages garnered sympathy, but the ensuing publicity about her divorces and her wealth made her seem hard and cold. Eames's femininity made her worthy of protection, yet her publicness made her a "dangerous woman." Contrast the early description of Eames as divinely "crowned by a mass of blonde fleece" with the scornful portrayal of her as "the other woman."

Public women also had to reconcile their public persona with their private feelings, a common dilemma during this period of carving out new public spaces for women. Eames, for example, felt obliged to overcome charges that she was an "operatic iceberg," but at the same time tried to protect her private life.[55] As a result, she confessed that she always played a role with her public. In a revealing comment made at the Cosmopolitan Club in Bath in 1913, Eames admitted that "when I began my career, I said to myself, I will have the public always see me perfectly well and happy and they have. That is what they want."[56]

The career demands of such a life also fostered among divas a competitive spirit that did not escape public scrutiny and was not always flattering. Publicly admired, divas were isolated because of their small numbers and hence did not form close, supportive relationships with other women. For instance, critics sensationalized a "squabble" between Nordica and diva Nellie Melba.[57] Similarly, Bath newspapers reported Eames's performance before Queen Victoria, in which the Queen decreed that Eames and her arch-rival Emma Calve could both sing for her only if they agreed to "bury the hatchet—or hair pins."[58] Throughout her career, Eames repeatedly referred to Melba as a "treacherous" rival who tried to keep Eames off the stage, and New York newspapers reported that "New York had a hotter climate with the two ladies [Eames and Melba] in residence; and also just about the best opera the city ever had." In 1905, Eames slapped another singer, Kathie Sanger-Bettaque, while they both waited in the wings during a performance of *Lohengrin*, apparently while arguing over who was to go on stage first. Eames later apologized.[59]

Pioneering can be hard. Singers like Nordica and Eames became successful female artists in a culture that constructed the artist as male. They showed that strength and ambition could coexist with glamour and femininity. Although they sang roles written by men, they did not make men the center of their lives. As Eliot's Armgart says, "Oh, I can live unmated, but not live / without the bliss of singing to the world."[60]

They were pioneers in another sense also. These outspoken women contributed to the modern feminist movement. In his study of Richard Wagner in American culture, cultural historian Joseph Horowitz correlates Wagnerism with "protofeminism"—a precursor to feminism. Horowitz argues that Wagner's heroines and singers like Lily Lehmann and Lillian Nordica were "influences enroute to liberation."[61] As historian John Dizikes explains in *Opera in America*, "a larger role was possible for women in the theater than in almost any field of endeavor, and especially in opera." Dizikes observes that women saw in the diva "a woman who had struggled and disciplined herself and made decisions and won through to fame and fortune."[62] The turn-of-the-century diva inspired other women to act and achieve. But beyond self-discipline and success, critics Susan Leonardi and Rebecca Pope locate that inspiration as modeling "women who have a voice—voice as metaphor of and vehicle for female empowerment. And not just empowerment of themselves, . . . but of other women as well."[63]

Willa Cather is a prime example of a woman inspired by opera singers. During Cather's long journalistic apprenticeship, she observed, loved, and learned from the artistic passion of the divas. Over and over in her reviews, Cather described how singers like Nordica and Eames conveyed essential artistic, womanly, and American values. Cather wrote that Nordica embodied "all that is best in American womanhood." She saw her as a symbol of the American character, comparing her to "our great Franklin, in his coonskin cap, . . . unawed by titles and splendors and the favors of kings."[64] According to Sharon O'Brien, these singers led Cather to discover her own unique female voice, a process she traces in *The Song of the Lark,* her novel about a singer, Thea Kronberg, whose career has many parallels with Nordica's.[65]

Eames and Nordica also influenced other women more directly. Both used their public voices to speak out for women and women's causes. Volunteering in Bath during World War I, Eames spoke on behalf of the American Red Cross: "Do you realize the woman power of the country? Woman is an enormous factor. She is being employed by the hundreds in ammunition factories, in freeing men in all kinds of labor that they may enlist."[66] Nordica was more radical. An outspoken and ardent suffragist in the years before the passage of the Nineteenth Amendment, she gave benefit concerts for the cause.[67] Nordica portrayed Columbia, an early representation of America, in a Washington, D.C., suffrage pageant on the steps of the Capitol (figure 7). In 1909 she exclaimed to a group of reporters:

> Smash windows? Yes! When men take the view that to gain an end warlike methods are excusable, they are heroes. . . . I think no great reform has been brought about without there being those willing to cast themselves into the breach and fight. . . . If we are to be heard, why, we have to make ourselves obnoxious.[68]

As an influential and wealthy proponent of women's rights, Nordica developed plans to help educate other women musicians and artists. Well aware of the difficulties facing talented young women, she proposed a school and concert house for their benefit. She envisioned a Lillian Nordica Festival House in Harmon, New York, modeled on Wagner's theater in Bayreuth. Unfortunately, she died before she was able to realize her dreams.[69] Nevertheless, we can deduce what kind of school she would have created. In her posthumously published *Hints to Singers,* Nordica focused on train-

Figure 7. Holding the flag, Lillian Nordica represents Columbia on the steps of the U.S. Capitol in a Washington, D.C. suffrage pageant.

ing the body, emphasizing the physical strength necessary for singing. She described the importance of "bodily strength and endurance" and warned against dieting. In an age of tight corseting and suffocatingly heavy dresses, she recommended loose, comfortable, non-restrictive clothing.[70] Interestingly, Nordica's advice echoed that of many female physicians who treated upper-class women whose health suffered from physical deformities caused by restrictive clothing.[71] Her educational theories not only promoted the physical culture of the singer, they were sound advice for women of her day.

In Cather's *The Song of the Lark*, Thea, the diva, says she has no personal life, but other experiences become a substitute. Thea says: "Your work becomes your personal life. You are not much good until it does. It's like being woven into a big web."[72] It is clear that these women gave their all to their careers. Eames often referred to her roles as her "babies." "Every artist dies twice," she asserted, "and the first time, the death of one's activities, is the most painful, when it suddenly came to me that my only source of real happiness lay in my career."[73]

Nordica also found joy in her art. "The reward of a singer is beyond my power to describe," she wrote. "Great compensations, quite aside from any material ones, and all that is refined and beautiful, go to constitute her lot. . . . Beyond, and above all, she gives pleasure to thousands as well as to herself, for if it is the delight of the hearer be great, how much greater must be the delight of the singer who bestows it."[74]

No doubt the divas also felt compensated by the regard they inspired in their native state. Mainers did not take art for granted. Local Maine newspapers followed the careers of both singers avidly. When Eames sang Elsa in *Lohengrin* in San Francisco in 1901, Bath residents read tales of her success under the headline "Our Bath Girl Sings." The paper offered a detailed review of each scene and aria and proudly pronounced her performance "the most poetic rendering of the part San Francisco has yet seen" while noting Eames's own modesty in refusing to appear alone during curtain calls.[75]

Beginning in 1905, Eames returned to Maine for several Maine Music Festivals, held both in Bangor and Portland. Advance Festival programs advertised that "the World's Favorite Prima Donna and Maine's Special Pride, will appear for the first time in Maine since she became famous."[76] One Maine newspaper devoted a full page to Eames' upcoming concert while the Portland newspaper proclaimed Eames's appearance at the Festival with the modest headline, "Madame Eames Given an Ovation Such as Was Never Bestowed in Portland."[77] News of concert appearances were often accompanied by detailed interviews with former classmates and family friends. The public seemed equally gratified at Eames's apparent pleasure at being in Maine. "Most fitting is it," Eames pointed out, "that as I made my first appearance in Bath at a small musical, I should come back to my first starting point for this tour."[78]

Media claims on Eames extended beyond the Maine border. New England music critics accounted for Eames's European training by expressing great pride in her combination of "Yankee ancestry and training with the superstructure of French education and accomplishment."[79] Eames herself viewed her career and life in terms of the dual influences of New England and Europe. She designed the monument that marks her grave to commemorate both continents—a ten-ton piece of Italian marble topped by an elegantly sculpted pine tree.[80] Eames died in 1952 and is buried in Bath.

Nordica was also admired in Maine and frequently returned. She sang in the first Maine Festival to a "breathless" audience who "drank up every tone."[81] In 1900, she was the first soloist to sing in the new Portland City Hall Auditorium with the Kotzszhmar Memorial Organ.[82] She also gave several concerts in Farmington. With the proceeds of one concert she donated kerosene streetlights for the town. On another occasion in 1911 she appeared in full operatic regalia, complete with jewels and gowns, and sang her most famous pieces at the State Normal School's Merrill Hall (now Nordica Auditorium at the University of Maine at Farmington). During this final Farmington concert she sang "Home, Sweet Home," turning slowly in the direction of the Norton homestead on the Holley Road.[83] In 1944 then-Congresswoman Margaret Chase Smith of Maine witnessed the launching of the first Liberty ship named for a musical artist, the S.S. *Lillian Nordica*, and the centennial of Nordica's birth, 1957, was proclaimed the Year of Lillian Nordica.[84]

Nordica's reputation extended far beyond Maine. The *New York Times* traced every nuance of her career, up to the round-the-world concert she announced in 1913 at the age of fifty-nine in hopes of recouping the money squandered by her third husband. But luck was not with her. After a shipwreck off the coast of Java, she died a lingering death in a hospital on the island of Batavia. A Portland newspaper reported she would be buried in Maine, but according to Glackens, she was cremated in London and her estranged husband, George Washington Young, laid claim to her ashes, carrying them to America, final destination unknown.[85]

Despite what Willa Cather said of Farmington—"Could a singer be born in a worse place, by the way?"[86]—Maine and Maine values shaped Nordica and Eames. As Cather gradually acknowledged the shaping power of her own rural Nebraska childhood, she recast Nordica as someone "wholesome and invigorating like the clean smell of the pine woods, mingled with the fresh sea breezes."[87] Cather's diva heroine Thea, in *The Song of the Lark*, leaves her prairie hometown, Moonstone, for studies in Chicago and then in Germany. When she returns to New York triumphant, she realizes that the roots of her art are in Moonstone, in what she calls her "rich, romantic past."[88] A 1930s carved wooden mural in the Farmington Post Office expresses something of the same idea. It shows Nordica as a child sitting by a brook listening to birds sing, suggesting that Nordica's Farmington childhood put her in touch with the source of her art.

These Maine artists have been embraced by the communities from which they came. Wayne's public library is named for Annie Louise Cary, and Nordica's birthplace in Farmington is a museum, containing her costumes and other memorabilia. The University of Maine at Farmington calls one of its public spaces "Nordica Auditorium." Eames's publicity photographs have been on display at the Patten Free Library in Bath.

These downeast divas challenge many assumptions about Maine and about Maine women in history. Historians have tended to place Maine on the periphery in terms of political and cultural significance. This assessment is beginning to change.[89] Alan Taylor's most recent work on the borderlands region of coastal Maine and New Brunswick, Canada, for instance, suggests that historians need to reexamine the connections that Maine has had to mainstream society.[90] Maine women have been praised by historians and novelists for being strong and independent. The example of the divas reinforces and extends those images. It seems clear that women like Nordica, Eames, and Cary, despite their rural upbringing, came from an environment that exposed them to high culture. Divas, moreover, paved the way for new generations of American women, helping them to become more comfortable with their public voice, and encouraging them to speak out and become part of the public conversation.

Photos of Emma Eames courtesy of Patten Free Library, Bath, Maine, and reproduced by Robert A. Miller. Thanks also to the Patten Free Library for their helpfulness and their research facilities, and to Rob Stevens for his curiosity about Emma Eames. Photos of Nordica courtesy of the Nordica Homestead, Farmington, Maine.

1. Emma Eames, *Some Memories and Reflections* (New York: D. Appleton and Co., 1927), 80. Nordica expressed this ambition to a reporter, according to Richard Hallett, in "Lillian Nordica Devoted Life to Operatic Career," *Portland Sunday Telegram*, 19 March 1944, 12B.

2. Hermann Klein, *Great Women-Singers of My Time* (New York: Dutton, 1931), 113.

3. Joan Jacobs Brumberg, in *Fasting Girls: The Emergence of Anorexia Nervosa as a Modern Disease* (Cambridge, Mass.: Harvard University Press, 1988) argues that in the late nineteenth century, young middle-class women developed a variety of health problems relating to non-eating. Brumberg writes: "Wasting was in style" (171). Also, Lillian Nordica specifically warned that thinness was detrimental to singing in *Hints to Singers*, William Armstrong, ed. (Mineola, New York: Dover Publications, 1998, orig. pub. New York: E. P. Dutton, 1923), 63.

4. William David Barry, "Maine and the Arts," in *Maine: The Pine Tree State from Prehistory to the Present*, ed. Richard W. Judd, Edwin A. Churchill and Joel W. Eastman (Orono: University of Maine Press, 1995), 486.

5. Joyce Butler, "Family and Community Life in Maine, 1783–1861," in *Maine: The Pine Tree State*, 225.

6. George Thornton Edwards, ed., *Music and Musicians of Maine* (Portland, Maine: Southworth Press, 1928), 194.

7. Ira Glackens, *Yankee Diva: Lillian Nordica and the Golden Days of Opera* (New York: Coleridge Press, 1963), 9–15.

8. Edwards, *Music and Musicians*, 206, 208, 216.

9. Eames, *Some Memories*, 18.

10. *Lewiston Journal*, 10 September 1905.

11. Lee Agger, *Women of Maine* (Portland, Maine: G. Gannett Co., 1982), 166.

12. *Bath Daily Times*, 12 March 1885.

13. Oscar Thompson, *The American Singer: A Hundred Years of Success in Opera* (New York: Dial Press, 1937), 174.

14. Eames, *Some Memories*, 21, 87.

15. Thompson, *American Singer*, 174.

16. Max De Schauensee, "A Tribute to Emma Eames," *Opera News Magazine* 27 (October 1952).

17. *Bath Daily Times*, 31 January 1887.

18. Barbara Sicherman and Carol Hurd Green, eds., *Notable American Women: The Modern Period* (Cambridge, Mass.: Belknap Press of Harvard University Press, 1980), 214.

19. Thompson, *American Singer*, 182.

20. Willa Cather, "Some Personages of the Opera," *The Library*, 29 March 1900, reprinted in *The World and the Parish: Willa Cather's Articles and Reviews, 1893–1902*, ed. William M. Curtin, 2 vols. (Lincoln: University of Nebraska Press, 1970), 2: 758.

21. "Nordica's Fierce Will to Win Recalled in Centennial Year," *Portland Press Herald*, 12 May 1957, 12C.

22. Glackens, *Yankee Diva*, 52–58, 90, 162.

23. Rebecca A. Pope, "The Diva Doesn't Die: George Eliot's *Armgart*," *Criticism* 32 (Fall 1990): 471.

24. Willa Cather, *The Song of the Lark* (Boston: Houghton-Mifflin, 1915, reprint 1988), 213.

25. John Dizikes, *Opera in America: A Cultural History* (New Haven, Conn.: Yale University Press, 1993), 86–87.

26. *The Story of a Hundred Operas* (New York: Grosset and Dunlap, 1940), 130, 152, 4.

27. Thompson, *American Singer*, 174.

28. "Nordica's Triumph," *Portland Evening Express*, 19 October 1897, 1.

29. Edwards, *Music and Musicians*, 239, 234.

30. Wayne Kostenbaum, *The Queen's Throat: Opera, Homosexuality and the Mystery of Desire* (New York: Poseidon, 1993), 155.

31. Willam Dean Howells, *The Lady of the Aroostook* (Boston: Houghton, Osgood, 1879), 120.

32. George Eliot, "Armgart," *Complete Poems by George Eliot* (Boston: Estes, 1870), 323.

33. Koestenbaum, *Queen's Throat*, 101.

34. Debra Cumberland, "A Struggle for Breath: Contemporary Vocal Theory in Cather's *The Song of the Lark*," *American Literary Realism 1870–1910* 28, 2 (Winter 1996): 63–65.

35. Cather, "Some Personages of the Opera," 2: 758.

36. Glackens, *Yankee Diva*, 160.

37. Cather, "Lohengrin and Die Walkure," *Lincoln (Nebraska) Courier*, 10 June 1899, 3, reprinted in *The World and the Parish*, 2: 620.

38. Klein, *Great Women-Singers*, 234.

39. Hallett, "Lillian Nordica Devoted Life," 12B; Edwards, *Music and Musicians*, 245.

40. Eliot, "Armgart," 822.

41. Rebecca Harding Davis, "The Wife's Story," *The Atlantic Monthly* 14 (July 1864): 16.

42. Elizabeth Stuart Phelps, *The Story of Avis* (Boston: Osgood, 1877), 195.

43. Cather, "Married Nightingales Seldom Sing," *Nebraska State Journal*, 27 January 1895, 13, reprinted in *The World and the Parish*, 1: 176.

44. Glackens, *Yankee Diva*, 124.

45. "Nordica Says Doehme Says He'd Kill Her," *New York Times*, 22 April 1904.

46. Willa Cather, "The Diamond Mine," *Youth and the Bright Medusa* (Vintage, 1975, 1916), 67–120.

47. Glackens, *Yankee Diva*, 265.

48. Richard Hallet, "A Great Maine Opera Star—Emma Eames," *Down East Magazine* 10, 1 (August 1963).

49. Sara M. Evans, *Born for Liberty: A History of Women in America* (New York: Free Press, 1989), 147.

50. Carroll Smith-Rosenberg, *Disorderly Conduct: Visions of Gender in Victorian America* (New York: Oxford University Press, 1985), 176–78.

51. *Bath Independent*, 1 May 1907.

52. Sicherman and Green, *Notable American Women*, 215.

53. *Bath Daily Times*, 13 December 1910.

54. Mary P. Ryan, *Women in Public: Between Banners and Ballots, 1825–1880* (Baltimore: Johns Hopkins University Press, 1990), 73; see also 58–94.

55. Harold Schonberg, *Glorious Ones: Classical Music's Legendary Performers* (New York: Times Books, 1985), 258.

56. *Bath Daily Times*, 5 December 1913.

57. Glackens, *Yankee Diva*, 185–97.

58. *Bath Independent*, 3 August 1895.

59. Schonberg, *The Glorious Ones*, 258, 259.

60. Eliot, "Armgart," 340.

61. Joseph Horowitz, *Wagner Nights: An American History* (Berkeley: University of California Press, 1994), 336.

62. Dizikes, *Opera in America*, 137–38.

63. Susan J. Leonardi and Rebecca A. Pope, "Screaming Divas: Collaboration as Feminist Practice," *Tulsa Studies* 13 (Fall 1994): 266.

64. Cather, "An Open Letter to Nordica," *Lincoln (Nebraska) Courier*, 16 December 1899, reprinted in *The World and the Parish*, 1: 646, 644.

65. Sharon O'Brien, *Willa Cather: The Emerging Voice* (New York: Oxford University Press, 1987), 166-73. See also Bernice Slote, *The Kingdom of Art: Willa Cather's First Principles and Critical Statements, 1893–1896* (Lincoln: University of Nebraska Press), 86; and Richard Giannone, *Music in Willa Cather's Fiction* (Lincoln: University of Nebraska Press, 1968).

66. *Bath Daily Times*, 18 April 1917.

67. "Mme. Nordica Sings for the Suffragists," *New York Times*, 17 June 1910. Her active role in suffrage is also mentioned in "Music World to Turn Eyes Toward Portland: Commemoration of 20th Anniversary of Lillian Nordica's Death," *Portland Sunday Telegram*, 19 November 1933, 1D.

68. Glackens, *Yankee Diva*, 241.

69. Ibid.

70. Nordica, *Hints to Singers*, 42, 54, 56, 63.

71. Regina Markell Morantz-Sanchez, *Sympathy and Science: Women Physicians in American Medicine* (New York: Oxford University Press, 1985), 37–38.

72. Cather, *Song of the Lark*, 392.

73. Eames, *Some Memories*, 285, 302.

74. Nordica, *Hints to Singers*, 78.

75. *Bath Independent*, 23 November 1901.

76. Program cover, Ninth Maine Festivals 1905, Folder on Emma Eames, Genealogy Room, Patten Free Library, Bath, Maine.

77. *Lewiston Journal*, 7 October 1905; *Portland Daily Press*, 12 October 1905.

78. *Portland Daily Press*, 12 October 1905.

79. *Bath Independent*, 25 February 1963.

80. Newspaper clipping, date unknown (1953?), folder on Emma Eames, Genealogy Room, Patten Free Library.

81. "Nordica's Triumph," *Portland Evening Express*, 10 October 1897, 1.

82. Hallett, "Lillian Nordica Devoted Life," 12B.

83. Glackens, *Yankee Diva*, 253.

84. *Portland Press Herald*, 18 March 1944, 1.

85. "Nordica's Ashes Here: Her Husband Brings Them From London in a Silver Urn," *New York Times*, 16 July 1914.

86. Cather, "Nordica," *Nebraska State Journal*, 13 December 1896, reprinted in *The World and the Parish*, 1: 383.

87. Cather, "An Open Letter to Nordica," 1: 646.

88. Cather, *Song of the Lark*, 396.

89. Richard W. Judd, "Introduction," in *Maine: The Pine Tree State*, 7.

90. Alan Taylor, speech given at Bowdoin College, Brunswick, Maine, 12 April 1997.

PART THREE

THE MID-TWENTIETH CENTURY

The United States assumed an international presence in the mid-twentieth century, a role inspired by winning World War II and growing confidence in its political traditions. Beginning with the first election of Franklin Roosevelt in the depths of the Depression and continuing for decades, Americans enjoyed a long stretch of optimism about themselves and their futures. Once the Depression was ended the nation's economy led the world in most measures of growth and development, although increasing postwar globalization would lead to a new awareness of economic vulnerability. Confidence and optimism came accompanied by other kinds of doubts as well; even as Americans looked forward to and then enjoyed prosperity and military superiority, they feared potential dangers from within and without. The dangers of fascism and especially communism lurked at home as well as abroad, so forms of dissent that had been tolerated, even encouraged, during the Depression now had to be quashed. Immigrants, unions, reform groups, Hollywood were all inspected to be sure that they conformed to the correct patriotic values. During the war, Japanese Americans were sent to internment camps because the government questioned their loyalty, while after it was over the Taft-Hartley Act prevented many kinds of union organizing, including by communists. Americans who believed their political system and economic arrangements to be the best in the world nevertheless feared they were in danger of toppling with only minor provocation.

Women experienced the middle decades of the century in similarly disjointed fashion. Denied the legitimacy of working for wages during the Depression because men were assumed to be the breadwinners, women turned to traditional ways of making ends meet. Yet because so many men were unemployed, women continued to take jobs outside their homes; no matter how discouraged or desperate, men were unwilling to work at jobs traditionally assigned to women. During the war, the same women who had been criticized for working outside their homes just a few years earlier were encouraged to take jobs in support of the war effort; some moved into jobs in heavy industry never before available to them. Women's wartime economic gains were not to last, however; once the war ended they were summarily dismissed and told, once again, that their place was in the home. Women were told once again that marriage and motherhood should define their existence; the rhetoric was so emphatic and the pressures for conformity so great that few were able to resist in an organized, public manner, although many did so privately.

These trends were deeply felt in Maine. Maine had experienced the Depression largely as a continuation of previous hard times, but the wartime boom brought unprecedented growth, especially in ship building. Improvements in transportation and communication, especially electricity and the radio, then television, brought the world within reach and eliminated much of the state's rural isolation. Tourists poured into the state while the young and ambitious fled. Even so, Maine remained something of an economic and cultural backwater. The prosperity enjoyed by the rest of the nation was not felt in many corners of the state, whose resource-based economy did not grow at anything approaching the national rate. Many in Maine were content with traditional ways of life, shunning anything that smacked of social change and refusing to raise taxes to support the kinds of programs in education, health, and social services that were common elsewhere. Maine, it seemed, was no longer at the cutting edge of anything, nor did it wish to be.

Maine women in the mid-twentieth century were no more adventuresome than the men of the state. They conformed to the national pattern of moving in and out of the paid labor force during and after World War II; some were employed at Bath Iron Works and other military industries. They continued to work in partnership with their husbands to ensure family survival. They were no more likely to object to traditional roles than were women elsewhere. Yet occasional signs pointed in a new direction. Although the votes women cast were little different from their husbands', women were standing for elective office in increasing numbers at mid-century— and winning. More of them were seeking higher education and planning to use that education in ways other than teaching. Still, for most these decades of conformity to traditional notions of women's roles meant limited opportunity to break free of convention. The state's economic backwardness limited the choices available to them; its avoidance of anything hinting at change made those who wanted something different for themselves recognize that their primary option was to leave. A more expansive future, in which women in Maine and the nation could choose from among more options and opportunities, would have to wait for the next generation.

The story of Native American history is often told in terms of their constant movement westward: away from the Atlantic coast, across the Appalachians and the Mississippi, eventually ending on reservations in isolated areas of the Great Plains. That story ignores the experiences of those in what is now the Southwest and along the Pacific coast, whose encounters with the Spanish were similarly destructive but in a rather different cultural and economic context. It also ignores the experiences of those who continued to live east of the Mississippi, in areas increasingly densely settled by whites. For them, the primary difficulties were not so much associated with removal as with pressure to assimilate into the dominant culture. That pressure came in many guises, from near-compulsion to adopt white languages, laws, education, religion, and other practices; to the economic pressure resulting from the inability to sustain a traditional livelihood; to the enticements associated with white culture, ranging from alcohol to cash, that were often particularly appealing to the young. Whether resisted or welcomed, however, assimilation generally meant the loss of traditions, of familiar ways of thinking and acting, from one generation to the next.

In Maine and elsewhere, those committed to resisting assimilation usually adopted an ambivalent attitude towards the white people among whom they lived. Sustaining cultural integrity in the face of the dominant society was difficult, yet by the turn of the century that society also developed a level of curiosity about Indians that some were willing to turn to their own advantage. This could entail enacting a measure of Indian-ness that met white assumptions, for example, or commodifying one's culture in order to appeal to white consumers. Such compromises simultaneously allowed Native people to preserve their own culture even as it was transformed under the pressure of white expectations.

For women, such dilemmas were especially troubling because Native society had such different gender expectations from those of whites. Native women, accustomed to positions of leadership and holding power within their communities, were reluctant to conform to the confined roles allotted to white women. Yet in some instances, they were pressured to do so not only by whites who claimed to have their best interests at heart, but also by the men of their own communities eager to enhance their status in the context of their own diminished power.

The situation for Maine's Native American women never reached anything near such a difficult level. Yet here, too, traditional gender arrangements along with ways of living were challenged by the proximity of an intrusive white society. Lucy Nicolar found one strategy for coping with these pressures while maintaining her sense of herself as a Native American woman; the women Pauleena MacDougall writes about, from the same background as Nicolar, developed another. Their story of changing responses to assimilation demonstrates the complexities of maintaining cultural integrity over several generations.

WEAVING A TRADITION: WOMEN BASKET MAKERS IN PENOBSCOT CULTURE

Pauleena MacDougall

> So many hours were spent picking berries, braiding sweetgrass, weaving baskets, chopping wood or shoveling snow and in return I gathered many a tale of my people, some old and legendary, and others the product of their own vivid imagination.
>
> —Molly Spotted Elk, Old Town, Maine, April 13, 1938[1]

Maine's Native American women (including Penobscot, Passamaquoddy, Maliseet, and Micmac) can be understood by considering the traditional stories that they have told for centuries in smoky wigwams during the long winter nights. Men and women told the stories to educate the next generation about the traditions, beliefs and history of the community. When we compare these stories with what we know about the industrious basket-making culture of late nineteenth- and twentieth-century Maine Indians, we find a complex transformation in which women's traditional roles and activities assumed new forms yet served familiar purposes. Women who had previously made baskets only to meet the needs of their families learned from the examples set in the stories they heard to aid their families by turning their skills in new directions.

Penobscot stories provided the community with cultural information or instruction about acceptable and unacceptable behavior, gender roles, and the knowledge and skills essential to subsistence. Anthropologist Frank G. Speck collected numerous samples of stories from Penobscot men and women during the first two decades of the twentieth century, soon after women were developing new roles as basket makers.[2] Other scholars collected similar tales among the Micmac, Maliseet and Passamaquoddy people around the same time.[3] The stories about Gluskabe[4] as well as other mythological beings demonstrate the cultural beliefs of the Native people of this region.

Gluskabe is the hero of epic tales that describe the transformation of the world from a place with giants and huge animals to a place suitable for human occupation. However, as important as Gluskabe is, he would be nothing without the woman who taught him all of the hunting and fishing skills he needed. Stories about Gluskabe's training as a young man feature a character known as Grandmother Woodchuck. She taught him the skills and knowledge that later become the core of traditional Penobscot belief. The Penobscots revered and sometimes feared her spiritual power and wisdom. She educated the male hero, teaching him life skills and social responsibility. She taught Gluskabe how to hunt, fish, and how to build a canoe and make arrows and spears—all the things a young man needed to know in order to provide food for his family. Grandmother passed on more than simple survival skills. When Gluskabe captured all the fish or all the game, she chastised him to leave some to reproduce for future generations.[5] In many of the stories Gluskabe took some action that would affect his descendants. Grandmother Woodchuck warned him to conserve resources, reinforcing the importance of kinship and community survival. Grandmother Woodchuck is the female archetype of mature womanhood. The activities she engaged in were those of most mature Penobscot women. The traditional stories depict women as independent, resourceful and knowledgeable, as well as the teachers and moral guides of men.

Grandmother Woodchuck is not the only woman or girl in Penobscot stories. One story about a woman has a ring of historical truth. In this story, a young woman was kidnapped by some Iroquois warriors and taken south. She had numerous adventures during her captivity. The Iroquois tortured her, burning the tips of her fingers. Her fingernails became deformed as a result, and she was subsequently named "Arrowhead Fingernails." She eventually escaped and returned to her community alone and with great difficulty.[6] Her ability to travel a long distance without assistance reinforces the understanding in Penobscot culture that women had the necessary skills to survive in the world without male protection when necessary.

The Penobscots also told numerous stories about abandoned women. Sometimes they were elderly, at other times wives abandoned by philandering husbands. But in all cases they were left alone on an island to die. However, in each case they found shelter, made a wigwam of bark, snared rabbits for food, tanned the rabbit skins and made clothing. After many years these women were either found by relatives or saved their starving relatives when the relatives returned. Clearly the stories speak to the skills and self-sufficiency of mature women. If they could survive abandonment, they were without a doubt resourceful enough to find solutions to all manner of difficulties, including the kind of political and economic deprivation Native women would find themselves facing in the late nineteenth and twentieth centuries.[7]

Some stories about mythological women reflect the ambivalence people felt about women's sexuality. The story of Skwehtemohs, "Swamp Woman," describes a hideous creature in the woods who transforms herself into a beautiful woman to save hunters lost in the woods by making them new clothes and snowshoes and directing them home. Other stories about woodland female sprites warn about the dangers of the woods. In these stories the mysteries of nature are equated with the mysteries of women. Pskegdemas longs for men and children. Hunters who encounter her lose interest in marriage. Maskikwesu, "Toad Woman," seduces men and children. She puts children in a deep sleep from which they cannot awaken. These stories engage people's fears of the negative aspects of women's strength and power. Pohkechin-skwehso, "Jug Woman," is old, sometimes foolish, and repulsive but very powerful. Her child is the Skunk Cabbage. Jug Woman takes on powerful shamans, including, at times, Gluskabe. In one story she holds Gluskabe at a standoff until she can release a terrible scourge of mosquitoes and other biting insects. She is described as having a stick for her husband, a joking reference to old women, usually widowed, who often get about with the aid of a walking stick.[8]

While the Grandmother stories portrayed women as skilled and wise, these stories of hideous women suggest that the Penobscot also considered them to be dangerous. These hideous and elderly women were threatening, but were also admired for their skills and power, suggesting a degree of ambivalence about their place in Penobscot culture. Audiences hearing tales about female protagonists such as these recognized the importance of female wisdom and resourcefulness to the continuation of traditions as well as survival of the community. Legendary females might be good or bad, valued or scorned but they were usually powerful, rarely victimized, and often possessed magical powers. Inspired by models such as these, Penobscot women sought to implement similar traits when faced with challenges in their own lives. In the late nineteenth and twentieth centuries, instead of using their strength and ability to snare rabbits for subsistence, women took the message of creativity and resourcefulness, skill and power and found a way to survive. They applied Grandmother Woodchuck's lessons about preserving community traditions and self-sufficiency to their own lives and turned to basket making as a source of income.

Basket making was just one of many subsistence activities that Penobscot women had taken part in before white settlers moved into Maine and began clearing the land and stripping it of game. Women were responsible for many tasks that helped to insure the survival of their communities. They set up houses, made warm clothes, gathered and prepared food, and bore and raised children. They also often helped men with fishing and hunting tasks, snaring rabbits and small game, butchering and cutting up meat, and processing skins and furs.

Women also made storage and cooking containers of birch bark. They sewed the bark of the white birch onto frames of ash. Weaving strips of ash, the first innovation in basket making during the early nineteenth century, led to modern basket technology. At that time men began making heavy storage baskets and travel cases or trunks and potato harvesting baskets to sell. Marketing first took place locally, with resident Catholic priests and state agents purchasing baskets for resale, but as the basket makers became more familiar with the rapidly growing

Figure 1. Birchbark with splint laced binder, wood bottom. Photo #6833, Northeast Archives of Folklore and Oral History (NAFOH), Maine Folklife Center, University of Maine.

Figure 2. Basket making at Indian Island, Old Town, Maine, circa 1908.
Courtesy of Maine Historic Preservation Commission.

dominant population, and as tourism grew after the Civil War, they began to do their own retailing off the reservation.

During the late nineteenth and early twentieth centuries, the Penobscots could no longer rely on traditional means of subsistence. Instead, men used their hunting skills to become guides and their boat handling skills to work on the river drives bringing logs to market, while women transformed their existing basket-making technology into a successful cottage industry in response to tourism. One reason for women's success was their astute response to a demand in the marketplace. Contact with the marketplace inspired women to alter the design of baskets, the methods and technologies used to manufacture them, and the marketing strategies used to sell them. Inspired by Grandmother Woodchuck and other female cultural heroes, Penobscot women transformed traditional skills in order to sustain themselves and their families and to preserve their culture. Where they once had been part of a subsistence economy, now they began to adapt traditional

Figure 3. The Penobscot Indian Agency Store. Courtesy of
Maine Historic Preservation Commission.

skills to a market economy. Always partners in a family
economy in which labor was divided by gender, Native
women wanted to earn money while still caring for their
homes and families.

Most women on Indian Island were listed as basket makers
by occupation in the U.S. census for 1910 as a sign of the
importance of this craft in their community. Men also made
baskets, usually the larger storage and pack baskets, and a
minority of men were identified as basket makers in the
same census. Usually these were men who also engaged in
other types of woodworking (in lumber mills) or were retired
from working on the river drives or in the woods.[9] Still, there
is no "basket maker" as such in Penobscot stories. Basket
maker is an occupation that women developed out of a need
to survive in a society with few opportunities.

Native women who turned to basket making as a means of
earning money found that they had to be resourceful and

inventive in order to do so effectively. Women performed most of the actual basket making tasks. Men provided the raw materials and sometimes pitched in with strip preparation. They went into the woods to cut the ash trees and pounded the logs until they could remove strips. They also helped by developing new tools such as gauges and forms. Some men continued to specialize in the making of pack baskets and other large utility baskets. However, the responsibility for developing basket making as a commercial activity belonged to women. A task-based division of labor was also adapted from American industry, with different parts of the basket making process being assigned to different women. While at first women would make whole baskets by themselves, using the materials men provided, they began to hire young women from the Maliseet and Micmac communities in Canada or the daughters of friends and relatives to assist them. The young women would just make the base or finish the edges. In this way families could more efficiently finish large orders for shipping or for the tourist trade. The work was not organized on a factory basis, but remained an extended family-based cottage industry.

Not only did women develop new, more efficient ways to manufacture baskets, they also found new ways to market them. Those who were literate in English learned new ideas for marketing their wares by reading newspapers and advertisements. They tailored their products to appeal to the public. After the turn of the century, the women's finely made "fancy basket" became the vogue among housewives who wished to decorate their homes with pretty things. Penobscot basket makers responded to the demand by manufacturing many items for this market. In keeping with the traditional gendered division of labor, women concentrated their efforts on fine work, thinning strips down to fine sizes, braiding sweet grass and developing new designs for the "fancy basket."

Women also organized the marketing of their families' work, seeking out new tourist areas in which to sell their baskets. Some women ran the stores or tent selling areas and made few baskets themselves. Instead, they hired other women and young girls to make baskets while they handled the retailing. One woman who adopted such a strategy was Madeline Tomer Shay's grandmother, Julia Saul Dana. Madeline Shay was a well-known Penobscot basket maker who worked in her grandmother's store at Poland Springs as a small child in the 1930s. Grandmother Dana expected young Madeline to follow her instructions and learn to be a basket maker. Her grandmother gave her all the gauges and the material and told her, "'Now you sit and you work; you learn how to make baskets.'" Dana followed the role of Grandmother Woodchuck as tradition bearer and teacher. But Julia Dana did not teach her granddaughter to make baskets herself. She had more important work to do and left that task to her employees so she could concentrate on marketing.

> My grandmother didn't do too much basketry. She did some, occa-
> sionally. Special orders, but she always had someone working for her.
> She had my father's aunt, Mary Ellen Mitchell, and she used to have
> Margaret Ranco. She worked for us quite a bit. Well, we had several
> different ones. I never went out anywhere. I always sat and watched
> them making baskets.[10]

Not only did Dana emulate Grandmother Woodchuck as teacher, she also imitated her resourcefulness and ingenuity.

Like Julia Dana, other Penobscot women brought their belongings and their children and set up large tents at various tourist destinations. Setting up camp throughout New England and eastern Canada in the late spring and early summer, they sold baskets until vacationers returned home in the fall. Native artisans and resorts cooperated in drawing

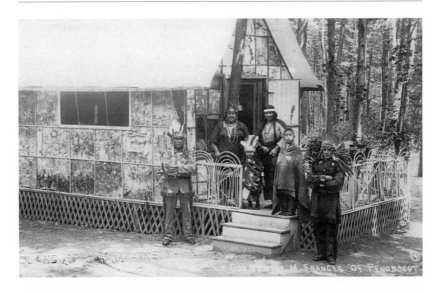

Figure 4. The Indian Camp at Poland Springs circa 1920. Left to right:
Newell M. Francis, Julia Saul Dana (Mitchell Newell), Madeline Poland
Francis Tomer (Shay), Edgar Tomer and Newell Tomer.
Collection of Michael S. Graham.

tourists. Penobscot families built birch bark covered cabins and donned culturally distinct clothing to attract summer visitors to buy their wares. Resorts advertised the presence of Native Americans in the "sylvan woods" of Maine to attract tourists who sought wilderness experiences as an escape from city life. Thus Native Americans cooperated with resort owners to commodify Native culture. Natives cooperated in this as a means of economic survival.

Women like Julia Dana who could not speak English engaged the young girls who were learning English in school to help them sell baskets. Shay remarked: "I was out in the store with her [Grandmother] because where she didn't talk English I had to help her. If anybody wanted to know anything I'd have to do all the tall explaining. Telling them what they wanted to know and telling her what they wanted to know and so I was in between."[11]

The younger generation of women born in the 1920s and '30s, including Madeline Shay, found themselves living "in between" two cultures, interpreting for each. Many women of Julia Dana's generation, though they spoke no English, knew that they needed to accept a degree of change in their lives in order to survive. So that they might sell their baskets they struck out for sometimes distant parts of New England where tourism thrived, and set up their businesses in the same location year after year, even generation after generation. They ranged as far as New Hampshire and Rhode Island, in addition to favorite spots in Maine such as Poland Springs and Bar Harbor. In doing so, they trained the next generation in basket making and marketing skills—and in women's traditional resourcefulness.

Demand for baskets increased as tourism grew and the antimodernist fascination with all things colonial led middle-class white people to a great interest in Native American culture and objects.[12] In response, Native women devised novel shapes for their baskets, often cleverly copying articles made from remarkably different materials. For example, their baskets imitated items usually made of cloth, china or glass such as workboxes, glove boxes, napkin rings, scissors' cases, candy dishes and creamers.[13] In adapting to the market, Native women continued to do fine basketwork; they simply found new expressions for their craft. By imitating items from the dominant culture, the basket makers reworked a traditional craft to fit the marketplace, thus insuring its survival.

Income from basket making became significant around 1864 when Indian agents began to report good returns. At first, this was probably due to their efforts to assist in subsistence activities by selling baskets in the agent's store. As the basket makers began to expand their markets to the tourist areas, Maine's Indian agent George Dillingham was able to report that by 1872 the home production of baskets had

Figure 5. Selection of sewing baskets and implement holders. Along outside edge, clockwise from top: birchbark canoe pincushion, sweetgrass and pointed porcupine pincushion, miniature sewing basket, brim edged sweetgrass pincushion, splint scissors holder, miniature sewing assortment. Center, clockwise from left: splint pincushion, miniature needle basket, miniature lidded basket. Photo #6814 NAFOH.

become the most important source of income for Penobscot families. "Many of the tribe have during the fall made improvements in their houses. This they are enabled to do from their savings in the result of their labor and profits in selling baskets and their other wares at the different watering places."[14] Basket sales brought in seasonal revenues large enough to make continued production throughout the winter not only possible, but also desirable in order to fill the demand of the summer trade. The need for materials also increased. Although families collected their own ash and

Figure 6. Indian Work at the Penobscot Indian Agency Store, Old Town, Maine, 1937. Courtesy of Maine Historic Preservation Committee.

sweet grass, at times demand grew so high that some had to purchase materials from other basket makers who had a surplus. As a result, some families began to specialize in obtaining raw materials for sale. Basket making seemed to offer a solution to the woes caused by erosion of the Penobscots' traditional means of subsistence.

But income from basket making was not always reliable. Sales were necessarily seasonal and the tourist market was subject to fluctuations due to weather, economic crises, social changes and warfare. Native artisans adapted to these changes but remained at the margins of mainstream society economically as well as socially and politically. Consequently, their efforts to survive in terms of economic welfare and ethnic integrity required constant struggle. Native people wanted and needed to use the skills they had to make a living despite limited opportunities. Making baskets was perhaps the most effective solution available. It allowed women to earn money to help support their families while continuing the traditional role of caring for children and husbands. It also allowed women to retain some measure of cultural integrity by remaining within their own communities for most of the year. If it required wearing feathers and being identified as stereotypical "Indians" in order to attract sales, they were willing to make the compromise.

In spite of the best efforts of Native people, basket making offered a sometimes precarious income. One business depression began in 1873 and lasted four years, resulting in plunging basket sales. An especially rainy or cold summer season would also reduce tourism and thus sales. Indian Agent Charles Bailey reported that during the 1881 summer season basket makers experienced "a failure of the revenues usually resulting to the tribe. . . . Owing to the unpropitious weather, it is well known that there was a greatly diminished atten-

Figure 7. Doll cradle. Photo #6842 NAFOH.

dance at these resorts. . . . Many were brought to need who had before been able to care for themselves and their families."[15] In the past, hunters and gatherers suffered hunger during hard winters and poor hunting seasons, while now Native people found themselves similarly suffering hardship due to weather that affected the tourist markets.

Another obstacle to economic well being was the seasonal nature of basket sales. A great deal of time and work was required to prepare all the necessary baskets and then to move family and belongings to resort areas each spring. Indian Agent John H. Stowe reported in 1888: "The preparations for these yearly trips often-times involve the labor of months and no little self-denial."[16] There was little in the way of a safety net available during the off season as the Indian agent doled out only meager subsistence rations from the Indians' own funds during emergencies. In addition, major events such as the presidential election campaign in 1888 and the Paris Exposition of 1889 drew patrons away from New England resorts. To offset losses, a few families began expanding their selling season by filling basket orders for the Christmas trade in 1891. Such fluctuations in demand made it difficult for Native families to control their financial circumstances.

Basket makers also suffered the consequences of racism. Often the reception Native artisans' families received from their white neighbors in tourist destinations mirrored the ambivalence white society demonstrated toward Native people. While large hotels and resorts welcomed the basket makers, sometimes the local community objected to sharing their Main Street and tourist dollars with Indians. A visitor's description of the Passamaquoddy encampment at Bar Harbor in 1894 suggests that local businesses wished to keep Native Americans in the background of their community.

> An element of the picturesque is supplied by an Indian Camp, which
> used for years to be pitched in a marshy field known as Squaw
> Hollow; but with the advent of a Village Improvement Society, certain
> newfangled and disturbing ideas as to sanitary conditions obtained a
> hearing, and the Indians were banished to a back road. . . . Their little
> shanties—some of them tents, some of them shanties covered with
> tarpaper and strips of bark—are scattered about.[17]

The identification of the Indian camp as "Squaw Hollow"
is a telling example of how dominant cultural stereotypes of
Native people were applied to basket makers. Hotel owners
and other tourist industry leaders recognized that the presence of "Indians" added to the allure of the country landscape
that attracted tourists. Local merchants who owned small
stores, especially those that sold souvenirs did not welcome
the competition from basket makers for tourist dollars.
However, shared economic rewards usually insured harmony.

During the 1930s, economic crises and social change
would again disrupt the basket making industry. American
businesses devastated by the Great Depression laid off many
workers and even the middle class had little money for extra
items, such as fancy baskets. Basket makers attempted to
market their goods to smaller numbers of tourists. One clever
strategy devised to meet the crisis was a summer pageant on
Indian Island, organized first by the Sodality of the Catholic
Church and later by the Indian Island Women's Club which
included several basket makers.[18] The pageant drew summer
visitors to Old Town. During the rest of this difficult time,
people got by as they did elsewhere in Maine by making do
and helping each other out.[19]

World War II brought prosperity, but at a high cost to
Native communities in Maine. Many Native people moved
away to Massachusetts and Connecticut to work in wartime
industries. Those who relocated often continued to make baskets to supplement their wages, yet the decline in the basket

making industry begun
during the Depression
continued during the
post-war era. Because
younger people left the
reservation, the older
generation was unable
to pass down its skills.
Older basket makers
were proud of their
craft and their ability
to provide money to
their families by selling
baskets and they want-
ed the practice to con-

Figure 8. Ribbon Curl Fancy Basket, early
twentieth century. Photo #6799 NAFOH.

tinue. To their lament, the younger generation was less interested in learning the craft, as they could earn money in other
ways, such as working in war industries. By 1950, few were
training to carry on basket making, instead rebelling against
the rigors of hard work, long hours, and piecework in a cottage industry with low wages and little opportunity. Able to
take advantage of abundant work opportunities away from
the reservation and higher wages characteristic of postwar
America, the new generation disdained a craft they viewed as
used by marginal people to scratch up an uncertain and sometimes meager income.

The dramatic social upheavals of the 1960s and 1970s
reversed the decline. An interest in their own culture among
Native young people brought granddaughters to their grandmothers' knees to learn to make baskets. As they began to
understand the place of basket making within a larger cultural context of values and institutions; of language, dancing,
and song; of kin networks and religious belief, this generation
increasingly recognized its importance. By 1990, with the

help of funding from the Maine Arts Commission and the National Endowment for the Arts, Maine instituted a program to support efforts to revive this and other traditional arts.[20] Today, contemporary Native artisans make baskets that sell for much better prices than they did in the nineteenth century. Individuals and museums seek these fine baskets for their collections and exhibits. Members of the Native communities in Maine are proud of their basket makers. They have organized into a cooperative known as the Maine Indian Basketmaker's Alliance and have recently opened a gallery in Old Town that features their baskets. Younger women learn fine basket making from those with particular skill, and in the process they also learn the stories and other traditions of their people.

Although women's knowledge of basket making waned during the middle of the twentieth century, it has since experienced a revival. Basket forms and shapes that were innovative during the nineteenth century have become the traditional forms, while young women now combine shapes and colors in original ways. Although Penobscot women today have many more options and opportunities in the market place, many young women wish to continue their tradition of basket making as a means of insuring cultural integrity in an increasingly homogenous world. When young women today approach the elderly basket makers who grew up during more difficult times and ask to learn to make baskets, they reinforce the traditional grandmother's cultural role. They are learning and relearning the lessons of women's strength, independence and resourcefulness.

★ ★ ★

Inspired by the stories they heard in their communities, mid-nineteenth-century Penobscot women learned to be self-reliant and independent from their mothers and grandmothers. When women found their hunting and gathering economy no longer viable, they used the message of women's resourcefulness taught by the stories to find ways to survive. They began making and marketing baskets, incorporating useful parts of white practices while retaining cultural distinctiveness by making a unique style of baskets identified as "Indian." They both accepted and resisted assimilation. They assimilated only those aspects of white society that were useful to them: education, marketing, and piecework. At the same time they resisted by retaining a separate identity as "Penobscot basket maker," preserving some independence by working for themselves, and continuing to pass on traditional knowledge by training the next generation of basket makers. By their resourcefulness, skill and adaptability, these women demonstrated the continuing influence of Grandmother Woodchuck in their lives.

1. Mary Alice Nelson, "'Katah-din: Wigwam's Tales of the Abnaki Tribes': The Penobscot Writing of Molly Spotted Elk," *Northeast Folklore* 27 (Orono: Maine Folklife Center, forthcoming).

2. Speck published stories in several journals and his book, *Penobscot Man* (Philadelphia: University of Pennsylvania Press, 1940; reprint Orono: University of Maine Press, 1997).

3. See for example: Silas T. Rand, *Legends of the Micmacs* (New York: Longmans, Green, 1894); W. H. Mechling, *Malecite Tales*, Canada Department of Mines, Geological Survey, Memoir 49, Anthropological Series no. 4, Ottawa, 1914; Walter J. Fewkes, "A Contribution to Passamaquoddy Folk-Lore," *Journal of American Folklore* 3 (1890): 257–80.

4. Spelled in various ways (Kluskabe, Glooscap, Klooscap) and pronounced slightly differently in the different Native communities in Maine, but the same cultural hero.

5. Frank G. Speck, "Penobscot Transformer Tales," *International Journal of American Linguistics* 1, 3 (1918): 199.

6. Frank G. Speck, "Penobscot Tales and Religious Beliefs," *The Journal of American Folklore* 48, 187 (1935): 11; and "Wawenock Myth Texts from Maine," *43rd Annual Report of the Bureau of American Ethnology* (Washington: Smithsonian Institution, 1928), 165–97.

7. Speck, "Penobscot Tales and Religious Beliefs," 84, 89.

8. Speck, "Penobscot Tales and Religious Beliefs," 16, 83.

9. Of 107 women listed, 85 were basket makers, 3 homemakers, 2 worked in retail sales and 17 had no occupation listed. For the men, 13 of 107 listed basket making as their occupation; most were listed as woods laborer. United States Census, 1910, Indian Island.

10. Madeline Tomer Shay, interview by author, Indian Island, Maine, 28 January 1993. Northeast Archives No. 2383, 3, Maine Folklife Center, University of Maine, Orono.

11. Northeast Archives 2383, 4.

12 Dona Brown, *Inventing New England: Regional Tourism in the Nineteenth Century* (Washington: Smithsonian Institution Press, 1995), 183–86.

13. Joan Lester, "'We Didn't Make Fancy Baskets Until We were Discovered': Fancy-Basket Making in Maine," *A Key Into the Language of Woodsplint Baskets*, ed. Ann McMullen and Russell G. Handman (Washington, Conn.: American Indian Archeological Institute, 1987), 53.

14. George Dillingham, *Report of the Indian Agent for the Penobscot Tribe* (Augusta, Maine: Sprague, Owen & Nash, 1873), 5.

15. Charles Bailey, *Report of the Agent of the Penobscot Tribe of Indians* (Augusta, Maine: Sprague & Son, 1881), 8.

16. J. N. Stowe, *Report of the Agent of the Penobscot Tribe of Indians for the Year 1888* (Augusta, Maine: Burleigh & Flynt, 1889), 7.

17. F. Marion Crawford, *Bar Harbor* (New York: Charles Scribner's Sons, 1894), 12.

18. Sadie Mitchell, interview by Dianne Ballon, 11 March 1987, Northeast Archives #1967, 14. Lucy Nicolar was the club's first vice president. See Bunny McBride's article, "Princess Watahwaso: Bright Star of the Penobscot," in this volume.

19. Theodore Mitchell, interview by author, 19 August 1993. Northeast Archives #2387.

20. Kathleen Mundell, *Basket Tree Basket Makers* (Augusta: Maine Arts Commission, 1992), 12.

The hardships brought by the Great Depression compelled women throughout the nation to adopt a range of unfamiliar roles. Some worked outside the home for the first time, taking jobs men scorned, primarily in the service sector. Others took on new responsibilities as heads of households, as discouraged men abandoned their families in record numbers. Some women were forced to negotiate with government relief workers and charitable agencies in an effort to care for their children. Since most Americans believed that whatever work was available rightly belonged to men in their roles as providers, women in large numbers lost their jobs, whether or not their husbands were present and employed. With only a tenuous legitimacy in the eyes of the public, professional women were particularly hard hit.

A few women were able to carve new opportunities for themselves out of the hardships of the Depression. Some government relief agencies hired women workers in small numbers, including the Civilian Conservation Corps and the Federal Writers' Project. Women served as labor organizers, particularly in the new industrial unions of the CIO, while others joined radical groups of all sorts from theaters to community organizing groups to health clinics to housewives' cooperatives. Still others, even smaller in number but dramatic in impact, worked for the federal government after 1932; Frances Perkins became the first woman cabinet member, while others assumed responsible positions in New Deal agencies and government offices.

Far more typical were the experiences of women who struggled to keep their families afloat. Women became experts at stretching limited resources, learning to bake without eggs or milk and to remake old clothing in inventive ways. Women grew gardens and preserved the crops, ensuring that families would not go hungry. In many households women's domestic production made the difference between at least an adequate standard of living and outright want. In addition, women's traditional place at the emotional center of family life became even more essential as Americans struggled with uncertainty in the present and anxiety for the future. Unemployed husbands were often discouraged and demoralized. With less money for entertainment, families were forced back on their own resources; this too could cause strain. The Depression disrupted family life in other ways as well, the absence of resources causing many to delay marriage and childbearing, others to double up in housing or disperse children to relatives better able to care for them. All of this put enormous pressure on women, who were expected to remain cheerful and provide comfort no matter what; that so many were able to rise to the occasion is testimony both to their strength and to the depth of the need. While in some parts of the country, including Maine, the Depression seemed little more than a continuation of hard times, its very pervasiveness called for inventive solutions. Dale Mudge offers a view of the ways in which one group of Maine women used traditional means to adapt to difficult circumstances.

WOOL YARNS:
TEXTILES AMONG ACADIAN WOMEN
IN THE ST. JOHN RIVER VALLEY

Dale Sperry Mudge

When Therese Albert was six months old, at the beginning of
the Great Depression, her father died, leaving her mother
with the responsibility of maintaining their farm in the St.
John Valley and supporting their family of fourteen children.
Alphonsine Deschaine Chasse and the children not only operated the farm, they also brought in necessary funds by selling
knitting. Albert explained how the family worked together to
produce mittens. "All the children were involved in the
process," she said. "We had to work all the time." Boys as
well as girls had assigned tasks, knitting cuffs, just the
thumbs, or the hands of the mittens as a way of dividing the
work load. The older daughters, who worked for families in
Bangor, sent the family discarded sweaters, mittens, and socks
which Chasse processed, recycling the wool back into yarn.[1]

The Chasses were practicing a community tradition of producing wool textiles at home that reached back to 1785 and the
settlement of the St. John Valley by Acadians, who had found
their way there after the British expelled them a generation
before from their homes in what had been French Canada.[2] The
Valley, which forms the border between Maine and the
Canadian province of New Brunswick, is home to the oldest
French-speaking community in Maine. Most descendants of

the original settlers continued to live along the St. John River, near Fort Kent, Madawaska, and Van Buren. The remainder lived in smaller towns, like Frenchville and St. Agatha, or in the back settlements, which were unorganized townships. In the isolated back settlements people lived without electricity well into the mid-twentieth century. Family members worked together as they had in the past to operate subsistence farms; everyone contributed to survival. In addition to their traditional household tasks, women made the wool textiles that were necessary in such a severe climate. They provided warm clothing for their families by producing wool, carding, spinning, knitting, and weaving for their families.

The long tradition of producing textiles for family use in the St. John Valley is first documented in an 1825 traveler's account of the people living in Madawaska. The traveler noted that the women manufactured a coarse cloth and kerseys "sufficient for their own consumption."[3] A report in 1831 confirmed that the women prepared wool and flax to make the family's clothing. The writer commented: "Men seem to have an easier life, working only from time to time. This is probably due to the productivity of the soil. The women, in all the homes, are busy spinning, making cloth and clothing."[4]

Census accounts from the mid-1880s show that most households in the valley raised sheep. The practice continued until the 1940s. Although sheep are dual purpose livestock, raised for wool and meat, most families did not raise sheep primarily for meat. The wool was a resource for the women; it was accessible and inexpensive. The priority and importance of supporting a flock of sheep was evident in the 1930s, when Fabienne Landry and her husband cleared the land for a farm near Edmundston, New Brunswick, Canada. They immediately added sheep because the animals could adapt to the sparse grasses and nibble around the stumps of the cleared woods. As they cleared more land, they increased their flock along with the numbers of other necessary farm animals.[5] Father Alphie Marquis, a retired pastor in Fort Kent, remembered that his parents received two sheep as a wedding present.[6] Sheep were essential to supporting large families. They provided a home-grown source of wool.

During the Great Depression, when prices for surplus crops produced by family farms in the St. John Valley plummeted, the men began to look for work elsewhere, often finding it in logging camps. Women's responsibilities in the family economy increased and they entered the market economy by producing and selling woolen textiles. This contribution to the survival of their families was compatible with their domestic responsibilities and allowed them to utilize the scarce resources that were available to them.

PRODUCING WOOLEN TEXTILES FOR THE FAMILY

Knitting fit well into a family economy, because women could do it along with other kinds of domestic work. Knitting could also be shared: different parts of the piece could be distributed among family members, sometimes including men and boys.

Fabienne Landry described her work day and said: "I knitted in the evenings until midnight. I knit to relax and was able to knit a sock or a mitten in an evening."[7] Knitting was done in the fall and winter when there was little outdoor work to do. It was portable and the only equipment needed were needles and yarn. Most women knitted when they visited friends, while cooking, and in between domestic chores. Knitting was not considered drudgery, but rather associated with socializing or freedom from hard work.

Working with wool textiles was divided seasonally. The sheep were sheared in the spring and the fleece washed and processed when time allowed. Washing was necessary to

Figure 1. An Acadian woman spinning wool.
Photo: Courtesy of Acadian Archives/
Archives acadiennes, University of Maine at Fort Kent.

remove all the accumulated dirt, but families did not usually have tubs for this purpose. Lillian Chasse remembered: "My father would take the fleeces to be washed in the summer to a brook behind our house. He would dig a hole in the brook and place stones at the ends to dam the water, creating a deep pool in the running water. The fleeces would be submerged in the water and left there for some time and then retrieved to be dried and picked through."[8] Some families would spread the wool on the grass and pour boiling water over the fleece to clean the wool.[9]

Once the wool was clean, it had to be carded and spun. Combing and carding fleece by hand was arduous and the short rovings produced were difficult to spin.[10] In 1895 a carding mill opened in Madawaska; it produced longer rovings that women found easier to work as they spent summer evenings on their porches spinning, after the rest of the day's activities were completed.

Because some Acadian women never had enough wool to meet their needs, they developed many ingenious methods of

Figure 2. Carding machine in the Corriveau Mill. Frenchville, Maine. Photo: Courtesy of Geon Corriveau.

recycling wool. Recycling traditions used by Therese Albert's mother, Alphonsine Chasse, had been passed down in her family for many generations. When she received discarded woolens from her daughters' Bangor employers, she gave the garments to her children to wear. But after the wool clothing wore out and became felted, the family recycled them into yarn. Chasse cut the knitted wool clothing into narrow strips

Figure 3. A *baratte*.
Photo: Dale Mudge.

that the children pulled apart and unraveled. They teased the short pieces of yarn and pulled the fibers apart. When they had collected enough wool, Chasse put it into a *baratte*, a machine resembling a butter churn. She filled it with hot water and homemade soap, and worked the paddle to break up the wool. When the wool was ready, she rinsed it and put it under a wood stove or outside on a wire fence to dry. She completed the recycling process by combing and spinning the wool back into yarn.

Chasse plied, or twisted, the finished yarn with a strand of newly spun white wool, producing what we recognize today as ragg wool. Because the ragg wool was not as strong as yarn made from two strands of new wool, it was generally reserved for home use. Alphonsine Chasse, however, had to rely on this source for the knitted socks she sold.[12] Father Marquis's mother, who sold mittens, plied her recycled wool with a strand of burlap from grain bags in order to extend her supply.[13]

Another form of recycling was to use unraveled yarn from knitted pieces to weave blankets, called *defaite* blankets (literally meaning "undone"). Widely produced in the Valley, they resemble blankets produced in Canada and Louisiana by other Acadians and French Canadians.[14] These were considered a utilitarian blanket for home use, as opposed to blankets woven from new wool which were given as wedding or christening presents. The *defaite* blankets were usually woven with thicker yarn, which was plied, compared to new wool blankets woven with a single strand. Because the used yarn was unraveled from knitted pieces that could be spared, the number of blankets a family could make was limited. The *defaite* blankets were usually woven in panels, in a twill or plain weave with the recycled wool as weft and a cotton warp. Completed by sewing two

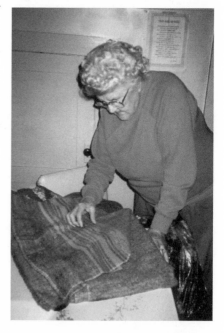

Figure 4. Bertha Voisine and her mother made the *defaite* blanket from recycled yarn. Fort Kent, Maine, 1997. Photo: Dale Mudge.

Figure 5. Bertha Voisine knitting in her kitchen. Fort Kent, Maine, 1997.
Photo: Dale Mudge.

woven panels side by side, *defaite* blankets are recognizable
by alternating bands and stripes of color.

The third form of recycling wool was carding and spinning
old and new wool together, producing a yarn similar to
tweeded wool. Although this practice extended the quantity
of new wool, it produced a yarn that was not as strong as
using only new wool fibers. Bertha Voisine and her mother
collected enough wool this way for a cherished blanket,
which was beige with orange bands at the ends. Voisine
remembered the pride they had at having the blanket made
and recalled, "It took a lot of work to provide the wool."[15]

Valley women worked constantly to provide warm clothing and blankets for their families. Fabienne Landry's efforts
are an example of the amount of work required to knit for her
sixteen children. Landry spun and knit the wool from their
flock of twenty ewes every year to provide each child with six
pairs of socks, three pairs of mittens, and a cap and scarf. Her

husband left the family to work in the woods in November and returned in March, leaving Landry to care for the animals and feed and clothe all of the children by herself. Although it was not unusual for men to work in the woods during the winter, women in Landry's position did not customarily assume dual roles of working on the farm and caring for their families for extended periods. Landry recollects that at that time, "I was always alone," perhaps a reflection of the responsibilities she felt, even with so many children to help her.[16] Her husband would resume working in the woods after the planting in the spring and return every three weeks to help with the farm. Father Alphie Marquis remembered his time with his mother: "We were always alone with her."[17]

DEVELOPING WOOL BUSINESSES

When the exigencies of the Great Depression stimulated the women of the St. John Valley to move beyond providing textiles for their families and enter the market economy, they were participating in a twentieth-century version of the traditional outwork system of nineteenth-century rural New England. Traditionally middlemen went out in wagons as agents for companies, bringing materials and offering money for finished goods. Sometimes rural storekeepers would act as middlemen, hoping that the money the women made would allow them to purchase goods in their stores. Historian Thomas Dublin discovered a flourishing outwork system in central and southern Maine in the nineteenth century. A firm in Fall River, Massachusetts, set up a store in Hallowell, Maine, as a center for putting its yarn out to be knitted by rural women. The practice declined when factory work developed.[18] There is no record of outwork in the St. John Valley for much of the nineteenth century because the area was so isolated, although it may well have existed on a small scale.

However, the development of the Bangor and Aroostook Railroad in 1891 allowed the practice to develop among Valley women, even though it had declined long before in the rest of New England in favor of factory production. By the 1930s, Valley women had developed extensive markets for their goods, knitting for manufacturers who then sold the goods throughout the nation.

Twentieth-century wool businesses in the St. John Valley took many forms and the limited amount of wool from the small farms was utilized in different ways depending on the resources, needs, and skills of individual households. Some women hooked and braided rugs from discarded woolen items, or did weaving on household looms. Others participated in knitting cooperatives.

WEAVING

Weaving required more work, space and resources than knitting, but remained a persistent tradition in the valley. According to the 1810 census, half of Maine households owned a loom.[19] In neighboring New Brunswick one household in three owned a loom in 1851.[20] A farmhouse had to meet many requirements in order to house a loom, including having a large room with high ceilings.[21] Looms took up valuable space in houses that were already crowded with large families.[22] Only comparatively wealthy families could afford a loom and devote the space to it as well as purchase the many supplies required. Amanda Hebert recalled that her mother kept her loom in the attic and brought it down to set up when it was needed.[23] Some women in the St. John Valley did custom weaving, either on location or at home.

Glorieuse LaChance Ouellette was a well-known weaver living in St. Agatha until 1984, when she died at the age of ninety-nine. She had always made things for her family; she

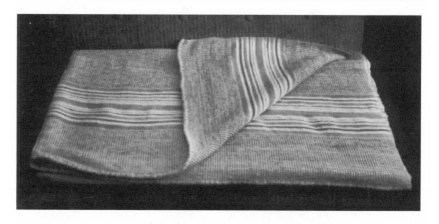

Figure 6. A woven rug made by Glorieuse LaChance Ouellette.
Photo: Dale Mudge.

wove, braided and hooked rugs, and sewed extensively. Ouellette developed a cottage industry weaving in her home for other people from wool yarn that they furnished, as well as doing custom spinning and dyeing. She produced hundreds of blankets from orders placed by northern Maine families. Her daughter, Edna Ouellette, remembers: "My mother wove all the time, devoting an upstairs back room to her loom and for storage of her wool supplies. I used to go there and see all the yarn stacked, with all the colors." Glorieuse Ouellette was always a weaver, but after her husband died, she developed the business to support her family. She worked steadily for thirty years, weaving most of the day, and produced a blanket panel a day. Edna Ouellette remembered that her mother never discussed how much money she earned, commenting: "What she made was enough. She was not able to make more." She thought her mother probably made around a dollar for a blanket and could weave several blankets a week.[24]

KNITTING MITTENS FOR SALE

Knitting, not weaving, became the main form of outwork for large numbers of women in the Valley during the 1930s and 1940s. It helped meet the need for cash to supplement meager incomes from agricultural products during the Depression. Before the development of the cooperative, women earned about twenty-five cents a day while knitting at home. Although it was a small amount, their work made an important economic contribution to their households. The wages of men who worked in the woods were also low.[25] Father Marquis remembered earning one dollar a day working in the woods cutting pulp in the 1930s.[26] Even the limited number of people who worked on federal projects in the area during the 1930s earned only $10.35 a week.[27]

Even before the Depression added to their need for income, women in the St. John Valley had found markets for knitted goods. When one New York merchandiser was on vacation in Maine, he noticed the well-knit children's clothing in the Valley. He sent his agents to contract with the women to knit for his markets. The company furnished yarn and patterns, agreed upon prices, and employed increasing numbers of women.[28] Railroads made agents' visits and shipping finished goods easy. The extra money women earned helped to build the local economy.

In 1912 Rose Corriveau realized the need for another carding mill and installed one beside her husband's grist mill in Frenchville. Women from area towns came to the mill and stayed for lunch before returning home, making it a social as well as an economic center.[29] Alphonsine Chasse used Corriveau's mill to process her wool and expand her output of mittens and socks. Her daughter Therese Albert remembered Chasse taking wool to the mill and then knitting more than twenty dozen pairs of socks just for one shop in a winter. She

Figure 7. Rose Corriveau spinning wool. Frenchville,
Maine. Photo: Courtesy of Geon Corriveau.

sold them to women in the Valley who were acting as agents
for manufacturers, as well as to local shopkeepers.[30]

One enterprising shopkeeper in Madawaska was Leona
Daigle, who sold knitted items made by the women in the
back settlements. Her daughter, Julie Daigle Albert, told how
her mother bought mittens to sell to manufacturers in
Boston. She stated: "Her reputation of paying $5 per dozen
mittens was well-known." Men from across the St. John
River in Canada brought their wives' knitting by canoes in the
summer and walked across the ice in the winter. After Daigle
had difficulties negotiating with the manufacturers over the
quality and pricing of mittens, she developed a market that
was no longer a system of outwork directed by manufacturers, but a system she could control.

Daigle's experience visiting a fishing camp led to the
expansion of her business. She read a want ad in a magazine
from a company in Alaska wanting knitters to make mittens
for fishermen. These oversized mittens were made from
white handspun one-ply wool to fit over leather mittens, to

prevent the leather from freezing and becoming slippery. Julie Albert described her mother's marketing procedures:

> The mittens were sold in dozen lots and the women would deliver mittens stacked one on top of another, tied with twine, to her store. Not all of the women complied with the quality standards of these orders. Since they were paid by weight, some of the women would put stones inside the mittens and some women who did not like to make the thumbs on the mittens, would eliminate knitting thumbs and stack those mittens in the middle.

Figure 8. Therese Albert holding a knitted fisherman's mitten. Madawaska, Maine, 1997. Photo: Dale Mudge.

Leona Daigle made handsome profits from her marketing efforts. Her daughter remembers her taking her boxes "by wagon in the summer, and on sleds in the winter," to send them to Alaska.[31]

Another opportunity was knitting directly for retail stores. L.L. Bean advertised hand-knit woolen socks and gloves made in Maine in their catalogues for 1917, 1926, and 1939.[32]

THE WOOL TEXTILE COOPERATIVE

The development of a cooperative, beginning in the late 1930s, allowed women knitters to achieve a much higher rate of pay for their work than ever before. Manufacturers had begun to

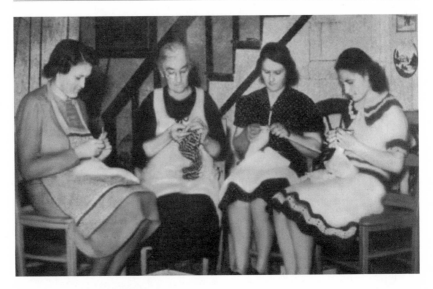

Figure 9. Acadian women knitting for the wool cooperative, Fort Kent,
Maine. Photo: Courtesy of Acadian Archives/Archives acadiennes,
University of Maine at Fort Kent.

take advantage of the women's reliance on their work and
slowly decreased their pay. By then, three thousand women
in the St. John Valley were knitting for them and receiving
twenty-five cents a day for their efforts. Every household had at
least one person knitting or crocheting—sometimes as many as
five or six including men and women. Father D. Wilfred Soucy,
a priest in Sinclair and Guerrette, was instrumental in starting the cooperative in the Valley. Through his study at a Nova
Scotia seminary, Soucy learned about producers' cooperatives.[33]
He organized the St. John Valley Handicraft Co-operative to
help the women negotiate with already-existing markets.

Soucy believed that a cooperative would encourage community cohesiveness and increase wages.[34] He lectured in
eighteen communities and traveled over one thousand miles
to speak about the virtues of cooperatives, always finding
receptive audiences. In his parish he set up teams of women
to instruct other women how to knit the designs and to help

them get established. He set up a central office at Fort Kent as a clearing house for orders and bought yarn at wholesale prices. Because the women were no longer subject to firms that regulated prices, their returns rose dramatically. Soon they were making five dollars a day.[35]

As a way of opening opportunities for the members of his parish, Soucy helped create a reliable communication system in the Valley. Providing electricity and telephones for the back settlements became a priority. When the telephone company resisted providing service to parts of Sinclair and Guerrette, he had the men in his parish cut poles, peel them, and set them up along seven miles of wilderness trail to the main road. After the poles had been erected, the telephone company agreed to put up the wires. Soucy was also responsible for building a road connecting the two towns, which helped women there get supplies and job orders for their handiwork.[36] The cooperative appealed to the roughly five thousand women from twenty-three parishes who participated, because of this democratic organization. No longer were they exploited by firms that regulated prices; they now worked together with a flexible doctrine that was non-threatening and effective.[37]

Figure 10.
Father D. Wilfred Soucy (on the right) is showing knitted goods made from the wholesale skeins of yarn.
Photo: Courtesy of Acadian Archives/ Archives acadiennes, University of Maine at Fort Kent.

Father Soucy's cooperative ran into trouble with the U.S. Department of Labor after the Fair Labor Standards Act was passed in 1938. At first officials assured him that the cooperative was exempt from the act that considered outwork illegal because it allowed employers to exploit their workers. Soucy believed the knitters should not be considered outworkers; in a cooperative, there were no employers or employees. Later, government officials revised their interpretation and ordered the cooperative dissolved. Father Soucy went to Washington to appeal, but was denied.[38] Even so, the women in the Valley continued to work together to knit for manufacturers.[39] The cooperative allowed women to enjoy higher incomes and increased independence from manufacturers. The women also enjoyed a new sense of accomplishment as they worked together and developed their skills. Even after the cooperative closed, women's earnings never dropped to the very low levels of the early years of the Depression.

Figure 11.
Father D. Wilfred Soucy's church in Sinclair, Maine. Parishioners went by horse and buggy and canoes.
Photo: Courtesy of Acadian Archives/ Archives acadiennes, University of Maine at Fort Kent.

Women's sympathetic attitudes towards collective movements contributed to the success of the cooperative. The concept was familiar—men had barn raisings and women had frolics to get work done. Theresa Violette remembers her mother inviting friends from across the river for a frolic two or three times a winter. She provided dinner and in return each woman would knit a pair of mittens made from wool she furnished. Violette remembers some of the women using needles fashioned from pieces of wire. For Violette's mother, hosting a frolic reunited her with her friends from New Brunswick where she was born, as well as serving as an expedient way to have many mittens knitted for her family.[40] Therese Albert remembers women taking turns going to neighbors' houses in Sinclair to knit.[41] Women also shared work with other women on a more informal basis. Doris Daigle Paradis's grandmother helped her daughter's family of eighteen children knit the supply of winter socks and mittens they needed.[42]

Women understood their production of wool textiles made an important contribution to family support. They all knew how; knitting had been practiced for generations. When they needed to join the cash economy, women in the Valley turned to this familiar skill to earn money. At first they sold knitted items that were extras from the household supply, but later they knit specifically to produce a salable surplus. Knitting was one of the only means for St. John Valley women in the 1930s and 1940s to earn money. When job orders arrived, Therese Albert said, "We put everything aside and got that work done."[43] There were few industrial jobs available and women's domestic responsibilities did not allow them to be away from the home for extended periods of time.

Early in the 1970s, twenty-five women knitters in the St. John Valley organized the Acadian Crafts Association. The association was an outlet, organized cooperatively, for growing numbers of women to sell their knitted and crocheted handiwork. The most profitable and numerous items were baby sets, which women could produce at the rate of one a day, earning just under $2.00.

KNITTING AS A CRAFT

Today, most women in the St. John Valley no longer knit for commodity exchange, but rather as a hobby. There are other jobs available for women who must work. Some older women who knitted for the cooperative still sell their handiwork. The Acadian Crafts Association has about twenty-five members, mostly older women. They continue to crochet and knit for stores throughout the country and continue to remain at home. When Bertha Voisine was asked if she went out, she replied: "I never go out in the winter. . . . I have my knitting."[44] She knitted for her family, and now knits socks, mittens, and *pichous* (slippers) to sell, as well as braided rugs. She is unaccustomed to going out; she lived on a farm and the responsibilities kept her at home.

Women still knit and crochet in limited quantities for their families or for presents to give away as well as for sale. The items are small, like mittens, socks, *pichous*, and caps; they are not time-consuming to produce and are readily salable. Women sell hand-knit items at church bazaars and fairs, small shops, laundromats, and general stores. Some women have built reputations for their fine handiwork and are well-known in their towns. One well-known knitter, Antoinette Ouellette, lived in a nursing home and sold her knitted items in a corner of the lobby entrance.

Wool yarn is difficult to obtain today in the Valley, so women knit with acrylic yarns. Since outdoor recreational activities have increased in popularity in recent years in Aroostook County, the knitted goods are still useful. Elderly women show great pride in their work. Bertha Voisine still knits all the time. She maintains a supply of socks to sell or give as gifts to family and friends. When she was asked how many pairs she knits a year, she answered: "I always have around eighty pairs."[45] Therese Albert remarked: "I am not knitting as much as I used to. I only knit 180 pairs of socks for the craft fair this year."[46]

The designs for knitted items have remained traditional. Each person has her own distinct method of knitting socks, turning the heels, creating the banding at the top of the sock, and extending the ribbing onto the top of the foot. Families have followed these patterns for generations. One reason the designs have persisted was that when women knitted for Father Soucy, the patterns had to be memorized; women learned the patterns by counting the stitches. There were few opportunities to learn new designs.

Knitting and the income it provided gave women a sense of self-reliance. They were independent and knew how to stretch scarce resources. When Therese Albert was asked if her mother ever talked about her deceased husband, she said: "My mother never talked about him. After he died, he was gone and she relied on herself."[47] The women have no regrets; they worked hard. Amanda Hebert, who is ninety-three and still makes homemade soap, claimed: "Women never lamented."[48] Catherine Morneault remembered: "We were happy because we didn't ask for more."[49] They are proud of their work, yet feel what they did was not unusual. Lucille Paradis said: "We didn't know anyone who complained. We were used to working."[50] When Marie Cyr talks about knitting for a family of twenty-seven children, she says: "I knit all the time." Her work was her life, and she does not feel that she worked harder than anyone else. She remarked: "All of my twenty-seven children were single births. I was lucky. Having twins would have been a lot of work."[51] As these women have aged, knitting has become a familiar form of creative expression that, according to Lillian Guerrette, "keeps me from being lonely."[52]

When these women were younger, making woolen textiles was a means of survival. They helped women contribute to the family economy by keeping their families warm as well as earning much-needed income. Knitting became an important means to bridge the gap between women's traditional roles and responsibilities and new realities. Unlike most work, it did not require women to leave their children and domestic responsibilities, yet it allowed them to make significant economic contributions, particularly during the lean years of the Depression. Knitting allowed women to participate in the market economy on their own terms. They developed marketing strategies that allowed them to increase their incomes while retaining a good deal of autonomy. Those strategies lessened the isolation of remote rural communities even as they encouraged women to maintain traditional roles. Commodity production for the market in the form of small items knitted by women in their homes was a traditional response to the needs of the family economy in changing times.

This paper is built on a series of interviews I conducted with Acadian women in the towns of Fort Kent, Madawaska, Frenchville, and St. Agatha, Maine and New Port Richey, Florida from 1996–1999. Also included in my research is a documentary with Maine Public Broadcasting in a segment of the television show *True North*, "Acadian Yarns," with on-air interviews and voice-overs, edited for broadcast July 12 and 18, 1999.

1. Therese Albert, interview by author, tape recording, Madawaska, Maine, November 1996.
2. Beatrice Craig, "Early French Migrations to Northern Maine, 1785–1850," *Maine Historical Society Quarterly* 25 (Spring 1986): 230.

3. Peter Fisher, *History of New Brunswick* (St. John, N.B.: The Society, 1921). Kerseys refers to woolen fabric for stockings or trousers.

4. John G. Deane and Edward Kavanaugh report to the government of the State of Maine in 1831.

5. Fabienne Landry, interview by author, tape recording, Edmundston, N.B., 8 February 1997.

6. Father Alphie Marquis, interview by author, tape recording, Fort Kent, Maine, 5 February 1998.

7. Fabienne Landry, interview.

8. Lillian Chasse, interview by author, tape recording, St. Agatha, Maine, 9 February 1997.

9. Father Alphie Marquis, interview.

10. Rovings are made with hand carders. Pieces of wool fleece are placed on the carders and combed until the fibers are straight. Then the wool is taken from the carders and rolled into tubes, about six inches by two inches. The rovings are used to spin wool.

11. Wool that is washed with too much agitation or in water that is too hot will shrink. Wool that has shrunk is called felted.

12. Therese Albert, interview.

13. Father Alphie Marquis, interview.

14. *Acadian Culture in Maine* (Boston: North Atlantic Region National Park Service, 1994), 51.

15. Bertha Voisine, interview by author, tape recording, Fort Kent, Maine, 8 February 1997.

16. Fabienne Landry, interview.

17. Father Alphie Marquis, interview.

18. Thomas Dublin, *Transforming Women's Work: New England Lives in the Industrial Revolution* (Ithaca, N.Y.: Cornell University Press, 1994), 38.

19. Paul Rivard reports an extensive amount of home weaving by women in southern and central Maine early in the nineteenth century. Paul E. Rivard, "Maine Manufacturers, 1820–80," in *Maine: the Pine Tree State from Prehistory to the Present*, ed. Richard W. Judd, Edwin A. Churchill, and Joel W. Eastman (Orono: University of Maine Press, 1995), 321–22.

20. For a discussion on the transformation from production to consumption in New Brunswick households, see Beatrice Craig, "Consumption and Economic Transformations in the North American Countryside in the Nineteenth Century," paper presented to the European Social Science History Conference, Noordwijkerhout, The Netherlands, 9–11 May 1996.

21. Amanda Hebert, interview by author, tape recording, St. Agatha, Maine, 8 February 1997.

22. Dublin, *Transforming Women's Work*, 45.

23. Amanda Hebert, interview.

24. Edna Ouellette, interview by author, New Britain, Conn., 1 March 1997.

25. *Portland Press Herald*, 29 March 1939.

26. Father Alphie Marquis, interview.

27. *Portland Press Herald*, 29 March 1939.

28. "No Relief or Unemployment Problems in Priest's Town," *Boston Sunday Post*, n.d., D. Wilfred Soucy Memoirs, Acadian Archives, University of Maine at Fort Kent, Fort Kent, Maine.

29. Cecile Dufour Pozzuto, *Madoueskak, 1785–1985: A Pictorial History, Recapturing the Past, An Acadian Bicentennial Project of the Madawaska Historical Society* (n.p., 1985), 53.

30. Therese Albert, interview by author, Madawaska, Maine, 31 January 1997.

31. Julie Daigle Albert, interview by author, Madawaska, Maine, November 1996.

32. Taken from the 1917, 1926, 1939 L. L. Bean catalogues, from the L. L. Bean archives, Freeport, Maine.

33. C. Stewart Doty, *Acadian Hard Times: The Farm Security Administration in Maine's St. John Valley, 1940–1943* (Orono: University of Maine Press, 1991), 58–60.

34. *The Catholic Mirror*, November 1940.

35. Father Denis Wilfred Soucy, interview by author, audio from a video production, New Port Richey, Fla., 5 February 1999.

36. Doty, *Acadian Hard Times*, 58.

37. *The Catholic Rural Life Bulletin*, 20 February 1940.

38. Letter from Phillip B. Fleming, Father Soucy's Memoirs, Acadian Archives.

39. "A Way of Life Is Threatened," source unknown, Soucy Memoirs, Acadian Archives.

40. Theresa Violette, interview by author, tape recording, Madawaska, Me., 8 February 1997.

41. Therese Albert, interview, 31 January 1997.

42. Doris Daigle Paradis, interview by author, tape recording, Fort Kent, Maine, 15 November 1996.

43. Therese Albert, interview, 31 January 1997.

44. Bertha Voisine, interview by author, tape recording, Fort Kent, Maine, 15 November 1996.

45. Bertha Voisine, interview, 15 November 1996.

46. Therese Albert, interview by author, tape recording, Madawaska, Maine, 12 February 1998.

47. Therese Albert, interview, 31 January 1997.

48. Amanda Hebert, interview.

49. Catherine Morneault, interview by author, tape recording, St. Agatha, Maine, 11 February 1998.

50. Lucille Paradis, interview by author, tape recording, Frenchville, Maine, 12 February 1998.

51. Marie Cyr, interview by author, tape recording, Edmundston, N.B., 7 February 1997.

52. Lillian Guerrette, interview by author, tape recording, St Agatha, Maine, 10 February 1998.

The mid-twentieth-century emphasis on conformity exacted a high price from all women, particularly those whose ambitions inspired a desire for public achievement. Postwar anxieties called forth sharp criticisms of anyone challenging dominant gender paradigms; women not content with domestic life were variously labeled neurotic and not well- adjusted or communist and un-American. Deviance from the norm was not easily tolerated.

In spite of the risks, women throughout the nation challenged rigid definitions of appropriate behavior in the postwar decades. Women organized against the arms race, objecting both to the threat of nuclear war and the toxic fallout from nuclear testing that poisoned milk and the environment. Other women became active in the civil rights movement: when Rosa Parks refused to give up her seat on a Montgomery, Alabama bus in 1954, she knew that she had the support of many of the women in her community, support that would continue to grow as the movement spread. Other women organized around community issues, improving schools, building parks and playgrounds, sustaining churches, neighborhood associations, cultural groups, and a host of other projects. Still others challenged convention in more idiosyncratic ways, as writers, participants in beat culture, and even by engag-

ing in pre-marital sexual behavior.

Women who participated in postwar organizations rejecting conformity often justified their behavior with arguments drawn from their traditional roles as wives and mothers. But familiar arguments could belie a more complex reality, as at least some women used the opportunities they created to push at the boundaries of acceptable behavior. For example, women claiming only to be protecting their children from nuclear danger were in reality protesting the nation's foreign policy, in the process challenging the very legitimacy of the arguments made by political and military leaders.

Such tactics offered women a way to participate in the public life of the nation without openly flouting the demands of domestic conformity, but they had real limits. Women who adopted them never successfully challenged postwar restrictions on their behavior; they were unable to legitimize their own participation in the public world except as the defenders of domestic virtues. As a result, they did not challenge conventional gender assumptions; that task would become the responsibility of their daughters in the 1960s and 1970s. Patricia Schmidt offers a closer look at one such woman who struggled to find a balance between ambition and convention, Margaret Chase Smith.

VIBRATING TO AN IRON STRING:
MARGARET CHASE SMITH AND HER
CONSTRUCTION OF GENDER
AT THE CENTURY'S MID-POINT

Patricia L. Schmidt

> Trust thyself: every heart vibrates to that iron string. Accept the place the divine providence has found for you, the society of your contemporaries, the connection of events. Great men have always done so, and confided themselves childlike to the genius of their age, betraying their perception that the absolutely trustworthy was seated at their heart, working through their hands, predominating in all their being.
>
> —"Self Reliance," by Ralph Waldo Emerson

Margaret Chase was a child of the nineteenth century and a product of the twentieth. When she was born in 1897, Queen Victoria still occupied the throne of England and the term "feminism" had not yet come into usage in America.[1] Shortly after Margaret's third birthday, the front page of the *New York Times* announced that Queen Victoria had died. "The most respected of all women, living or dead" passed away peacefully at Osborne House on the Isle of Wight.[2] President William McKinley sent condolences to the new king, the U.S Senate and House passed resolutions, and Senator Henry Cabot Lodge of Massachusetts, "voicing the sentiment of most of his colleagues" (according to the *Times*), claimed that the reign of Queen Victoria "has been a great and memorable one, but . . . perhaps nothing [has been] greater or more memorable than her own ability and purity of character, her fidelity to her high duties, and her devotion to those ideals of conduct and domestic life which appeal most profoundly to all English-speaking people."[3] This easy link between domesticity and gender, with its suggestion of separate spheres based on gender, preceded Smith into the world and lingered long after the "Victorian age" ended. In fact, until the 1950s and later, despite significant strides toward sexual equality, domestic ideals continued to limit women's choices and narrow their vision.[4]

At the same time, growing numbers of women were becoming involved in a variety of activities that promoted full equality with men. From 1910 to 1920, the birth control movement and the struggle for woman suffrage dominated, followed by a variety of campaigns and causes that were often united only by a shared belief "in equality of opportunity regardless of sex."[5] Set in motion by these swirling currents were backlashes against those who were perceived to be involved in undermining the social order. Such cross-currents could not be breached by the faint of heart. Since women who sought elective office were by their actions weighing in on the side of equality between the sexes, they opened themselves to all kinds of criticism and questions, not the least of which was whether they were "sexually adjusted."[6]

Margaret Smith would not be deterred. Schooled in the art of politics by her husband Clyde Smith, one of the most successful practitioners in Maine, Smith seized the opportunity to run for office as soon as it was presented. She knew that the state Republican power brokers were not in her corner; they had already picked out their candidate. But she ran in spite of them, and when she won she owed them nothing. Clyde had taught her how to court votes and how to count them, and she knew that she could not afford to appeal to only one-half of the electorate. So she ran a campaign that reached out to mainstream voters of both sexes. Instead of drawing attention to the fact that her candidacy was "unique" or "symbolic," she avoided any suggestion that she had chosen an unconventional path. Her choices—from platform to persona—reinforced the impression that she was a "safe" choice. Finally, in an irony that was a constant in her complex career, she drew heavily on the Maine chapter of the National Federation of Business and Professional Women, a group that was founded in the twenties to foster sexual solidarity and advance the interests of women, an impulse at the very heart of feminism. These Maine women provided both the organizational backbone and steady grass roots support that comprise the core of every successful political campaign, and they enabled her to cultivate mainstream men and speak directly to women without appearing to be a feminist.

Margaret Chase Smith understood well—at least intuitively—the nature of the social construction and regulation of identity. And that understanding was a key ingredient in her electoral success. Her construction of self telegraphed a conventional view of femininity that was central to her viability as a political operative. But beyond efficacy, it also met a deeper, psychic need, glimpses of which could be caught when Smith was only a child.

Agnes Staples, her childhood babysitter, remembered vividly how "particular" Smith always was. On outings, Smith would make sure that her doll, which she took with her "when she went to call," was as spotlessly clean as her own dress and leather shoes, which she rubbed with handkerchiefs tucked into her apron pocket.[7] Not too great a leap is required to infer that even at a young age she valued propriety and sought social acceptance. By the time she took her seat in Congress, her clothing, speech, and bearing conveyed the manner of an aristocrat, not a poor girl from North Street, Skowhegan, who had struggled to complete high school. The process that produced such a thoroughly poised Washington figure is as complex as it is prototypical of a society that rewards success with upward mobility, in Washington as well as Maine. Through it, her persona took on a transformative function, projecting not only who she wished to be, but shaping the woman she was in the process of becoming.

*　*　*

The terrain that motivated Smith's quest for standing was a society whose cultural practices established more than one dominant group and many subordinate groups. But the gap between greater and lesser was wide. Criteria for inclusion in the former included wealth, ancient roots and lineage. Smith's family met two of the three criteria, though the issues of longevity and lineage were confused slightly by the marriage of Smith's father—a descendant of two Puritan lines—to her mother, daughter of a recent immigrant from Quebec province. Wealth, or the lack of it, was the primary reason the Chase family had neither prominence nor influence by the twentieth century.

Skowhegan had been carved out of the wilderness by Smith's forebears and others like them—tough-minded descendants of Puritan fishermen and farmers who had set out from Massachusetts early in the nineteenth century for the Maine frontier. They left "civilization" behind, lured by the promise of cheap land in a "bran-new country [where] the only rooms were of Nature's working"— in many instances carrying with them little more than a sense of adventure, love of order, and a wide streak of practical idealism.[8] Their expansive view of the future, fueled by a vision of themselves as autonomous freeholders, bound these people together and kept the murderous winters and epidemics from crushing them.[9] By the time Smith was born, several generations of Chases had survived these rigors and acquired their cherished plot of land just outside of Skowhegan—only to lose it when Smith's grandfather, John Wesley Chase, died of pneumonia at thirty-nine and their 150 acres were sold for taxes. By the start of the twentieth century, the Chases were no better off than when they had first arrived in Maine.

This circumstance explains in part the quest for standing that dominated Smith's life—instrumental perhaps in her decision to marry a wealthy older man and, upon his death in 1940, to run for his House seat. But being a congressman (her preferred title) did not satisfy her for long, and in 1947 she decided to risk it in order to run for the United States Senate, a choice that suggests there was more at stake than mere standing. Much to the surprise of nearly everyone and the delight of women across the nation, she emerged victorious. The contest was thought to be uneven—a woman against two powerhouses of the Republican establishment—one a sitting governor, the other a former governor, both well-heeled and extraordinarily well-connected. Smith would rarely be underestimated afterwards. During the course of her twenty-four-year Senate career, she became a powerful advocate for a strong national defense and a proponent of equal benefits for women in the armed services. Twice she emerged as a potential vice presidential nominee, and in 1964 she made a bid for the Republican presidential nomination. In 1972, after winning a bitter primary contest—which focused on her age (seventy-five)—she lost the general election. After returning to Maine to "retire," she maintained a rigorous schedule, not unlike the one she had followed in Washington. Margaret Chase Smith was a woman who chose—in the words of Carolyn Heilbrun—to "invent her own destiny" and "to live a quest plot, as men's stories allow, indeed encourage them to do."[10] How she accomplished such a feat within the narrow boundaries then delineating woman's sphere is the focus of this inquiry.

* * *

For many, Margaret Chase Smith's very presence on the hustings challenged traditional notions of woman's place. In her first race, her candidacy was somewhat sanctified because she was Clyde's widow, but widowhood did not justify a second and third term, and it certainly could not insulate her from criticism when she declared for the senate seat of retiring Senator Wallace White. Instead, her chief protection came from a personal style that exuded traditional femininity and left critics little room to claim, apart from her candidacy itself, that she was a threat to the existing sexual and social order. From her first campaign and through subsequent campaigns, she consistently displayed fidelity to prevailing conceptions of woman's "place" in costume and demeanor, even as she simultaneously created a self that thrived outside of the culturally prescribed role for women. In this way, Margaret Chase Smith was a composite of tradition and eccentric quest. But the only face the public saw—at least for quite some time—was a model of gender-appropriate behavior that both short-circuited criticism and enabled her to reach the widest range of voters.

The fact that Smith's image of polished gentility struck exactly the right note for her times is suggested by the press coverage she received from the time she plunged into elective politics. In August 1940—one month before the election that would send her to Washington for her first full term—the widow Smith held a reception in the large Fairview Avenue house in which she and Clyde had taken up housekeeping ten years earlier. The Skowhegan *Independent Reporter* described the event in minute detail. Summer flowers filled the rooms: gladioli and zinnias in the living rooms, lilies and white petunias in a huge centerpiece in the dining room, a brilliant flash of red nasturtium in the reception room. Smith wore white— a white dress, a corsage of white begonias. The reader could almost see it—a lone woman, framed against the house's dark interior, splashes of color like fireworks announcing the presence of that slender, white-clad figure. At sunset, the company adjourned to the broad lawn. Smith addressed them briefly from the front portico and then presented the candidates for office in Somerset County. The guests paid tribute to her, and then to her deceased husband, as someone who had effectively represented the "laboring men."[11] One month later, the *Independent Reporter* described her successful campaign for the House of Representatives as "energetic in the extreme, and yet she found time to act as the gracious hostess, which she always is, at intervals during her hasty visits to her Fairview Avenue home."[12]

As adaptive as Smith's use of convention was in creating her public self, its deeper psychic function was to establish and revivify her sense of herself as a "lady." Thus not only did her traditional femininity serve her well on the stump, it performed an important transformative function. The impulse for something grander—to be someone who "counted"—was already evident when she was a young woman. She was consistently drawn to activities of transformation—to the theatre and costumes, trips to the "city," and flights in the still-novel airplane—as well as to organizations that offered an opportunity for self-improvement. When she became the president of the local Business and Professional Women's Club, she learned how to run a meeting and speak effectively in public. Later, as state president, she had the opportunity to travel widely and meet a spectrum of women across Maine. Their view of her—as a charming and attractive young woman—

provided important validation of her worth; later, they became the cornerstone of her political organization. A central link in this transformative process was Smith's choice of husband, the fifty-four-year-old Clyde Smith. After their marriage, Clyde not only schooled her in the ways of politics but taught her how to entertain. With the help of one of Clyde's closest friends, she was proposed and accepted for membership in the socially prestigious Daughters of the American Revolution. When the couple moved to Washington, D.C., Smith spent much of her time honing her social skills and widening her network. She even took public speaking lessons. From childhood to widowhood, her activities were a sustained dress rehearsal for a role that diluted her birthplace on blue collar North Street as the defining factor of her identity and enabled her to pursue both an inward and an outward quest. Her "hidden personal myth"—a term coined by biographer Leon Edel—thus was more than mere ambition. That was the obvious myth. The hidden part of the myth was the inadequacy that drove the myth—an inadequacy that was reinforced, as is often the case, during adolescence.

In high school, Smith played running center on the women's basketball team. In her senior year, the team traveled to Augusta for a game with Cony High School, where she was assigned to spend the night in the large home on Western Avenue that belonged to the Millikens, whose eldest daughter was her hostess.[13] Although Smith later described this trip as "pleasant," her stay made her acutely aware of the social distance between herself and the Milliken children, a memory that remained fresh even sixty years after the event. A few years after her visit, Carl Milliken was elected governor of the state, but in 1916 his children already took for granted the privileges and luxuries of an upper-middle class official family. Smith inevitably compared herself with such girls. Augusta's Cony High School team, she recalled, "was made up of fast and well-trained girls—girls who dressed well." And although the poised and unflappable "lady" of later years may already have existed in her mind's eye, Smith remembered herself then as "just a little poor girl up there in Skowhegan, and all these girls wore raccoon coats and all that type of thing."[14] While that poor girl never really left Smith's side, the forty-two-year-old who buried her husband in 1940 and then ran for his seat had already become a person of standing. Once she was elected to the House, people outside of Maine widely assumed that the slim, well-dressed Republican had attended college (probably at one of the seven sisters) and was a New England blue blood, a perception reinforced by her speech, her demeanor and her clothing. From her soft-spoken delivery to her erect posture to her signature pearls, red rose and dressmaker suits, she was the portrait of a lady, a card-carrying member of the Establishment.

The impression was heightened by her choice of female friends, many of whom could be described as "old money." When Margaret and Clyde Smith first arrived in Washington, Dorothy Brewster—the wealthy and socially prominent wife of Maine Congressman Owen Brewster—introduced her to Washington society, picked her up regularly in a chauffeured automobile and took her to call on other prominent women. She was also instrumental in helping Smith win the treasurer's post at the Congressional Club, a social club for wives of senators, congressmen, cabinet officers, and other political leaders. Another friend, Maine native Marion E. Martin, was the daughter of a well-to-do Aroostook County potato farmer. In the thirties, while Smith was adjusting to married life, Martin was travelling around the world with a party of Wellesley classmates.[15] After Clyde Smith's death, and during Martin's stint as head of the Women's Division of the Republican National Committee, she became Smith's link to the National Committee and a source of information to which only the inner circle was privy. Theirs was a small, but vitally important power base in the closed political world in which they moved. The wealthiest of Smith's friends, Representative Frances Bolton, was a Republican from Ohio who had won her husband's seat after his death. While they were in the House, the two forged a lifetime friendship. On the heels of Smith's stunning Senate primary victory in 1948, Bolton introduced her to a cheering Republican National Convention, and in 1964 seconded her nomination for president at the Republican National Convention in San Francisco. Over the years, Smith was a frequent guest in Florida at Bolton's Palm Beach estate.

In addition to her choice of friends, Smith's sense of self was revealed by the name she selected for herself. In the forties, a widow was expected to show respect for her husband by using his name socially in every way. The "rules" of etiquette were quite clear on this. The "correct" choice was "Mrs. Clyde Smith," not "Mrs. Margaret Smith," no matter how long she survived her husband.[16] Throughout her first term, her letters carried the typed name "Mrs. Clyde Smith" under the signature "Margaret Chase Smith." After her first term—but without violating "the rules"—she dropped the typed signature and used only "Margaret Chase Smith," explaining that when she used "Margaret Smith" people did not recognize her. In naming herself she had invented an identity. "Chase" was a name with Puritan antecedents; "Smith" a name ubiquitous throughout New England, proudly borne by families far more distinguished than her husband's. The name had an upper-class resonance. It echoed with the voices of her culture far better than the less prepossessing and more alien (to her) "Mrs. Clyde Smith." "Margaret Chase Smith" was the name of someone who mattered and someone who belonged. By 1940, "Margaret Chase Smith" was in fact who she had become.

In Margaret Chase Smith's career can be seen many of the themes and possibilities inherent in the conflicting aspirations of twentieth-century American women. Today's feminists are divided by identity politics and fragmented by issues such as pornography and abortion. No less conflicted are large numbers of women who do not identify themselves as feminists but have profound doubts as to how they *should now* behave because they are women. On one side are feminists like Judith Butler, professor of rhetoric and comparative literature at the University of California at Berkeley, whose influential work *Gender Trouble*—a critique of fixed gender identities—has been described by the *Chronicle of Higher Education* as an "instant classic," and by others as "brilliant," "innovative," and "subversive."[17] On the other side are women like Margaret Chase Smith, whose careers would neither have been launched, nor sustained, by explicitly challenging traditional constructions of gender. The gap between these two groups illustrates the continuing instability and volatility of the concept of "woman's place." In Butler's experience, "to make trouble was, within the reigning discourse of . . . childhood, something one should never do precisely because that would get one *in* trouble. The rebellion and its reprimand seemed to be caught up in the same terms," she observes. "The prevailing law threatened one with trouble, even put one in trouble, all to keep out of trouble." Thus she concluded *"that trouble is inevitable and the task [is] how best to make it, what best way to be in it."*[18] In contravention to this view, Margaret Chase Smith's goal was *not* to be seen as a troublemaker, a dilemma historically shared by virtually all women with aspirations for public office. She began by keeping her distance from "feminists," a strategy adopted by other public women as well.

Despite her well-deserved reputation for helping to forge "a women's constituency in Washington," even Eleanor Roosevelt was careful to avoid the label of "feminist," a decision that seems to echo Smith's circumspection. During the 1930s, writes historian Susan Ware in *Beyond Suffrage: Women in the New Deal,* the "network" of women within the New Deal not only shied away from the label "feminist," but used it in "a fairly narrow (and slightly pejorative) sense." She further reports that "after spending an entire year mobilizing to get women appointed to the Platform Committee of the Democratic Party for the first time," Molly Dewson asked journalist Ruby Black, "'Don't you think that, *for one not a feminist, I* get in some pretty good licks for the girls?'"[19]

Margaret Chase Smith and Eleanor Roosevelt were mirroring the choices of many of the women who successfully won elective office early in the century. (Mrs.) Dora Pinkham, the first woman elected to the Maine Legislature, offers a case in point. When a reporter asked why she had decided to run for public office, Pinkham replied demurely that it was "because the men . . . thought they could not spare the time from their livings." When it was observed that she did not seem too interested in the cause of suffrage, she protested. "On the contrary, I was never more interested in any cause as anybody who knew me personally would testify."[20] Interested perhaps, but no more publicly identified with it than Margaret Chase Smith would be with Women's Liberation thirty years hence, despite her campaign for equal benefits for women in the military and her continuing support of the Equal Rights Amendment. Like Pinkham, Smith's efforts to publicly acquiesce to gender expectations distanced her from those who openly rejected the social order and publicly challenged its assumptions. Paradoxically, that same conformity became the means by which she was able to carve out a life course and pursue a quest plot that had historically been the prerogative of males.

* * *

Margaret Chase Smith's "conventional" choices would be a great deal less interesting had her personal style foreshadowed an indifferent career in the Senate, similar to that of Hattie Caraway of Arkansas. Although Caraway served in the Senate for over a decade, she is credited with no major legislation and is remembered as a quiet, dowdy woman whose electoral success was attributable in large part to the energetic campaigning of neighboring Louisiana Senator Huey Long, with whom she voted 99 percent of the time.[21] In contrast to Caraway, Senator Smith became known for her independence, her courage, and her trouble-making potential.

On 1 June 1950, Margaret Chase Smith—a freshman senator—became the first in that body to challenge Wisconsin Senator Joseph R. McCarthy on the floor of the senate. Five months earlier, McCarthy had electrified America with a speech in Wheeling, West Virginia in which he claimed to hold in his hand a list of 205 names "that were known to the Secretary of State [Dean Acheson] as being members of the Communist Party and are still working and shaping policy in the State Department."[22] By the time McCarthy returned to Washington, he had shot overnight from the back bench of the Senate into national prominence. Since World War II, Americans had grown increasingly fearful of a worldwide Communist conspiracy. In 1949 alone, fifteen states passed anti-subversive laws, and the United States Chamber of Commerce suggested the establishment of sub-committees on the local level to expose Communists and "Commie sympathizers."[23] Had America been "sold out" at Yalta?, asked Republicans. Was the State Department riddled with Communists? The stage was set for a Red scare and for the rise of a Republican who would convert "public fear about Communism into a winning issue against the Democrats."[24]

Former chicken farmer and prize fighter McCarthy was just the man for the job—or at least that is what the Republicans decided after they observed the public's response to his Wheeling speech. But McCarthy was a liar and a bully, two facts that were obvious to Smith almost immediately, even though it took most of America over four years to see through him. His spurious evidence, combined with his presumption of guilt and his use of guilt-by-association as emotional blackmail were anathema to Smith's independent spirit. And so she decided to challenge him, hurling herself in the role of hero to battle the forces of darkness, a script that had all but vanished for women with V-E Day. The decision was an extension of her search for a larger life and the natural outcome of decades spent in pursuit of a quest plot.

It was also an act for which she would pay a high price. Overnight she went from a rising star and frequently-mentioned vice-presidential candidate to the sidelines. Even in Maine, her challenge to McCarthy was to have long-term deleterious effects. Wrote a Portland man some time after the speech: "While he [McCarthy] ridiculed you, he was charitable enough not to embarrass you as much as he could have if he knew what your own generation of Maine people say about *Maggie Chase*."[25] And from Lewiston came this message: "You remind me of a snake who hiss [sic] at a mountain in your narrow-minded attempts to degrade [him]. . . . Many of us in Maine really know you, don't we Margaret?"[26] Nonetheless, for Smith, the contest had irresistible allure. Obscured by her genteel exterior was the ferocious spirit of a competitor. In contrast to the qualities projected through her persona, she warmed to the challenge of navigating through "a symbolic action system, a structure of statuses and roles, customs and rules for behavior, designed to serve as a vehicle for earthly heroism," even though as an American woman, she was by definition no "hero."[27] Yet she was not divided against herself any more than her persona was a complete fiction. Instead, in both instances, she achieved a delicate balance of rhetorical adaptation, deep meaning, and primary impulse toward fully evolved personhood. How she achieved such an outcome is important not only in assessing her career, but in understanding more fully the relationship of women and public power. Is it reasonable to expect women's style or substance to mirror the style of males, for instance? Or rather, since women had been so long excluded from political power, is it not more likely that women's ethos would have its own special warp and weft?

*   *   *

One reason that Margaret Chase Smith was able to carve out a unique place for herself in the public domain was that she understood what had to be done to get where she wanted to go. A dramatic illustration of her ability to pursue her own course successfully, all the while functioning in accordance with gender expectations, can be seen in her 1956 debate with Eleanor Roosevelt on CBS' "Face the Nation." From Smith herself one learns that she and her administrative assistant William Lewis, Jr. paid close attention to the selection of her simple, dark dress, softly waved hair, and "demeanor or conduct—air or style some might say." Their focus was less on issues and more on Roosevelt's "towering height, top-heavy appearance, and decidedly partisan manner"—all of which, they believed, would give Smith an edge so long as she answered the questions "as briefly as possible, slowly, deliberately, in a low, even-pitched tone." What they wanted was a "favorable sharp contrast" with Roosevelt, and that is what they got.[28] The soft, feminine persona, signified by a rose and pearls which so effectively blurred Smith's non-traditional pursuit of political power, played to her advantage against a woman whose white blouses, hats, and tweed suits looked to one observer "as though she rushed in and bought them while waiting for the traffic light to change."[29]

Also linked to Smith's success was her fierce self-protectiveness. From friends, family, supporters and even newspapermen, she insisted on privacy and total loyalty, and she "punished" lapses by stony withdrawal. Perhaps as a respite from always being "on stage," and certainly as a first line of defense against gossip and leaks, she staffed her Senate office with close friends like Blanche Bernier (who began her career as the Smiths' Washington housekeeper) and family members like Joseph "Spike" Bernier, Blanche's brother and the husband of Smith's sister Laura—all people she could count on to protect her image and with whom she could "be herself." Chief among this group of intimates was William Chesley Lewis, Jr.

The two first met during Smith's third year in the House in 1943 when she was appointed to a subcommittee of the Naval Affairs Committee. Lt. Lewis, on assignment from the Navy as staff to the sub-committee, quickly earned the gratitude of its members (including Smith) by his even-handed solicitousness and his unswerving efforts make them all look good.[30] Very quickly his capacity for loyalty and gift for public relations began to fill a void for the barely-more-than-freshman congresswoman. After Smith's successful run for the United States Senate in 1948, he "officially" became her administrative assistant. By that time, he had also become her best friend, confidante, and housemate. For over twenty years, no hint of scandal about the nature of their relationship appeared in the newspapers. Then, on 9 December 1971, when Lewis was stricken with a severe heart attack (from which he later recovered), Smith missed thirteen consecutive roll call votes to stay by his side in the VIP suite at Walter Reed Hospital.[31] Soon their "close 23-year association" was made public in the *Portland Press Herald* by the its Washington correspondent, Don Larrabee. He further referred to Lewis as "a queenmaker" and "master strategist" and revealed that Lewis had recently been introduced at a fundraiser as the "prime minister." As Larrabee wrote, "The name of William C. Lewis, Jr. may not have been a household word in Maine these past 23 years. In Washington, it is synonymous with Senator Margaret Chase Smith. . . . Lewis is treated with all the courtesy, honor and respect accorded to the senator herself. He is universally recognized as her alter ego without whom no major decision has been made for almost a quarter of a century."[32] The story was picked up by *Washington Post* columnist Maxine Cheshire, who drew attention to Lewis's ownership of their getaway houses at Cundy's Harbor, their living arrangements in Lewis's Silver Spring house and their "close, 23-year association."[33] In my recent conversation with Larrabee, he recalled that there had been quite a bit of gossip about them in Washington, and Larrabee himself had once speculated that they were "husband and wife." But so long as Lewis was healthy, nothing of the sort ever made it into print—in part because such revelations were not in fashion in those pre-Watergate years, and in part because of Lewis's successful protection of the Margaret Chase Smith image.[34]

One year later in 1972, when Smith lost her bid for re-election, Larrabee again raised her ire by reporting that she would not open her office door or answer phones. He also reported that a Senate Office Building worker saw "Republican Senator Strom Thurmond (S.C.) pounding on her office door and yelling, 'Margaret! Margaret! If you're in there, let me in!'"[35] Larrabee's persistence in trying to reach her finally paid off when Bill Lewis answered the phone. "You're never going to talk with her again," Lewis told him. "Bill, for heaven sakes," protested Larrabee, "all I wrote was what everybody was saying." But Lewis was furious. "You've turned on her," he said, and hung up. UPI's Mike Posner, who had covered Smith's 1964 presidential campaign, believed—as did Larrabee—that "Margaret Chase Smith [n]ever really trusted anyone except Bill Lewis." Observed Posner, "He built the Margaret Chase Smith image, and they both wanted it to remain sacrosanct."[36] But of course Smith's image was a work in progress, begun long before she had an administrative assistant, and she was no less zealous in guarding it than was Lewis.

A major casualty of this tendency was Marion Martin. In contrast to the close friendship that had flowered in the forties, by 1982 Smith was citing Martin as an example of one of her most strongly held views—that women are their own worst enemies. Smith believed that in the 1948 senate race, Martin had supplied negative campaign information to fellow senate hopeful Horace Hildreth, who as governor had appointed Martin Commissioner of Labor and Industry after she lost her job with the Republican National Committee in 1946. During the 1948 contest, smear sheets painting Smith as a radical, if not a "fellow traveler"—sheets that she believed Martin had helped to author—popped up all over Maine, posing a real threat to her chances. Though she had no proof, the mere suspicion that Martin had helped to produce such information led Smith to sever their relationship. Queried as to why such a close friend would have turned on her in this way, she replied, "You'll have to find that answer. The only thing that I can think of is . . . she owed it to Hildreth."[37] Later I discovered among her papers a memo from William Lewis that implicated Martin in a rumor spread by someone else about Smith's sexual preferences.[38] Given the date of this rumor (1949), it could not have caused the Smith-Martin rupture, but it probably validated Smith's (earlier) hasty conclusion, for which I could find *no* evidence.

This tendency to rush to judgement without corroborating evidence reveals a woman beleaguered and much less sure-footed than her persona suggests. Her well-arranged exterior was in sharp contrast to an insecurity that produced such ferocious self-protectiveness. And yet, there was good reason for her to see phantom enemies, for the real ones were real enough and numerous.

Margaret Chase Smith had virtually no natural allies in the Maine or Washington power structures. Among women in the political limelight, she was an odd duck —different from women like Eleanor Roosevelt, whose power was derivative, and even Frances Perkins, who did not have to worry about re-election. To many power brokers—with the notable exception of Massachusetts congressman Joe Martin, who for a time presided over the House as Speaker—she was a "lone woman," not "one of the boys" but an exotic hybrid. Men who were indifferent or bore her no ill gave her a wide berth because they could not escape their own conventional assumptions about women. Believing women to need things other than what men needed, they could not conceive of her journey as a quest, part of a great adventure similar to their own. Denied this context, her political career could be reduced simply to a series of successful, if somewhat anomalous, election victories. Surprisingly, even the brilliant critic Lionel Trilling mirrors such a failure of imagination. In his 1957 introduction to the Riverside edition of Jane Austen's *Emma*, he reveals a great deal about his own and (arguably) his culture's assumptions about women. "The extraordinary thing about Emma is that she has a moral life as a man has a moral life," he wrote with obvious surprise. "And she [Emma] doesn't have it as a special instance . . . but quite as a matter of course." Women do not "exist as men exist—as genuine moral destinies," continued Trilling. "No change in the modern theory of the sexes, no advances in status that women have made, can contradict this. The self-love [equated by Trilling with hubris] that we do countenance in women *is of a limited and passive kind, and we are troubled if their self-love is as assertive as man's is permitted, and expected to be."*[39] And that does not begin to suggest the almost palpable hostility that Smith faced daily from the Pentagon to the Justice Department. Into this stiff wind Smith sailed throughout her career. "People thought I was sensitive," Senator Smith told me one day. "I was not sensitive, but I was quite conscious of it and perhaps have been on my guard because I have not had it easy."[40]

Being on guard ranged from the intense self-protectiveness noted earlier, to harmless deceptions, such as claiming to shun Washington's social whirl in favor of work and quiet—lest she be thought of as a social butterfly—even though countless photos in the Margaret Chase Smith Library attest to an ongoing and glamorous Washington social life. Her balancing act included both the "forbidden" and the required, the audacious and the inconspicuous. A particularly intriguing illustration of protective coloration can be seen in her unusual friendship with Secretary of Labor Frances Perkins.

So far as her constituents knew, Margaret Chase Smith and Frances Perkins moved in different orbits, though in 1965 when Perkins passed away, Smith referred to her in remarks to the Senate as a "personal friend" and someone of whom she was proud, "for the very warm human being that she was and for the dedication of her life for the betterment of all human beings."[41] Similar expressions cannot be found by Smith in the thirties or forties. From the time Perkins became the first woman appointed to the cabinet, she sparked controversy. "When she arrived in Washington," notes historian Nancy Woloch, "no one save Grace Abbott and Mary Anderson sent notes of welcome; the Gridiron celebrants excluded her . . . Congress called on her endlessly to testify. . . [and] organized labor was suspicious of her, since she had never been a union leader, or even a union member."[42] Many of Smith's constituents were likely to have seen Perkins as too pro-labor, too pro-black, and only one step removed from espousing the Communist Manifesto—all ample reason for the "conventional" Margaret Chase Smith to keep her distance, at least publicly. But they became friends. In 1946 Perkins' name appears in Smith's campaign diary as an invitee on one of Smith's "Party List[s]." Later, her name appears under "To Entertain," with a "D" after it— Smith's code for those on her dinner list. In 1945, on the eve of Perkins' departure from the cabinet, Smith sent her a note. "I had planned to ask you for an evening this week but after inquiring about your program, did not have the courage to crowd any more into your busy life," she wrote. "I shall look forward, however, to see you when you return to Washington from time to time and trust on one of the occasions you will have dinner with me. In the meantime I am looking forward to spending a little time in Maine and shall hope to have an opportunity to chat with you."[43] An earlier letter, presumably written just after Smith heard of Perkins' decision to leave the cabinet when Truman became president, displays uncharacteristic feeling. "I have wanted to write to you or call and talk with you personally about your resignation as Secretary . . . but words seem futile when trying to express my feelings about the services you have rendered. I feel fortunate to have had the benefit of your counsel and friendship."[44] The relationship continued even after Perkins left Washington. In 1948 when Smith won the Republican nomination for the Senate, Perkins wrote to congratulate her. "I am delighted with your note," replied Smith warmly, "both because I appreciate your friendship, and because you know as I do the difficulties confronting women and what a victory like mine means to women. I hope you will be at home [in Newcastle,

Maine] when I get into your section sometime during the summer. I would like so much to visit with you for at least a few minutes."[45]

Smith's concession to caution was that their friendship was not widely broadcast. Though she was ordinarily almost "chatty" when it came to important women she met in Washington, Smith made little reference to Perkins, nor was Perkins highlighted in Smith's newspaper column as someone with Maine ties, as were Massachusetts Representative Edith Nourse Rogers and Ohio Representative Frances Bolton. In Smith's political biography, no comments about Perkins can be found, even though Eleanor Roosevelt is accorded fifteen. Common sense, if nothing else, counseled such a fiction, for the political costs of a perceived alliance with the woman who occupied the New Deal's "hot seat" could have been quite costly for Smith, both in Maine and in Washington's male world of power politics.[46] A balance between impulse and self-discipline enabled Smith to survive in the political arena. Why should it be otherwise in her relationships? Her marriage to Clyde—an event thought by some to have been preceded by a long affair—as well as her unconventional living arrangement with Lewis and a romantic involvement with a married man during World War II—all suggest a perilous balancing of convention with nonconformity, compliance with rebellion, acceptance of some parts of the existing sexual and social order while rejecting others. The strategy was the only one suited to an age with a still-vigorous cult of domesticity. Smith therefore constructed a public self that met the needs of society, while stubbornly refusing to barter away her need for adventure.

But there was a quality of pathos about her journey, a loneliness deeper than that of male heroes, in part because there were no comrades with whom to share it and cheer her on, to witness her achievements and validate her choices, and in part because she had to travel in disguise. The trick was not to let a persona that telegraphed conventional womanhood and thereby facilitated genuine access to the movers and shakers of her world (white males) turn into a trap of disempowerment and passivity. Margaret Chase Smith's lasting legacy was her wager on transcendence and her quest to cross over into full personhood on her own terms. By using convention, she became the most dangerous kind of troublemaker—one whose disguise was so complete that for thirty-two years she eluded capture and hanging as "a spy in the enemy's country."[47] Who can say with certainty whether success was possible on any other terms?

1. See discussion in Nancy F. Cott, *The Grounding of Modern Feminism* (New Haven, Conn.: Yale University Press, 1987), especially 13–22.

2. *New York Times*, 23 January 1901, 1.

3. Ibid.

4. See Barbara Welter, "The Cult of True Womanhood: 1820– 1860," *American Quarterly* 18 (Summer 1966); Eleanor Flexner, *Century of Struggle: The Women's Rights Movement in the United States* (Cambridge, Mass.: Harvard University Press, 1959); Aileen S. Kraditor, *The Ideas of the Woman Suffrage Movement, 1890–1920* (New York: Anchor Books, 1965); William P. O'Neill, *Everyone Was Brave: A History of Feminism in America* (New York: Quadrangle, 1976); William H. Chafe, *The American Woman: Her Changing Social, Economic and Political Role, 1920–1970* (New York: Oxford University Press, 1975).

5. Cott, *Grounding*, 275, 16. Cott dates modern feminism as beginning about 1913. Her description of the complex legacy inherited by twentieth-century feminists is instructive. "Nineteenth-century women . . . had sought diverse means and ends to assert their share in directing the world's public as well as private destinies. . . . One, begun very early in the century, lay in service and social action, motivated variously by noblesse oblige or by neighborly or altruistic intent. . . . Another comprised more overtly self-interested, more focused campaigns for 'woman's rights'—rights equivalent to those that men enjoyed on legal, political, economic, and civic

grounds. The third included more amorphous and broad-ranging pronounce-
ments and activity toward women's self-determination via 'emancipation'
from structures, conventions, and attitude enforced by law and custom."
6. Ibid., 145–65.
7. Oral history, Anecdote File, Margaret Chase Smith Library, Skowhegan,
Maine.
8. Henry David Thoreau, *The Maine Woods* (New York: Harper and Row,
1987), 20; Perry Miller and Thomas H. Johnson, *The Puritans* (New York:
American Book Co., 1938), 46–51.
9. Alan Taylor, *Liberty Men and Great Proprietors: The Revolutionary
Settlement on the Maine Frontier, 1760–1820* (Chapel Hill: University of
North Carolina Press, 1990), 59.
10. Carolyn G. Heilbrun, *Writing a Woman's Life* (New York: Ballantine
Books, 1988), 49.
11. *[Skowhegan] Independent Reporter*, 8 August 1940, 3A.
12. *[Skowhegan] Independent Reporter*, 12 September 1940, 3A.
13. On 17 March 1916, the Skowhegan girls' high school basketball team
soundly defeated the widely-favored Cony team 6 to 2. They went on to
win the Central Maine championship, after slipping past Waterville 5 to 4,
trouncing Oakland 6 to 1 and Anson 13 to 3. Trumpeted the Skowhegan
Independent Reporter: "The 1915–1916 Girls Basketball team . . . has without doubt established a precedent in Athletic History of the school by winning every game out of the fourteen played." *[Skowhegan] Independent
Reporter*, 23 March 1916, 1.
14. Margaret Chase Smith, interview with author, 13 August 1983,
Cundy's Harbor, Maine.
15. *Lewiston Evening Journal*, 22 January 1931, 9.
16. Amy Vanderbilt, *Complete Book of Etiquette* (New York: Doubleday,
1952), 564–65; Patricia L. Schmidt, *Margaret Chase Smith: Beyond
Convention* (Orono: University of Maine Press, 1996), 119–20.
17. *The Chronicle of Higher Education*, 23 May 1997, A1.
18. Judith Butler, *Gender Trouble: Feminism and Subversion of Identity*
(New York: Routledge, 1990), vii. Italics mine.
19. Susan Ware, *Beyond Suffrage: Women in the New Deal* (Cambridge,
Mass.: Harvard University Press, 1981), 16. Ware's italics.
20. *Daily Kennebec Journal*, 6 January 1923, 2.
21. House Committee on House Administration, Joint Committee on
Arrangements for the Commemoration of the Bicentennial Print, *Women
in Congress*, 94th Cong., 2d sess., 1976, 15.

22. Thomas C. Reeves, *The Life and Times of Joe McCarthy: A Biography* (New York: Stein and Day, 1982), 224.

23. David Caute, *The Great Fear: The Anti-Communist Purge Under Truman and Eisenhower* (New York: Simon and Schuster, 1978), 70–81.

24. George Mayer, *The Republican Party, 1854–1966* (New York: Oxford University Press, 1967), 478.

25. _____ to Margaret Chase Smith, n.d., Declaration of Conscience Correspondence File, Margaret Chase Smith Library.

26. _____ to Margaret Chase Smith, n.d., Declaration of Conscience Correspondence File, Margaret Chase Smith Library.

27. Ernest Becker, *The Denial of Death* (New York: The Free Press, 1973), 4.

28. Margaret Chase Smith, *Declaration of Conscience* (Garden City, New York: Doubleday, 1972), 205–6.

29. Nancy Woloch, *Women and the American Experience* (New York: Alfred A. Knopf, 1984), 425.

30. Anecdote file, Margaret Chase Smith Library.

31. Until she underwent hip surgery in 1969, she held the record for 2941 consecutive floor votes, an accomplishment of which she was justifiably proud and to which she referred often in her news releases. For this reason, her absence inevitably invited comment.

32. Donald R. Larrabee, "Illness of Senator Smith Aide May Shorten Her Career," *Maine Sunday Telegram*, 19 December, 1971, 1; see also Donald R. Larrabee, "Mrs. Smith keeps Vigil at Stricken Aide's Bed," *Daily Kennebec Journal*, 17; Donald R. Larrabee, "Sen. Smith Aide Has Heart Attack," *Portland Press Herald*, 12 December 1971, 1.

33. Maxine Cheshire, "Veteran Aide's Illness may Revise Plans of Maine Sen. Smith," *Boston Sunday Globe*, 9 January 1972, A-10.

34. Donald R. Larrabee, phone interview with author, 5 July 1997.

35. Donald Larrabee, "75, Clearing Out," *The Washington Post*, 15 December 1972, E-5.

36. Patricia Wallace, *The Politics of Conscience: A Biography of Margaret Chase Smith* (Westport, Conn.: Praeger, 1995), 189, 171; see also Wallace's discussion of Smith's general relations with the press, 167–72.

37. Margaret Chase Smith, interview with author, 27 December 1982, Skowhegan, Maine. At one point, Smith attributed the sheets to Senator Owen Brewster, and at another to Governor Hildreth.

38. Marion Martin file, Margaret Chase Smith Library.

39. Jane Austen, *Emma*, ed. Lionel Trilling (New York: Houghton Mifflin

Co., Riverside Editions, 1957), x–xi, italics mine. I am indebted to Carolyn Heilbrun, whose recent discussion over National Public Radio led me to the 1957 introduction.

40. Margaret Chase Smith, interview with author, 28 December 1982, Skowhegan, Maine.

41. Frances Perkins File, Margaret Chase Smith Library.

42. Woloch, *Women*, 456.

43. Margaret Chase Smith to Frances Perkins, 29 June 1945, Frances Perkins Papers, Butler Library, Columbia University Library, New York, N.Y.

44. Margaret Chase Smith to Frances Perkins, 8 June 1945, Frances Perkins Papers.

45. Margaret Chase Smith to Frances Perkins, 10 July 1948, Frances Perkins Papers.

46. Woloch, *Women*, 456.

47. Ralph Ellison, *The Invisible Man* (New York: Vintage Books, 1980), 16.

Historians trying to understand women's identities in the mid-twentieth century have a rather different task from those who study earlier generations. By the middle decades of this century, awareness of identity had achieved a new self-consciousness. Inspired perhaps by the influx of large numbers of immigrants early in the century, ethnicity and particularly ethnic pride became a cornerstone of identity for many. No longer did immigrants and their children seek to remove all traces of their origins in an effort to assimilate and Americanize as quickly as possible. While that had always been more the hope of those who viewed America as the great melting pot than it had been the goal of immigrants themselves, by mid-century it was giving way to a more complex vision that celebrated difference even as it encouraged patriotism and a sense of belonging.

Ethnic awareness was not the only newly self-conscious aspect of identity at mid-century. Aware of the homogenization of culture inspired by movies, radio, and later television, community leaders sought to sustain and revive local loyalties. In Maine, towns sponsored "old home days" designed to encourage those who had left to return, if only for a summer weekend. Local historical societies, genealogical groups, and historical re-creation sites flourished as never before. While most of these activities were as much the product of the tourist industry as anything else, they nevertheless point to Americans' growing interest in cultivating their roots.

This continuing attention to identity did not exclude gender. While many hoped that winning the vote in 1920 would eradicate the significant political differences between men and women, experiences during the Depression and beyond demonstrated that gender remained a potent factor shaping people's lives. While few new groups designed to improve women's status as women were formed, gender remained at the heart of individual identity and women were never allowed to forget that they were women, different from men.

All of this attention suggests that over the course of the century covered by the essays in this book, questions of identity continued to be shaped by gender, ethnicity, place, and all of the other characteristics used to describe individuals. While the content of those characteristics changed over time, often quite dramatically, their ability to shape the individual and her experience did not. What it meant to live in Maine, to be a woman, to practice a particular religion, to be identified with an ethnic group, class, and occupation—the content of all of these changed over time, yet all continued to define identity. They continued to resonate with one another in fluctuating ways that complicated efforts to describe group experiences, requiring historians not just to explore each characteristic, but also the ways in which these influenced and shaped one another. In this volume's final essay, Celeste DeRoche explores the changing characteristics of identity for mid-century Franco-American women.

Celeste DeRoche

At 14,
My grandmother walked toward the red sky
Toward the sun glancing its gold at every mill window
She saw how, over the border, her dreams had flocked
And flown ahead . . .
                          –Susann Pelletier, "Red Sky"[1]

* * *

Back then, the city where I was born
Gave little comfort.
It shook me with the clatter of looms
And night machines,
Blinded me with that immigrant dream
                          –Susann Pelletier, "Immigrant Dreams I"[2]

It is easy to forget Maine's industrial history. Most of the
mammoth brick mill buildings no longer churn out the textiles or shoes that once provided the foundation for the state's
economy. The buildings, if they are used at all, are now retail
space or offices. With their "waterfront" locations, the buildings are picturesque and many are now admired for the solidity of their construction. The air the present-day office workers breathe is cleaner than the damp lint-filled air that

clogged the workers' lungs when the looms clattered and shook the building.

Women were at the center of Maine's industrial history and French-Canadian women were integral to the success of companies like Pepperell and Bates. The history of the French-Canadian women who traveled to Maine specifically to find work tells us much about not only the development of Maine's economy, but the evolution of the peoples of Maine as well.

By the end of the nineteenth century and well into the middle of the twentieth century, French-Canadian women were the mainstay of the often poorly paid labor force that kept the textile looms and shoe machines, paper-sorting machines and woolen factories running from Biddeford to Lewiston and Westbrook to Dexter. The first-generation immigrants often made the difficult overland trip from the farms and small towns of Quebec to southern Maine expressly to find work in the growing mills and factories. While many times they hoped that their daughters and sons would be able to forego the demands of millwork for more skilled jobs, many Franco-American women of the second and third generations found that millwork offered their best hope for decent wages.

THE CLATTER OF LOOMS

The French Canadians who came to Maine developed a close association with the textile industry. By 1860, cotton textiles employed the largest number of Maine wage earners. And by the turn of the century, when French Canadians represented twelve percent of Maine's population, they were largely concentrated in the textile centers of central and southern Maine.[3] French Canadians from the Beauce region of Quebec traveled the "Kennebec Road" either on foot or in horse-drawn wagons, while the Grand Trunk and Maine Central railroads carried the majority of Maine's other Franco-Americans from a much broader area of Quebec.[4]

Lewiston was an early destination for many French Canadians. Between 1880 and 1910 competitive capitalism added 28,000 new jobs to the work force. Native-born and immigrant alike were leaving their rural homes for better futures in industrial centers. In 1890, 26 percent of all Mainers lived in urban areas; forty years later the urban population stood at 40 percent.[5] Lewiston was part of this tremendous shift in population and industrial growth.

Estelle Bouchard grew up in Lewiston in the early twentieth century and clearly remembered how the rhythms of millwork provided the cadence for life.

> I was brought up in the Hill Block in Lewiston. You see, there were three major mills. There was the Bates Mill, the Hill Mill and the Androscoggin Mill. And then one street lower was the Continental Mill. And each of these mills built a big block of apartment buildings directly in back of the mill so that the people they brought in could live in those apartment buildings. At 3:00 PM everybody would come out, and the whole of Canal Street was invaded with workers. We were playing in the yards there, and the people would come by with their lunch boxes. This was very much a part of what I grew up with, the mill workers going in at 2:30, the other shift coming out at 3:00. Then, later that night, we would hear them on summer evenings at 11:00 coming out. This was very much a part of my surroundings— my mother's stories about how it was to work in the mill . . . and how hard they would work.[6]

The working conditions inside the mill were far from pleasant. Besides the monotonous and tiring nature of the work, there was the ever-present cotton dust suspended in the air and the constant noise of the machines. Alice Blais described the wearing noise that accompanied the workers eight to ten hours a day.

There was not a lot of socializing going on in the mill. We worked very hard, and you didn't leave [your work] a lot. There was a lot of noise in the mills. It was worse than the noise in the shoe shops. If someone wasn't used to it, he was nearly deaf when he left. When there were fifty to sixty machines in the same room, they all made the same noise. What a racket that made![7]

Cecile Doyon, who worked in the mill from the time she was a child, found the mill sounds especially tiresome. She recalled a strategy the operatives used to combat the relentless noise.

If you wanted to talk to someone, you had to talk in his ear. It came to a point where there was a rhythm to it, and we'd start to sing to that rhythm when the work was going fine, but when the work was going badly, there was no singing.[8]

And for a city dependent on one industry, there was no singing if the industry experienced problems. With the Depression of 1929 came work slow-downs and layoffs. Franco-American families like Cecile Doyon's were faced with difficult choices. As often happened, it was the women who bore the brunt of the hard trade-offs.

We suffered some. . . . I can remember one time, right after the last boy in the family was born. I had just had him, and my husband wasn't working at all. I saw the second man (one of the bosses) in the mill go by. After the baby was born, I couldn't go back to work right away, so I said to my husband, "Go ask him (the boss) if he will give you a job." He hadn't worked for two weeks, and so he went. And I said, as he started to go, "If he doesn't have any work for you, ask him if he has any for me." The man didn't want to take my husband, and he said, "Tell your wife to come. Tell her to come Monday." He knew I had more experience than my husband. I'd been working in the mill since I was fourteen years old. My husband hadn't worked long in the mill, so the boss knew I could do the work better than he could. My husband didn't like it too much because he had to take care of the

baby. The baby was eight weeks old. The man doing the hiring wanted me to work the third shift. During the day, I took care of the kids
and the baby, and at night I had to work. My husband helped me in
the daytime because then he wasn't working. I tried to sleep in the
day when he was in the house. I could sleep once in awhile — two or
three hours sometimes. Then I'd go to work, and when I came home,
I had to make the bread.[9]

The investigation done in 1908–9 by the Immigration
Commission, appointed by the U.S. Senate, draws a compelling portrait of the extent of French-Canadian women's
participation in the textile industry in Maine and New
England. The Commission generated much controversy during its tenure, yet the forty-one volumes of findings remain
an important source of empirical data. It gathered information from about 40 percent of the active workforce in cotton
manufacturing, including 13,000 foreign-born French-Canadian workers.[10] The Commission's data demonstrate the
prominent role French Canadian women played in the industry. Women workers were far more numerous than men in
the 14-to-24 age bracket, representing 47 percent of their sex
group, whereas the men of that age bracket represented only
28 percent of their sex group. Women's presence in the workforce declined in the 25-to-34 age bracket and rose significantly in the 35-to-44 bracket.[11]

The Commission's data also uncovered the importance of
the "family income" as opposed to a single-breadwinner
income for French-Canadian immigrants. When compared to
other ethnic groups included in the Commission's survey,
only the Portuguese had a higher proportion of wives at work.
For French-Canadian families, both working wives and working children contributed to the income necessary for the family's survival. The image of the male breadwinner providing
through his work for the economic sustenance of the family
was far from the reality.[12]

Claudia Emond knew first-hand the rigors of a family income. She was the last of twelve children born to Bellesemere and Eugene Breton on a one-hundred-acre tract in Thetford Mines, Quebec. The farm was a spacious one and Emond remembered her childhood fondly: *"J'ai une belle enfance; jamais les troubles* (I was a child without a care)." She grew up on the farm with her parents, three sisters and one brother. The seven others were married and gone. Some had children before Emond was born.[13]

Emond and her family moved between Biddeford and Thetford Mines several times before returning to settle in 1927. When she returned to Biddeford she was sixteen. She found a job at the York Mills where she worked sixty-four hours a week as a weaver, for nine dollars per week. As a weaver, she was required to stand before the giant looms from six in the morning until five-thirty in the afternoon. She received a thirty-minute break for lunch and two other ten-minute breaks. She quit her weaving job after one year and returned to Thetford Mines for a four-month respite. When she returned to Biddeford she married Amedeé Emond but did not return to millwork until after the births of her four children. In 1935 she began working again, this time as a winder in the Bates Mill, which was formerly the York Mill.

The tremendous migration of people to Maine did not go unnoticed in Quebec. Many politicians and priests in Quebec condemned the phenomenon as a serious threat to the continued vitality of the French-Canadian people. Some leaders in the province dealt with the loss by disparaging the immigrants. Georges Etienne Cartier, Prime Minister of Canada from 1857–1862, is alleged to have said: *"Laissez-les partir: c'est la canaille qui s'en va* (Let them depart: it's the rabble who are leaving)."[14]

While Cartier's remarks may have been apocryphal, the concern for the loss of cultural values and allegiance was real.

Franco-American leaders, especially priests, business leaders, and other professionals, emphasized the cultural cohesion of Franco-American communities.[15] Franco-Americans were often viewed as choosing ethnic closeness over class allegiances. Some labor history studies have focused on the Franco-Americans as submissive and unsympathetic to labor's causes.[16] Following the lead of vocal anti-union priests, many Franco-Americans chose *survivance* over worker solidarity.

Other labor historians have found a quite different picture by asking similar questions from a different angle. John Cumbler in his study of Fall River, Massachusetts, found that French Canadians originally migrated to the city as strikebreakers. In the early 1870s, Fall River's French-Canadian population was generally non-militant and maintained a closer association with agrarian Canada than with industrial Fall River.[17]

Yet Cumbler also uncovered splits within the ethnic community. Unable to relate to the conservative and older leadership, which was becoming dominated by clerics and the small white-collar middle class, younger and unskilled French Canadians searched for new leadership. Unions provided this new leadership. These young French Canadians slowly began to participate across ethnic lines as they found more in common with other wage earners than the elite ethnic leadership of their own community.[18]

Cumbler's research raised an important issue: shared ethnicity did not necessarily mandate harmony. A homogeneous ethnic culture was not as prevalent as early studies of Fall River had concluded. Cumbler's findings pointed to a deficiency in Franco-American historiography which has been too quick to assume a singular Franco-American experience without paying sufficient attention to intra-ethnic differences. Yet Cumbler missed a central point. His inattention to women serves to highlight the centrality of gender and generational differences in the formation of ethnic consciousness.

GOLD AT EVERY MILL WINDOW

Work outside the home occupied most working-class Franco-American women for some portion, if not all, of their adult lives. Grace Pedneault Curtis remembered in quite specific detail her first job:

> I started to work when I was a senior in high school. Trying to work in the dime store which was Woolworth's uptown, to earn money for an evening—no, no—a graduation dress. But I didn't last there very long, and the manager was overly friendly to a very unsophisticated young girl. And all I had to do was to go home and tell my mother, "I don't want to work there anymore." And she didn't say one other word. That's fine. So she must have heard of the man's reputation. So that was my first job. I was very uncomfortable. I was not too sophisticated, and we won't go into. . . . Besides families did not discuss sex or sex problems in my generation. Maybe they did in other. But you didn't; you just went along and did the best you could, and so I was relieved I didn't have to explain because it was making me very uncomfortable.[19]

Curtis' recollection is not an unfamiliar one. The story she relates of her first job while still in high school is information historians have long collected about ethnic women. The importance of her story is that it furnishes the complicating feature of the sexual harassment she experienced. This detail expands what historians have known: "women have always worked." What has been missing are the particulars Curtis provides—what the experience of work really meant in the life of a seventeen-year-old young woman.

Curtis' memory reveals the dominance of family in the lives of Franco women. It is not simply this obvious fact, the importance of the family, that needs to be examined. The less visible aspects of family in the Franco experience need to be explored. The actual meaning, content and boundaries of family relationships are crucial to understanding the role the family played in Franco women's lives. Paying attention to the family while keeping in mind gender, generation, and family dynamics means that the issues of family hierarchy, conflict, and power struggles within the family can be examined.

A family dynamic that played a significant and compelling role in the lives of Franco-American women was the impact birth order had on their lives, choices, and opportunities. In order to find meaning in their work, Franco-American women often referred to the role they played in their families. Responsibilities within Franco-American working class families varied depending on where they came in the birth order. Older children all took on additional responsibilities. And older daughters often assumed even more. Tasks fell unevenly along gender lines and older daughters were expected to do more and to do different things from their brothers.

Josephine DeRoche LaBrecque, her older sister Victoria DeRoche Guitard, and Grace Pedneault Curtis were all older daughters. As such, they were expected to put the collective needs of the family before their individual goals or desires. Their reaction to this reality was mixed. Curtis insisted, "You felt good to be able to help your parents." She was proud that her paycheck contributed in essential ways to her family's welfare. Yet as she told the stories that documented her pivotal role in the economic support of her parents and siblings a further meaning to the circumstances of her work history emerged.

> When I got out of high school, it was 1936, and I applied at S. D. Warren and couldn't get a job right off, so I babysat. So that was my first job outside of home. And then in October I got a job in S. D. Warren, and everybody was pleased because you make a lot of money, but the job that I was trying—given a job on sorting paper. . . . I worked running a paper cutter — a great big machine. I detested machinery.[20]

Grace Curtis remembered her pride and used it to cope with the more distressing recollection of the difficult work conditions she endured in order to assist her family. Josephine LaBrecque, like Grace Curtis, was a "providing daughter."[21] Her contributions also exacted a painful price.

> I got out of school, and I worked in the Dana Warp Mill. I quit high school for the same reason Rita [her elder sister] quit. It sounds as though my father was an old tyrant. You know, he had all this money coming in, but he didn't because Vickie was away, Mary was doing housework, Annie, I think was working in the Mill, but she got married in 1930 something. That was right after the Depression. So actually those three—and Madeline worked at the Snow Laundry. It was a—they did washings and ironing and you know. Then she went away—she did housework after she got through school, and she didn't graduate from high school. So I went to high school until my third year. I started my third year, and for the same reason that Rita quit, we didn't have no clothes. In fact, Rita was working in the Dana Warp Mills, and I would go by in the morning [on her way to school], and I'd have to take—I wore one of her jackets, because she was "wealthy," you know, she had money, and I'd wear one of her jackets, but I had to kind of hurry by the Mill because she could be looking out the window and see me. So then I quit school in the beginning of my third year. It was just before Christmas I think, and I went to work in Dana's.[22]

Elder daughters were also older sisters. By dropping out of school and going to work, these women gave their younger siblings the opportunity to gain more education.

Victoria DeRoche Guitard, LaBrecque's older sister and the eldest child and daughter in the family, remembered that even after leaving home for work in Boston she still provided for the family in Westbrook by paying special attention to younger siblings.

> I said to him [her younger brother] if you get on the honor roll—I was working in Boston then, and I did a lot of hockey, and he liked hockey

too—so I promised him if he got on the honor roll, I would send him a ticket. And so he did make the honor roll. He got on the train and came to Boston. I met him in Boston and we went to a hockey game.[23]

Grace Pedneault Curtis also had a younger brother who benefited from her being older and out in the world earning an income.

The other thing is my brother was younger than we were, and my sister and I would keep him well dressed. He was going to—he was two years behind me in school. And he was going to Gorham, which was a teacher's college at the time. And we'd chip in together to get him a sports jacket because it—you know, boys wore sports jackets and ties. So it helped him look like the other boys; and anything that needed money, my sister and I helped with. You know. Christmas was a pure delight, because we—you know—we really had a lot of fun at Christmas time.[24]

As second-generation daughters and sisters, these working-class Franco women contributed to the economic survival of their families. Along with their parents, they fed, clothed, and helped house siblings and at times more distant relatives. These second-generation women respected and even revered the preceding generation. Franco-American women knew firsthand the challenges their parents faced in the workplace. Emma Tourangeau remembered: "My mother often told us of her long days at Dana Warp Mills; she and her sister had to carry a small stool or box to stand on and tending to the bobbins was tedious . . . and one day when mother had to leave early, she lost a few pennies when she was paid the small weekly wage, which I believe was fifty cents."[25] The valiant efforts of their parents were not unappreciated. Dorothy Hawkes described her parents and their peers as "gutsy people." She acknowledged their fortitude and their ability to "never complain." "They weren't wealthy," Hawkes remarked, "but they were gutsy. And they were good people."[26]

Like Tourangeau's mother, the women who worked the unskilled jobs at the Warren paper mill found the work required, more than anything else, fortitude. For some Franco-American women, millwork did bring satisfaction. Annie DeRoche Downes worked at the Dana Warp Mill for fifteen years. In her words: "I was very privileged to work in the cotton mill."[27] Yet Downes's sisters who also worked at the Dana Warp described the experience differently. One agreed that Downes had a good job, but concluded, "I wouldn't have wanted to do that kind of work." Another sister noted, "The cotton mill wasn't the best. It was hard on your lungs. When I worked there, we started coughing up blood."[28]

Most of the DeRoche sisters worked at the S. D. Warren mill. By the 1920s and 1930s, jobs at the mill were in short supply. It was especially difficult for women to get hired. The jobs that were available went to men. The sisters agreed that "knowing someone" helped you get in at the mill. One of the sisters had worked for a local doctor who happened to be the doctor for the mill, and he helped her get a job at Warren. Another sister had done housework for the man who was the supervisor of the finishing department, and this connection helped her get hired. Ultimately, though, they all agreed that what was really needed to get a job at the mill was persistence. "I went down there every morning. That's what we used to have to do. We used to have to go down every morning. We wanted the work."[29]

The sisters were clear in their understanding that they needed to work and were willing to contribute to the family economy. But the need to work was still difficult to reconcile with the normal events of a young woman's life. Josephine DeRoche LaBrecque recalled an event in the life of her older sister that clearly focused the conflict between wanting to participate in the usual high school events and needing to work.

Rita was a junior in school, and she was working at the mill in West-brook; and she asked our father, she said—well, course she would have liked to have gone to the Prom, but she knew she wouldn't have the money to buy the clothes she needed to wear—so she asked my father what should she do. Well, he said, you know what you would like to do, what you feel you should do, but she said she knew he needed the money.[30]

Mary DeRoche Daley worked as a paper sorter for fourteen years. Alice DeRoche worked at the Warren mill for thirty-two years. Alice described her work as "a nice job. I worked in the lab. Testing paper. And it was very interesting because we had to use a lot of different machines. I didn't have a high school education, but I did—it came to me, and I just made up my mind that I was going to learn what I needed to know." Theresa DeRoche Hebert worked at the mill for two years, until she married and got pregnant. "Then I quit." Josephine DeRoche LaBrecque remembered trying to get a job at the mill, "I would go to S. D. Warren with my friend Dot Hawkes and we would go to Mr. Lincoln [mill hiring agent] and ask for work and Mr. Lincoln would say, 'I'm sorry ladies, the situation is just the same.' Meaning, no work."[31]

LaBrecque was more successful at the Dana Warp Mills. Quitting high school after her junior year, LaBrecque got a job at the textile mill. This was just at the start of the Depression and her family needed another wage earner. Learning several different jobs at the textile mill increased your job security. LaBrecque explained it this way: "At Dana Warp I was a winder and I doffed. When you worked there you did several jobs. If you could do several jobs, you'd be better off. You were more secure of a job."[32]

Mostly what the sisters remember is that they just worked. As Mary DeRoche Daley put it: "I always worked." Another sister said: "We were just glad we had a job then. We didn't care what we did."[33] Employed outside the home even after marriage and bearing children, work was an ever-present reality for the DeRoche sisters. The camaraderie of friends could relieve some of the tedium, but paid labor brought them little personal satisfaction.

Grace Pedneault Curtis found paid labor an often-frustrating challenge. Like most of the DeRoche sisters, Curtis worked at S. D. Warren. Curtis explained: "There was never any question, if you went to work in the Mill, you went to work at S. D. Warren." She got a job sorting paper. "I was very small, and the paper—some of the sheets—were so large, it was—I didn't complain—but they must have noticed it was no job for a woman my size sorting the papers." The most redeeming feature of work at the mill was the presence of relatives. Curtis's sister was a secretary in the finishing department and a cousin also worked at the mill. As Curtis expressed it: "So it was like being among your own people to work there."[34] The nearness of relatives mitigated some of the strain of large machinery and treacherous work.

Most of Curtis's paycheck went towards helping with family expenses. Even so Curtis found a way to treat herself. "I was able to afford a leopard coat." For a long time, Curtis's secret longing was for a leopard coat: "Boy, if ever I . . . and oh, boy, to have a leopard coat, I'd wear only forest green with it, and stuff like that." Curtis's older sister, a working woman herself, told her how the purchase of such a coat could be possible. The story is about a coat but it also suggests the new values and choices Curtis was putting on in 1938 when she wore it.

> So after I'd been working — let's say six or eight months or whatever, my sister says, "you know there's a way to do it." And she explained how you could buy the coat with a down payment, and you pay $5.00 a week. That was what I did. That was the grandest thing in my life to have that leopard coat.

The purchase of the coat made work palatable. And the joy of owning the coat provided a special pride. "I wore it to church every Sunday and to the movies and to any kind of an evening affair. I really didn't save it for anything. I just really enjoyed it." The pride, joy, and relief that the leopard coat brought for this hard-working Franco woman was still evident many decades later as she added, "I've got part of it upstairs."[35]

Not even a leopard coat could make millwork interesting. Curtis minded the danger of millwork less than the tedium. "I felt I was wasting my time not getting ahead mentally and just doing a drab job that someone that doesn't know very much can do, you know. And I wanted to get out in the world. I loved to go out and sell and meet people. This kind of stuff. But I did my job in the mill and I never downed it while it was providing me with the income I wanted to help the family and to get a leopard coat."[36] Finding a way to have work provide personal satisfaction and not just economic survival was the dilemma of Curtis's work career. More often than not the exigencies of family needs took precedence over personal goals.

For Emma Tourangeau this became even more true when her father died in 1910 from injuries sustained in a work-related accident. Tourangeau and the two sisters who followed her became the primary wage earners in the family. Tourangeau was twenty-six at the time, while her sisters Virginia and Delia were twenty-two and eighteen, respectively; none was married. They worked at S. D. Warren. Between their earnings and their mother's careful management, Tourangeau remembered that they survived financially. The three younger children still at home were sixteen, fourteen, and ten. As Tourangeau said: "It was a 'toss up'—to feed, clothe, and educate—took love, understanding."[37] From week to week the Tourangeau women could never be sure if there would be enough resources to insure that all the family members were fed and clothed.

Taking care of younger siblings and making sacrifices for their benefit was not unknown to the older DeRoche sisters. As soon as they were old enough, they quit school and went to work fulltime. They gave their salaries to their parents. With the older sisters working, the younger children could stay in school. Consequently, only the three youngest children out of the eleven in the family were able to graduate from high school.

The older sisters did not seem to begrudge this sacrifice. What seemed to affect them more was remembering that while their father emphasized the importance of education to them, it was really the boys he had in mind. LaBrecque recalled: "One thing that he [her father] always said, and I never forgot it; he always talked to the boys to get an education. So they wouldn't have to do the work that he was doing."[38] Their father's emphasis on education did not extend to the women in the family.

Emma Tourangeau also found herself at odds with her father over education. Like the senior DeRoches, Tourangeau's father did not emphasize education for his daughters. He had assumed that she would work at the S. D. Warren mill, as he did. Tourangeau's desire for more education, while not actively blocked by her father, was not encouraged either. Tourangeau's commitment to education continued to be a priority that she extended to include her younger siblings. She worked hard to ensure that they would have access to higher education if they wanted it, even after her father's death curtailed her own ambitions.

In 1919 I sent Ted to U of M at Orono — he stayed five years, and it cost me $3500.00—this I paid week to week. . . . I had a Falmouth and Loan Book to pay the U of M and can truly say I was always borrowing and paying back through S. D. W. Co. and good old Westbrook Trust Co. I gave Ted a "paid in full" receipt for his education and Irene [Ted's wife] and he never had this debt over their heads.[39]

These experiences make clear two important issues in family dynamics. Not only were there gender differences in families, with males being given different and often better opportunities than females. In addition, the females' experiences in the family were not the same. A woman's place in the birth order could significantly affect her chances for opportunity and autonomy. Being an older daughter brought different and usually more strenuous responsibilities than being a younger son or younger daughter.

Emma Tourangeau, Victoria DeRoche Guitard, and Grace Curtis took obvious pleasure in being "providing women" for their younger siblings.[40] This pride notwithstanding, birth order made a tremendous difference in their lives. Age played a decidedly important role in the lives of these oldest daughters. Yet gender was also critical. It took Josephine LaBrecque many years, but she finally understood something her mother said in her final illness. "When she was sick," LaBrecque said, "Mama said, 'I wished I had all boys.' I don't think she realized how that sounded." LaBrecque continued, "Now I know why she said that. Really, I do. I think she figured the women would go through a lot more than the men. I really felt that."[41]

HER DREAMS HAD FLOCKED AND FLOWN AHEAD

Emma Tourangeau of Westbrook, Maine did not expect that her life would be linked with that of the S. D. Warren Company. She had explicitly decided that she did not want to work at the mill. Given the stories her mother had told her of her years at the Dana Warp Mill, Tourangeau knew that millwork was not what she wanted for herself. As the eldest in a family with seven younger siblings, there was never any question that she would go to work and contribute to the family economy. She was able to stay in school long enough to receive her high school diploma. After she graduated, her father took her to S. D. Warren where he worked. He wanted her to see the young women sorting paper. Tourangeau remembered, "One glance convinced me that I just did not want to spend days doing that kind of work."[42]

Despite her father's insistent desire that Tourangeau join him in working at the mill, Tourangeau decided she wanted more education. She had ambitions for a different kind of life than millwork would afford. She gave piano lessons and played in a band with her father and brother and saved the one hundred dollars required for tuition at Miss Elinor Moody's Private Business School. She studied bookkeeping, shorthand, typewriting, and advanced English. Successfully completing this one-year program, Tourangeau secured a job in the freight office of the Maine Central Railroad at Union Station in Portland. Her salary was $7.00 a week.

Yet Tourangeau's resolute goal of avoiding employment at S. D. Warren, or any mill for that matter, was interrupted by the gendered exigencies of family life and responsibility. In 1906, Tourangeau's father was permanently disabled in an accident at the mill where he had worked since 1883. John E. Warren, agent of the Warren mill, approached Tourangeau. He asked her to come to work at the mill. Warren's motives were not completely altruistic or beneficent. Shortly after Tourangeau's father's accident, Warren visited the family and insisted that Mr. Tourangeau sign a paper stipulating that he would never sue the mill. Tourangeau remembered this as a traumatic moment for her father: "My father cried. He said, 'Mr. Warren, you did enough for me and my family. Why do you ask me—why do you fear that I'm going to sue—I'd never sue the Company.'" Tourangeau recalled that while the mill paid her father's doctor bills, he did not receive any salary or worker's compensation. Instead, he received a promise from Warren. "Well, he [John E. Warren] said, 'I'll tell you, Mr.

Tourangeau, I'll promise you that as long as there is a Tourangeau, they'll get a job at S. D. Warren Mills.'" Tourangeau was the first Tourangeau to benefit from this promise. At the time, she remained unconvinced that it was a positive move. She recalled her move to S. D. Warren and all the ambivalence and apprehension that surrounded the decision.

> They sent for me, you know, to go down and see him [John Warren]. So I had to go on a Saturday when I wasn't working. I told Mr. Warren, "I don't want to go down — to come down here to work. I like where I am." "Yes, you're paying carfare, and you have to wear better clothes, and you have to bring your lunch. Why not come in here, and you can go home to lunch." And I said, "No. I don't want to come."[43]

Tourangeau found other considerations besides the ability to go home for lunch more critical. Central to these was the pride she felt at having carved out for herself a professional identity, and she liked having to wear "better clothes." Tourangeau respected her current boss, and commented, "I liked to go downtown at noon, walk to the stores. I used to love to go to the library to get some books." Mr. Warren continued to insist. He wanted Tourangeau to leave her job immediately and come to the mill. Perhaps he felt some guilt at the accident; perhaps he really thought a job at the mill was a better opportunity for Tourangeau. Yet Tourangeau remained cautious and concerned. She told Warren, "I'd have to give them two weeks notice. I can't leave them this way, because I might want to come back here." But to her great niece, seventy-six years after this difficult period in her life, Tourangeau admitted the more complicated nature of her anxieties, a poignant and telling acknowledgement of the imbalance of power between a prominent businessman and a young ethnic woman with a primary commitment to the well-being of her family.

I made all kinds of excuses. I didn't want to go down. I was scared of
the Warren people. To me they were just like the King. You know?
My father worked there, and my father had a good position. We had
a good home. I was afraid the whole thing would crumble up if I went
down to work. I said, "What if I can't do the job and they discharged
me?" I had all kinds of bad dreams about the job.[44]

Tourangeau tried to allay her uneasiness by getting Warren
to "make it all right with Mr. Fletcher that if I don't like the
job [at S. D. Warren] that I could come back." Through a combination of her sheer doggedness and tenacious determination to maintain some control over her future while meeting
her family obligations, Tourangeau convinced Warren to agree
to her terms. She worked a two-week notice at her job with
the Maine Central Railroad and then went to work at S. D.
Warren. Her tenure at the Warren mill almost ended before it
even began. On her first day of work, Tourangeau reported to
a Mr. Caldwell, the office manager. When Tourangeau
inquired about Warren on her first day on the job, Caldwell
was quick to assert his authority. He answered her inquiry by
saying, "Well, Missy, you won't have nothing more to do
with Mr. Warren. He's the agent. I'm the one that runs the
office. I'm going to put you to work."[45] Caldwell then
assigned Tourangeau to her new job on the switchboard.

And, so believe me—you wouldn't believe this—he took me to this
little room. There was a high chair. It was a switchboard. A switchboard. I said, "Well, I didn't come here to be a switch operator—to be
a telephone operator. I never saw a switchboard before," I said. And
there was a sign there that said telephone and the number and all
that. "Yes, you see, but you're going to learn. We're going to have
someone teach you." I said, "I don't want to have anybody teach me.
I don't want to be a switchboard operator. I didn't come here to be a
switch-telephone operator." So he said, "You are certainly one person
that knows what you want." "I don't want to be a switch operator," I
said, "I'll go right back to Portland where I belong. I'm a secretary," I

said. "I want to do what I like to do." Well, he said, "All right. Get out."

So what was I going to do when a man tells me the first day of work to get out? I went in and sat in Mr. Warren's office, and so I waited about—a long time. Finally, he came in. Well, he says, "Hello, Emma. Well, what can I do for you?" "I came in to tell you that I'm going back to Portland. Mr. Caldwell put me on the switchboard and I don't want to be a switch operator. Haven't you got any other job for me?" He said, "I didn't tell him to put you on the switchboard." I said, "What do you want me to do? I came here to be—you know what I came here to do." So then he called in Mr. Barrow. He was the Assistant Superintendent of the mill. So I met him, and he took me in his office—private office, and, "Well, let's have our first letter, Emma." And he gave me the first letter, and "Come with me," and there was a desk with the typewriter. I was there for 46 years. I came home, when I retired and I brought home with me that desk and my chair.[46]

Maybe Caldwell was just establishing his authority as the boss and meant Tourangeau no harm. With the chasm of time gone by, it is difficult to attribute motives and intentions. Yet a true fact is that Tourangeau was the first French or Catholic person to work in the front office at S. D. Warren. Her father had been the first French man hired at the mill. Tourangeau's father encouraged her to be a paper sorter because he was sure she would never get hired to work in the front office.[47] Tourangeau was willing to risk losing her job in standing up to Caldwell. It is not clear from her interview with her great niece or her memoir what compelled Tourangeau to take this risk. Did she know Warren would back her up? Did Tourangeau think Warren would fear her father would file a lawsuit if Tourangeau were fired? Perhaps Tourangeau's business school training had instilled a professional sense of her abilities, allowing her to stand her ground. Whatever the reason or reasons, Tourangeau was able to negotiate a successful outcome for herself.

For the women who worked unskilled jobs at the Westbrook mills, life was quite different. Most Franco-American women in Westbrook found work at the textile mill. While they did not face the outright discrimination that marked Tourangeau's encounter with Caldwell, the owner of the textile mill made clear his position by saying that he hoped when he got to heaven there would be only Republicans and Congregationalists.[48]

Franco-American women in Maine were not reluctant to join the paid labor force, if it meant their families would be fed and younger siblings could stay in school. Paid labor did not provide exciting careers. Work was tedious and at times physically dangerous. And if a job brought a measure of prestige, as it did for Emma Tourangeau, it also required the employee to work long hours to sustain an intangible reward. Franco women coped with the unpleasantness of their work lives by focusing on their sense of pride and accomplishment in enabling their families to survive. Work was a means to an end rather than an end in itself. Franco-American women did not ignore the reality of low wages or discrimination. They focused instead on the dignity they found in surviving and shaping their lives to the best of their ability.

THAT IMMIGRANT DREAM

Franco-American women in Maine were community builders. Whether at work in the mills, hanging laundry in their backyards or tenement porches, or attending church functions, they were keenly attuned to developing bonds that would sustain themselves and their families through the often uncertain flow of everyday life. It is usually to institution-building rather then community-building that historians give their greatest attention. Institutions are more visible. Community can be intangible, vague, and difficult to pinpoint. For the most part historians do not like vagueness. Yet the effort to capture the experiences of people who leave behind little documentation of their community work causes historians to examine issues and questions that previously have been deemed of little importance.

In an effort to understand the culture and community Franco-American women created and sustained, one place to start is their neighborhood life. Especially for working-class Franco women who usually had little time to join organizations, neighborhood life provided a pivotal connection.

Grace Pedneault Curtis sketched a cartography of "Frenchtown," Westbrook's Franco-American neighborhood, that demonstrated in vivid strokes the neighborhood's significance in her life. The axes of her days were mapped along lines stretching up hills, across streets, and around corners to a community, which in conscious and unconscious ways kept her connected.

> There were no organizations that I chose to belong to. Let's put it that way. Because my needs at home—you see I was married just about—not quite two years when Newt [her husband] left for the service. So I had no time for social activities. I live[d] alone for all the time that Newt was in the service. And I lived in an ideal place for someone. I lived right in the heart of Frenchtown. Behind me, downhill in King Street my grandmother lived and my aunt. And I lived directly across from the beer parlor on Brown Street. I was surrounded with relatives and never had to use them. And across the street I had another aunt, and my father lived up the street. So that it was a kind of snug feeling.[49]

Using census data, historians have been able to map with precision the geography of ethnic and immigrant neighborhoods. The adaptive role of the neighborhood is well-documented, and more and more understood by historians. Yet neighborhood life was important for other reasons as well.

Historians of ethnic women are just beginning to understand the layered meanings of neighborhood. Ardis Cameron, in her study of the working women who went on strike in Lawrence, Massachusetts in 1882 and again in 1912, found that a common neighborhood life prepared these women to organize on their own behalf. Sharing recipes, childcare, shopping strategies, and recreation, the immigrant women of Lawrence created links with one another across ethnic lines.[50] It was in the neighborhoods, at the ground level of daily life, that the familiar and the routine became powerful weapons of protest and resistance. At the center of this activity were female-centered networks. Female networks were based on relationships rather than memberships. In Westbrook's Frenchtown there were no strikes. The neighborhood was not the site of intensive organization. Yet the Franco women who lived there disclosed the importance of female networks. From purely social gatherings to a more intentional reliance on relationships with family and friends, these Franco women existed in a latticework of relationships that the census could not enumerate.

Most of the emphasis on ethnic neighborhoods in Franco-American historiography has been to determine how the "Little Canadas" protected and sustained ethnic identity.[51] Neighborhood connections had a gendered dimension in addition to an ethnic component. Uncovering the neighborhood networks that women created and the female traditions of reciprocity and association that women utilized in their day-to-day lives can break open the myriad and prolific ways that Franco women created community and adapted it to their own needs. In Lawrence, women trained and protected children, cared for the sick, fed the hungry, "kept" house, and provided for families and neighbors.[52] Franco-American women in Westbrook, Lewiston, Biddeford, Dexter, and all the "Little Canadas" in between used their ethnic enclaves to improve life for themselves, their families, their neighbors, and the larger community.

Looking out for one another, helping one another, and just enjoying each other's company—elements of ethnic neighborhood life long ignored by historians—created a sense of power and autonomy that was lacking in other areas of women's lives. Denied choice or freedom in their work lives, women formed neighborhood relationships that ultimately empowered them to take active roles in the larger community. Franco women encountered political power within the ties of social relations. Grace Curtis remembered her mother as a prominent figure at election time. "In those days—you may know this—but in those days it was very important to have someone that could speak two languages work for the election because a lot of the people could only speak French." Curtis's mother, who was respected and admired in Frenchtown, was wooed by candidates seeking the French vote. "Whoever was fortunate enough to get my mother to work for them," Curtis recalled with obvious pride and satisfaction, "Republican or Democrat, usually won the election."[53] Franco-American political history will not be complete until we know how many Franco women, like Curtis's mother, were courted for their influence and the authority they represented among the women and men up and down their street. Whether functioning as midwife for her neighbors, political consultant for aspiring candidates seeking the French vote, or simply as a member of a neighborhood club, the Franco woman remembered a history often overlooked because it did not involve permanent institution building. The pulse of life in the "Little Canadas" was monitored closely by Franco women. Paying attention to its daily beat enriched and expanded their lives.

Emma Tourangeau remembered Sundays best. "My father and my mother entertained people every single Sunday.

Every single Sunday we had people for dinner at our house."[54] Social gatherings provided the backbone of neighborhood life and family gatherings were its centerpiece. These gatherings were an occasion to have fun together, but they also cemented relationships that were essential to the family's well-being. *Family* was understood broadly, so family gatherings included friends, neighbors, and co-workers as well as blood relations.

Tourangeau remembered in careful detail the elements of these Sunday events, which always included a meal.

> I loved to think of Sundays. My mother with her white apron on, cold roast pork, a lovely dinner. And then we would wash the dishes. We were four girls, you know, and we got along so well. And, then, people used to come. My mother used to make molasses candies. She used to make white candy. Popcorn balls in the wintertime. My father would have men in to play cards, and the women used to get together and talk.

Tourangeau recalled that this social life included both family and friends. If you did not have much family, friends became even more important and visiting became a vital tradition.

> We didn't have much family. My mother only had a sister. Her brothers had gone. My father didn't have no relatives. Had an old uncle. My old uncle used to come. But I used to bring my friends, and I would—it was a kind of tradition among the French people. If you went calling on Sunday afternoon, they asked you to stay for supper. So I was very fussy where I used to go Sunday afternoons. I'd always go someplace that would be better than I was going to have at home. I'd pick out different houses, you know, to go to.[55]

Later in her life, Tourangeau took all these memories of Sunday gatherings, with their special foods and meals and created a cookbook. With an emphasis on old French-Canadian recipes, *Aunt Emma's Island Cookbook* featured all the food Tourangeau remembered best and associated with the web of relationships that sustained her and her family. Collecting and saving the recipes seemed to be Tourangeau's way of maintaining a connection with this central experience in her own history. Tourangeau's recipes were one of her most treasured inheritances. She considered them "some sort of heirloom, like the old 'spinning wheel,' and the mother's 'wedding ring.'"[56]

Tourangeau found a permanent way to mark the significance of food and social gatherings in her life, but for many other Franco-American women, visiting also provided the cornerstone of their recreation. Dottie Hawkes remembered that visiting and playing cards often went hand-in-hand.

> Back then I remember when we were young, my mother used to play cards a lot. They would go to the Old Westbrook Tavern and play cards; and the Sliscos lived down below us, and she used to like to play. We've always played cards and we still play cards. I remember mother used to have Aunt Clara—she wasn't our Aunt, but, you know, people you know so well—she used to—they'd come upstairs, and my mother would go downstairs, and they'd play cards. My mother and father and Clara and Carl with the Guitards or, you know.[57]

Josephine DeRoche LaBrecque remembered the sustaining importance of getting together.

> That's all there was in those days. You know? There was no radio, no TV, dirt roads, so they got together. And what got me is when they would get together, everyone would bring their kids, and they were small babies. They'd lay them on the bed, you know. They'd have a ball—they'd have a dance in the house. It was really fun. You couldn't see them do that today.[58]

Like Dottie Hawkes' memory of her parents, LaBrecque remembered how important friends were to her mother.

LaBrecque's mother belonged to a group of women who gathered weekly to visit. As LaBrecque put it, "They had something like a club." LaBrecque's mother did not drive, so LaBrecque would drive her to the gathering. Playing cards, talking, and just enjoying each other's company, this weekly social event brought women together and into each other's lives. LaBrecque related that spirits ran high for these women when they got together. "They went to this one house, and there was a circular—it was an apartment house. There was a circular stairway. I'll never forget it. They laughed. Coming down they—somebody dared my mother to ride the rail. She did!"[59]

LaBrecque continued the tradition of her mother's social group. She joined a group in the late 1930s that met weekly to socialize and to knit together. The club, which does not have a name, started before she was married and is still in existence. For most of that time LaBrecque, like her mother, attended every week. She said, "The only reason I don't belong to it now is because I don't drive at night."[60]

The importance of leisure underscored the weekly gatherings of Franco women. Life in Westbrook's Little Canada offered Franco women different possibilities for creating values and behaviors that would afford a sustaining way of life. Their leisure time offered them the opportunity to affirm the value of relationships and spending time together. Women's time differed from men's. Women's leisure was often intertwined with the rhythms of household labor and the relations of kinship.[61] For Franco women, Sunday dinners, visiting, and playing cards cleared a space and created a culture that enabled them to survive and even find some delight in the shadow of the mills.

The process of creating community found these second-generation women demarcating the edges of a new identity. They encountered ways in which they differed from their parents. There was movement away from the unquestioning attachment to first-generation interpretations of appropriate behavior for women. These second-generation Franco women, like ethnic women in other places, observed the changing times and absorbed new ideas. Josephine DeRoche LaBrecque came face-to-face with these changes when she realized that her religious beliefs differed not only from her mother's but also from the parish priest's.

> My Uncle Joe lived in Rumford, he was a woodsman. And we went up to see him; and, of course, he didn't go to church. And, of course, my mother you know. [She said] "If he didn't go to church, I'll feed you when he'd stop at the house. I'll give you something to eat, but you can eat on the porch and leave." She told her own brother that! And, course, we thought it was terrible at the time but religion was everything to her and my father. So anyway, when he was on his deathbed, she said, "Go up and see him." Well, we went up, and we had—he had a table by his bedside. He was in a private room—a room by himself, of course. Two candles and there was a crucifix there. And we went in, and we just told him we were Salina's daughters. Rita and I went up. We borrowed a car. He was—he vaguely recognized us. "Oh, yes, Salina, Salina." And he held up the Rosary that she had given him. Well, that pleased my mother [when we told her about the visit.] Well, then when he died his daughter come down, and she wanted to know if we could give him a Catholic burial. I went to see my mother, and she said, "You go see Father Finn." I went to see Father Finn. I went—I called Father Finn first, and I wanted to make an appointment to see him with Mary Proctor, Uncle Joe's daughter. She lived up in Standish. Father Finn says, "Well, you come along." Cause I told him, you know, that he hadn't been practicing, but he received the Last Rites, and Father Finn says, "I wouldn't even say a prayer over his grave."

The identity that Josephine LaBrecque was forging called for a more inclusive definition of religion and religious practices. The rigid and unyielding compliance that her parents understood as their duty and only available choice made LaBrecque "mad."[62]

The traditional approach to Franco-American history is no longer sufficient. It is not enough to simply describe immigrant and ethnic communities. As immigration and ethnic history has demonstrated after a half-century of scholarship, we may have a vast treasure trove of data, but we do not know very much about how people made sense of their experiences. The hidden issues of women's lives, internal family dynamics, informal social networks, how women understood their lives, all require careful attention.

There exists a subtlety in the texture of family life that we need to understand better for its historic meaning. We need to illuminate the web of family connections in the lives of Franco-American women. In this way we can begin to broaden our understanding of the lives of these second-generation ethnic women. Attending to these matters will enable historians to chart the passage of time in the lives of Franco women and to probe the forces of change.

WALKING TOWARD THE RED SKY

Being a student of Maine's working-class Franco-American women requires a special diligence. Despite historians' best efforts, the history of these ethnic women remains fragmented and limited. Instead, historians of the Franco experience have emphasized the centrality of *la survivance* to the immigrant generation's migration and acculturation experience. Historians recount the institution-building that became the centerpiece of a heroic effort to maintain French-Canadian cultural, religious, and ethnic integrity even as the process of becoming Franco-Americans was underway.

A variety of community studies and projects examining specific issues and events provide rich details of the challenges and opportunities the first generation faced.[63] Guided by a powerful elite of clerics and professionals, businessmen, newspaper editors, and doctors, the first generation set out to establish ethnic communities, *"les petits canadas"* where the principles of *la survivance* could hold sway. Devoted to preserving Franco cultural values, and emphasizing religion and language as integral to French Catholic identity, *la survivance* provided critical structure and support for a generation adjusting to a new way of life.

This initial emphasis on *survivance* enabled historians to write a much-needed history. However, in its concentration on formal institutions and organizations, historians missed working-class French-Canadian immigrants, and most especially, women. A continued emphasis on *survivance*, especially one that insists on a definition of *survivance* as language retention, ethnic organizations, and strict allegiance to the Catholic Church, only serves to obscure and neglect the history of both the working-class immigrant generation and the experience of the second generation.

For Franco-American women, *la survivance* did not provide a neat or tidy solution to life in a new country. Despite what the leaders of the immigrant generation may have thought, a hermetic Franco-American culture did not develop. Rather, permeable *cultures* rooted in generation, gender, and region, class and personal experience evolved. Franco-American women not only survived, but they flourished because they made choices. They and their children selected, borrowed, retained, and abandoned as they created distinctive cultural forms.[64] The history of Franco-American women underscores the need for a broader perspective on the shaping of Franco-American culture.[65] If we are to capture the experience of Franco women, we need to look beyond the traditional foci of formal organizations like church and school. We need to expand our search for *survivance* to include informal organizations, like neighborhood networks, which often provided extensive mutual assistance. The usual feminist edifice of "separate spheres" does not apply in the lives of immigrant women or those of the second generation. The "inextricable nature" of family life and wage work, which lies at the heart of the histories of immigrant women, explodes and exposes the false oppositions of the public/private dichotomy.[66] It is the texture of Franco women's lives that needs to be captured. How did they see themselves? How did they socialize their children? How did they participate in neighborhood life? How did they create their own sense of values within the home and in the neighborhood?[67]

La survivance could not contain the experience of the second generation. It especially could not do justice to the experience of Franco-American women. Often relegated to "landscape roles,"[68] Franco women remain a vague presence in Franco-American historiography. Nearly invisible in most descriptions of Franco-American communities, Franco women are rarely acknowledged as cultural or community leaders.

The second generation of Franco-American working-class women has much to tell us about the nexus of ethnicity and gender in Maine history. The elite paradigm of *la survivance* did not and could not provide a clear path for them. Reliance on religion and language would not safeguard their passage through work in the mills, raising a family and negotiating an increasingly complex world. These twin pillars did not enable working-class women to develop new definitions of womanhood and femaleness. Yet second generation Franco women did not jettison religion and language or awareness of their ethnic past. Instead, an examination of the history of these women reveals an intricate and complex melding of the values and priorities of the first generation with the changing world of the second.

Ultimately, these women wrestled with their inheritance of being second-generation Franco-American and women, and distilled an identity that was distinctly their own. Loyal to traditional ways and values, they also embraced the many contradictions of their second-generation status. Their reflections reveal a complex and nuanced understanding of ethnic life. Their lives reflect the limitations of what it meant to be female, even as they subverted traditional ideas to expand their own possibilities. Hundreds of French-Canadian women learned how to be Franco-American in Maine's mills and factories and in its homes and neighborhoods from the late nineteenth century to the middle of the twentieth. Maine history is incomplete without their experiences.

1. Susann Pelletier, *Lives in Translation* (Lisbon Falls, Maine: Soleil Press, 1991), 89–91.

2. Susann Pelletier, *Immigrant Dream and Other Poems*, Soleil Press Chapbook Series, Vol. 1 (Lisbon Falls, Maine: Soleil Press, 1989), 5.

3. Robert H. Babcock, Yves Frenette, Charles A. Scontras, and Eileen Eagan, "Work and Workers in the Industrial Age, 1865–1930," in *Maine: The Pine Tree State from Prehistory to the Present*, ed. Richard W. Judd, Edwin A. Churchill, and Joel W. Eastman (Orono: University of Maine Press, 1995), 450, 453.

4. Gerard J. Brault, *The French Canadian Heritage in New England* (Hanover, N.H.: University Press of New England; Kingston, Ont.: McGill-Queen's University Press, 1986), 56.

5. Babcock et al., "Work and Workers," 452.

6. *Immigrants from the North: Franco-Americans Recall the Settlement of Their Canadian Families In the Mill Towns of New England*, collected and written by The Franco-American Studies Class, Hyde School, Bath, Maine, 1982, 19.

7. Ibid., 22.

8. Ibid., 25.

9. Ibid., 26.

10. *Reports of the Immigration Commission: Immigrants in Industries* (in twenty-five parts), Part 3: Cotton Goods Manufacturing in the North Atlantic States. Senate Documents, 61st Congress, 2d Session, 1909–10, vol. 72 (Washington, D.C.: Government Printing Office, 1911), 13, 15.

11. *Report on Condition of Woman and Child Wage-Earners in the United States*, 19 vols., vol. 1: Cotton Textile Industry. Senate Documents, 61st Congress, 2d Session, 1909–10, vol. 86 (Washington, D.C.: Government Printing Office, 1910), 623.

12. *Reports of the Immigration Commission*, 112–14.

13. Anne Lucey, "Memere: The Life of a Franco-American Woman," in *"Je suis franco-americaine et fiere de l'être* [I am Franco-American and proud of it]: An Anthology of Writings of Franco-American Women," ed. Rhea Côté Robbins, Lanette Landry Petrie, Kristin Langellier, and Kathyrn Slott, manuscript, 1995, Special Collections, Fogler Library, University of Maine, Orono, Maine.

14. Brault, *French-Canadian Heritage*, 65.

15. A work that adheres largely to the *survivance* model is Michael Guignard, *La foi, la langue, la culture: The Franco-Americans of Biddeford* ([New York?]: M. J. Guignard, c. 1982).

16. Philip T. Silva, Jr., "Neighbors from the North: French-Canadian Immigrants vs. Trade Unionism in Fall River, Massachusetts," in *The Little Canadas of New England*, ed. Claire Quintal (Worcester, Mass.: Assumption College, 1982), 44–48.

17. John T. Cumbler, *Working-Class Community in Industrial America: Work, Leisure, And Struggle in Two Industrial Cities, 1880–1930* (Westport, Conn.: Greenwood Press, 1979), 120–30.

18. Ibid., 159.

19. Grace Pedneault Curtis, interview by author, tape recording, Westbrook, Maine, 18 August 1993.

20. Ibid.

21. Carole Turbin, *Working Women of Collar City: Gender, Class and Community in Troy, New York, 1864–86* (Urbana: University of Illinois Press, 1992), 85–87.

22. Josephine DeRoche LaBrecque, interview by author, tape recording, Westbrook, Maine, 30 October 1993.

23. Victoria DeRoche Guitard, in joint interview with DeRoche sisters: Victoria DeRoche Guitard, Annie DeRoche Downes, Josephine DeRoche LaBrecque, Alice DeRoche, Theresa DeRoche Hebert, and Mary DeRoche Daley, interview by author, tape recording, Westbrook, Maine, 16 August 1993.

24. Curtis, interview.

25. Emma M. Tourangeau, "The French Canadian," 2, unpublished manuscript, copy in author's possession, original owned by Albert Duclos, Portland, Maine.

26. Dorothy Harnois Hawkes, interview by author, tape recording, Westbrook, Maine, 19 August 1993.

27. Annie DeRoche Downes, in DeRoche sisters, interview.

28. DeRoche sisters, interview.

29. Ibid.

30. Josephine DeRoche LaBrecque, in DeRoche sisters, interview.

31. DeRoche sisters, interview.

32. Josephine DeRoche LaBrecque, interview by author, tape recording, Westbrook, Maine, 10 October 1993.

33. DeRoche sisters, interview.

34. Curtis, interview.

35. Ibid.

36. Ibid.

37. Emma Tourangeau, "These Lines of my Life," 9, unpublished memoir, copy in author's possession, original possessed by Albert Duclos, Portland, Maine.

38. LaBrecque, in DeRoche sisters, interview.

39. Tourangeau, "These Lines," 12.

40. Turbin, *Working Women of Collar City*, 85–87.

41. LaBrecque, in DeRoche sisters, interview.

42. Tourangeau, "These Lines," 7.

43. Emma Tourangeau, interview by Catherine Walker, tape recording, Portland, Maine, 7 November 1982.

44. Ibid.

45. Ibid.

46. Ibid.

47. Ibid.

48. Marian Dana, interview by Vaun Born, tape recording, Westbrook, Maine, 15 June 1976.

49. Curtis, interview.

50. Ardis Cameron, *Radicals of the Worst Sort: Laboring Women in Lawrence, Massachusetts, 1860–1912* (Chicago: University of Illinois Press, 1993), 111.

51. Quintal, *The Little Canadas of New England*.

52. Cameron, *Radicals of the Worst Sort*, 110.

53. Curtis, interview.

54. Tourangeau, interview.

55. Ibid.

56. Emma Marie Tourangeau, *Aunt Emma's Island Cookbook: Featuring*

Old French Canadian Recipes (Iowa Falls, Iowa: General Publishing and Binding, 1967), 85.

57. Hawkes, interview.

58. LaBrecque, interview, 30 October 1993.

59. Ibid.

60. Ibid.

61. Kathy Peiss, *Cheap Amusements: Working Women and Leisure in Turn-of-the-Century New York* (Philadelphia: Temple University Press, 1986), 4, 5.

62. LaBrecque, interview, 30 October 1993.

63. Important examples of community studies include Quintal, *The Little Canadas of New England;* Cumbler, *Working-Class Community in Industrial America;* and Guignard, *La foi, la langue, la culture.* For a general Franco history, see Brault, *The French-Canadian Heritage in New England.* Addressing the issue of union-building in a Franco community is Gary Gerstle; *Working-Class Americanism: The Politics of Labor in a Textile City, 1914–1960* (Cambridge, England: Cambridge University Press, 1989).

64. Vicki L. Ruiz, *From Out of the Shadows: Mexican Women in Twentieth-Century America* (New York: Oxford University Press, 1998), xvi.

65. Yves Frenette, "Understanding the French-Canadians of Lewiston, 1860–1900: An Alternate Framework," *Maine Historical Society Quarterly* 25, 4 (1986): 198–229, 199.

66. Ruiz, *Out of the Shadows,* xvi.

67. Sydney Stahl Weinberg, "The Treatment of Women in Immigration History: A Call For Change," *Journal of American Ethnic History* 11, 4 (Summer 1992): 25–69, 34.

68. Vicki L. Ruiz, *Cannery Women, Cannery Lives: Mexican Women, Unionization, and the California Food Processing Industry, 1930–1950* (Albuquerque: University of New Mexico Press, 1987), xiv.

There is every reason to believe that identities based on gender and place will continue to resonate in powerful ways for Maine women in the new century. As Mainers continue to grapple with the polarization brought by unequal economic opportunity within the state, and as men and women continue to explore the implications of gender in their daily lives, what it means to be a Maine woman will continue to change. Today, Maine women enjoy unprecedented economic opportunities in ever-expanding fields; they are no longer limited to traditionally female jobs, but are making inroads in technology, construction, and other areas once deemed the province of men. Maine women have been elected to high office in numbers large enough to preclude the label of tokenism. More than ever before, Maine women are able to determine their own paths in life, paths that may or may not include husbands, children, or traditional domestic arrangements.

At the same time, Maine women's lives retain aspects that would have been familiar to many of the subjects of the essays in this book. Women still experience multiple identities based on class, ethnicity, race, and religion as well as on gender, identities that continue to divide as well as unite them. Maine is still divided between areas of relative prosperity and economic stagnation, with corresponding opportunities for women's employment. Some women still struggle alongside family members to wrest a living from land and sea, working at multiple tasks in the process. Many still feel the need to leave the state in order to improve their prospects. Others continue to work together to reform aspects of society they consider problematic, usually doing so along with men.

Gender remains a potent force shaping women's experiences. While access to birth control and abortion and less restrictive social mores have freed women to express their sexuality, women far more than men still face the threats of rape, domestic violence, discrimination, and sexual harassment; they also experience hate crimes. In Maine like the rest of the nation, women still earn less money than men and, along with their children, live disproportionately in poverty. Access to child care and health care remains limited for many women, largely because of cost. In spite of the significant accomplishments of individuals, women are still under-represented in politics, in the professions, in management positions. As Maine's population ages, women in ever larger numbers will struggle with the difficulties of living on fixed incomes and without adequate social services.

Even so, the assumptions about identity that limited women for much of the time period covered in this volume are no longer as powerful as they once were. Maine women need no longer choose between leaving the state and making the best of a bad bargain. Women today are perhaps more diverse in their experiences than in the past, choosing from a greater array of options and defining themselves with more freedom. That they are able to do so is a testament to the efforts of their predecessors described in this book.

Polly Welts Kaufman

Even as the reader begins to consider the new scholarship presented in *Of Place and Gender*, it is useful to examine the research that has come before. The following bibliography presents a variety of sources that describe different aspects of the story of Maine women. Although the works listed are primarily historical studies and personal accounts, a selected list of classics by such notable Maine women writers as Sarah Orne Jewett and Ruth Moore is also included. Because only their best known works are listed, the reader is encouraged to look for their other books as well.

The essays in *Of Place and Gender,* combined with the titles listed below, lead to new themes and illuminate old understandings. What are the prevailing images of Maine women that exist in the public mind? How do these works change or support a traditional view? What future research do these new studies suggest?

The picture of a Maine woman, in fact, conjures up different and even contradictory views. On the one hand, Maine women are known for their participation in public life. Maine is the only state in the union that has selected three women to the U.S. Senate without their having first served on an interim basis, and since 1953, Maine women have ranked consistently in the top ten in the nation in numbers of women serving in state legislatures.[1] A recent index of political participation ranked Maine women fourth nationally and first in the New England region. On the other hand, the same study found Maine women falling only in the middle nationally in an index of economic health and last in the New England region.[2]

In order to bring meaning to these competing definitions of Maine women, writers have looked to the past as well as the present. The economic status of Maine is linked both to the health of the state's economy and to the characteristics of that economy. With a few exceptions, Maine's largest employers have been connected to industries largely employing men: lumbering and paper mills, fishing, shipbuilding, and agriculture. The exceptions were the textile mills, where nineteenth and early twentieth century women operatives outnumbered men, and shoemaking where women made up one quarter of the employees.[3] Yet the political participation of Maine women not only reveals a continuing history of community service, but also a long tradition of women working as partners in the family economy.

Both the new essays in *Of Place and Gender* and existing research reveal the extent of shared responsibilities. Laurel Ulrich's *Midwife's Tale* set the stage by revealing partnership on the Maine frontier. The new essays demonstrate that partnership continued: among the wives of sea captains, women knitters on Acadian farms, Irish women immigrants in urban centers, rural women conservationists, and through Franco-American women's neighborhood networks.

Yet another traditional image of Maine women is their reputation as independent thinkers. Studies of Kate Furbish, a botanist;[4] Sarah Jane Foster, a teacher of the freedmen after the Civil War;[5] and Senator Margaret Chase Smith[6] provide evidence. The new essays in *Of Place and Gender* reveal lesser known independent Maine women: a Utopian thinker in antebellum Bangor, Penobscot Indian performer Lucy Nicolar, divas Lillian Nordica and Emma Eames, early sportswomen in the Maine woods, and single working women of the Portland Business and Professional Women's Club.

This volume has expanded the reader's view of the role of women in the history of Maine, but much more research is needed. One potentially promising area is local politics. What difference has it made that there is so high a proportion of women in the Maine state legislature? What kinds of legislation have women proposed and supported? What is the extent of the gender gap? Have women's policies changed over time? Research on the state's African American women is in its early stages.[7] Franco-American women are beginning to tell their stories.[8] Although writers have portrayed the lives of poor rural women in modern fiction,[9] only one account presents their stories in a woman's own words.[10] Still, this new volume of essays, added to works previously published, does provide a good overview of the diversity of Maine women's lives and their contributions to the state.

1. Elizabeth M. Cox, "Maine (1923–1995)," in *Women State and Territorial Legislators, 1895–1995* (Jefferson, N.C.: McFarland & Co., 1996), 135–44.

2. Institute for Women's Policy Research, *The Status of Women in Maine* (Washington, D.C. and Portland, Maine: Women's Development Institute and YWCA of Greater Portland, 1996).

3. [Flora E. Haines], "Working-Women," in *Second Annual Report of the Bureau of Industrial and Labor Statistics for the State of Maine, 1888* (Augusta, Maine: n.p., 1889), 64–148.

4. Ada and Frank Graham, Jr., *Kate Furbish and the Flora of Maine* (Gardiner, Maine: Tilbury House, 1995).

5. Wayne Reilly, ed., *Sarah Jane Foster, Teacher of the Freedmen* (Charlottesville, Va.: University Press of Virginia, 1990).

6. Patricia L. Schmidt, *Margaret Chase Smith: Beyond Convention* (Orono: University of Maine Press, 1996); Janann Sherman, *No Place for a Woman: A Life of Senator Margaret Chase Smith* (New Brunswick, N.J.: Rutgers University Press, 2000).

7. Stan Clough, "Zion Upon a Hill: Portland's A. M. E. Zion Church and Social Uplift in the Progressive Era" (master's thesis, University of Southern Maine, 1994); *Anchor of the Soul*, narrated by Barbara Jordan (Shoshana Hoose and Karine Odlin, 1994), film.

8. Kristin Langellier, Rhea Côté Robbins, Lanette Landry Petrie, and

Kathryn Slott, "An Anthology of Franco-American Women's Voices from *Le Forum*," unpublished manuscript, Franco-American Center, University of Maine, Orono, Maine, 1995; Rhea Côté Robbins, *Wednesday's Child* (Brunswick, Maine: Maine Writers and Publishers Alliance, 1997).

9. Carolyn Chute, *The Beans of Egypt, Maine* (New York: Ticknor and Fields, 1985); Cathie Pelletier, *Weight of Winter* (New York: Viking, 1991).

10. Cedric N. Chatterley and Alicia J. Rouverol with Stephen A. Cole, *"I Was Content and Not Content": The Story of Linda Lord and the Closing of the Penobscot Poultry* (Carbondale: Southern Illinois University Press, 2000).

HISTORY AND PERSONAL ACCOUNTS

Abbott, Berenice. *A Portrait of Maine.* New York: Macmillan, 1968.

Agger, Lee. *Women of Maine.* Portland, Maine: Guy Gannett Publishing Co., 1982.

Albee, Parker Bishop, Jr. *Letters from Sea, 1882–1901: Joanna and Lincoln Colcord's Seafaring Childhood.* Gardiner, Maine: Tilbury House, 2000.

Arlen, Alice. *She Took to the Woods* [Louise Dickinson Rich]. Camden, Maine: Down East Books, 2000.

Balano, James W. *Log of the Skipper's Wife* [Dorothea Moulton Balano]. Camden, Maine: Down East Books, 1979.

Barry, William David. *Women Pioneers in Maine Art, 1900–1945, April 9–May 19, 1985: The Joan Whitney Payson Gallery of Art.* Portland, Maine: Westbrook College, 1985.

Battick, John F. "The Searsport 'Thirty-six': Seafaring Wives of a Maine Community in 1880," *American Neptune* 44 (Summer 1984): 149–54.

Beam, Lura. *A Maine Hamlet.* New York: Wilfred Funk, 1957.

Beedy, Helen Coffin. *Mothers of Maine.* Portland, Maine: The Thurston Print, 1895.

Blanchard, Paula. *Sarah Orne Jewett: Her World and Her Work.* New York: Addison-Wesley, 1994.

Bonta, Marcia Myers. *Women in the Field: America's Pioneering Women Naturalists* [Kate Furbish, Cordelia Stanwood, Rachel Carson]. College Station: Texas A & M University Press, 1991.

Bourne, Miriam Anne. *The Ladies of Castine: From the Minutes of the Castine, Maine, Woman's Club.* New York: Arbor House, 1986.

Bridges, Doris A. *Growing Up Way Downeast.* Ed. Gail Menzel. Mt. Desert, Maine: Windswept House, 1997.

Brown, Elspeth. "Gender and Identity in Rural Maine: Women and the Maine Farmer, 1870–1875." *Maine History* 33 (Fall 1993): 120–35.

Burns, Connie. "Margaret Jane Mussey Sweat and the Expanding Female Sphere," *Maine History* 33 (Fall 1993): 106–19.

Butler, Joyce. "The 'Single-Parent' Households of Portland's Wadsworth-Longfellow House." In *House and Home* (Dublin [N.H.] Seminar Annual Proceedings, 1988). Ed. Peter Benes. Boston: Boston University, 1990.

Carr, Sister Frances A. *Growing Up Shaker.* Sabbathday Lake, Maine: United Society of Shakers, 1995.

Carrigan, D. Owen. "A Forgotten Yankee Marxist" [Martha Moore Avery,] *New England Quarterly* 42 (March–December 1969): 23–43.

Carson, Rachel. *The Edge of the Sea.* Boston: Houghton Mifflin, 1955.

Chase, Mary Ellen. *A Goodly Heritage.* New York: Henry Holt, 1932.

Chatterley, Cedric N. and Alicia J. Rouverol with Stephen A. Cole. *"I Was Content and Not Content": The Story of Linda Lord and the Closing of the Penobscot Poultry.* Carbondale: Southern Illinois University Press, 2000.

Clifford, Mary Louise and J. Candace. *Women Who Kept the Lights: An Illustrated History of Female Lighthouse Keepers.* Williamsburg, Va.: Cypress Co., 1993.

Clough, Stan. "Zion Upon a Hill: Portland's A. M. E. Zion Church and Social Uplift in the Progressive Era." Master's thesis, University of Southern Maine, 1994.

Coatsworth, Elizabeth. *Maine Memories.* Woodstock, Vt.: Countryman Press. 1968.

Coburn, Louise H. *Kate Furbish, Botanist: An Appreciation.* N.p., [1924]. Available in the Maine State Library, Augusta, Maine.

Colcord, Joanna. "Domestic Life on American Sailing Ships," *American Neptune* 2 (July 1942): 191–202.

Cox, Elizabeth M. "Maine (1923–1995)" in *Women State and Territorial Legislators, 1895–1995*, 135–44. Jefferson, N.C.: McFarland & Co., 1996.

Doty, C. Stewart. *Acadian Hard Times: The Farm Security Administration in Maine's St. John Valley, 1940–43.* Orono: University of Maine Press, 1991.

Foley, Edward. "The Third Maine's Angel of Mercy: Sarah Smith Sampson," *Maine History* 36 (Summer–Fall 1996): 38–53.

Fournier, Constance Anne. "Navigating Women: Roles of Nineteenth Century Maine Women at Sea," *Maine History* 35 (Summer–Fall, 1995): 46–61.

FreeHand, Julianna. *A Seafaring Legacy: The Photographs, Diaries, Letters and Memorabilia of a Maine Sea Captain and His Wife, 1859–1908.* New York: Random House, 1981.

Graham, Ada and Frank Jr. *Kate Furbish and the Flora of Maine.* Gardiner, Maine: Tilbury House, 1995.

Greenlaw, Linda. *The Hungry Ocean: A Swordboat Captain's Journey.* New York: Hyperion, 1999.

[Haines, Flora E.] "Working-Women." In *Second Annual Report of the Bureau of Industrial and Labor Statistics for the State of Maine, 1888*, 64–148. Augusta, Maine: State of Maine, 1889.

Hamlin, Helen. *Nine Mile Bridge: Three Years in the Maine Woods.* New York: Norton, 1945; Camden, Maine: Down East Books, 1973.

Hendrichsen, Margaret K. *Seven Steeples.* Boston: Houghton Mifflin, 1953.

Higgins, Mary Raymond, R.S.M. *For Love of Mercy.* Portland, Maine: Sisters of Mercy, 1995.

Institute for Women's Policy Research. *The Status of Women in Maine.* Washington D.C. and Portland, Maine: Women's Development Institute and YWCA of Greater Portland, 1996.

James, Edward T. and Janet Wilson James, eds. *Notable American Women.* Cambridge, Mass.: Harvard University Press, 1971. [Articles on: Martha Moore Avery, Annie Louise Cary, Kate Furbish, Sarah Orne Jewett, Edna St. Vincent Millay, Lillian Nordica, Sarah Payson Willis Parton, Elizabeth Oakes Prince Smith, Lillian Ames Stevens, Ellen Gould Harmon White, Kate Douglas Wiggin, Sally Sayward Barrell Keating, and Abba Woolson.]

Jones, Dorothy Holder and Ruth Sexton Sargent. *Abbie Burgess, Lighthouse Heroine.* Camden, Maine: Down East Books, 1976.

Judd, Richard, Edwin Churchill and Joel Eastman, eds. *Maine: The Pine Tree State from Pre-History to the Present.* Orono: University of Maine Press, 1995.

Karmen, Abbe L. "Putting the House in Order: Women's Cooperative Extension Work in the Early Twentieth Century," *Maine Historical Society Quarterly* 32 (Summer 1992): 30–50.

Kaufman, Polly Welts, ed. *Apron Full of Gold: The Letters of Mary Jane Megquier from San Francisco, 1849–1856.* Albuquerque: University of New Mexico Press, 1994.

_____. *Women Teachers on the Frontier.* New Haven, Conn.: Yale University Press, 1984.

Langellier, Kristin, Rhea Côté Robbins, Lanette Landry Petrie, and Kathryn Slott. "An Anthology of Franco-American Women's Voices from *Le Forum.*" Unpublished manuscript, Franco-American Center, University of Maine, Orono, Maine, 1995.

Lear, Linda J. *Rachel Carson: Witness for Nature.* New York: Henry Holt, 1997.

Leonard, Elizabeth. "Civil War Nurse, Civil War Nursing: Rebecca Usher of Maine," *Civil War History* (September 1995): 190–207.

Litoff, Judy Barrett and Hal Litoff. "Working Women in Maine: A Note on Sources," *Labor History* 17 (1976): 88–95. Also published as a pamphlet: *Recognition: A Source Book on Working Women*. Orono, Maine: Bureau of Labor Education, University of Maine, 1974.

MacCaskill, Libby and David Novak. *Ladies in the Field: Two Civil War Nurses from Maine to the Battlefields of Virginia* [Isabella Morrison Fogg of Calais and Sarah Smith Sampson of Bath]. Livermore, Maine: Signal Tree Publishing, 1996.

Mackenzie, Scotty. *My Love Affair With The State of Maine*. New York: Simon and Schuster, 1955; Camden, Maine: Down East Books, 1997.

Macmillan, Miriam. *Green Seas and White Ice*. New York: Dodd, Mead, 1948.

McBride, Bunny. *Molly Spotted Elk: A Penobscot in Paris*. Norman: University of Oklahoma Press, 1996.

_____. *Our Lives in Our Hands: Micmac Indian Basketmakers*. Gardiner, Maine: Tilbury House, 1990.

_____. *Women of the Dawn*. Lincoln: University of Nebraska Press, 1999.

Mikulski, Barbara, ed. *Nine and Counting: The Women of the Senate*. New York: William Morrow, 2000. [Includes biographical statements by Maine U.S. Senators Olympia J. Snowe and Susan Collins.]

Milford, Nancy. *Savage Beauty: The Life of Edna St. Vincent Millay*. New York: Random House, 2001.

Morrison, Jane. *Master Smart Woman: A Portrait of Sarah Orne Jewett*. Unity, Maine: North Country Press, 1988.

Nearing, Helen. *Loving and Leaving the Good Life*. New York: Chelsea Green, 1992.

_____. *Continuing the Good Life*. New York: Schocken Books, 1979.

Norwood, Vera. *Made from This Earth: American Women and Nature* [Rachel Carson, Celia Thaxter, Cordelia Stanwood]. Chapel Hill: University of North Carolina Press, 1993.

Ogilvie, Elisabeth. *My World is an Island*. New York: Whittlesey House, 1950; Camden, Maine: Down East Books, 1990.

Peary, Josephine. *My Arctic Journal; A Year Among Ice-Fields and Eskimos*. New York and Philadelphia: The Contemporary Publishing Co., 1893; New York: AMS Press, 1975.

_____. *The Snow Baby: A True Story with True Pictures*. New York: Fred Stokes, 1901.

Peary, Marie Ahnighito. *Snowbaby's Own Story*. New York: Fred Stokes, 1934.

Peladeau, Marius B. *Chansonetta: The Life and Photographs of Chansonetta Stanley Emmons, 1858–1937*. Waldoboro, Maine: Maine Antique Digest, 1977.

Petroski, Catherine. *A Bride's Passage: Susan Hathorn's Year Under Sail*. Boston: Northeastern University Press, 1997.

Phippen, Sanford, ed. *High Clouds Soaring, Storms Driving Low: The Letters of Ruth Moore*. Nobleboro, Maine: Blackberry Press, 1993.

Porter, Marion. "Employment of Women in Maine Stores." In *Third Biennial Report of the Department of Labor and Industry, State of Maine, 1915–1916*, 50–60. Augusta, Maine: State of Maine, 1917.

Reilly, Wayne, ed. *Sarah Jane Foster, Teacher of the Freedmen*. Charlottesville: University Press of Virginia, 1990.

Rich, Louise Dickinson. *We Took to the Woods*. New York: Lippincott, 1942.

Richmond, Chandler S. *Beyond the Spring: Cordelia Stanwood of Birdsacre*. Lamoine, Maine: Latona Press, 1978.

Robbins, Rhea Côté. *Wednesday's Child*. Brunswick: Maine Writers and Publishers Alliance, 1997.

Risen, Celia C. *Some Jewels of Maine: Jewish Maine Pioneers*. Pittsburgh, PA: Dorrance Publishing Co., 1997.

Sargent, Ruth. "Gail Laughlin and Maine Politics." In *Maine, A History through Selected Readings*, 552–60. Ed. David C. Smith and Edward O. Shriver. Dubuque, Iowa: Kendal/ Hunt, 1985.

Sarton, May. *A House by the Sea: A Journal.* Boston: G. K. Hall, 1977.

Schriver, Edward, "'Deferred Victory': Woman Suffrage in Maine, 1873–1920"; and "From Rule 25 to the ERA: Women in the Maine Legislature." In *Maine, A History through Selected Readings*, 409–20, 561–70. Ed. David C. Smith and Edward O. Shriver. Dubuque, Iowa: Kendal/ Hunt, 1985.

Schmidt, Patricia L. *Margaret Chase Smith: Beyond Convention.* Orono: University of Maine Press, 1996.

Seguino, Stephanie. *Living on the Edge: Women Working and Providing for Families in the Maine Economy, 1979–1993.* Orono, Maine: Margaret Chase Smith Center for Public Policy, University of Maine, 1995.

_____. *Struggling to Make Ends Meet in the Maine Economy.* Augusta, Maine: Women's Development Institute and Maine Center for Economic Policy, 1998.

Sewall, Abbie. *Message through Time: The Photographs of Emma D. Sewall, 1836–1919.* Gardiner, Maine: Harpswell Press, 1989.

Shain, Charles and Samuella. *The Maine Reader: The Downeast Experience from 1614 to the Present.* Boston: Godine Publishing, 1991.

Sherman, Janann. *No Place for a Woman: A Life of Senator Margaret Chase Smith.* New Brunswick, N.J.: Rutgers University Press, 2000.

Sherman, Sarah Way. *Sarah Orne Jewett, an American Persephone.* Hanover, N.H.: University Press of New England, 1989.

[Shorey, Eva L. and Elsie Clark Nutt], "Women Wage Workers: Portland" and "School Teachers." In *Twenty-first Annual Report of the Bureau of Industrial and Labor Statistics for the State of Maine, 1907*, 138–289. Augusta: State of Maine, 1907.

Sicherman, Barbara and Carol Hurd Green, editors, *Notable American Women, The Modern Period*. Cambridge, Mass.: Harvard University Press, 1980. [Articles on Rachel Louise Carson and Gail Laughlin.]

Small, Connie. *The Lighthouse Keeper's Wife*. Orono: University of Maine Press, 1986. Revised edition 1999.

Smith, Samantha. *Journey to the Soviet Union*. Boston: Little Brown, 1985.

Souliere, Yvonne A. "Education and Gender: The Misses Martin's School for Young Ladies." *Maine History*. Forthcoming.

Sprague, Laura Fecych, ed. *Agreeable Situations: Society, Commerce, and Art in Southern Maine, 1780–1830*. Kennebunk, Maine: Brick Store Museum, 1987.

_____. "My Best Wearing Apparel: Maine Women and Fashion, 1800–1840," *Maine Historical Society Quarterly* 30 (Spring 1991). Includes Nan Cumming, "Collecting Early Nineteenth-Century Costumes at the Maine Historical Society," 6–11; and Kerry A. O'Brien, "'So Monstrous Smart': Maine Women and Fashion, 1790–1840," 13–43.

Stanton, Elizabeth Cady, Susan B. Anthony, and Matilda Gage. "Maine." In *History of Woman Suffrage*. New York: Arno, 1969, V. 3 [1876–1885]: 352–66; V. 4 [1883–1900]: 689–94; V. 6 [1900–1920]: 236–47.

Strom, Deborah. *Birdwatching with American Women* [Sarah Orne Jewett, Cordelia Stanwood, and Celia Thaxter]. New York: W. W. Norton Co., 1986.

Sudlow, Lynda L. *Vast Army of Women: Maine's Uncounted Forces in the American Civil War*. Gettysburg, Penn.: Thomas Publications, 2000.

Trickey, Katherine. "A WAC from Maine in the South: The World War II Correspondence of Katherine Trickey." Ed. Judy Barrett Litoff and David C. Smith. *Maine History* 34 (Winter–Spring 1995): 194–209.

Ulrich, Laurel Thatcher. *A Midwife's Tale: The Life of Martha Ballard, Based on Her Diary, 1785–1812.* New York: Random House, 1990.

Vallier, Jane E. *Poet on Demand: The Life, Letters, and Works of Celia Thaxter.* Portsmouth, N.H.: Peter Randall, 1994.

Wallace, Patricia Ward. *Politics of Conscience: A Biography of Margaret Chase Smith.* Westport: Praeger Press, 1995.

Whitten, Jeanne Patten. *Fannie Hardy Eckstorm, A Descriptive Bibliography.* Orono: Northeast Folklore Society, 1976.

_____ with Elizabeth Ring. "Fanny Hardy Eckstorm, Maine Woods Historian." *New England Quarterly* 26 (March 1953): 45–64.

SELECTED LITERATURE AND MODERN FICTION

Carroll, Gladys Hasty. *As the Earth Turns.* New York: Macmillan, 1933; Nobleboro, Maine: Blackberry Books, 1995.

Chute, Carolyn. *The Beans of Egypt, Maine.* New York: Ticknor and Fields, 1985.

Jewett, Sarah Orne. *A Country Doctor.* 1884. New York: Penguin, 1986.

_____. *The Country of the Pointed Firs and Other Stories.* 1896. New York: Doubleday Anchor, 1956.

Millay, Edna St. Vincent. *Renascence and Other Poems.* 1917. New York: Dover, 1991.

Moore, Ruth. *Spoonhandle.* New York: Morrow, 1946; Nobleboro, Maine: Blackberry Books, 1986.

Ogilvie, Elisabeth. *High Tide at Noon.* New York: Crowell, 1944; Camden, Maine: Down East Books, 1971.

Pelletier, Cathie. *Weight of Winter.* New York: Viking, 1991.

Stowe, Harriet Beecher. *The Pearl of Orr's Island: A Story of the Coast of Maine.* 1862. Hartford, Conn.: Stowe-Day Foundation, 1990.

Thaxter, Celia. *An Island Garden.* 1894. Bowie, Md.: Heritage Books, 1978.

FILMS

Anchor of the Soul. Narrated by Barbara Jordan. Produced by Shoshana Hoose and Karine Odlin. 1994.

And You from Yours. Produced by Lynn Robinson. 1993.

Master Smart Woman [Sarah Orne Jewett]. Produced by Jane Morrison. 1984.

A Midwife's Tale. Produced by Laurie Kahn Leavitt. 1997.

On the Job: Women Launching a New Tradition. Narrated by Elizabeth Mitchell. Produced by the Center for Diversity and the Spring Point Media Center at the Southern Maine Technical College. 1997.

Rachel Carson's Silent Spring. Produced by Neil Goodman for *The American Experience,* Corporation for Public Broadcasting. 1993.

Renascence: Edna St. Vincent Millay, Poet. Produced by Vanessa Barth and Doreen Conboy. 1994.

The Sins of Our Mothers: The Story of Emmeline. Produced by David Hoffman for *The American Experience,* Public Broadcasting Service. 1988.

SPECIAL COLLECTIONS

Maine Women Writers' Collection, Abplanalp Library, Westbrook College, University of New England, Portland, Maine.

Northeast Archives of Folklore and Oral History, Maine Folklife Center, University of Maine, Orono, Maine.

NAN CUMMING was Assistant Director and curator of exhibitions at the Maine Historical Society in Portland, Maine, until 1999. Nan believes that today's city dwellers need nature and open space in their lives even more than the Victorians she writes about, so she became Executive Director of Portland Trails in December 1999. Portland Trails is an urban land trust whose mission is to create a network of multi-use trails in Greater Portland. "Following Diana: The New Woman in the Maine Woods" is derived from her 1995 master's thesis, "Fin-de-Siècle Diana: The New Woman Discovers the Maine Woods" (American and New England Studies, University of Southern Maine).

CELESTE DEROCHE is a third generation Franco-American and native Mainer. She grew up in Portland, Maine. Her article is derived from her master's thesis on Franco-American women in Westbrook, Maine. Her doctoral dissertation, "How Wide the Circle of We: Cultural Pluralism and American Identity, 1910–1954" (History, University of Maine, 2000), examined the efforts of immigrant ethnic women and native-born women to implement cultural pluralism. Celeste now lives in Florida, where she writes entries for the Dictionary of Unitarian and Universalist Biography; her current research examines Sophia Lyon Fahs and the nexus of cultural pluralism and the liberal religious impulse.

EILEEN EAGAN is Associate Professor of History at the University of Southern Maine. She is one of the developers of the Portland Women's History Trail as well as the Portland Labor History Trail and exhibit "Building: A Celebration of Maine's Working-Class History." Her Ph.D. is from Temple University.

PATRICIA FINN is one of the co-founders of the Portland Women's History Trail and the Portland Labor History Trail. She is a member of the Southern Maine Labor History Project committee that developed the Labor History Trail 2000 and the exhibit "Building: A Celebration of Maine's Working Class History." She is currently enrolled in the Master of Science in Adult Education graduate program at the University of Southern Maine. She is a staff person at the University of Southern Maine in the History Department.

CONSTANCE FOURNIER received her M.A. and Ph.D. in American Studies from the University of Hawaii at Manoa in 1993. A "sea wife" herself, she taught American Studies and English as a Second Language at the University of Hawaii and at other schools and colleges during her fifteen-year residence in Honolulu. Having returned home to Maine, Connie is revising her dissertation on the experiences of nineteenth-century New England maritime women for publication. She is currently involved in a Maine island project for the Maine State Museum, writes historical articles, teaches English composition, and works as a fund-raiser for Maine Public Broadcasting.

ALLISON L. HEPLER is Associate Professor of History at the University of Maine at Farmington and has lived in Woolwich, Maine since 1983. She has published articles on women and occupational health history, and is the author of *Women in Labor: Mothers, Medicine, and Occupational Health, 1890–1980* (Ohio State University Press, 2000). She is currently researching the history of rural hospitals.

MAZIE HOUGH is the Associate Director of the Women in the Curriculum and Women's Studies Program at the University of Maine. She received her Ph.D. in American

History from the University of Maine in 1997. The title of her dissertation was "'I'm a Poor Girl in Family and I Want to Know if You be Kind': The Community's Response to Unwed Mothers in Maine and Tennessee, 1876–1954."

NORMA JOHNSEN is originally from New Hampshire but has lived in Maine since 1969. She is an Associate Professor Emeritus of English at the University of Maine at Farmington where she taught English Composition and Women's Studies. She has published articles on women artists in literature and is presently teaching and studying art.

CANDACE A. KANES has a master's degree from SUNY Buffalo in Women's Studies and a doctorate from the University of New Hampshire in Modern American History. She teaches at the Maine College of Art and has taught at Bates College, the Westbrook College Campus of the University of New England, and the University of Southern Maine. She is a former journalist.

POLLY WELTS KAUFMAN teaches history at the University of Southern Maine. Among her books are two that include Maine women: *Apron Full of Gold: The Letters of Mary Jane Megquier from San Francisco, 1849-1856* (University of New Mexico Press, 1994) and *Women Teachers on the Frontier* (Yale University Press, 1984). She is the Project Director for Women's History Trails in Portland and Brunswick. Her most recent book is *National Parks and the Woman's Voice: A History* (University of New Mexico Press, 1996). She spent the academic year 1999–2000 as a Fulbright Roving Scholar in Norway.

PAULEENA MACDOUGALL, Associate Director of the Maine Folklife Center, received her Ph.D in American history from the University of Maine in 1995. She is also Faculty Associate in Anthropology at the University of Maine, where she teaches courses in linguistics and Native American folklore. Since 1979, MacDougall has published numerous papers on the Penobscot Indian language, culture and history, and a book, *The Penobscot Dance of Resistance: Tradition in the History of a People* (Durham: University Press of New England, 2004). She is editor of the Maine Folklife Center's annual monograph series, *Northeast Folklore* and currently is writing a biography of Maine folklorist and historian, Fannie Hardy Eckstorm.

BUNNY MCBRIDE is a writer with a master's degree in Anthropology. Much of her work focuses on cultural survival and wildlife conservation themes. She is the author of *Women of the Dawn* (Friends of American Writers Literary Award recipient, University of Nebraska Press, 1999), *Molly Spotted Elk: A Penobscot in Paris* (Pulitzer nominee, University of Oklahoma Press, 1995), *Our Lives in Our Hands: Micmac Indian Basketmakers* (Tilbury House and Nimbus, 1990), and co-author of *The Audubon Society Field Guide to African Wildlife* (Knopf, 1995). Bunny is an adjunct lecturer of anthropology at Kansas State University and has taught at the Salt Institute for Documentary Field Studies in Portland. In 1999 the Maine state legislature gave her a special commendation for her research and writing on the history of Native women in the state, an honor initiated by tribal representatives in the legislature.

DALE MUDGE started her academic career living on a sheep farm with her four children in Lincolnville. She commuted for fourteen years to the University of Maine and received her B.A. in Anthropology with high distinction. After working on textile exhibits at the Peabody Museum in Salem, Massachusetts and the Carnegie Museum in Pittsburgh, she pursued her interest in historic preservation. Her involvement with textiles and the desire to document traditions in Maine influenced her decision to research textiles among Acadian women. She conducted oral histories for four years in Aroostook County and produced and edited a segment for the documentary program *True North* on Maine Public Broadcasting. She developed three photographic exhibits of the Navajo people and collaborated with C. Stewart Doty on *Photographing Navajos: John Collier, Jr. on the Reservation, 1952–1953* (Albuquerque: University of New Mexico, 2002).

JOAN N. RADNER teaches Literature, American Studies, Women's Studies, Folklore, and Celtic Studies at American University in Washington, D.C., and publishes in these areas. She is President of the American Folklore Society and a member of the Board of Trustees of the American Folklife Center in the Library of Congress. Her publications include *Fragmentary Annals of Ireland* (Dublin Institute of Advanced Studies, 1978), *Irish Drama, 1900–1980* (Catholic University of America Press, 1990), and *Feminist Messages: Coding in Women's Folk Culture* (University of Illinois Press, 1993). Her current book project concerns manuscript literary newspapers in postbellum rural northern New England.

TINA ROBERTS received her B.A. in Environmental Studies and Political Science from the University of California, Santa Barbara and, after traveling the world for several years and settling in Maine, her M.A. in History from the University of Maine. She speaks often to classes and community groups about her research on Maine's conservation and recreation history; women climbers, hikers and out-doorswomen; and the evolution of outdoor clothing. She is currently a domestic abuse advocate at Spruce Run Associates in Bangor.

PATRICIA L. SCHMIDT is the author of *Margaret Chase Smith: Beyond Convention* (University of Maine Press, 1996). The book was nominated for the Joan Kelly Memorial Prize in Women's History, the John H. Dunning Prize in U.S. history, and the MLA prize for a first book. She is currently working on her second book, a study of the Scranton family of Pennsylvania. She resides in Gainesville, Florida, where she is a Professor of English at the University of Florida.

KATHRYN TOMASEK teaches U.S. and Women's History at Wheaton College in Massachusetts. She is currently at work on a manuscript about women, Fourierism, and the public sphere.

MARLI F. WEINER is Professor of History at the University of Maine. She is the author of *Mistresses and Slaves: Plantation Women in South Carolina, 1830–1880* (University of Illinois Press, 1998) and *Heritage of Woe: The Civil War Diary of Grace Brown Elmore, 1861–1868* (University of Georgia Press, 1997).

Indian Island. *See* Nicolar, Lucy

Indian pageants: 111-16

Indians. *See* Native Americans; Nicolar, Lucy; basket making and marketing

industrialization: nineteenth century, 83; in Maine, 85, 401-2

Ingersoll, Henrietta Crosby, 31

Jackson, Ruby: as professional woman, 216

Jewett, Sarah Orne, 5

Joyce, Barbara Carey, 255-6

Katahdin: MFWC support for protection of, 193

Kent, Edward: gender anxiety of, 27, 30, 33-9

King, Helen M.: and BPW, 212, 219, 224

knitting. *See* textiles: knitting

Knowles, Belle Smallidge: on conservation, 196-7

Knowles, Mrs. J. H.: and conservation, 196, 200-1

Koestenbaum, Wayne: on sexuality of divas' performances, 296, 297

Ku Klux Klan (KKK), 84; and anti-Catholicism, 250-1

L. L. Bean: and marketing of Acadian knitting, 359

Landry, Fabienne: and textiles as part of family economy, 348-9, 353

Landry, Leonie: and professional success, 222-3

Larrabee, Don: and MCS, 389-90

LeBrecque, Josephine DeRoche: and family economy, 409, 410, 413; and community, 427-8, 429

Lewis, William Chesley, Jr.: and MCS, 387, 388-90

Lewiston: and French-Canadian immigration, 403

Lieurance, Thurlow: performs with Lucy Nicolar, 104, 105

Little Chief, Tommie: performs with Lucy Nicolar, 107

Lord, Mabel: as professional woman, 215-16

Loring, Frank, 95-6

lumber industry, 29

lyceum newspapers: power of women as editors of, 140-2; humor in, 142-5; courtship portrayed in, 145-55

Maine Central Railroad: promotion of Maine wilderness by, 270, 271, 272-4

Maine Federation of Women's Clubs (MFWC), 93, 109, 111, 135-6; rural orientation of, 188-90, 203-4; and support for forestry, 190-2; and Mount Katahdin Park, 193-4; and bird conservation, 194-6; and water issues, 197-9; opposition of, to billboards, 199-200; and gardening, 201-3

Maine guides, 269; women as, 270

Maine Indian Basketmakers's Alliance, 342

Maine Outings: promotion of hunting and fishing for women, 271-2

Maine: regional divisions, 6-7; rural nature of, 8-10, 12, 164, 165, 285-6; attitudes of Mainers to social change, 9-10; wilderness mystique of, 268

mariners. *See* seafaring

Marquis, Alphie, 354; on textiles as part of family economy, 349; and woods work, 357

marriage: changing gender relations in, 51-2; companionate, 54, 55, 66-7, 72-3; as portrayed in lyceum newspapers, 151-2; "New Women" and, 287; problems with, for career women, 300-2

Martin, Joe, 391